2014

THE ELECTION
THAT CHANGED
INDIA

RAJDEEP SARDESAI

2014

THE ELECTION THAT CHANGED INDIA

PENGUIN
VIKING

VIKING

Published by the Penguin Group

Penguin Books India Pvt. Ltd, 7th Floor, Infinity Tower C, DLF Cyber City, Gurgaon 122 002, Haryana, India

Penguin Group (USA) Inc., 375 Hudson Street, New York, New York 10014, USA

Penguin Group (Canada), 90 Eglinton Avenue East, Suite 700, Toronto, Ontario, M4P 2Y3, Canada

Penguin Books Ltd, 80 Strand, London WC2R 0RL, England

Penguin Ireland, 25 St Stephen's Green, Dublin 2, Ireland (a division of Penguin Books Ltd)

Penguin Group (Australia), 707 Collins Street, Melbourne, Victoria 3008, Australia Penguin Group (NZ), 67 Apollo Drive, Rosedale, Auckland 0632, New Zealand

Penguin Books (South Africa) (Pty) Ltd, Block D, Rosebank Office Park, 181 Jan Smuts Avenue, Parktown North, Johannesburg 2193, South Africa

Penguin Books Ltd, Registered Offices: 80 Strand, London WC2R 0RL, England

First published in Viking by Penguin Books India 2014

All the quotations in the book are substantially correct but some may not be verbatim.

The views and opinions expressed in this book are the author's own and the facts are as reported by him which have been verified to the extent possible, and the publishers are not in any way liable for the same.

ISBN 9780670087907

Typeset in Sabon by R. Ajith Kumar, New Delhi
Printed at Thomson Press India Ltd, New Delhi

A PENGUIN RANDOM HOUSE COMPANY

To Sagarika, for keeping the faith

Contents

Introduction

On a hot, steamy day on the campaign trail in Varanasi, I was given another reminder of the enduring attraction of an Indian election. Stopping for a cool drink at the city's famous Pehelwan Lassi shop, we asked the owner whom he was going to vote for. Twirling his luxuriant moustache, Pehelwan Chacha looked at us. *'Jo Baba Jagannath aur dil kahe!'* (Whatever God and my heart tell me.) I tried to press him further—Narendra Modi or Arvind Kejriwal? As he lovingly laced the lassi with sinful dollops of *rabri*, he shot back, *'Dekhiye, sir, vote hamara hai, aap ko kyon batayein?'* (The vote is mine, why should I tell you?)

For more than five decades now, millions of Indians like Pehelwan Chacha have lined up across the country to exercise their franchise with hope and resolve. It is the one day when the gap between the *khaas aadmi* and the *aam aadmi*, between the *lal-batti* car and the auto rickshaw, between a Forbes billionaire and a BPL family, dissolves. We all stand in line waiting to have our fingers inked. If someone tries to break the queue—as actor-MP Chiranjeevi tried to in Hyderabad this time—you can find your voice and ask them to get back in line.

It is a truism that the higher income groups in India tend to vote less than the poor—the quest for equality is a constant motivator for the have-nots. Georgina from north Bengal, mainstay of our household for two decades, had never voted in her life and didn't have a voter card for the Delhi assembly elections. When we finally managed to get her one before the 2014 elections she was overjoyed. On voting day, she just couldn't stop smiling, showing her finger to anyone who would care to see. Her twinkling eyes reflected a sense of feeling genuinely empowered. '*Sir, hamne bhi vote daala*' (I voted too), she reported to me triumphantly.

In *India After Gandhi*, historian Ramachandra Guha suggests that the first election in 1952 was an 'article of faith' for our Constitution makers. The first election commissioner, Sukumar Sen, described it as the 'biggest experiment in democracy in human history'. A Chennai editor was less kind: 'a very large majority will exercise their votes for the first time; not many know what the vote is, why they should vote and for whom they should vote; no wonder the whole adventure is rated as the biggest gamble in history'.

Sixty-two years later, we can proudly say the faith has triumphed; the experiment has succeeded; the gamble was well worth it. The 2014 elections, in a sense, were a reaffirmation of the process that started in 1952. More than 550 million Indians voted in these elections, larger than the entire population of the world's oldest democracy, the United States. I shall never forget what a Pakistani friend once told me. 'In Pakistan, when we want to change the government, we bring in the army; in India, you just use the ballot box.' Indeed, we do.

Each of the sixteen general elections in this country has been special, though some are more significant than others. The first election was obviously a landmark one—a leap in the dark for a country that many western commentators were convinced would rapidly disintegrate. Nineteen seventy-seven was a historic election as well—in the aftermath of the Emergency, it restored public confidence in democracy and was a resounding rejection of creeping dictatorship. I was just twelve years old at the time, but I do remember reading the bold headlines: 'Indira Gandhi is defeated by the people of India'. I am sure it must have been a remarkable election to track as a journalist—just imagine profiling Raj Narain after he had defeated Indira.

I would rank 2014 in the same league as 1952 and 1977. Having had a privileged ringside view of Indian elections as a journalist since 1989, I do believe that the sixteenth general elections mark a tectonic shift in Indian politics. It has been, and I use the word judiciously, a political tsunami (or 'tsuNamo'). It's a term that was first used by the key BJP strategist Amit Shah to suggest that this was more than just a 'wave' election—it was something bigger, much bigger.

Tsunami in India is associated with the terrible disaster that hit the southern coast of the country in December 2004, spreading death and destruction. This election did not result in deaths, but it did destroy certain rigidly held beliefs about politics in this country. It was the death in a way of long-held orthodoxies about voting patterns. The death of a conventional rural–urban divide, of traditional caste and regional loyalties, of family ties, of paternalistic governance, maybe even of the Nehruvian consensus that had dominated Indian politics for decades. To quote Guha from a column written a day after the verdict: 'The sometimes noble, sometimes ignoble, "structure of renown" erected by Motilal Nehru and his descendants is now merely a heap of rubble.' Stereotypes of which social groups voted for the Congress, which for the Bharatiya Janata Party and which for caste-based parties have been demolished. The political earth of India shook, moving the centre of gravity of an Indian election from identity politics to aspirational politics. It's a new 'plus' factor that now gets you the crucial additional support, beyond narrow appeals to caste and community vote banks.

Election 2014 saw a shift in outcomes, processes and personalities. The outcome itself was staggering. The BJP became the first non-Congress party to win a clear majority on its own (the Janata Party in 1977 was a collection of several parties). In its original avatar as the Jana Sangh, the party had won just three seats and 3.1 per cent of the vote in the 1952 election. Now, it has won 282 seats and 31 per cent of the national vote—astonishing figures when you consider that the BJP's catchment area of winnable seats was less than 350 seats. The lotus has truly bloomed and come a very long way from the time when it was pigeonholed as a Brahmin–Bania party.

In six states, the BJP won each and every seat on offer. Its strike rate across north and west India was over 80 per cent, with the party winning more than four of every five seats it contested in this belt. It is in Uttar Pradesh and Bihar—two states that we believed were locked into an enduring caste matrix—that the BJP achieved some of its more dramatic results. Almost every community, except the Muslims, voted overwhelmingly for the BJP. Not only was there strong upper-caste consolidation, even Other Backward Castes (OBCs), Dalits and tribals voted for the BJP in large numbers. The BJP was, at least in 2014, the new rainbow coalition.

In contrast, the 129-year-old Congress party, with its roots in the freedom movement, has been decimated, its monopoly over power challenged like never before. Even in the 1977 elections, the party at least managed to save face south of the Vindhyas. This time, Kerala is the only state where the Congress won more than ten seats. Its final tally of forty-four seats and just 19.3 per cent of the vote—the first time its percentage slipped below 20—represents a critical inflexion point in its history. The Congress performance has also been the subject of rather cruel jokes. Returning on a flight to Delhi in June, my co-passenger said, 'Looks like the national capital's temperature will soon be more than the seats the Congress has in the Lok Sabha!'

But it's not just the final result that made this 2014 election so distinctive. The election has unleashed a chain of processes—latent and overt—that could change the way elections are fought in the future. Never before has so much money been spent in fighting an Indian election—inflation doesn't just affect the price of tomatoes, it also influences the cost of an election. The BJP, bolstered by unflinching corporate support, easily outspent its rivals, but the more worrisome aspect is just the quantum of money that is now needed by every member of Parliament to win an election. Because, with every rupee donated, the IOUs need to be encashed post-election.

A candidate in Andhra Pradesh admitted to me that he needed 'at least Rs 15 to 20 crore to just stay in the fight'. The massive inflow of cash suggests that a level playing field is simply not possible any longer. It is practically impossible to win an Indian election unless you are a *crorepati* several times over, or have funders to back you. The case for state funding could not be stronger.

The brazen use of money power imperils democracy and shrinks the basket of choices before the voter. Not that every Indian voter is complaining. In Mumbai, I met a fisherwoman at the Sassoon Docks who said she had been offered Rs 1000 by the Congress and Rs 1500 by the BJP candidate for her vote. 'I will take money from both and then decide whom to vote for!' she laughed.

If money is a threat, technology is not. In the first election, the ballot boxes stuffed with votes were carried by camels across deserts and by horses over mountains. The counting went on for weeks. Now, in the age of the electronic voting machines (EVMs), the process is faster, surer and cleaner. Yes, there are still complaints of malfunctioning EVMs, of names missing from rolls, of occasional intimidation. But the *bahubalis* (musclemen) have less of a role to play in an Indian election. The musclemen have been replaced in 2014 by the machine men—technology whiz-kids who are able to plot every constituency down to the last booth. The level of micro messaging in this election, with the aid of technology, is unprecedented. Never before has an SMS got a political party as many volunteers as it did for the BJP this time.

Indeed, one of the more fascinating aspects for me while researching this book was meeting several young men and women who designed the BJP's strategy using technology solutions. Many of them were alumni from top institutes—IITs and IIMs—who had given up lucrative jobs to be part of the election planning. It was almost as if you were in a business school and were being asked to assist in a corporate management plan. Certainly, there is enough reason to believe that the BJP's 'Mission 272' was the first time an Indian election was strategized like a business venture. Even caste arithmetic has now been given a professional edge. One of the young men I met had each caste voting in a booth mapped out on an Excel sheet with precise detailing on which household voted for whom in the previous elections.

The emergence of technology as an electoral weapon has been

accompanied by the almost irresistible rise of media power. There were times in the 2014 elections when it seemed as though the locus of the electoral battle had shifted from the heat and dust of the maidan to the air-conditioned comfort of a multi-media universe. It is no longer enough to hold a massive rally; the rally must play in a 360-degree spin across media platforms—live television, Internet, social media, mobile applications.

We aren't yet a tele-democracy in the American style. Nor is media spin enough to turn an election. Indian elections are still won and lost on a complex interplay of local-level allegiances and a robust organizational machinery on the ground. But while your debating skills on prime time won't prove decisive, they are a useful weapon to possess on the electoral battlefield. News television can set the agenda—it may be awfully noisy, but it is heard.

Many years ago, a veteran Congress politician, the late V.N. Gadgil, had lamented that he no longer felt suited to be a party spokesperson. 'I speak for thirty minutes—you reduce it to a thirty-second sound bite,' he told me. We are becoming a sound-bite society—short, sharp quotes are preferred to any long-winded manifesto. I sometimes wonder if anyone these days reads party manifestos before they go to vote.

It's not just the sound-bite age—it is the era of marketing. The year 2014 marks a coming-of-age moment for political advertising. Yes, we've had ad campaigns—most notably in the 1984 elections—that did create a flutter, but the kind of sustained hype we've witnessed this time is unmatched. Hoardings, billboards, news and entertainment channels, newspapers, radio—if you spent eight weeks in India between March and May, you'd think politics was the only 'product' on sale. Like television, advertising won't make or break an election verdict, but like the rest of the media, it can help create the 'surround sound', the election *mahaul* (atmosphere). The BJP's ad line—'*Achhe Din Aanewale Hain*' (Good Days Are Coming)—has now stuck in public consciousness. When India won a Test match at Lords in July 2014, the Hindi commentator was ecstatic. '*Achhe din aa gaye,*' he exulted.

But elections, above all else, are made by personalities, or, as in the 2014 elections, by a clash of personalities. Narendra Modi versus Rahul Gandhi—the *pracharak* versus the prince, the 'outsider' versus the 'insider', the meritocrat versus the dynast, the small-town tea boy versus the child of elite privilege. We love a Hindi film where two sharply contrasted individuals are pitted against each other (Rajesh Khanna and Amitabh in *Namak Haraam*, for example); or a tennis contest that offers similar variety (Federer versus Nadal). Politics is no different—conflicting chemistries make for a great election battle.

Sure, there were other subplots playing right through this election—the sudden rise of the Aam Aadmi Party and its doughty leader Arvind Kejriwal; the power plays of regional supremos like Mamata, Naveen Patnaik and Jayalalithaa; the break-up of Andhra Pradesh; the antics of feisty caste leaders of the north; the Nitish Kumar ideological challenge. But these were sideshows—the principal narrative remained Modi versus Rahul.

Many political experts reject the idea that a parliamentary-style democracy is actually presidential in nature. A senior Congress leader accused me on a television show of failing to understand the logic of an Indian election. 'Five hundred and forty-three constituencies and you are obsessing about two individuals,' was his angry comment. Truth is, that's how Indian general elections have always played out. The 1952 election in the end was about the overwhelming charisma of Jawaharlal Nehru. In the 1970s, it was Indira Gandhi's dominant image that set the terms of the political debate. In 1984, Rajiv Gandhi offered himself as the fresh-faced hope for the future. In 1989, it was V.P. Singh who was projected as 'Mr Clean'. In the 1990s, the BJP coined the slogan '*Abki Baari Atal Bihari*'. Why, even the silent bureaucrat-politician Dr Manmohan Singh was transformed into 'Singh is King' ahead of the 2009 elections.

The 2014 election was, in the end, about the '*chhappan* inch *kee chhaati*' machismo of the politician from Vadnagar in Gujarat. To quote right-wing columnist Swapan Dasgupta: 'For some he was a modern-day Chhatrapati Shivaji who would finally make Hindus come into their own; to others he was the poor boy next door who had made it big in the ugly and cruel world of Delhi, and to still yet others he was the great liberator of the economy from sloth and socialist incompetence. What united these divergent strands was the belief that his victory would usher in the proverbial happy days.'

Indeed, Modi's biggest success was that he made the mandate about himself and the high growth rate he had achieved in Gujarat, about rising incomes and the 'Gujarat model' of governance, a model whose grey edges remained surprisingly unchallenged till nearly the very end of the election campaign. He represented, in a sense, the 'audacity of hope'—a charismatic orator, a state chief minister who was spinning a dream for a positive future at a time when the country was burdened with negativism. Leaders emerge in a context—at a time of an economy in turmoil and a political class riddled with corruption, Modi was, as one senior Congress politician conceded, 'the right man at the right time with the right rhetoric'.

In the process, he was able to discard his own spotted legacy and that of his party. The 2002 post-Godhra riots and the fact that more than a thousand people died under his watch were simply not an issue in 2014 because Modi was able to artfully change the terms of the political discourse to a more 'inclusive' vision premised on effective governance. Or maybe that's how a majority of Indians preferred to see him—not as an ideologue of religious nationalism but as a tough, no-nonsense administrator.

Hindutva politics can never be disconnected from the Sangh Parivar's ethos and the RSS (Rashtriya Swayamsevak Sangh) is part of Modi's DNA, but there was a conscious attempt to keep any overtly religious appeal on the backburner. The RSS did fully throw itself into the campaign and their cadres were the BJP's last-mile warriors, especially in the crucial battleground of Uttar Pradesh. But this election wasn't going to be about building a Ram mandir in Ayodhya, unlike the 1991 and 1996 elections where the BJP made its first serious bid for power. It wasn't about a core ideological agenda that pushed for a uniform civil code or Article 370. Nor was this election going to be decided by communal polarization, unlike Modi's first win as Gujarat chief minister in 2002. That election was fought in the backdrop of riots and Modi's claim to be a Hindu Hriday Samrat (Emperor of Hindu Hearts). This election was fought in the context of an India itching for change and Modi being its principal agent of transformation.

Yes, the BJP did get a substantial Hindu vote, especially in UP and Bihar (see chapter 5 and appendix 2), but this can be best described as the result of 'identity plus' politics. The party had a core Hindutva vote, but to win a national election, it needed a wider base. In a sense, Modi did a Tony Blair. Like the former British prime minister made a struggling Labour party more 'electable' by discarding its ideological dogmas and creating 'New Labour', Modi, too, reinvented the BJP. This was almost a new, freshly minted BJP—market-friendly, not pushing swadeshi economics. Governance, not religious politics, became its distinctive appeal for those Indians who remained sceptical of the Bajrang Dal–VHP (Vishwa Hindu Parishad) foot soldiers. Of the seventy seats where voter turnout increased by 15 per cent or more, the BJP and its allies won a staggering sixty-seven. Modi's other great success was in understanding the changing demographics of India—a younger, aspirational society that is easily the most upwardly mobile in the world. Modi likes to see the core of this new India as a 'neo-middle class' society which is tiring of state-sponsored welfarism and simply wants market-driven growth As a *Wall Street Journal* article points out, 'Modi tapped into the frustration of a generation of Indians who climbed out of poverty in the past decade, but who have been prevented from joining the middle classes by slowing growth and a lack of employment.'

Modi has presented himself as India's first post-liberalization politician (I refer to this in some detail in chapter 8), someone who has sought to combine a certain cultural rootedness with the vaulting desire of millions of Indians to get onto the superhighway to prosperity. He tapped into this yearning for *parivartan* (change), especially by offering himself as a muscular leader in contrast to the weak leadership of Manmohan Singh and the dynastical legacy of Rahul Gandhi. He was aggressive and communicative—qualities that go down well with young Indians in particular. How often did one hear on the campaign trail a young voter saying he would vote for Modi because 'at last, we will have a prime minister who talks!' Of the 810 million electorate, first-time voters in the eighteen to twenty-three age group were around 120 million, or almost 15 per cent. The CSDS (Centre for the Study of Developing Societies)-Lokniti national election study suggests that 42 per cent in this age group wanted Modi as prime minister, with just 16 per cent preferring Rahul. The BJP got twice as many votes as the Congress did amongst first-time voters—an estimated 36 per cent versus 17 per cent (see appendix 2). In a cynical India tiring of its politicians, Modi offered a priceless four-letter word to a young and restless India—HOPE.

Rahul was twenty years younger than Modi, blessed with the most enduring family surname in Indian politics. He was well intentioned but that is never enough for an India living by the '*Dil Maange More*' slogan. Through the campaign, he appeared to speak the language of an older India—of handouts, of entitlements, even vote banks. At times, you almost felt a reversal of roles—it was Modi who would harp on rapid development, it was Rahul who would focus on issues tending to spread fear and insecurity amongst the minorities.

While Modi spoke of the twenty-first century belonging to India, Rahul would often talk of the past—of the sacrifices, for example, which his family had made. He did not offer a vision for the future. Even his 'Bharat versus India' divide appeared to suggest a stagnant nation that lived in two separate universes. His listless, almost dull, campaign never had a chance against the vigorous energy that Modi exuded. Not surprisingly, it was among India's first-time voters that the Rahul–Modi gap was widest. The role models of a new India aren't dynasts but self-made achievers.

Of course, it wasn't ever going to be easy for Rahul. He had to bear the baggage of the ten years' rule of the United Progressive Alliance (UPA). The Sonia–Manmohan diarchy had promised much initially, but an uneasy ruling coalition was bound to implode eventually. A unique power-sharing arrangement between a bureaucrat prime minister and a status quo-ist Congress president rapidly degenerated into sloth, corruption and, above all else, untamed inflation. The

Indian voter can be rather tolerant of corruption, but what they are notoriously unforgiving of is rising prices. In every election tracker we've done, price rise has always been the top concern for the electorate. Almost five years of slow growth and high inflation is a recipe for political suicide. In the end, it was 'the economy, stupid'—which meant that for many voters it became a case of 'anyone but Congress'. P. Chidambaram, former finance minister, put it aptly when he told me post-election, 'The economy destroyed us in the 2014 elections. Had we got growth back on track and inflation under control, everything else might have been forgotten.'

And yet, no election is determined overnight by a single issue or even by one towering individual. This book is, therefore, about much more than just Modi and Rahul. Like a multi-starrer, it contains many characters who played a role in the eventual shaping of the verdict. I have tried to locate some of them in the wider context of the constantly evolving Indian political landscape.

Elections are not a one-day match. While the final act may have been played out on 16 May when the results were announced, the build-up began much before, in fact quite a few years before D-Day. And it is by tracing those roots that we can make sense of the present. I do firmly believe, for example, that the Congress-led UPA lost the 2014 elections in 2011 itself, the year corruption caused a volcanic eruption in public anger. After that, the party and the government were like a comatose patient on slow drip—the end was preordained. Similarly, the rise of Modi wasn't instant magic—it was the outcome of a deliberate, well-crafted campaign that evolved over several years. Indeed, my central premise is that when the UPA's decline began four years ago, Modi had already begun planning for his daring Delhi bid. It was a long, single-minded journey to the top, not an overnight coup.

This book, I must warn you, isn't written by a political scientist or a psephologist. I belong to the more humble tribe of news reporters—every time I look in the mirror, I see a sleeves-rolled-up reporter first, only then a preachy editor or jacket-and-tie anchor. As pen-pushers or sound-bite warriors, we perhaps lack the conceptual base of academics or the number-crunching skills of pollsters. But what journalism does provide is the best seat in the house—you can meet, observe, understand all kinds of people you report on. Your sources share stories and anecdotes that years later can actually be spun into a long narrative. This book is built on the edifice which twenty-six years of journalism have so kindly provided—the chance to report the politics of this remarkable country where no two days (at times, no two hours!) are ever the same.

I am no soothsayer, even though journalists and editors like to believe they can give you a glimpse into the future. If you had asked me when I first met Narendra Modi in 1990 whether he'd be the fifteenth prime minister of India, my answer would have been firmly in the negative. If you ask me today whether Rahul can make a comeback, I'd again be hard-pressed to give an answer in the affirmative. No one can predict the future with any certainty, and especially not for India and Indian elections—this is the enduring fascination of this country.

Democracy is also the ultimate leveller. One of the great joys of anchoring live television shows on counting day is just to watch the crestfallen faces of mighty politicians who had taken the electorate for granted. I remember deriving almost sadistic pleasure on meeting Narasimha Rao after his loss in 1996. The prime minister who would treat television journalists with contempt had just got his comeuppance from the Indian voter—his pout was now even more pronounced.

The first election that I have a distinct memory of was the 1976 US presidential elections. As an eleven-year-old, I sat all day in the USIS building in Mumbai watching the results unfold in another continent. I had wanted Jimmy Carter to win that one over Gerald Ford—don't ask me why, maybe I just like peanuts! When Carter was declared the winner, I let off a scream of delight. That same feeling of exhilaration has accompanied every Indian election I have had the good fortune to report on since 1989. From Pehelwan Chacha in Varanasi to the fisherwoman in Sassoon Dock, it's that tingling excitement that only the festive spirit of an Indian election can bring to life. It's that great Indian story in all its rainbow colours that I have tried to capture in this book—the story of the 2014 elections, a mandate which has the potential of changing India and its politics forever.

1

Narendrabhai, the Man
from Gujarat

Counting day in a television studio. A bit like a T20 match. Fast, furious, the excitement both real and contrived. The 16th of May 2014 was no different. It was the grand finale of the longest and most high-decibel campaign in Indian electoral history—this was the final of the Indian Political League, the biggest show in the democratic world. In the studio, we were preparing for a long day with packets of chips and orange juice to stay energized. But even before we could settle our nerves, or go for a 'strategic break', it was all over.

By 9.30 a.m., it was certain that Narendra Modi would be India's fourteenth prime minister. In our studios, Swapan Dasgupta, right-wing columnist and a proud Modi supporter, was cheering. 'It's a defining moment in Indian history,' he exulted. His sparring partner, the distinguished historian Ramachandra Guha, who disliked Modi and Rahul Gandhi in equal measure, had a firm riposte. 'I think Modi should send a thank you card to Rahul for helping him become prime minister of India!'

As we analysed the scale of the win, my mind went back to the moment when I believe it all began. The 20th of December 2012 saw another T20 match, another counting day. The results of the Gujarat and Himachal Pradesh assembly elections were streaming in that morning. Himachal was an also-ran. Gandhinagar was where the action was. By noon, we had the breaking news—Narendra Modi had scored a hat-trick in Gujarat. The margin was a bit lower than many had predicted, but with 116 seats in a 182-member assembly, Modi was once again the self-styled 'sher' of Gujarat.

That evening, Modi addressed a large gathering of the party faithful in Ahmedabad's JP Chowk. 'If there has been a mistake somewhere, if I have erred somewhere, I seek an apology from you, the six crore Gujaratis,' said the Gujarat chief minister. 'Gujarat is a role model for elections,' he added. 'The entire election was fought here on the plank of development. Gujarat has endorsed the plank of development. This victory is not the victory of Narendra Modi but of the six crore Gujaratis and those Indians who aspire for prosperity and development. This is a victory of all those who wish the country's good.'

This was clearly no routine victory speech. Showing a characteristic alertness to the political moment, it was delivered in Hindi and not Gujarati, designed for a national audience way beyond Gujarat. In the frenzied crowds, posters had sprung up: 'Modi chief minister 2012; prime minister 2014'. One Modi supporter even went to the extent of claiming 'Modi is India, India is Modi', reminiscent of Congress slogans for Indira Gandhi in the 1970s. As the 'PM, PM' chant echoed amidst the crowd throughout the speech, Modi obligingly said, 'If you want me to go to Delhi, I shall go there for a day on 27 December.'

In our studios that day too, Swapan Dasgupta was elated. It wasn't just a self-congratulatory 'I told you so' reaction—most exit polls had predicted a Modi win. He was convinced that Modi was now poised to take the great leap to the national capital. 'This is the beginning, we will now see a clear attempt to redefine Mr Modi's role in national politics', was his verdict. Modi's triumph carried the edge of a victory over the 'left liberals', a muffling of those critical voices which seemed to have dominated the mainstream. India's right-wing voices were waiting to burst through the banks and sweep aside the so-called 'secularists' who in their view had monopolized the discourse on Modi. Swapan seemed not just excited at Modi's victory but inordinately pleased at being able to cock a snook at his ideological opponents.

Others in the studio panel were a little more sceptical. After all, Modi wasn't the first chief minister to score a hat-trick of wins. Odisha's Naveen Patnaik, Sheila Dikshit in Delhi and, of course, the redoubtable Jyoti Basu in Bengal had shown it was possible. Was Modi, then, sui generis? Was there something in the saffron-hued Ahmedabad air that evening which suggested this was a watershed moment in Indian politics?

Later that night, as the dust settled and the television talking heads made their exit, I telephoned Mr Modi's residence in Gandhinagar to congratulate him. A little after midnight, he returned the call. 'Congratulations on your victory,' I said. His response was in Hindi. *'Dhanyawaad, bhaiya!'* I asked him whether his decision to deliver a victory speech in Hindi was the clearest sign yet that he wanted to make a pitch for prime minister. *'Rajdeep, jab aap reporter editor ban sakte ho, toh kya chief minister, pradhan mantri nahi ban sakte kya?'* (If a reporter like you can become an editor, why can't a chief minister become a prime minister.) Stated with his trademark gift of quick-witted repartee, there was my answer.

~

The first time I met Narendra Damodardas Modi, I was a young reporter with the *Times of India* in Mumbai. The year was 1990 and I had been in the profession for less than two years. My hair had not greyed nor had Modi's. He was wearing a loose, well-starched kurta–pyjama and greeted us warmly. Almost instantly, he became Narendrabhai for all the journalists.

The occasion was the Ram rath yatra of L.K. Advani from Somnath to Ayodhya. I had been assigned to cover one leg of the yatra as it wound its way from Gujarat into Maharashtra. Actually,

I was the secondary reporter, tasked with looking for some 'colour' stories around the main event. I joined the yatra in Surat as it moved across south Gujarat and then into Maharashtra. For me, it was a big opportunity to gain a ringside view of a major national political event, away from the local Mumbai politics beat.

It was a big occasion for Narendra Modi too. He was then the BJP's organizing secretary in Gujarat, the RSS's point person for the state, looking to carve an identity for himself well beyond being just another pracharak. If the rath yatra provided me an opportunity for a front-page byline, it gave Modi a chance to take a step up the political ladder. His role was to ensure the yatra's smooth passage through Gujarat and create an atmosphere and a momentum on which the BJP could capitalize in the rest of the country.

Gujarat at the time was poised to become, as subsequent events would confirm, a 'laboratory' for political Hindutva. The BJP had just made an impressive showing in the assembly elections that year, winning sixty-seven seats and forging a coalition government with Chimanbhai Patel's Janata Dal (Gujarat). The alliance didn't last long as Patel merged his party with the Congress, but it was clear that the BJP was the party of the future with a solid cadre and a strong popular appeal across the state.

Under Advani's leadership, the BJP had abandoned the 'Gandhian socialism' plank for a more direct appeal to religious nationalism. The idea of a Ram temple in Ayodhya was central to this new line of thinking. From just two seats in the Lok Sabha in 1984, the party had won eighty-five in 1989. There was a fresh energy in its ranks, with an emerging group of young leaders giving the party a sense of dynamism missing from an earlier generation. Modi, along with the likes of Pramod Mahajan and Sushma Swaraj, was part of this Generation Next of the BJP.

As a Mumbai journalist, I had got to know Mahajan first. He had a debonair flamboyance that marked him out amidst the BJP's conservative and rather nondescript cadre. He may have got his early inspiration from the RSS but appeared to have little time for its austere lifestyle. He was the first politician I knew who wore

Ray-Ban, who never hid his affiliations to big business houses and who openly enjoyed his drink. One of my unforgettable journalistic memories is of sitting in a rooftop suite of Mumbai's Oberoi hotel with Bal Thackeray smoking a pipe while Mahajan drank chilled beer. To think that the pipe-sucking Thackeray and the beer-swilling Mahajan were the architects of the original 'conservative' Hindutva alliance indicates sharply how ideological Hindutva was in fact tailor-made for hard political strategy.

Mahajan was every journalist's friend. He was always ready with a quote, a news break and an anecdote. He was also, in a sense, the BJP's original event manager. The 1990 rath yatra, in fact, was his brainchild and he was made the national coordinator of the event.

Modi was in charge of the Gujarat leg, and was to accompany the procession from Somnath to Mumbai. Which is how and where we met. My early memories of him are hazy, perhaps diluted by the larger-than-life image he acquired in later years. But I do remember three aspects of his persona then which might have provided a glimpse into the future. The first was his eye for detail. Every evening, journalists covering the yatra would receive a printed sheet with the exact programme for the next day. There was a certain precision to the planning and organization of the entire event which stood out. Modi would personally ensure that the media was provided every facility to cover the yatra. Fax machines were made available at every place along the yatra route, with the BJP local office bearing all expenses. Modi even occasionally suggested the storyline and what could be highlighted! Micromanagement was an obvious skill, one he would use to great effect in later years.

The second aspect was his attire. Without having acquired the designer kurtas or the well-coiffured look of later years, he was always immaculately dressed and well groomed. He may have lacked Mahajan's self-confidence, but Modi's crisply starched and ironed kurtas marked him out from the other RSS–BJP *karyakartas* (workers) who sported a more crumpled look. Rumour had it that he spent at least half an hour a day before the mirror, a habit that suggests early traces of narcissism.

The third lasting impression came from Modi's eyes. Sang Kenny Rogers in his hit song 'The Gambler': '*Son, I've made a life from readin' people's faces, knowin' what the cards were by the way they held their eyes.*' In my experience, those with wide twinkling eyes tend to play the game of life gently, perhaps lacking the killer instinct. Modi in those early days smiled and laughed a lot, but his eyes at times glared almost unblinkingly—stern, cold and distant. They were the eyes of someone playing for the highest possible stakes in the gamble of life. His smile could embrace you, the eyes would intimidate.

The dominant image of that period, though, was the yatra itself. It wasn't just another roadshow—this was religion on wheels that was transformed into a political juggernaut. Religion and politics had created a heady cocktail. Mahajan and Modi were the impresarios, Advani was the mascot, but the real stars were the Hindutva demagogues Sadhvi Rithambhara and Uma Bharti. I shall never forget their speeches during the yatra, seeking Hindu mobilization and loaded with hate and invective against the minorities. Feverish chants of '*Jo Hindu heet ki baat karega wahi desh pe raj karega*' (Those who speak of benefits to Hindus, they alone will rule the country) would be accompanied by powerful oratory calling for avenging historical injustices.

Uma Bharti, a natural, instinctive politician and mass leader, appeared to me breezily bipolar. At night-time rallies, she would deliver vitriolic and highly communally charged speeches, and the very next morning, she would lovingly ask me about my family and offer to make me *nimbu pani* (she is a terrific cook, I might add). Years later, when Modi was sworn in as prime minister, Uma Bharti was made a minister and Sadhvi Rithambhara was a special invitee—the wheel appeared to have come full circle for these stormy petrels. As I watched first as a reporter in his twenties, through the decades to an editor in his late forties, the Hindutva movement rose up from street-side clamour and charged-up rath yatras to claim its place finally at the national high table, with these indefatigable agitators always at hand to lend their shoulder to the slowly rolling saffron wheel as it turned corner after corner.

~

The next time my path crossed with that of Modi we had both, well, moved a step up in life. I was now a television journalist while Modi was a rising star in the BJP in Gujarat. It was March 1995 and I was covering the Gujarat assembly elections for NDTV. It was the early days of private news television and we had just begun doing a daily news programme for Doordarshan called *Tonight*. For the BJP, too, the assembly elections were new, uncharted territory. For the first time, the party was in a position to capture power on its own in Gujarat.

As the results began to trickle in—and this was the pre-electronic voting machine era, so the counting was much slower—there was an air of great expectancy at the BJP party headquarters in Khanpur in Ahmedabad. By the evening, it was becoming clearer that the BJP was on its way to a famous win. The party eventually won a two-thirds majority with 121 of the 182 seats. The leaders were cheered as they entered the party office. Keshubhai Patel was the man anointed as chief minister; other senior leaders like Shankersinh Vaghela and Kashiram Rana all shared traditional Gujarati sweets and *farsan*. In a corner was Modi, the man who had scripted the success by managing the election campaign down to the last detail. The arc lights were on the BJP's other senior leaders, but I remember an emotional Modi telling me on camera that 'this is the happiest moment in my life'. The almost anonymous campaign manager seemed to sublimate himself to his party with the fierce loyalty of the karyakarta.

On 19 March 1995, Keshubhai Patel was sworn in as the first BJP chief minister of Gujarat at a function in Gandhinagar. Again, Modi wasn't the focus, but already the whispers in party circles projected him as the 'super-chief minister'. The sweet smell of success, though, would quickly evaporate. The Sangh Parivar in Gujarat became the Hindu Divided Parivar and the party with a difference began to weaken because of internal differences. By October that year, a rebellion within the BJP led by Vaghela forced Keshubhai to resign. A compromise formula was evolved—Suresh Mehta was made the chief minister of Gujarat, and Modi, who was accused by his detractors of fomenting the politics of divide and rule in the state, was packed off to north India as the national secretary in charge of Haryana and Himachal Pradesh.

These were Modi's years in political *vanvas* (exile). He could have dived into his new challenge, but his heart was always in Gujarat. 'He still wants to be the chief minister of Gujarat one day, that is his ultimate ambition,' a common friend told me on more than one occasion. If that was his final destination, Modi kept it well concealed. Once ensconced in Delhi, Modi liked to speak out on 'national' issues. Private television was just beginning to find its voice and political debates on television had just begun to take off. Modi, as an articulate speaker in Hindi, was ideally suited as a political guest for prime-time politics on TV.

Modi took to television rather well at that time in the late 1990s. I recall two telling instances. Once I was anchoring a 10 p.m. show called *Newshour* on NDTV with Arnab Goswami. (Arnab would later anchor a similarly named prime-time show on Times Now with great success.) At about 8.30 p.m., our scheduled BJP guest, Vijay Kumar Malhotra, dropped out. We were desperate for a replacement. I said I knew one person in Delhi who might oblige us at this late hour. I rang up Modi and spoke to him in Gujarati (I have always believed that a way to a person's heart is to speak to them in their mother tongue, a tactic that every reporter learns while trying to charm the power food chain from VIPs down to their PAs and PSs).

'*Aavee jao, Narendrabhai, tamhari zarrorat chhe*' (Please come, Narendrabhai, we need you). Modi hemmed and hawed for all of sixty seconds and then said he was ready to appear on our show but didn't have a car. Modi at the time lived in 9, Ashoka Road, next to the BJP office along with other pracharaks. I asked him to take a taxi and promised that we would reimburse him. Arnab and I sweated in anticipation as the countdown began for 10 p.m. With minutes to go, there was still no sign of Modi. With about five minutes left to on-air, with producers already yelling 'stand by' in my ear, a panting Modi came scurrying into the studio, crying out, 'Rajdeep, I have come, I have come!' He was fully aware he was only a last-minute replacement but so unwilling was he to give up a chance at a TV appearance, he made sure he showed up, even at the eleventh hour. As far as Arnab and I were concerned, we had our BJP guest and our show was saved.

In July 1999, when General Musharraf came visiting for the Agra Summit, Modi came to our rescue again. We were on round-the-clock coverage of the event, and needed a BJP guest who would be available for an extended period. Modi readily agreed to come to our OB van at Vijay Chowk, the designated site for political panellists outside Parliament. But when he arrived, it began to rain and the satellite signal stopped working. Without creating any fuss whatsoever, Modi sat patiently through the rain with an umbrella for company and waited for almost two hours in the muddy downpour before he was finally put on air.

At one level, the determined desire to be on television perhaps smacked of a certain desperation on Modi's part to stay in the news and in the limelight. This was a period when he had lost out to other leaders of his generation. Mahajan, for example, had become prime minister Atal Bihari Vajpayee's right-hand man and a leading minister in the government. Sushma Swaraj was a great favourite with the party's supporters for her oratorical skills, and her decision to take on Sonia Gandhi in Bellary had given her a special place as a fearless political fighter. Arun Jaitley was also slowly emerging as one of the party's all-rounders—a crisis manager, a highly articulate legal eagle and a credible spokesperson on TV.

Modi, by contrast, was struggling to carve a distinct identity. He had been virtually barred from Gujarat, a state where a theatre of the absurd was being played out with four chief ministers in four years between 1995 and 1998. In Delhi, Modi was being accused of playing favourites in Himachal Pradesh and mishandling the political situation in Haryana. Moreover, as a pracharak, he was expected to remain content as a faceless organizer and a backroom player. I would meet Modi often in this period, and sometimes over a meal of *kadhi chawal* (he ate well but liked to keep his food simple), I got the sense of a politician struggling to come to terms with his seeming political isolation. For an otherwise remarkably self-confident man, he often gave way to a creeping self-doubt over his immediate political future. I remember we once did a poll in 1999 on who were the BJP leaders to watch out for in the future. Mahajan, Swaraj, even another pracharak-turned-politician Govindacharya, were mentioned; Modi didn't even figure in the list. *'Lagta hai aap punditon ne desh mein bhavishya mein kya hoga yeh tay kar liya hai!'* (Looks like you political pundits have decided the country's future), was Modi's sharp response.

Which is why news television became an ally, almost a political weapon, for Modi in this period. It gave him a national profile in a crowded political space. It also ensured that he remained in public memory, both in Gujarat and in Delhi. He was a good party spokesperson—clear, direct, aggressive, often provocative. He did not pussyfoot around the party's commitment to Hindutva and never shied away from a joust.

When the Twin Towers were attacked in New York in September 2001, I was looking for a guest for my weekly *Big Fight* show to discuss the new buzzword—Islamic terror. The BJP leaders in the Vajpayee government were for some reason reluctant to appear on the programme. Modi had no such compunctions as he came and spoke out strongly against what he said was one of the biggest threats to the country. 'It has taken an attack like 9/11 for India's pseudo-secular media to finally use a word like Islamic terrorism and wake up to the reality of how some groups are misusing religion to promote terror,' thundered Modi in the programme.

Little did I know then that Modi's position on Islam and terror would subsequently come to define his political identity. I also could not have foreseen that the man who was one of my 'go to' BJP netas for a political debate would never again appear on a television show of this kind. Life for Modi, the country and even for me as a journalist was about to take a dramatic twist.

~

Less than four weeks after appearing on *The Big Fight* show on the 9/11 terror attack, Narendra Modi was sworn in as Gujarat's chief minister. It was a remarkable change in fortune for a leader who had found himself on the margins of national politics till then. The change in leadership in Gujarat had been in the offing for some time. Keshubhai Patel's second term as chief minister had been disastrous. The BJP had lost a series of municipal elections and assembly by-elections in the state in the 2000–01 period. On 26 January 2001, as the country was celebrating Republic Day, Kutch and Ahmedabad had been shaken by a devastating earthquake. Instead of seeing this as a wake-up call, Patel's government became even more somnolent. The relief and rehabilitation measures were widely criticized. Modi himself once told me in March that year, 'Yes, we need to do more, else people will not forgive us.' Nature had delivered its verdict—the political leadership of the BJP was left with no choice but to heed the message. It wasn't easy—a strong section of the state leadership remained opposed to Modi. In the end, it was the Advani–Vajpayee duo who pushed the decision with the support of the RSS.

On 7 October 2001, Modi became the first full-time RSS pracharak to be made a state chief minister. It hadn't been an easy ride. Born in a lower middle-class family in Vadnagar in north Gujarat's Mehsana district, Modi came from the relatively small Ghanchi community, an OBC caste involved in oil extraction. This was a state whose politics was dominated by the powerful landowning Patels. In early conversations, I never heard Modi speak of his caste background or his years in Vadnagar. He did speak, though, of his RSS mentors with great fondness. 'Lakshman Inamdar, or Vakilsaab, is a Maharashtrian like you, he guided me always,' Modi told me. 'You should then speak better Marathi!' I teased him.

A few days after he became chief minister I interviewed Modi on the challenges that were now before him. 'We have to rebuild Gujarat and restore confidence in the people in our leadership,' he said, sounding almost sage-like. I sensed that he had been waiting for this moment for years. Some of his critics have suggested that Modi 'conspired' to become chief minister. Veteran editor Vinod Mehta has claimed that Modi had met him with files against Keshubhai which he wanted him to publish. Clearly, this was one pracharak who was adept at the power game.

A pracharak, or 'preacher', is the backbone of the RSS-led Sangh Parivar. Mostly bachelors, they are expected to live a life of austerity and self-discipline. Modi wasn't a typical pracharak—he was intensely political and ambitious. I had met several Gujarat BJP leaders who insisted Modi was constantly plotting to 'fix' them. Modi was also a loner—when I met him in the BJP central office in his wilderness years in the late 1990s, he was often alone. His contemporary, Govindacharya, would be surrounded by admirers; Modi preferred to be in the company of newspapers.

Which is why becoming chief minister was a major transition point in his life. As an organizational man, Modi had proved himself as hard-working, diligent and passionate about his party and its ethos. Now, he needed to show that he could actually be a politician who could lead from the front, not just be a back-room operator who had never even contested a municipal election.

Modi's big chance came on 27 February 2002. I was showering that morning when a call came from an old journalist friend from Gujarat, Deepak Rajani. Rajani managed a small evening paper in Rajkot and had excellent contacts in the police. '*Rajdeep, bahut badi ghatna hui hai Godhra mein. Sabarmati Express mein aag lagi hai. Kaie VHP kar sevak us train mein thhe. Terror attack bhi ho sakta hai*' (There's been a big incident at Godhra. The Sabarmati Express with many kar sevaks aboard has caught fire. It could even be a terror attack). In the age of instantaneous breaking news, it isn't easy to separate fact from hyperbole. What was clear, though, was that a train compartment had caught fire and several kar sevaks (volunteers) were feared dead.

A few hours later, as the information became clearer, it was apparent that this was no ordinary train fire. A mob of local Muslims in Godhra had attacked the train, a fire had started and several people had died. The backdrop to this tragedy had been an attempt by the VHP to reignite the Ram temple movement by launching another *shila pujan* (foundation stone-laying ceremony) in Ayodhya. Several kar sevaks from Gujarat had joined the programme and were returning from Ayodhya when the train was attacked. That evening, Modi, visiting the site in Godhra, suggested that the kar sevaks had been victims of a terror conspiracy. The VHP was even more aggressive—a bandh was called in Gujarat the next day.

Television journalists like to be at the heart of the action. A few of my action-hungry colleagues rushed to Ayodhya because there were reports of a potential backlash to the train burning, in UP. The Union budget was to be announced the next day, so a few journalists remained parked in the capital. My instinct told me to head for my birthplace, Ahmedabad. A senior police officer had rung me up late that evening after the train burning. 'Rajdeep, the VHP is planning a bandh. The government is planning to allow them to take the bodies home in some kind of a procession. Trust me, there could be real trouble this time,' he warned. The next day, along with my video journalist Narendra Gudavalli, we were on the flight to Ahmedabad.

The Ahmedabad I travelled to that day was not the city I had such happy memories of. As a child I spent every summer holiday in the comforting home of my grandparents. Hindi movies, cricket, cycling—Ahmedabad for me was always a place to savour life's simple pleasures. Sari-clad ladies zoomed by on scooters, their *mangalsutras* flying. The *sitaphal* ice cream and cheese pizzas in the local market were a weekend delight. My memories were of an endlessly benevolent city, full of neighbourly bonhomie and friendly street chatter. But that day in February, I saw a smoke-filled sky, closed shops and mobs on the street. The city frightened me—the Ahmedabad of my joyous childhood dreams had turned into an ugly nightmare. I can claim to have had a ringside view to India's first televised riot, a riot in the age of 'live' television. From 28 February for the next seventy-two hours, we were witness to a series of horrific incidents, all of which suggested a near complete collapse of the state machinery. We listened to tales of inhuman savagery, of targeted attacks, of the police being bystanders while homes were looted and people killed. For three days, with little sleep, we reported the carnage that was taking place before our eyes even while self-censoring some of the more gruesome visuals.

On 1 March, I was caught in the middle of a 'mini riot' in the walled city areas of Dariapur–Shahpur. This was a traditional trouble spot in Ahmedabad—Hindu and Muslim families lived cheek by jowl and even a cycle accident could spark violence. That morning, neighbours were throwing stones, sticks, even petrol bombs at each other, with the police doing little to stop the clashes. One petrol bomb just missed my cameraperson Narendra by a whisker even as he bravely kept shooting. I saw a young girl being attacked with acid, another boy being kicked and beaten. We managed to capture much of this on camera and played out the tape that evening while carefully excising the more graphic visuals. A riot is not a pretty picture. We had filmed a family charred to death inside a Tata Safari, but never showed the images. We did exercise self-restraint but clearly the government wanted a total blackout. 'Are you trying to spark off another riot?' Pramod Mahajan angrily asked me over the phone. I felt it was important to mirror the ugly reality on the ground—an impactful story, I hoped, would push the Centre into sending the army to the battle-scarred streets.

I did not encounter Modi till the evening of 2 March when he held a press conference at the circuit house in Ahmedabad to claim that the situation was being brought under control with the help of the army. That morning, though, he had rung me up to warn me about our coverage which he said was inflammatory. In particular, he told me about the report of an incident in Anjar, Kutch, of a Hanuman temple being attacked, which he said was totally false. 'Some roadside linga was desecrated, but no temple has been touched. I will not allow such malicious and provocative reporting,' he said angrily. I tried to explain to him that the report had come through a news wire agency and had been flashed by our Delhi newsroom without verifying with me. A few hours later, the chief minister's office issued orders banning the telecast of the channel.

Modi's press conference also took place against the backdrop of a front-page story in that morning's *Times of India* indicating that the chief minister had invoked Newton's law to suggest that the violence was a direct reaction to Godhra. 'Every action invites an equal and opposite reaction', was the headline. Modi denied having made any such remark to the reporter. Naturally, the mood at the press conference was frosty and hostile.

After the press conference, I reached out to Modi, assuring him we would be even more careful in our coverage. I offered to interview him so that he could send out a strong message of calm and reassurance. He agreed. We did the interview, only to return to the office and find the tape damaged. I telephoned Modi's office again, explained the problem and managed to convince him to do another interview, this time in Gandhinagar later that night.

We reached the chief minister's residence in Gandhinagar a little after 10 p.m. We dined with him and then recorded the interview. I asked him about his failure to control the riots. He called it a media conspiracy to target him, saying he had done his best, and then pointed out that Gujarat had a history of communal riots. I asked him about his controversial action–reaction remark. He claimed what he would later repeat in another interview, to Zee News, '*Kriya aur pratikriya ki chain chal rahi hai. Hum chahte hain ki na kriya ho na pratikriya*' (A chain of action and reaction is going on. We want neither action nor reaction).

We came out of the interview almost convinced that the chief minister was intent on ending the cycle of violence. Less than an hour later, the doubts returned. Barely a few kilometres from his Gandhinagar residence on the main highway to Ahmedabad, we came upon a roadblock with VHP–Bajrang Dal supporters milling about, wielding lathis, swords and axes. It was well past midnight. Our driver tried to avoid the blockade when an axe smashed through the windscreen. The car halted and we were forced to emerge. 'Are you Hindus or Muslims?' screamed out a hysterical youth sporting a saffron bandana. For the record, we were all Hindus, except our driver Siraj who was a Muslim. The group, with swords threateningly poised in attack mode, demanded we pull down our trousers. They wanted to check if any of us were circumcised. In the pursuit of male hygiene, at my birth my rationalist parents had ensured I was.

The crowd confronting us was neither rationalist nor normal. They were in fact abnormally enraged, feverishly excited youth, hopping about with their swords and axes, drunk on the power they had over us. Their raised swords were repeatedly brandished above our heads. Pushes, shoves and lunges towards us indicated that we were in serious danger from a militia both neurotic and bloodthirsty.

When in danger, flash your journalist credentials. Even though I did not feel particularly brave at the time, I gathered up my courage for the sake of my team and drew myself up to my full six feet—thankfully I was at least a head taller than most of them. I aggressively yelled that I and my team were journalists, we were media and, guess what, we had just interviewed the chief minister. Such behaviour a short distance away from his house was unacceptable and a disrespect to the CM's office. How dare they disrespect their own CM? 'Agar aap kisi ko bhi haath lagaoge, toh mein chief minister ko complain karoonga!' (If you touch anyone, I will complain to the chief minister), I said, trying to sound as angry as possible.

The gang wasn't willing to listen. 'Hamein chief minister se matlab nahi, aap log apna identity dikhao' (We don't care about the chief minister. Show your identity cards). I showed my official press card and got my cameraperson Narendra to play a clip from the interview with Modi. 'Look,' I shouted, 'look at this interview. Can't you see we are journalists?' After fifteen tense minutes and after watching the tape, they seemed to calm down a bit and we were finally allowed to go. Our trembling driver Siraj was in tears. My own fear at a near-death experience was now replaced by a seething rage. If, just a few kilometres from the chief minister's house, Hindu militant gangs were roaming freely on the night of 2 March, then how could the chief minister claim the situation was under control? We were unnerved and visibly shaken. Images of those crazed faces and their shining weapons haunted me for days afterwards.

My coverage of the riots ruptured my relationship with Modi. Till that moment, we had been 'friends' (if journalists and netas can ever be friends!). We had freely exchanged views and would happily speak in Gujarati to each other, and he would regularly come on my shows. Now, a wariness crept in. As a politician who didn't appreciate any criticism, he saw me as emblematic of a hostile English-language media, and I always wondered if he had wilfully allowed the riots to simmer. A relationship based on mutual respect turned adversarial. He could not 'forgive' me for my riot reporting and I could never separate his politics from what I had seen in those bloody days. When my father passed away in 2007, Modi was the first politician to call and condole, but somehow the ghosts of 2002 would always haunt our equation.

With the benefit of hindsight, and more than a decade later, I have tried to rationalize the events of the 2002 riots. Was chief minister Modi really trying to stop the riots? Is the government claim that in the first three days of violence, sixty-two Hindus and forty Muslims were killed in police firing not proof enough that the Modi government was not allowing the rioters to get away scot-free? I shall not hasten to judgement, but I do believe the truth, as is often the case, lies in shades of grey. And the truth is, no major riot takes place in this country without the government of the day being either incompetent or complicit, or both.

My verdict is that the Modi government was utterly incompetent because it was aware that the Godhra violence could set off a cycle of vengeance and yet did not do enough to stop it. In the places from where I reported in Ahmedabad, I just did not see enough of a police presence to act as a deterrent to the rioters. The violence only really began to ebb once the army stepped in; the Gujarat police was caught with its khaki uniform betraying a saffron tinge. I remember asking the Ahmedabad police commissioner P.C. Pande about the failure of his force. His reply on a live television show stunned me. 'The police force is part of the society we come from. If society gets communalized, what can the police do?' I cannot think of a greater indictment of our police constabulary by its own leadership.

There was a personal angle as well. My grandfather P.M. Pant had been a much-admired and decorated police officer in Gujarat for more than three decades, eventually retiring as its chief in the 1970s. He had the reputation of being a tough, no-nonsense officer and had seen the 1969 riots in Ahmedabad. He died in 1999, but my stoic, self-contained grandmother was still in Ahmedabad in an apartment block dominated by Bohra Muslims—a Hindu Brahmin lady who lived in neighbourly solidarity with her Bohra neighbours, each feasting on the other's biryani or *patrel*. I told her what Mr Pande had told me about the situation in the city. Her reply was typically direct. 'Well, you go and tell him that your baba [grandfather] would have never allowed any such excuse.'

The other question—whether the Modi government was complicit—is slightly more difficult to answer. Lower courts have cleared Modi of any direct involvement and though there are troubling questions over the nature of the investigations, I shall not quarrel with the judicial system. It is never easy to pin criminal responsibility for a riot on the political leadership, be it Rajiv Gandhi in 1984 or Modi in 2002. Modi had, after all, been in power for just five months when the riots occurred, Rajiv for less than twenty-four hours. Modi's supporters claimed to me that their leader was not fully in control of the administration when the violence erupted. 'He wanted to stop it, but he just did not have the grip over the system. Not every minister would even listen to him,' claimed one Modi aide, pointing out that the chief minister had won his by-election only a few days before Godhra happened. Modi himself claimed to me that he wanted the army to be brought in right away, but the forces were tied up at the border because of Operation Parakram which had been launched in the aftermath of the terrorist attack on Parliament.

What is probably true is that in February 2002, the real boss of Gujarat was not Modi but the VHP general secretary Praveen Togadia. If there was a ringmaster for the 2002 riots it was Togadia, a doctor-turned-Hindutva demagogue. The moustachioed Togadia with his whiplash tongue was the one who called the shots—several ministers were beholden to him, and the street cadres were his loyalists. At the time, maybe even Modi feared him.

The VHP and the Bajrang Dal had built a strong network in Gujarat from the Ram Janmabhoomi movement in the 1980s, and Togadia, the rabble-rousing doctor-demagogue had emerged as an alternative power centre in the state. On the streets, the VHP's foot soldiers were most visible and led the attacks against the minorities. In the Naroda Patiya massacre in Ahmedabad in which ninety-seven people were killed, the list of those arrested (and later convicted) included a roll call of prominent VHP members of the area. Unlike Modi, who would not accept any involvement in the violence, Togadia was more forthright and declared he was 'proud' of his role. 'If we are attacked, you expect us to keep quiet? These Islamic terrorists have to be taught a lesson,' he told me in an interview.

In later years, Modi successfully reined in Togadia, even managed to virtually isolate him, but in the bloody days of 2002, he failed to do so. Whether that was deliberate or otherwise is a question only he can answer, but the political benefits of a consolidated Hindu vote bank were obvious. Modi will perhaps never answer the question, but it is very likely that barely five months into his tenure, he decided that it was wise political strategy, or perhaps rank opportunism, not to take on someone who reflected the blood-curdling desire for revenge on the street. Even if he wanted to stop the violence, he chose to play it safe by not challenging the VHP goons right away. Moreover, Togadia was part of the wider Sangh Parivar which claimed proprietorial rights over the BJP government in the state. Togadia and Modi had both cut their teeth in the same Parivar.

The violence perpetrated by their own cadres also meant that

Modi's benefactors in Delhi, Vajpayee and Advani, were faced with the tough choice of whether to act against their chief minister. The closest Vajpayee came to ticking off Modi was almost a month after the riots when he visited Ahmedabad and spoke of a leader's 'raj dharma' to keep the peace.

The immediate aftermath of the riots did, however, spark off a churning within the BJP and the political system. The Opposition was baying for his blood; international human rights agencies were demanding a full inquiry; the media and judiciary were relentlessly raising discomfiting questions. Matters needed to be settled one way or the other at the BJP national executive in Goa in April that year. I followed Modi from Gujarat to Goa, again a journey with a slight personal touch. While I was born in Ahmedabad, my late father had been born in Margao in Goa. It was in the balmy air of Goa that Modi's destiny was to be settled.

~

The plush Hotel Marriott in Panaji's Miramar Beach area was the rather unlikely setting for deciding the fate of the Gujarat chief minister in early April 2002. It was faintly amusing to see old-time RSS leaders in their dhotis and kurtas slinking past bikini-clad women sunbathing by the hotel swimming pool. But there were no poolside distractions for the gathered denizens of the Sangh whose focus of attention was squarely on Modi. He arrived at the conclave of the party's national executive, and claimed to me that he was ready to resign. I recall sending out what we call a 'news flash', even as Modi delivered a short speech at the meeting. 'I want to speak on Gujarat. From the party's point of view, this is a grave issue. There is a need for a free and frank discussion. To enable this, I will place my resignation before this body. It is time we decided what direction the party and the country will take from this point onwards.'

Was this offer of resignation spontaneous, or was it part of an orchestrated strategy to force the party to support him in its hour of crisis? The top BJP leadership had been divided on the issue while the RSS had put its weight behind Modi. L.K. Advani was clear—if Modi resigned, the party could not face the electorate in Gujarat. 'The "pseudo-secularists" may not approve, but Modi has emerged as the defender of "Hindu interests" in the aftermath of Godhra—he is a hero for our cadres,' was the gist of Advani's argument. Vajpayee was equally clear—Modi's failure to control the riots was a blot on the ruling coalition at the Centre, the National Democratic Alliance (NDA) and would only lead to its break-up. In the end, the Advani logic won out—the national executive rejected Modi's offer to resign. The party had re-emphasized its faith in its core Hindutva ideology—the ideology that unites and galvanizes its cadres, the voter-mobilizing machine, far more effectively than any other plank.

Years later, I sat over a drink at the India International Centre bar with Brajesh Mishra, Vajpayee's all-powerful principal secretary, to find out why the former prime minister fell in line so easily. 'Make no mistake, Vajpayee wanted Modi to resign. But while he may have been in charge of the government, the party did not belong to him. The BJP is not the Congress. If the party and the RSS come together even a prime minister like Vajpayee cannot have his way,' said Mishra, a trifle wistfully. In a television interview after his surprise defeat in the 2004 general elections, Vajpayee admitted that not removing Modi at the time was a mistake. I see it slightly differently. I believe that in the madness of the summer of 2002, Vajpayee could not have afforded to force Modi to resign. Godhra and the riots which followed had transformed Modi into a Hindu Hriday Samrat—he now represented the soul of the brotherhood in saffron. Through the trauma of the riots, a new leader had been born. Vajpayee, by contrast, was simply the acceptable public face of a coalition government.

The decision to reject Modi's offer of resignation electrified the Goa gathering. Cries of 'Modi Zindabad', *Desh ka neta kaisa ho, Narendra Modi jaisa ho*' (A nation's leader should be like Narendra Modi) rent the air. Foreign guests in the Marriott lobby must have wondered if they had strayed into a victory rally. That evening, I managed to catch up with Modi. The trademark aggression was back. 'Some people in the media and pseudo-secular elite have been carrying on a conspiracy against the people of Gujarat. We will not allow it,' he said with a triumphant firmness.

Modi had rediscovered his mojo and also his campaign plank. From that moment onwards, he would inextricably identify himself with six crore Gujaratis, their sense of hurt and their aspirations. By targeting him, Gujarat was being targeted; he was not the villain of 2002 but its victim. He had defended the state against 'terrorists' and had protected the people, and yet 'pseudo-secularists' were gunning for him. He didn't even need to directly refer to the riots and Hindu–Muslim relations; Godhra had ensured the underlying message was clear to the voters. If it needed to be amplified, the likes of Togadia were always there.

The political narrative in place, Modi decided to call for elections in July that year, eight months ahead of schedule. When the Election Commission rejected the call for an early election, citing law and order concerns and the continued need to rehabilitate riot victims, Modi chose to confront the commission. The chief election commissioner was no longer just J.M. Lyngdoh, but was derisively referred to by Modi as James Michael Lyngdoh, the emphasis being on his Christian identity. It was to be the beginning of a phase in Modi's politics where the lines between what constituted politically correct behaviour and what was simply politically expedient would be routinely crossed.

Itching for a confrontation, Modi decided to embark on a statewide Gujarat Gaurav Yatra ahead of the elections which had been rescheduled for December that year. Modi claimed he wished to invoke a sense of Gujarati 'pride' which he said had been unfairly tarnished by the criticism over the riots. What he really wanted to do was remind the predominantly Hindu electorate of the state how he had 'defended' their interests even at great personal cost. A new slogan was invented—'*Dekho, dekho kaun aya, Gujarat ka sher aya*' (See, see, the lion of Gujarat has come). Modi was now pitched as a Gir lion and a modern-day Sardar Patel rolled into one.

The Gaurav Yatra was launched from the Bhathiji Maharaj temple in the village of Fagvel in early September. I was seated in the front row in the press enclosure when Modi spotted me. Pointing to me in his speech, he said, 'Some journalists come from Delhi and target our Gujarat. They say we failed to control the riots and damage the image of peace-loving Gujaratis; but you tell me, will we allow this conspiracy against Gujarat to continue?'

The combative tone had been set. For the next four weeks, Modi used the Gaurav Yatra to portray himself as the 'saviour' of Gujarat. When the Akshardham temple was attacked on 24 September while the yatra was on, Modi turned adversity into opportunity. It gave him a chance to attack Pakistan, and in particular, its president Pervez Musharraf. In every speech, he would refer to 'Miyan' Musharraf and blame him for terrorism. The public target may have been Musharraf, but the message was really aimed at local Muslim groups—the Godhra train burning, after all, was still fresh in public memory.

The distinctly communal edge to the Gaurav Yatra surfaced in its most vitriolic form during a rally in Becharji on 9 September. This is where Modi referred to the riot relief camps as 'baby-producing centres' with his infamous one-liner, '*Hum paanch, hamare pachhees*' (We five, our twenty-five). In an interview to his admirer Madhu Kishwar, Modi later claimed that he was not referring to relief camps but to the country's population problem. He told her, 'This phrase was not uttered just to target relief camps. I say it even now that the population of our country is increasing rapidly. Today, if a farmer has five sons, they will soon, between them, produce twenty-five.'

Few will buy Modi's explanation. The entire Gaurav Yatra was taking place against the backdrop of the riots. The tone of Modi's speeches was set by the fragility of communal relations and the climate of fear and hate that had been sparked off by the violence. That he was allowed to get away with such blatant appeals to religion reflects the limitations of the law and the bankruptcy of the Opposition Congress in the state. The agenda had been set; only the people's verdict remained to be delivered.

That verdict was delivered on 15 December 2002. The night before, the Congress general secretary in charge of Gujarat, Kamal Nath, had rung me up exuding complete confidence. Nath is now a nine-time Lok Sabha MP, and had a swagger which is rapidly disappearing from the Congress. 'Rajdeep, let's do a dinner bet. You've got this one horribly wrong. We are winning it,' he said boastfully. Only a day earlier, I had predicted on our election analysis programme on television that Modi might win a two-thirds majority. Most exit polls had been a little more conservative in their estimates. My logic was simple—the post-Godhra riots had divided Gujarat on religious lines and the Hindu vote bank had been consolidated by Modi. Nath preferred to focus on micro details of constituencies and regions.

On that occasion, I was proven right and the veteran politician wrong (though he still has to buy me the dinner!). The BJP won an impressive 126 seats, the Congress just fifty-one. The BJP swept the riot-hit belt of north and central Gujarat, lending further credence to the theory that the violence had only served to polarize the electorate. Modi's strategy had worked. Only, he wasn't quite done yet.

That evening at the BJP headquarters, Modi agreed to do a 'live' interview with me. The mood amongst the cadres was not just jubilant but vengeful too. A large mob that had gathered outside wanted to 'teach a lesson' to those who had tried to 'malign' Gujarat and its chief minister. Some of the journalists were forced to escape through the backdoor of the office to avoid the mob. Rather than calming the situation, Modi proceeded to sermonize. 'Today, all of you must apologize to the people of Gujarat who have given you a befitting answer.' Surrounded by his supporters, Modi was an intimidating sight—steely eyes, a finger pointing at the camera, the face impassive. It was one of the most difficult interviews I have ever done.

That year, Modi was chosen by *India Today* newsmagazine as its Newsmaker of the Year. In a cover story on the Gujarat chief minister in its April 2002 issue, he was described as 'The Hero of Hatred'. Its tag line said: 'A culpable Modi becomes the new inspiration for the BJP even as this offends the allies, infuriates the

Opposition and divides the nation.' After almost three decades in public life, the organizational man turned television spokesperson turned chief minister was now a national figure. An RSS pracharak who was once accused of lacking a mass base, who had only fought his first election earlier that year, finally had an identity.

~

Modi's victory in 2002 gave him the chance to establish himself as the Supreme Leader of Gujarat. He did not squander it. Over the next few years, he set about systematically decimating all opposition within and outside the BJP. The ageing Keshubhai Patel was confined to the occasional rumbling at being sidelined. Suresh Mehta, another former chief minister, was too gentle to offer any real threat. Kashiram Rana, a former state BJP president, was denied a Lok Sabha ticket. Gordhan Zadaphia, who was minister of state for home during the riots and was close to Togadia, was forced out of the party and eventually formed his own group. 'Modi is the ultimate dictator—he will not tolerate anyone even questioning his decisions or leadership,' Zadaphia once told me. Ironically, just before the 2014 elections, Zadaphia returned to the BJP and was forced to publicly acknowledge Modi as his leader.

Even Togadia, who had played a crucial role as a rabble-rouser during the 2002 elections, was completely marginalized. Modi even went to the extent of razing roadside temples in Gandhinagar built by local VHP karyakartas, if only to send out the message that he wasn't going to do any special favours to the VHP for supporting him. Senior VHP leader Ashok Singhal likened Modi to Mahmud Ghazni for the demolition—ironical, since the rise of Modi had begun in 1990 during the rath yatra from Somnath to Ayodhya. Years later, an incensed Togadia told me in an interview, 'We have nothing to do with Modi. He may be Gujarat's chief minister, we stand for all Hindus!'

Perhaps the most controversial challenge to Modi's leadership came from Haren Pandya, the BJP strongman from Ahmedabad.

Pandya, like Modi, was strong-willed and charismatic. He was a two-time MLA and had been home minister in the Keshubhai Patel government when Modi became chief minister. Modi wanted Pandya to vacate his safe Ellisbridge seat in Ahmedabad for him. Pandya refused and a rather ugly battle ensued.

Pandya's own role during the riots was questionable—more than one account claims that he was among the mob leaders in the city. And yet, a few days after the riots, he dropped into our office in Ahmedabad with what sounded like a potential bombshell of a story. 'I have evidence that Modi allowed the riots to fester,' he claimed. On the night of 27 February, he said, Modi had called senior officials and told them to allow 'the public anger' to express itself. I asked him to come on record. He refused but gave me a document which showed that the Gujarat government was carrying out a survey to find out how the riots would politically influence the electorate.

What Pandya did not tell me on record, he told a Citizens' Tribunal headed by a retired judge in May that year. In August 2002, Pandya was removed from the government for breaching party discipline. In December, Modi ensured that Pandya was denied a ticket to contest the elections, even going to the extent of admitting himself to hospital to force the party leadership to agree to his demand. On 26 March 2003, while he was on his morning walk, Pandya was gunned down. The killers have not been caught till date, even as Pandya's family pointed a finger at Modi. A senior police officer told me, 'It was a contract killing, but who gave the contract we will never know.'

Remarkably, through all the chaos and controversy, Modi remained focused on his own political goals. He had won the battle within the BJP; he wanted to make an impact beyond. In this period between 2003 and 2007, Modi spent a considerable time understanding governance systems. Working a punishing eighteen-hour schedule at times, he was determined to chart a new path. He did not trust his fellow ministers, but he developed an implicit faith in the bureaucracy. Maybe he felt bureaucrats were less likely to challenge his authority. He collected around himself a core team of bureaucrats who were fiercely loyal. 'Modi gives clear orders, and then allows us the freedom to implement them. What more can a bureaucrat ask for?' one of the IAS officers told me. No file would remain on his table for long. Fastidious about order and cleanliness, he liked a spotless, paper-free table.

Three IAS officers, K. Kailashnathan, A.K. Sharma and G.C. Murmu, formed a well-knit troika—'Modi's men' is how they were perceived. Another bureaucrat, P.K. Mishra, guided him through the early period. All low-profile, loyal and diligent, they were just the kind of people Modi liked around him. 'They are more powerful than any minister in Modi's cabinet,' was the constant refrain in Gandhinagar. It was true—Modi's cabinet meetings lasted less than half an hour; he would spend a considerably longer time getting presentations from bureaucrats. For an outwardly self-assured individual, Modi seemed strangely paranoid about his political peers. At one stage, he kept fourteen portfolios with him—his ministerial colleagues, naturally, were unhappy.

One of the disgruntled ministers came to see me once in Delhi. 'Rajdeepji, I am planning to leave the government. Modiji doesn't trust me, he still thinks I am a Keshubhai man,' the senior minister said. A few months later, when I met the minister, I asked him why he hadn't resigned yet. 'Well, I have realized that in Gujarat, if you want to remain politically relevant, you have no choice but to be with Modi,' he said.

The minister was right. The ever-pragmatic Gujarati's business, they say, is business. The brightest minds find their way into *dhanda* (entrepreneurship)—politics hardly attracts any talent. The Congress, in particular, was a party in sharp decline, haunted by the familiar malaise of not empowering its local leadership. Their main leader, Shankersinh Vaghela, had spent most of his career in the BJP. 'How can we take on the RSS when we have made an RSS man our face in Gujarat?' Congressmen would often tell me.

Compared to his political competition, Modi was not only razor-sharp but always quick to seize on new ways to motivate his administration and push them towards goals. Whatever the political benefits he gained from the riots, it seemed as if he was always anxious to rewrite his record, reinvent his personality, his tasks made even more urgent by the desire to forget and even obliterate events which paradoxically and fundamentally shaped his political persona.

His bureaucrats were given twin tasks—implement schemes that would deliver tangible benefits to the people in the shortest possible time, and ensure the chief minister's persona as a development-oriented leader gets totally identified with the successful projects. In this period, the Gujarat government launched multiple projects, from those aimed at girl child education to tribal area development to irrigation and drinking water schemes. The aim was clear—show Gujarat as a state committed to governance and its leader as a *vikas purush* (man of development).

A good example of the extent to which Modi was willing to go to push the '*bijli, sadak, shiksha aur pani*' (electricity, roads, education and water) agenda was his Jyotigram Yojana, designed to ensure twenty-four-hour power supply, especially to rural Gujarat. A flat rate, approximating to market costs, was to be charged. Farmers who refused to pay would be penalized while power theft would lead to jail. RSS-backed farmer unions protested; the Opposition stalled the assembly. Unmindful of the protests, Modi went ahead with the scheme, convinced of its long-term benefits. 'Only someone with Modi's vision could have pulled off Jyotigram,' says one of his bureaucrat admirers. The Gujarat Model was born and would pay rich dividends to its leader in the years ahead. Today, Gujarat's power supply compares favourably with other states as does a double-digit agricultural growth rate. And even if there are dark zones as reflected in troubling child malnutrition figures, the overarching impression is of a state on the fast track to prosperity.

But the Gujarat Model was not just about growth rates and rapid development. It was also about recasting the image of the man who was leading Gujarat. It was almost as though development was Modi's shield against his critics who still saw him through the prism of the riots. For example, Modi took great pride in his Kanya Kelavani (girl child education) project. Every year from 2003, in the torrid heat of a Gujarat summer, IAS officers would fan out to convince parents to send their children, especially girls, to school. Modi himself had laid out the blueprint. In his book *Centrestage*, Ahmedabad-based journalist Uday Mahurkar says that Modi told his officers, 'Why should a child cry when she goes to school for the first time? We need to bring a smile on their face.' Cultural programmes were started to make the toddlers feel at home in school. Dropout rates fell and the enrolment percentage rose from 74 to 99.25 per cent in a decade. 'Why don't you show positive stories about Gujarat? *Kab tak negative dikhate rahoge?*' (How long will you keep showing only negatives?), Modi asked me on more than one occasion.

It seemed as though Modi wanted to constantly prove a point. The riots had left a big question mark on his administrative capability, and he now wanted to undo the damage. This wasn't just about his national ambitions—it was also about conquering the demons that nestled within, a yearning to prove his critics wrong.

An interesting aspect of this was Modi's relationship with industry, well documented in a *Caravan* magazine profile in 2012. In March 2002, barely a few weeks after the riots, at a Confederation of Indian Industry (CII) meet in Ahmedabad, Cyrus Guzder, a much-respected industrialist, had raised a pointed question—'Is secularism good for business?'—and likened the attacks on Muslim homes to a 'genocide'. It didn't stop there. I was speaking at a panel discussion at the CII annual summit in Delhi in April 2002 on 'Gujarat at the Crossroads' when Anu Aga of the Thermax group, who later became a member of Sonia Gandhi's National Advisory Council, lashed out, 'The Gujarat riots have shamed all of us.' She got a standing ovation from an audience that is normally very careful in displaying its political preferences openly.

In February 2003, the confrontation between Modi and industry appeared to worsen. Rahul Bajaj and Jamshed Godrej, two of the country's seniormost corporate leaders, spoke out on the 2002 riots in the presence of the Gujarat chief minister. Describing 2002 as a 'lost year' for Gujarat, Bajaj asked, 'We would like to know what you believe in, what you stand for, because leadership is important.'

Modi listened to the rush of criticism and then hit back. 'You and your pseudo-secular friends can come to Gujarat if you want an answer. Talk to my people. Gujarat is the most peaceful state in the country.'

Modi was now seething. He carried this sense of hurt and anger back with him to Gujarat; this rage would become a driving force channelized towards greater self-reinvention, towards revenge on those who questioned him critically. *'Een Dilliwalon ko Gujarat kya hai yeh dikhana padega'* (We have to show these Dilliwallas what Gujarat is), he told one of his trusted aides. Within days, a group of Gujarati businessmen led by Gautam Adani established a rival business organization—the Resurgent Group of Gujarat—and called on the CII's Gujarat chapter to resign for 'failing to protect the interests of the state'. The CII was on the verge of a split, forcing its director general Tarun Das to broker peace through senior BJP leader Arun Jaitley. Das was forced to personally deliver a letter of apology to Modi. 'We, in the CII, are very sorry for the hurt and pain you have felt, and I regret very much the misunderstanding that has developed.' Modi had shown corporate India who was the boss.

That year, the Gujarat government launched its Vibrant Gujarat summit, designed to showcase the state as an investment destination and re-emphasize the traditional Gujarati credo—'Gujarat's business is business'. I attended the summit in 2005 and was struck by the precision with which the event was organized. This was not just another government initiative—it was a glitzy event where one individual towered over all else. Every speaker would begin their speech by praising the chief minister, some a shade more effusively than others—Anil Ambani of Reliance Communications even going to the extent of likening Modi to Mahatma Gandhi and describing him as a 'king of kings'.

While corporate India fell in line, the media was proving more recalcitrant. On 12 October 2007, a few weeks before the Gujarat assembly elections, I had the occasion to moderate a session with Modi at the *Hindustan Times* Leadership Summit. Dressed, appropriately perhaps, in a saffron kurta, I was looking forward to the dialogue. The topic was 'Regional Identity and National Pride'. While Modi spoke eloquently on Mahatma Gandhi and development, I could not resist asking whether he had transformed from the politician of 2002 when he had been described by his opponents as a 'hero of hatred' and even a 'mass murderer'. The question touched a raw nerve—a combative Modi questioned my credentials as an anchor and wondered whether I would ever change and be able to look beyond the post-Godhra riots even while my kurta colour had changed!

At least, Modi did not walk out of the gathering. Less than ten days later that's precisely what happened when senior journalist Karan Thapar was interviewing him for CNN-IBN's *Devil's Advocate*. I had warned Karan before the interview that Modi was still very sensitive about Godhra and the riots and maybe he should broach the subject a little later in the interview. But Karan has a deserved reputation as a bit of a bulldog interviewer—relentless, unsparing and direct. Less than a minute or two into the interview, he raised the question of Modi's critics viewing him as a mass murderer despite his reputation as an efficient administrator, and whether he would express any regret over the handling of the riots. There was only one way the interview was going from that point on. Asking for a glass of water, Modi removed his microphone, thanked Karan and ended the interview. 'The friendship should continue. You came here. I am happy and thankful to you. These are your ideas, you go on expressing these. I can't do this interview. Three–four questions I have already enjoyed. No more, please,' was the final word.

The walkout might have embarrassed any other politician. Not Modi. When I rang him up a short while later, his response was typically sharp. 'You people continue with your business, I will continue to do mine.' The Gujarat assembly election campaign was about to begin and Modi wasn't going to be seen to be taking a step backwards.

A few days later, Sonia Gandhi on the campaign trail said those 'ruling Gujarat are liars, dishonest and *maut ka saudagar*' (merchant of death). Modi was enraged. It was one thing for a journalist to refer to him as a mass murderer in an interview, quite another for the Congress president to call him a 'killer'. The positive agenda of development was forsaken—in every speech Modi now claimed that the Congress had insulted the people of Gujarat. 'How can a party which can't act against terrorists talk about us?' thundered Modi. 'They call us maut ka saudagar. Tell me, is it a crime to kill a terrorist like Sohrabuddin?' The reference was to a killing by the Gujarat police that had been labelled a fake encounter. Muslim terrorism, Gujarati pride, Modi as a 'victim' of a pseudo-secular elite and the 'saviour' of Gujarat—it was almost 2002 all over again.

The election results in December 2007 confirmed that the Congress had self-destructed once again and Modi's strategy had worked brilliantly. The BJP won 117 seats, the Congress just fifty-nine. Chief minister once again, Modi was now brimming with confidence. '*Gujarat ki janta ne mere virodhiyon ko jawab diya hai*' (The people of Gujarat have answered my critics) was his firm response while flashing the victory sign. He was now the unrivalled king of Gujarat. But like all ambitious politicians, he wanted more.

~

There are two dates that define Narendra Modi's twelve-year chief ministership of Gujarat. The first was 27 February 2002—the Godhra train burning and the riots conferred on Modi, for better or worse, the image of a Hindutva icon. The second was 7 October 2008. On that day, the Tata group announced that they would be setting up the Tata Nano plant at Sanand in Gujarat. Its small car project had faced massive opposition over land displacement at its original choice of Singur in Bengal, fuelled by Mamata Banerjee's Trinamool Congress. Looking for an alternative site, the Tatas plumped for Gujarat as Modi offered them land at a very nominal rate.

That day, Ratan Tata, the Tata chairman, held a joint press conference with Modi. 'This is an extremely momentous day for us. We have been through a sad experience, but so quickly we have a new home,' said a delighted Tata, adding, 'there is a good M (Modi) and a bad M (Mamata)!'

A beaming Modi responded, 'I welcome the Tatas. For me, this project entails nationalistic spirit.' The truth is, it was more than just a business deal or even 'nationalism' for Modi. This was a symbolic victory, the moment when he finally got what election triumphs alone could not win for him—credibility as a trustworthy administrator. His attitude during the 2002 riots had won him the hearts of the traditional BJP constituency who saw him as a leader who had stood up to 'Islamic terrorists' and 'pseudo-secularists'. Being endorsed by Ratan Tata and rubbing shoulders with him gave Modi the legitimacy he secretly craved for amongst the middle class and elite well beyond Gujarat.

The Tatas, after all, are not just any other corporate. They are seen as one of India's oldest and most respected business brands, the gold standard, in a way, of Indian business. Their Parsi roots can be traced to Gujarat. As Tata admitted, 'We are in our home. *Amhe anhiya na chhe* (We are from here).' Modi, never one to miss an opportunity, also reminded the audience of how a hundred years ago Jamshedji Tata had helped Gujarat by donating Rs 1000 during a famine to save cattle. It was all very cosy and convenient. Tatas desperately needed land; Modi thirsted for reinvention.

That year, Ratan Tata was chosen the CNN-IBN Indian of the Year in the business category, principally for the manner in which he had established a global presence for the Tatas. I asked him for his views on Modi. 'He is a dynamic chief minister who has been good to us and for business in general,' was the answer. CII 2002–03 seemed far, far away.

This was, then, the moment when Modi's ambitions began to soar beyond Gujarat. A new self-confidence shone through, of a leader who believed his isolation was over. In this period, Modi travelled to China and Japan, countries whose economic and political systems he had long admired. This was also when Modi's public relations machinery began working overtime to make him more 'acceptable' across the world. The US had denied him a visa in 2005 in the aftermath of the riots, but his NRI supporters, including the Overseas Friends of the BJP, began to vigorously lobby for him at Capitol Hill.

In 2007, Modi had reportedly hired a global PR agency, APCO, at a cost of $25,000 a month. The brief was simple—market Modi globally and sell the Vibrant Gujarat image. Modi insisted that he had not hired any PR company for his personal image building. But it's true that he was undergoing a visible makeover. His speeches became more deliberate; the chief minister's office would release well-sculpted images of a 'softer' man—reading a book, playing with children, flying kites—all designed to showcase a New Age politician. Select journalists and opinion leaders were flown to Gandhinagar and would write glowing reports on Modi's capabilities. Modi even got a book on climate change ghostwritten which was released by former president A.P.J. Abdul Kalam. He also took his first tentative steps towards a social media outreach by signing into Facebook and Twitter in 2009.

Always a natty dresser, he became even more trendsetting with his Modi kurtas, designed by the Ahmedabad tailoring shop Jade Blue. At different functions on a single day, he would always be dressed for the occasion, often changing three or four times a day. He was always fond of pens, only now the brand in the pocket was Mont Blanc, the sunglasses were Bulgari, the watches flashy and expensive. A former aide told me at the time, 'Narendrabhai sees himself not just as the chief minister of Gujarat—he is the CEO of Gujarat Inc.'

This was also a period when the Gujarat government launched an aggressive campaign to promote tourism. In December 2009, the Amitabh Bachchan starrer *Paa* was released. The film's producers were pushing for an entertainment tax exemption. Bachchan met the Gujarat chief minister who readily agreed on one condition— Amitabh would have to be a brand ambassador for the Gujarat tourism campaign. Till then, Bachchan was seen to be firmly in the Samajwadi Party (SP) camp—his wife Jaya was a party MP, as was his close friend Amar Singh. He had even done a *'UP Mein Hain Dum'* (UP Is Strong) campaign for the SP in the 2007 assembly election. Now, he would be identified with *'Khushboo Gujarat Ki'*

(The Scent of Gujarat), with Ogilvy and Mather being hired for a massive ad blitz. Modi had scored another political point.

While Modi was repositioning himself, the BJP was caught in a time warp. The party had chosen L.K. Advani as its prime ministerial candidate for the 2009 elections in the hope that he could be projected as a 'tough', decisive leader in contrast to Manmohan Singh's softer, gentler image. The voter, however, did not seem enthused by the prospect of an octogenarian leader spearheading a new India. Moreover, in the aftermath of the Indo-US nuclear deal, 'Singh is King' was the refrain, especially among the urban middle classes. The UPA-led Congress scored a decisive victory in the polls. The BJP was left wondering if it would ever return to its glory days.

Modi may not publicly admit it, but this is where he began sensing his chances as a potential BJP prime ministerial candidate. The Advani–Vajpayee era was drawing to a close and there was an emerging leadership vacuum. Pramod Mahajan, the man I had expected to lead the BJP into the future, had died in tragic circumstances in 2006, killed by his own brother. Sushma Swaraj was a crowd-puller but appeared to lack the political heft to lead the party. Arun Jaitley was not a mass leader and needed Modi's support to get elected to the Rajya Sabha. Rajnath Singh as party president had just led the BJP to a defeat in the general elections. Modi was, in a sense, the natural choice.

That Modi was now looking squarely at Delhi became clearer in September 2011 when he launched a Sadbhavana Yatra (Peace Mission), aimed primarily at reaching out to the Muslims. The yatra was the most direct attempt made by Modi to shed the baggage of the post-Godhra riots. It was shadowed by controversy when Modi refused to wear a skullcap offered to him by a Muslim cleric, Maulvi Sayed Imam. When I asked him about it later, Modi's answer was emphatic. *'Topi pehenne se koi secular nahi banta!'* (You don't become secular by wearing a cap.) The words would cross my mind later when during the 2014 campaign, Modi wore different headgear, including a Sikh turban, at almost every public meeting.

The larger message being sent out during the Sadbhavana Yatra, though, was obvious—the Hindutva icon was unwilling to be a prisoner of his origins. He wanted to position himself as a more inclusive leader. The overarching slogan was '*Sabka Saath, Sabka Vikas*' (Together with Everyone, Development for All).

Zafar Sareshwala, a BMW car dealer in Ahmedabad, was among those involved in the execution of the yatra. Once a fierce critic of Modi—he claims to have suffered financial losses during the 2002 riots—he had become Modi's Muslim 'face' on television. Whenever he came to Delhi, he'd bring me Ahmedabad's famous mutton samosas and insist that Modi had evolved into a new persona. 'Trust me, Modi is genuine about his desire to reach out to Muslims and has even met several ulemas in private. Even the VHP and the BJP cadres were opposed to the yatra, but Modi did not buckle. He wants to forget the past and only look to the future,' Sareshwala would tell me.

On the streets of Gujarat, opinion was more divided among minority groups. If you met someone who had been personally affected by the riots, like Baroda university professor Dr J.S. Bandukwala, he would tell you that Modi needed to at least show some remorse for failing to stop the violence. 'My home was destroyed by the rioters. Not once did Modi even try and contact me to express any sense of solidarity for our loss,' says the professor with quiet dignity.

In February 2012, I did a programme on the tenth anniversary of the riots. My journey took me to Gulberg Society where sixty-nine people had been killed, with several in the list of those missing. Among the missing was a teenage boy Azhar, son of Dara and Rupa Mody, a devout Parsi couple. Along with my school friend, film-maker Rahul Dholakia, I had met the Modys just after the riot flames had been doused. On the wall of their tiny house was a picture of young Azhar with the Indian tricolour at the school Republic Day parade just a month before the riots. Rahul had decided to make a film on the Mody family's struggle to locate their son. The film *Parzania* would go on to win a slew of national awards, but couldn't be released in Gujarat because the theatre owners feared a backlash.

I had stayed in touch with the Modys and was shooting with them at Sabarmati Ashram. No one from the Gujarat government had even tried to help them all these years. Their only support had come from human rights activists, such as Teesta Setalvad, who were branded as anti-national by Modi's men. 'Couldn't such a big man like Modi come even once and speak to us?' Rupa Mody asked me tearfully. As a father of a lanky teenage son myself, I couldn't hold back my tears.

For the same news documentary I also travelled to a slum colony, Citizen Nagar, on the outskirts of Ahmedabad. Here, the riot-affected families had been literally 'dumped' in subhuman conditions near a large garbage mound into which the city's waste flowed. 'Modi talks of Vibrant Gujarat, but for whom is this Vibrant Gujarat, only for the rich?' one of the locals asked me angrily. In Juhapura, a Muslim ghetto in the heart of Ahmedabad—sometimes referred to as the city's Gaza Strip—the mood was equally unforgiving. 'Modi goes everywhere marketing himself, why doesn't he come to Juhapura?' was a question posed by many out there.

Interestingly, the more affluent Muslims had made their peace with Modi. Many Gujarati Bohra Muslims are traders and businessmen—they were ready to break bread with Modi so long as he could assure them a return to communal harmony and rapid economic growth. In my grandmother's building in the walled city, there were many Muslim middle-class families who had reconciled themselves to a Modi-led Gujarat. 'We have no problem with Modiji so long as we get security,' one of them told me. Many younger, educated Muslims too seemed ready to give him a chance. 'It's ten years now since the riots, it's time to move on,' was how a young management graduate explained his position.

And yet, how do you move on when your house has been razed and your relatives killed? Modi has claimed that his government's track record in prosecuting the guilty was much better than the Congress's in 1984. One of his ministers, Maya Kodnani, was among those who had received a life sentence. And that Gujarat had seen no major communal outbreak since 2002.

The truth is a little more bitter and complex. Yes, 1984 was a terrible shame, but then so was 2002. Any comparisons in death toll figures would reduce human lives to a tragic zero-sum game—'my riot' versus 'your riot'. Yes, Gujarat has also seen more successful prosecutions, but many of these were achieved only because of the tireless work done by a Supreme Court-supervised Special Investigating Team (SIT) and indomitable activists like Setalvad, and not because of the efforts of the Gujarat police. Honest police officers who testified against the government were hounded. Lawyers who appeared for the victims, like the late Mukul Sinha, were ostracized. As for Gujarat being riot free, I can only quote what an Ahmedabad-based political activist once told me, 'Bhaisaab, after the big riots of 2002, why do you need a small riot? Muslims in Modi's Gujarat have been shown their place.'

A Sadbhavana Yatra was a good first step but clearly not enough to provide a healing touch. Nor would a token apology suffice. In my view, Modi needed to provide closure through justice and empathy. He did not provide Gujarat's riot victims with either. Their sense of permanent grievance would only end when they were convinced that their chief minister wasn't treating them as second-class citizens. In the end, the high-profile, well-televised yatra only served as a conscious strategy to recast Modi's image as a potential national leader who was now ready to climb up the political ladder.

How should one analyse Modi's complex relationship with Muslims? Reared in the nursery of the RSS, political Hindutva had been at the core of his belief system. His original inspiration was the long-serving RSS chief Guru Golwalkar, whose rather controversial writings, especially *Bunch of Thoughts*, see the Indian Muslim as anti-national. Modi had been careful not to endorse Golwalkar publicly after becoming chief minister, but one sensed he could never distance himself fully from his early training (not a single Muslim was ever given a ticket by Modi in Gujarat).

Gujarat, too, had seen decades of Hindu–Muslim conflict. In the land of the Mahatma, the Gandhian values of religious tolerance and pluralism coexisted uneasily with a xenophobic hatred for the

'Mussalman'. Certainly, every time I visited Sabarmati Ashram in the heart of Ahmedabad, it felt like an oasis of harmony amidst the prevailing communal separateness. For the socially conservative Gujarati middle class, Modi seemed to represent a Hindu assertiveness they could identify with.

A year after his Sadbhavana Yatra, in September 2012, Modi had hit the road again. Ahead of the December 2012 assembly elections, there were concerns that a poor monsoon and anger against local MLAs could hurt the Modi government. Modi realized the need to directly connect with the voter. He launched a statewide Vivekananda Yuva Vikas Yatra, ostensibly meant to celebrate the 150th birth anniversary of the saint, but primarily designed to set the stage for the Gujarat election campaign to follow. Modi had long claimed to be inspired by Vivekananda, and by publicly identifying with him, he was looking to appropriate his legacy of 'inclusive' religiosity. This was again typical of Modi—he had this instinctive ability to create a well-marketed political event that would raise his profile.

I met Modi on the yatra in Patan district of north Gujarat. The choreography of the interview, not just the content, was fascinating. We had travelled around 150 kilometres to catch up with Modi. Dressed in a colourful turban, he was surrounded by supporters. When we finally got time with him in his spacious van, we set up to do the interview in a fairly large space at the rear end of the vehicle which allowed for proper seating and lighting. Modi refused to do the interview there. 'I will be sitting next to the driver—you will have to do the interview where I am!' he said. 'But there isn't space for me to sit next to you, so how do I do the interview?' I asked. Modi smiled. 'That is for you to work out!'

The interview was eventually done with me on the footboard of the vehicle, the cameraperson seated on the dashboard. It was perhaps Modi's rather characteristically perverse way of reminding me of my station in life as a humble journalist who was interviewing a Supreme Leader. Or perhaps of putting the English-language television media, which had haunted him all these years, in its place. To this day, Modi's relationship with the English-language media continues to be adversarial, even though there are many in its ranks who would be happy to be counted as his cheerleaders.

While he predictably stayed silent on any question related to an apology for the riots, turning away rudely from the camera, he did answer my question on whether he planned to move to Delhi if he won the Gujarat elections a third time. His answer was typically combative. 'Have people of this country assigned you and the media the task of finding the next prime minister'?' When I repeated the question of whether the next PM would be from Gujarat, his answer was cryptic. 'I am only focused on Gujarat and dream of building a strong state.'

Interestingly, I had asked him a similar question about his prime ministerial ambitions during the *Hindustan Times* Summit in 2007. Then, too, he had spoken of his love for Gujarat and how he was not looking beyond the state. Then, I had believed him. Now, his responses seemed to be more mechanical and lacking conviction. As he turned away from me, I could see a celebratory glint in his eyes—it suggested to me that, with victory in Gujarat almost assured, Modi was now ready to stake a claim for the biggest prize in Indian politics.

2

Prisoner of a Family Legacy

As with Narendra Modi, 2012 was a crucial year for the Congress's heir apparent Rahul Gandhi as well. He was turning forty-two, still 'young' by Indian political standards but no longer a novice in public life. If the Gujarat assembly election battlefield at the end of that year was Modi's Kurukshetra, then the Uttar Pradesh elections at the start of it were a severe test for the man blessed with the most famous surname in Indian politics.

Uttar Pradesh was, after all, not just the most populous state in the country—it was the *karmabhoomi* of the Gandhi–Nehru family stretching back several generations. The family tag had bestowed him with a 'national' leader status almost instantly, but Rahul Gandhi needed to prove himself on home turf to the Congress party and beyond. Rahul understood that, which is why through much of the summer of 2011 he had slogged it out in the heat and dust of UP, courting arrest during a farmers' agitation over land acquisition in the western UP village of Bhatta Parsaul and then starting off on a *padyatra* through the affected areas. Sleeves rolled up, both literally and metaphorically, he seemed ready for a big fight.

As the build-up to the UP elections continued, Rahul was drawing crowds and eyeballs. His Hindi had visibly improved, his speeches appeared less staccato and there was a definite energy in his campaign. Through this period, I had been attempting to contact him for an interview. But chasing Rahul is never easy—ensconced in a feudal political structure, the heir to the Congress family fortune would hardly ever reply to email and phone queries. A wall of deafening silence existed between him and me. Which is why I was pleasantly surprised one late evening in the middle of February, while UP was in the midst of a seven-phase marathon election, to receive a call to say that Mr Gandhi would be pleased to have breakfast with me the next morning.

There was only one slight hitch—I was in Mumbai doing a live show on the city's civic elections when the call came. My appointment, I was told, was at 8 a.m. sharp. No early morning Mumbai–Delhi flight would get me back on time and I was too late to take the late-night flight. Thankfully, I discovered that there was an international flight at 2.30 a.m. which ferried hordes of migrant workers from Mumbai via Delhi and Lucknow to the Gulf. So, seated amidst a large crowd of sleepy, rather desperate looking Indians heading out to make their future in the Saudi capital, I finally reached our national capital. A few hours' sleep and I was on my way to Rahul's office-cum-residence at 12, Tughlak Lane, bleary-eyed but hopeful that my long vigil for an interview was over.

On arrival, I realized I wasn't the only editor who had been summoned to the 'court' of Mr Gandhi. What I presumed was an interview was actually an informal press conference. Chai and idlis had been laid out and Mr Gandhi's man Friday Kanishka Singh was bustling around making sure every journalist was feeling comfortable. When Mr Gandhi arrived, he apologized for the last-minute invitation but mentioned he'd been awfully tied up criss-crossing UP. 'But I shall be happy to take all your questions,' was the earnest assurance.

Editors in a group can be terribly competitive and self-important. Each one of us was attempting to outdo the other by asking that one question which would be seen as truly 'newsy'. I asked two questions. The first was whether Rahul had ever considered putting himself up as the Congress's chief ministerial candidate for Uttar Pradesh. After all, Mayawati was the Bahujan Samaj Party's (BSP) incumbent chief minister, Akhilesh Yadav was the face of a potential SP government, why should anyone vote for the Congress when the party didn't even have a chief ministerial nominee? Even Jawaharlal Nehru had cut his teeth in Allahabad politics and had even been the city's mayor, so why didn't Rahul Gandhi offer himself to the UP voters as their man in the Lucknow hot seat? 'Good question,' said Mr Gandhi. 'I would be very happy to do that, but my party is a national party and won't allow me to just focus on one state.' Matter closed.

My second question was a little more controversial. Was it true that the Congress party was waiting for Rahul to take over as prime minister, and Dr Manmohan Singh as prime minister was a bit like Bharat in the Ramayana doing a holding job for Ram? The question was perhaps framed rather crudely or was considered inappropriate. Either way, it touched a raw nerve. 'I resent that, Mr Sardesai!' was the terse, angry response. 'The prime minister is doing a fine job and a question like this only belittles Dr Singh in a manner that I find unacceptable.' I had been suitably admonished. For the next hour, Mr Gandhi took other questions and lectured us on how UP was caught in caste and community politics, and how he could have easily lived abroad but had chosen instead to serve the people of the country—almost it appears out of a sense of noblesse oblige. I silently ate my idlis.

When the session was over, some of us asked if we could carry quotes from the interaction on the channels. I had already mentally conjured up a headline: Rahul wants to be chief ministerial candidate for Uttar Pradesh but his party won't let him! But we were all in for a severe disappointment. Just as we were all drafting headlines and working out the pitch, bang came the spoiler. 'Sorry, this is all off the record, I don't want any controversy in the middle of an election,' we were commanded by the Gandhi scion. My 2.30 a.m. flight with the bleary-eyed Gulf-bound breadwinners had been in vain.

So why had a galaxy of editors been summoned in the first place? The answer came from an old Congress source. Apparently,

Mr Gandhi had found the ground was slowly slipping away from the Congress in UP. Yes, his rallies had attracted sizeable crowds, the television cameras had focused on him, but the votes, not surprisingly, seemed to be going elsewhere. The enthusiasm of the previous summer when Mr Gandhi had led a farmer agitation had given way to the harsh realities of a UP winter where it was becoming increasingly obvious that the SP was in pole position to gain from the anger against the Mayawati government. The meet-the-press was designed almost as an anticipatory bail application. Mr Gandhi wanted to tell media leaders that he had tried, and tried hard, but that rebuilding the Congress in UP was a long-term project that would require more than one election to fructify.

A few weeks later, on 7 March, the UP results were out. The SP swept the elections. Akhilesh Yadav, not Rahul Gandhi, was the new great hope of UP. The Congress ended up with twenty-eight seats in the 405-member assembly, just six more than what it had got in the 2007 elections. The Rahul factor, if there ever was one, had failed. If this was a cricket match, the captain would perhaps have been dropped. But this was the Congress party, where the Gandhi family were not just the captains but the coach, manager and chief selectors too. As the enormity of the Congress defeat sunk in, the enduring image for the television cameras was a rather forlorn-looking Rahul Gandhi being consoled by sister Priyanka as the two of them, arms around each other, walked into the forbidding gates of 10, Janpath. If 2012 was the year that Narendra Modi's national ambitions began to crystallize, it was also the moment when Rahul Gandhi was given a rude wake-up call. A durable family name was not enough to overcome serious deficiencies in his political persona.

~

A boyish-looking Rahul Gandhi made his political debut in 2004. The decision to formally enter politics, like so much else in the Gandhi family, was taken at the dinner table with Sonia Gandhi and sister Priyanka in attendance. Rahul, we were told, was the apple of his mother's eye—'She just can't say no to him and he can be very obstinate,' is what a family friend told me—and Sonia was keen to see him take over what, for all purposes, had become a family business. Till then, he had zealously guarded his privacy. There was the occasional gossip item of a Latin American girlfriend he had been photographed with but little else. Rahul, we were told, was working with a management consultancy firm in London, was not particularly enamoured of politics and was still debating whether to live abroad or return to take forward the family legacy. He had seen his grandmother and father assassinated while still in his teens, had been forced to change his surname at Cambridge to ensure security, and had consciously shunned the limelight. And yes, he was still a bachelor.

His mother and sister had adopted different trajectories. Sonia Gandhi had entered politics in 1998 after a bloodless but rather unseemly coup in which veteran Congressman Sitaram Kesri had been removed overnight as party president. Rahul's sister Priyanka Gandhi had married young, was a mother of two and had also acquired a slight political profile while handling Sonia's campaign in 1999. I had spent a day filming with her at the time and must confess was thoroughly charmed. Forthcoming and attractive, with a striking resemblance to her grandmother Indira, Priyanka had then come across to me as a potential leader for the future. I still remember a local UP Congress leader, Akhilesh Singh, telling me, *'Dekhna, ek din Priyankaji bahut badi neta banegi!'* (Priyanka will one day become a big leader.)

All that changed in 2004 when it was formally announced that Rahul Gandhi would be the Congress candidate for Amethi, the seat from where his father Rajiv and uncle Sanjay had contested. That general election was expected to offer little hope to the Congress's declining fortunes. The BJP, under Atal Bihari Vajpayee, was the overwhelming favourite for a hat-trick of victories. India Shining was the buzzword and most opinion polls were predicting a comprehensive win for Vajpayee, the BJP's original vikas purush.

After we broadcast the results of one such pre-poll survey, I was called for an informal chat with Sonia Gandhi to her residence at 10, Janpath. It was only the second time I had visited the home of the Congress leadership; the previous occasion was an interview with Sonia Gandhi after a court order had exonerated Rajiv Gandhi in the Bofors case. With life-size pictures of Rajiv Gandhi on the wall and photographs of Nehru and Indira, the main room in 10, Janpath is an in-your-face reminder of the family tree that has dominated the country's post-independence politics. It can also be a little intimidating since there is an almost eerie silence when you enter. 'Are you sure we are doing so badly as your polls suggest?' was Mrs Gandhi's pointed query. I was about to explain our poll methodology, when a rather shy, tentative-looking Rahul entered the room, and was promptly introduced by his mother.

We shared polite smiles. Slightly nervously, I began to show our data to mother and son. Mrs Gandhi seemed concerned, the son a trifle dismissive. 'How can anyone do serious polling in a country of India's size with such a small sample? I've done market research and know how difficult it can be to get these things right,' was Rahul's initial response. He struck me at first sight as someone who didn't have too much time for pollsters or journalists. In fact, he almost deliberately demonstrated his scorn for urban election pundits in the usual fashion of a newly minted grass-roots embracer. As I attempted to defend my case, Rahul's mobile rang. He excused himself and did not return. Mrs Gandhi remained attentive to our presentation. The contrast was striking.

The family picture was complete when Rahul filed his nomination for the 2004 elections. Son with mother and sister next to him and brother-in-law Robert Vadra just behind—the nomination ceremony in Amethi was a family affair. Watching it was an audience which, in Amethi at least, appeared umbilically tied to the family. We were attempting a 'follow the leader' programme, which essentially involved tracking a leader for twenty-four hours. It was a terribly hot April and the team's energy was flagging badly in the heat. To make matters worse, the Special Protection Group (SPG) had created a firewall between Rahul and us. We spent four days in Amethi, seeking to speak and film with Rahul but with virtually no success.

Rahul just didn't seem interested in speaking to us. We even chased him on a late-night walk with his brother-in-law, but to no avail. 'Look, if I speak to you, I will have to speak to every news channel, and I don't want to do that at this stage,' was his firm response. When he finally did address the media in Amethi, it was almost as if he had been coerced into it. 'I just want to take my father's legacy forward and fulfil the work and dreams he had for Amethi,' was his answer to most questions. Any slightly loaded political question was deflected. 'I am not the leader of the Congress—you must ask Soniaji about this.'

Political novice or simply a shy recluse, the family surname was enough for Rahul to win his first election from Amethi very easily. What was more surprising was that the Congress and its allies emerged as the leading pre-poll grouping, leaving all opinion pollsters wondering where they'd gone so horribly wrong. The 'aam aadmi' plank had got the better of India Shining, and flawed alliances in Andhra and Tamil Nadu contributed to the Vajpayee government's shock defeat. That wasn't the only surprise. In a political masterstroke, Sonia Gandhi decided she would forego her prime ministerial claims, and chose Manmohan Singh as her nominee. She had listened, she claimed, to her 'inner voice'. With that one decision, she buried the debate over her foreign origins, achieved the halo of apparent renunciation and blunted, at least for the moment, the BJP's searing attack on her.

While Mrs Gandhi continued to wield enormous power as the UPA chairperson, Rahul did a disappearing act of sorts. Between 2004 and 2007, he was hardly seen in and outside Parliament. In the fourteenth Lok Sabha, Rahul participated in just five debates, asked just three questions, did not present a single private members' bill, and attended only 63 per cent of the Lok Sabha proceedings, well below the average attendance. In an interview to *Tehelka* magazine at the time (the Congress later denied that any interview was given, saying it was only a 'casual conversation'), Rahul was quoted as saying, 'I don't ask questions in Parliament because I like to think things through. Just look around at the questions that are asked in Parliament and you will know why I don't ask questions!' Sounding condescending and arrogant in equal measure, Rahul even controversially claimed in that interview, 'I could have been prime minister if I wanted at the age of twenty-five years!'

The one memorable Rahul intervention in Parliament came in 2008 during the Indo-US nuclear debate. Linking poverty to energy security, Rahul invoked the hardships of a Dalit woman Kalavati whom he had met during a tour of Maharashtra's drought-prone Vidarbha region. Kalavati's husband had committed suicide like hundreds of other farmers, and Rahul spoke passionately of the need to empower Kalavati. In a foreign policy debate on nuclear energy, Rahul had struck an emotional chord. But the moment remained typically fleeting because there was no sustained follow-up action to alleviate agrarian distress.

I met Kalavati a few years later when an NGO brought her to Delhi for a 'guided tour'. It was almost as though she had become a 'mascot' for Vidarbha's plight. Had her life changed, I asked. She nodded her head in a manner that suggested there hadn't been any dramatic transformation. Had she met Rahul Gandhi? More silence. Did she trust politicians? She didn't seem to want to answer. Kalavati's story, in a sense, appeared to typify Rahul Gandhi's politics—well intentioned but lacking the focus and stamina to convince the sceptics that he was a genuine 24/7 politician.

On 24 September 2007, another famous chapter in Indian cricket was scripted when Mahendra Singh Dhoni's team won the inaugural T20 World Cup, defeating Pakistan in the final. That win sparked the emergence of a new cricket hero in Dhoni. Rahul Gandhi perhaps was hoping for a similar political metamorphosis when on the same day he was anointed the Congress general secretary in charge of the Indian Youth Congress and the National Students' Union of India (NSUI). While the rest of the country was celebrating the cricket triumph, Congressmen were rejoicing in the fact that Rahul Gandhi had finally decided to take up a specific political responsibility.

On the face of it, it wasn't such a bad idea. The Youth Congress and NSUI were in desperate need of revival. The Congress was perceived as an ageing party in a 'young' country. Politics per se was seen as having no space for the youth even though 60 per cent of the population was under the age of thirty-five. As a young politician still in his thirties, Rahul Gandhi was, in a sense, ideally placed to effect a demographic shift in the Grand Old Party. If he could inspire the young to join politics, he was assured of a dedicated vote bank that would cut across traditional caste and community divisions. The last time a Congressman had attempted to build the Youth Congress was when Sanjay Gandhi took over the organization in the 1970s, leading to much controversy during the Emergency years. Rahul later told an aide in an unguarded moment, 'I am not my uncle. He tried to destroy the Youth Congress, I want to build it.'

A few months after taking over, Rahul met some of us at his residence (once again, off the record, of course!). Through the meeting, he spoke passionately about his desire to revamp the student bodies of the Congress, how he wanted to 'democratize' the organizations by ushering in new faces. He spoke of holding free and fair elections to these bodies, of organizing 'talent hunts' where necessary, of questionnaires that were being prepared to identify the right people for specific tasks. 'We will transform the Congress party bottom-up in a manner that will be truly revolutionary!' he said, with almost missionary zeal. For the old-timers amongst us, it was a near-rewind to Rajiv Gandhi's famous speech in the 1985 Congress centenary session in Mumbai when he had vowed to rid the party of 'power brokers'.

He also reflected on his other big idea—the need to bridge the divide between 'Bharat' and 'India', between the 'poor' and the 'rich'. I had heard him speak on the 'two Indias' at a public rally during the Congress plenary session in November 2007; now he was giving us a detailed exposition on his social and economic world view. 'You cannot have one India that travels on a bullet train and another that takes a bullock cart,' he said in a tone of controlled aggression. I couldn't decide whether he was astoundingly platitudinous or earnestly sincere, whether the lectures on the Indian predicament were his own eureka moments, or whether in fact he had charted out a long-term agenda of inclusive growth for a more compassionate India.

I must confess emerging from that meeting with a sense that we had perhaps underestimated Rahul Gandhi. Here was a young man from India's most durable political family promising to end the dynasty cult and open up the closed shop that Indian politics had become. His economic thoughts were more dodgy—they appeared almost a straight lift from some 1970s thesis, echoing a certain old-world socialist viewpoint that was completely at odds with the massive changes taking place in post-liberalization India. The growing interlocking between the countryside and the market economy seemed to have missed him altogether. And yet, I was inclined to give him the benefit of the doubt—if he could show the same fervour in transforming his ideas into a concrete plan of action, then we were really witnessing the start of a new innings in Indian politics.

In the next two years—2007 to 2009—Rahul Gandhi kept up this image of being a youth leader who stood for 'change'. NSUI conventions were organized across the country where Rahul Gandhi would reiterate his desire to bring in a new order of politics by ridding his party of the 'nomination' culture. Images of enthusiastic students greeting him were seen on TV screens. His critics called it a 'discovery of India' tour, suggesting that Rahul Gandhi was still struggling to get acquainted with the real India. When he visited a Dalit home for a night, Mayawati accused him of 'opportunism' and a desire to pander to Dalit voters. 'He has used a special soap and incense to purify himself,' she thundered at a rally in April 2008. The visits may have smacked of tokenism, perhaps even of poverty tourism, but at least a Gandhi finally seemed to be readying himself for a fierce political battle.

It didn't take long, though, for the bubble to burst. On a visit to

Mumbai, a few Youth Congress members expressed a desire to meet me. I asked them about the electoral process that had been initiated in the organization. 'What elections, sir, everything is being fixed and a lot of money is changing hands. You must expose it,' was their plea. Apparently, the main candidates in the fray were all sons of leading Congress politicians from the state. Eventually, the Maharashtra State Youth Congress 'elected' as its president Vishwajeet Kadam, son of a powerful state minister who owned a chain of private education institutes. The pattern was repeated in other states with the children of top politicians dominating key positions. When it came to Lok Sabha seats too, most of the younger candidates had family links with senior leaders. Attempts at fostering inner-party democracy could not break the well-entrenched cliques of patronage within the party system.

In a sense, Rahul Gandhi was a prisoner of the very system that had spawned him. Once the top leadership of the party observes the dynastical principle, it is difficult to impose a different set of rules for those down the line. The deep paradox remained that Rahul could not radically alter the Congress and yet insist on quasi-royal status for himself—the road to genuine glasnost would have to include his own abdication. He may have genuinely wanted to change the organizational structure, but in a party as old as the Congress, as ossified and as crowded with big egos, rival camps, an entrenched old guard and byzantine intrigue, no quick fixes were possible.

But the problem was not just with the Congress party—it was also with the method adopted by Rahul Gandhi to try and effect change. In her book, *Decoding Rahul Gandhi*, author Aarthi Ramachandran claims that Rahul Gandhi wanted to adopt a Japanese style of management to revamp the NSUI and Youth Congress. 'The Toyota Way' is how Gandhi saw the future, urging his team to develop the right 'processes' and 'systems' which would make standardization of practices possible. Apparently, a few of his team members were even sent to the Toyota factory in Japan to get first-hand experience of how the auto company was able to arrive at a zero-error system of production.

Rahul Gandhi failed to recognize that a political party is not a corporate house. Business practices that worked in the automobile industry simply could not be replicated in the Congress party. A senior MLA from Maharashtra told me how he had to wait almost a month in Delhi for an appointment with Rahul. 'In a business, you can interact on the computer. In a political party, there must be direct contact. What is the point of having a "system" when I cannot even get access to my leader? A party worker feels on top of the world when his leader talks to him; he doesn't want to be told to fill in a form first and wait in a queue!' The frustrated politician later joined Sharad Pawar's National Congress Party (NCP). In fact, more than one Congressman complained that if they rang up Rahul's office, they would be put through to a voice recording machine.

The people chosen by Rahul Gandhi to implement his agenda reflected a desire to have strategic consultants, management-oriented corporate types and well-meaning scholars around him rather than full-time politicians. The one member of Team Rahul whom I met on a couple of occasions was Kanishka Singh. A slight, bespectacled, soft-spoken young man, he was the son of a former foreign secretary, S.K. Singh, who later became a governor. Kanishka had a degree in international studies and business from the University of Pennsylvania, a degree in economics from St Stephens College and had even done a stint in an investment bank in New York. In other words, he was the perfect child of Delhi's elite Lutyensland, complete with well-connected parents, a foreign degree and a CV that would probably have got him a top job in corporate India. But was he the right man to be strategizing politics for the Congress's future?

Kanishka had, interestingly, written about the need to restructure the political system in an article in *Seminar* magazine in December 2005: 'Our leaders are older than they ought to be. Our citizenry is young. A severe and visible disconnect exists between the separate time horizons that each of the two groups are focused on and invested in . . . If India is to leapfrog into the millennium we live in, we need to be proactive in demonstrating that political and organizational capital is being invested in the domain of future-oriented implementation.' The words sounded perfect, echoing Rahul Gandhi's similar desire for change. But in the cut and thrust of electoral politics, what did these high-sounding fancy words really mean in practice?

On one social occasion, Kanishka and I got down to discussing UP politics. He rattled out impressive statistical data on caste and community equations in the state, but you could easily sense this was the kind of knowledge that one acquires on the Internet. He couldn't, or so I sensed, have intimate knowledge of the local leaders of the Congress in each district of UP, the kind of personal information that makes a Mayawati or a Mulayam such a formidable opponent in the state. The roaring, rumbustious subaltern leaders of the Hindi belt can hardly be combated through an academic grasp of caste combinations.

The other member of Rahul Gandhi's A-Team was Sachin Rao. Like Kanishka, he, too, was foreign educated, having got an MBA in international business and strategy from the University of Michigan. He was deeply influenced by management guru C.K. Prahlad's 'Bottom of the Pyramid' philosophy. He had returned to India with a desire to build a culture of 'social entrepreneurship', to reach out to those poor and marginalized sections who needed access to markets and technology. His NGO-like approach to politics appeared to mirror Rahul Gandhi's 'two Indias' philosophy.

Interestingly, during this period, Rahul Gandhi also sought out prominent left-leaning academics as part of his 'political learning' process. Professor Sudha Pai of Jawaharlal Nehru University (JNU), an expert on BSP and UP politics, was one such academic. Rahul even attended a seminar at JNU on 'UP in the 1990s: Critical Perspectives on Politics, Society and Economy' and invited Prof. Pai to speak to a Congress youth training camp in Chitrakoot in UP. Dalit Bahujan scholar Kancha Ilaiah, known for his controversial anti-Brahminical views, was also engaged with. Caste politics in particular had, it seems, captured Rahul's imagination.

Gandhi clearly was looking for intellectual sustenance to shore up dwindling political self-confidence. One academic told me that Rahul would often ask him to suggest books he should be reading. 'When I gave him a list, he promptly asked his assistant to get the books as soon as possible,' the academic claims.

Another academic wooed by Rahul was Prof. Yogendra Yadav of CSDS, best known for his psephology and election analysis on television. 'I was most impressed with Rahul when I first met him,' Yogendra confessed to me once. 'He came across as good-hearted and well read.' Then why did Yogendra eventually not bite the bait and become part of Rahul's think tank? 'I think one eventually realized that for all his good intentions, he couldn't really change the system as he was promising. The Congress party was too set in its ways to change,' says Yogendra, who in 2013 joined the Aam Aadmi Party (AAP).

Yogendra may have stayed away, but Rahul appeared to find an intellectual mentor in Dr Mohan Gopal, director at the Rajiv Gandhi Institute of Contemporary Studies (RGICS) and a former director at the National Law School in Bangalore. Gopal joined RGICS in 2011 and began providing Rahul with key inputs on political and constitutional issues. It is Gopal who is believed to have suggested to Rahul that he should target the 'Not Rich, not Middle class, not BPL' (referred to as NRMB) constituency, sandwiched between poverty and middle-class incomes. This idea would lead Rahul in the 2014 elections to seek out the unorganized sector social groups like street vendors, farm labour and daily wage earners as a potential vote bank (see chapter 8).

Gopal has an interesting CV. He was one of the founders of the Congress's student wing, the NSUI, in the 1970s. He even became president of the NSUI between 1974 and 1976 before leaving party politics to do a law doctorate at Harvard, then work for twenty years in legal administration at the World Bank and then head the prestigious National Law School in Bangalore.

I met Gopal for this book and asked him to describe his relationship with Rahul. 'No, I am not an adviser or mentor to Rahul, I am only a colleague,' is how he described the equation. He claimed that Rahul had 'genuine empathy and goodwill for the poor' and was looking to provide them with a *dhancha* (support). 'Long before Aamir Khan discovered Bezwada Wilson and the *safai karmachari*s in *Satyamev Jayate*, Rahul was already in dialogue with them on what needed to be done for manual scavengers,' claims Gopal.

I wondered whether the kurta-clad Gopal had drawn Rahul into the NGO–*jholawallah* circuit, in a sense, and thereby retarded his political growth. 'I think that is a spurious argument. Don't forget, a political party is also an NGO that is meant to serve the aam aadmi,' he countered.

Rahul, though, clearly seemed to lead two lives. In the day he would engage with thinkers and activists, but at night he seemed to draw comfort from being in the company of family friends from the glamorous Page Three set. Perhaps the India–Bharat divide was most in evidence in his own personality, a split he was perpetually trying to reconcile both with himself and with his view of India. Delhi's gossip bazaars would endlessly speculate on who his latest girlfriend was and on the mysterious foreign trips he would often take off on. I found it amusing that every year in June when Rahul celebrated his birthday, the Congress faithful would line up outside his Tughlaq Lane residence with cakes and garlands. Only the birthday boy was never there—he was beating the summer heat abroad with undoubtedly much more fun folk than Congress netas!

Rahul, it appeared, had very few close friends in politics. There were a few MPs who the media scornfully referred to as the *babalog* MPs (the word 'babalog' was first used for Rajiv Gandhi's coterie, his Doon School–Cambridge buddies like Arun Singh, Suman Dubey, Vivek Bharat Ram and Romi Chopra) whom he would occasionally hang out with. The likes of Jyotiraditya Scindia, Milind Deora and Jitin Prasada were in the same age group as Rahul Gandhi. Like him, they, too, came from illustrious political families, spoke fine English, were educated abroad, and had perhaps similar cultural tastes and hobbies. Jyotiraditya's father Madhavrao had been a close family friend and a Cabinet minister in Rajiv Gandhi's government. Deora plays a rather swinging rock guitar and Rahul Gandhi has been spotted at Deora's gigs. His father Murli was a Rajiv loyalist who had stood by the Gandhi family. Prasada's father had fought for the Congress presidency against Sonia Gandhi in 1999 and lost. The shared past perhaps made it easier for this Congress Generation Next to bond with one another.

One of the few exceptions to this 'people like us' syndrome encircling Rahul was Meenakshi Natarajan, a rare young Congress leader to rise in the party hierarchy without a famous surname. Natarajan who won the Lok Sabha elections in 2009 from Mandsaur was proof that Rahul's experiment to break the Congress's traditional structures could work only if it was pushed through with firmness at every level. Sadly, that did not happen.

Perhaps, Rahul Gandhi needed that comfort factor in being surrounded in his private life by people with similar values and upbringing. He was happiest in the company of those with whom he could be himself, with whom he could go gymming, cycling and biking (he has a fascination, I am told, for Harley-Davidson bikes). After witnessing terrible tragedy within the family at an early age, he had lived a sheltered life and had spent an extended period of his early adulthood out of the country. He had every right to his privacy, but forgot a cardinal principle of contemporary politics—a full-time politician has almost no private life. Genuine mass leaders will keep their doors open for one and all round the clock. I once sat with Lalu Prasad in his bathroom while he was shaving, while Mamata Banerjee will SMS you at 2 a.m. with a news point!

Rahul, it appears, prefers the corporate 9 a.m. to 6 p.m. working style, ill-suited to a political world where every party member should have a right to your time. An old Congressman who knew Rajiv Gandhi well draws a fine contrast. 'Rajiv liked to take his Sundays off, but the rest of the week, he would work a punishing schedule, often till late in the night. Rahul is ready to work hard, but wants to switch off all too often. He doesn't understand he is not working in a foreign bank but is in politics in India.'

Rajiv was also a naturally warm and open-hearted person. Rahul, though, tends to be reserved and lacking the easy charm of his father. I had met Rajiv once in 1990 at a function organized by the then South Mumbai MP Murli Deora. His ready smile had floored the audience within minutes. Rahul, I was told, could have mood swings. 'He can be gracious and attentive one moment, and seem rude and stand-offish the next,' is how a Congress MP described his behaviour. Apparently, when Rahul once visited Chennai for a Youth Congress function, a senior Congress leader from Tamil Nadu suggested he might wish to pay a courtesy call on M. Karunanidhi who was then chief minister and a Congress ally. 'I am here for a Youth Congress function, I can meet him some other time,' was the terse reply. He eventually never met the DMK chieftain.

Unlike Rajiv, who was blamed for relying on a tiny cabal for political advice, Rahul does seek wider counsel. He would, for example, as regularly consult Sam Pitroda, the flamboyant technology adviser to Rajiv, as he would a university academic or a business leader. 'He is much brighter than you think,' Pitroda once told me, a shade defensively.

But the truth is, Rahul has miserably failed to build a political team of substance. He gave important posts to relatively minor politicians like Madhusudhan Mistry (general secretary in charge of UP) and Mohan Prakash (general secretary in charge of Maharashtra and a former Janata Dal leader). 'These are netas who can't win a seat in their home states—how will they win some other state for us?' a senior Congress MP told me caustically, adding, 'Just because they look and talk like NGOs doesn't make them leaders, for God's sake.'

This is perhaps where he should have taken a cue from M.S. Dhoni. As India captain, Dhoni built a culture of excellence by bridging the gap between the senior legends like Sachin Tendulkar, Anil Kumble and Rahul Dravid and a new generation led by Yuvraj, Suresh Raina and Virat Kohli. It was that unique combination of young and old with merit as the great unifier which saw India become the number one test Team in the world. Sadly, Rahul Gandhi was never able to create a similar enduring team spirit in the Congree Party. The older generation Congressmen couldn't fathom him, the younger ones didn't feel empowered enough. Party loyalists may have accepted his leadership, but one sensed that they didn't really respect him. It is a crucial difference. Respect, even in the sycophantic Congress culture, has to be earned—it isn't conferred by birth.

~

By the time the 2009 general elections arrived, Rahul Gandhi was established as a 'national' leader even though he still hadn't proved his vote-catching abilities beyond Amethi. In 2004, Sonia Gandhi had dominated Congress posters. Now, she was sharing space with her son and the prime minister, Dr Manmohan Singh. In 2004, the Congress had almost given up on the elections. Now, five years later, there was a greater sense of self-belief. You could see it in the body language of Rahul as well. Where five years ago he had hesitated to step out of Amethi, he was now actively campaigning across the country. I managed to get a sound bite from him while he was on the campaign trail in Mumbai. 'We're winning this one, and winning well,' he said with a cheery, dimpled smile.

He was right. The Congress won 206 seats, its best performance since its landslide win in 1984. Its UPA alliance won 262 seats which put it in a comfortable position to form a government once again. Manmohan Singh would be India's prime minister once again, the first to win two successive five-year terms since Jawaharlal Nehru. But the credit, unsurprisingly, went to Rahul Gandhi. Every Congress leader who appeared on television on counting day hailed Rahul's 'dynamic' leadership. Dr Singh's contribution as the incumbent prime minister seemed but a footnote. The fact that the Congress had won as many as twenty-one seats in Rahul's home state of Uttar Pradesh only added to the euphoria around the Congress's 'yuvraj'. It only seemed a matter of time that the 'prince' would be crowned. 'Just you wait and see, in a year or two Dr Singh will step aside and Rahul will take over,' was a refrain one heard from more than one Congressman. Sycophancy Congress-style had just received a new lease of life.

There was another group within the Congress which felt that Rahul should become a minister in the new government. They suggested that Rahul become either rural development or human resource development minister since he had strong views on rural uplift and education. 'He refused us point-blank,' says a member of that group. 'His view was that he could only focus on one thing at a time and at that moment he was obsessed with "democratizing" the Youth Congress and NSUI.' The truth is, the idea of a Gandhi family member working under another prime minister also made some Congressmen uneasy, though Indira Gandhi did serve briefly as information and broadcasting minister under Lal Bahadur Shastri in the 1960s.

It wasn't just loyal Congress family courtiers who were heaping praise on Rahul. There were enough of us in the media who were praising Rahul's youthful enthusiasm as a crucial factor in the ruling alliance's triumph. That year, the CNN-IBN Indian of the Year award in the category of politics was awarded to Rahul Gandhi. At the jury meeting chaired by eminent jurist Soli Sorabjee, the verdict was unanimous. 'For galvanizing the Congress cadres, for reaching out to young India and enthusing millions of Indians to vote for the Congress, the CNN-IBN Indian of the Year award goes to Rahul Gandhi,' read the citation.

In hindsight, we were wrong. Yes, Rahul had worked hard; yes, the Gandhi family name had helped the Congress in Uttar Pradesh where the voter was looking for an alternative at the national level to the BSP and the SP. But the real credit for the Congress's strong performance in 2009 should have gone to the prime minister. Only a year before, he had dared the left parties to withdraw support to his government over the Indo-US nuclear deal, stitched an alliance with the SP and won a contentious vote on the nuclear issue in Parliament. Indians like it when their leaders get tough—the nuclear vote, no matter how briefly, transformed Dr Singh into a prime minister who was ready to sacrifice his chair for a principle. 'Singh is King' became the theme song that carried the UPA to victory. The BJP's L.K. Advani, by contrast, looked liked a tired leader, well past his prime. Yet, the self-effacing prime minister was forgotten and Rahul was hailed as the game changer.

The CNN-IBN Indian of the Year awards were held in December that year. The prime minister was the chief guest, Rahul one of the winners. Every other winner—be it A.R. Rahman (who was chosen as the overall Indian of the Year for his Oscar-winning compositions in *Slumdog Millionaire*) or badminton player Saina Nehwal who won the award for sports—was present at the ceremony. Rahul chose not to attend. For weeks before the event, we had tried to convince him to receive the award. Several phone calls and emails went typically unanswered. We had even asked his sister Priyanka to remind him that it would appear inappropriate for Rahul to stay away when the prime minister was the chief guest. 'He is very busy, you can read out a message on his behalf,' was the official response from Team Rahul. The fact is, Rahul was in Delhi, but apparently did not see any reason to attend the function. A message was read out on his behalf.

Why did Rahul choose to avoid receiving an award from the prime minister? Priyanka claimed that Rahul didn't believe in awards. 'He likes his work to do the talking,' was her explanation. Maybe Rahul realized what some of us hadn't—he still hadn't done quite enough to deserve the label of 'politician of the year'.

Giving Rahul the major credit for the 2009 victory was not the only misreading of the electoral result. The Congress party believed that the win was a triumph of their 'inclusive' social and economic agenda. The government's flagship scheme for rural jobs—the National Rural Employment Guarantee Act (NREGA)—had been projected as reflecting the vision of Rahul and Sonia Gandhi. Rahul, in fact, had led a Congress delegation to the prime minister in 2007 to have the scheme extended to the entire country. Within two days, the government followed Rahul's wishes at an additional cost of Rs 8000 crore. Rahul had also fully backed the Rs 60,000 crore farm loan waiver scheme that was introduced in the 2008–09 Union budget. NREGA and farm loan waiver—Congressmen were convinced these were the twin planks that had propelled them back to power.

The truth is, the Congress actually performed much better in urban, rather than rural, India in the 2009 elections. The UPA alliance swept to power in every major metropolis, except Bangalore. The alliance won around 130 of the 200 seats which could be seen to have an 'urban character'. It was the urban middle class which was the backbone of the UPA's electoral growth, yet Congress strategists convinced themselves that their rise was in the countryside.

Rahul Gandhi, too, was convinced of the Congress's rediscovery of rural India. In October 2009, he again met some of us (again, need I say, an interaction that was off the record) to expand on his political theories. Invoking his grandmother, he said, 'Indiraji taught us this in the 1970s with her *Garibi Hatao* slogan. The core Congress vote lies amongst the poor and marginalized, among farmers, Dalits and tribals. That vote is our strength. We need to preserve it and then get an incremental vote amongst other sections. Once we do that, we will be unbeatable.'

There was a second argument he made that day. 'All of you see this as a victory of an alliance. I see it differently. I believe that the Congress party has to strengthen itself. Our future is not in alliances, it is in making the Congress party the dominant force of Indian politics once again,' he said emphatically. I tried to point out how the Congress was still in no position to call the shots without allies in key states like Bihar, UP, Bengal, Tamil Nadu and Maharashtra. 'The problem with political journalists is that you think short term. I prefer to have a long-term vision!' was his sharp response. We realized it wasn't easy winning an argument with a leader who didn't have to deal with too many dissenting voices. And who, frankly, liked to talk more than listen.

In the next five years leading up to the 2014 elections, Rahul's 'twin vision' shaped his and the Congress party's strategy. 'Inclusiveness' was the new mantra chanted almost routinely while debating economic policy. 'Congress first' became the dominant political philosophy in place of coalition dharma and the idea of a common minimum programme of UPA-I.

In the next two years, Rahul tried to consciously project himself

as the *aam aadmi ka sipahi* (common man's soldier)—his heart,
we were told, did not lie in the bright lights of the big cities. When
he went to Mumbai, he travelled by a local suburban train as if to
suggest to the daily commuters that he shared their concerns. When
the British foreign secretary David Miliband visited India, Rahul
took him for another night stay in a Dalit home in a UP village,
and to Amethi to introduce him to the women's self-help groups he
had set up there. Critics saw many of Rahul's efforts as tokenism;
his image-makers saw it as defining Brand Rahul as a leader of the
aam aadmi.

Perhaps the best example of what Rahul was attempting was his
intervention in the contentious debate over mining and environment
rights in Niyamgiri in Odisha's Kalahandi district. At the heart of
the debate was whether the local Dongeria Kondh tribals had rights
over their land which had been acquired by the Vedanta group for
setting up a $1.7 billion aluminium refinery. The Niyamgiri hills were
flush with bauxite deposits but were also part of a rich biodiversity
zone. Moreover, the local tribals believed the hill to be sacred and
an abode of their deity, Niyam Raja.

Visiting Niyamgiri in March 2008, Rahul grandly announced,
'Kalahandi ka aur Adivasiyon ka Delhi mein ek sipahi hai aur uska
naam hai Rahul Gandhi' (Kalahandi and the tribals have one soldier
in Delhi, and his name is Rahul Gandhi). At a press conference
in Bhubaneshwar, Rahul underlined his stand. 'I am not against
industrialization per se. What I am for is fairness. My personal
view is that doing mining there will destroy the environment. It will
destroy the water supply of thousands of people. It will destroy their
culture. And I am against that personally.'

On 24 August 2010, more than two years after Rahul had
spoken out, the environment ministry refused to grant clearances
to Vedanta's proposed bauxite mine. The environment minister at
the time was Jairam Ramesh, a nominee of Sonia and Rahul Gandhi
to the Union Cabinet. An IIT graduate, the silver-haired Ramesh is
erudite and intellectual, rare qualities for a Congressman. He is not a
traditional politician and has never contested a Lok Sabha election. A

man of ideas and policy, not of the masses, he likes to see himself as an old-style Nehruvian liberal. His critics see him as an opportunist. He had worked as a back-room boy in the governments of V.P. Singh, Narasimha Rao, the United Front and even served as an economic adviser to Chandrababu Naidu. His big move up came when he strategized the Congress's 2004 election campaign successfully. He was credited with fashioning the winning slogan—'*Congress Ka Haath, Aam Aadmi Ke Saath*'. During UPA-I, Ramesh was the key member of Sonia Gandhi's National Advisory Council—a clutch of NGOs and public intellectuals who shared a left-of-centre ideology. In UPA-II, Ramesh was given independent charge of the environment and forests ministry.

Tech-savvy, policy-driven, English-speaking, a left-leaning liberal—Jairam perhaps was attractive to a Rahul with similar inclinations. I asked Jairam of his equation with Rahul, and whether he had helped shape his economic and social vision. 'I was not his adviser. Whenever he needed inputs I was there for him. But his ideas were his own in the end,' he says.

One such idea led to the successful setting up of women's self-help groups in Amethi. 'Early on in his political career, I took him to Andhra Pradesh. He met and saw the work being done by self-help groups. Till then, he was sold on microfinance but that visit changed him. So, he was ready to learn all the time,' says Ramesh. A similar experience with the milk cooperative movement in Gujarat saw the setting up of similar milk producing centres in UP.

Ramesh claims that Rahul was driven by a desire to root for the underdog and provide justice to the marginalized. 'All the agitations he supported were driven by the idea that the world needed to be a fairer place, be it in Niyamgiri, Bhatta Parsaul, or in Mahuva, Gujarat, against a Nirma cement plant,' points out Ramesh.

Land acquisition in each of these instances had pitted tribals, Dalits and farmers versus big corporates. Rahul saw this as part of a greater Bharat versus India battle—he wanted to be seen on the side of the 'small guy'. He was labelled a 'jholawallah', more comfortable in the company of activists than corporate leaders.

Mamata Banerjee, too, had taken a similar anti-corporate stance in Bengal—her land agitations in Singur and Nandigram revived her political career. Mamata was a natural streetfighter. Rahul was, in the end, part of the ruling establishment. His agitational mode, therefore, lacked credibility and consistency. He almost seemed to flit in and out of a movement without actually taking a confrontational path that would reap political benefit. 'He felt a little trapped,' admits a senior Congressman. 'It wasn't easy to be seen as an activist and a powerful ruling party politician at the same time.'

Rahul's 'Bharat versus India' world view was perhaps shaped in his Cambridge years where he studied development economics as one of his 'core' papers. He also met and had dinner there with Nobel laureate Amartya Sen who was then Master at Trinity College. Sen later claimed that he was impressed with Rahul. 'He seemed deeply concerned about deprivation in India and wanting to make a change in that,' he told *Outlook* magazine in an interview. Interestingly, while looking back at his Cambridge years, Rahul told *Varsity* magazine, 'I'm a lot less left wing now than I was.' But in the Indian context, Rahul was firmly placed on the political left. While the Manmohan Singh government spoke of growth and market reforms, Rahul's language was one of rights and entitlements. It only created a certain fuzziness in policy approach at a time when the country needed clarity.

If Ramesh was seen as Rahul's economic fellow-traveller, then his early political guru was Digvijaya Singh. A former Madhya Pradesh chief minister, Singh had rather dramatically claimed after an electoral defeat in 2003 that he was taking 'sanyas' from political office for ten years. Submitting to political sanyas did not stop him, however, from becoming a Congress general secretary, entrusted with the task of reviving the Congress in the key state of Uttar Pradesh. Singh was an old-style Congressman—a firm believer in social engineering and in a vision of secular politics that gave the minorities a special status. He was strongly anti-RSS, but was also deeply religious and ritualistic; a proud Thakur who flaunted his Hindu identity but routinely attacked 'communal' forces; a public-school alumnus from Daly College, Indore, who was just as comfortable in a five-star hotel as he was in a village panchayat. As Madhya Pradesh chief minister, he had built a strong equation with NGO groups and was seen to occupy the 'secular' space within the Congress once occupied by his political guru and another former Madhya Pradesh chief minister, Arjun Singh.

Rahul turned to him because he needed a strong political 'face' from the Hindi heartland to guide him through the maze of caste and community politics. For Singh, proximity to Rahul became the source of an independent power base at a time when his political career was staring at a dark tunnel. He promised to 'deliver' UP—the key prize that had eluded the Congress for two decades—to Rahul. The strategy was premised on reconstructing the Congress's traditional electoral alliance—upper castes, Muslims and Dalits.

Singh took up the case of Muslim youth arrested in terror cases, questioning the role of the police in the 2008 Batla House encounter in Delhi, in which two suspected terrorists and a senior police officer were killed. The accused were from Azamgarh in UP, and Singh promised to deliver justice to them. He targeted the Sangh Parivar, accusing them of promoting 'saffron terror'. He also reached out through a back channel to Hindu and Muslim religious leaders in an effort to break the Ayodhya deadlock.

This was politics from an earlier era—of vote banks, appeasement and allurements. Only that the space Singh was attempting to recapture was already firmly with parties like the BSP and SP. The politics of north India had changed, perhaps irreversibly, with the political rise of OBC and Dalit politicians through the 1980s and 1990s. Singh, though, remained confident that his strategy was working. On the eve of the 2012 UP elections, he had a dinner bet with me that our opinion poll predicting an SP victory would be proven horribly wrong. 'We will win a minimum of 100 seats, if not 150,' was his brave prediction. When the Congress barely squeaked past the twenty-five-seat mark, he was honest enough to admit his failure. And he kept his promise and bought me dinner!

For Rahul, though, there was no such consolation. The dependence on the Digvijaya Singh brand of politics had brought him no political return. Instead, he had been exposed as amateurish in his attempt to revive the Congress in the Hindi heartland. Take, for example, a speech he made in Phulpur during the UP election campaign in 2012 while claiming that UP-ites had been forced by failed governments to go and beg in Mumbai. *'Aapko Mumbai jaakar bheek mangna padta hai. Kab tak bheek mangte rahoge?'* (You have to go and beg in Mumbai. How long will you do so?), he asked the audience. No one likes to be called a beggar. Least of all an economic migrant looking for a better future in the big city. The defeat in UP in 2012 was a hammer blow.

In 2010, Rahul had suffered a similar debacle in neighbouring Bihar. He had made Bihar the test case for his *'ekla chalo re'* (go it alone) political belief—no alliances, the Congress would fight the elections on its own. Lalu Prasad had wanted to revive his Rashtriya Janata Dal's (RJD) alliance with the Congress. Rahul did not want one. He had spurned Lalu before the 2009 elections as well. *'Lagta hai ladke ko mera chehra achha nahi lagta!'* (Looks like the boy doesn't like my face), Lalu told me at the time.

The former Bihar chief minister had enjoyed an excellent equation with Sonia Gandhi. He was the one politician who had stood by Mrs Gandhi when she had been targeted for her foreign origins. In 2004, the Congress–RJD alliance had won twenty-nine of the forty seats in Bihar, and Lalu Prasad was made railway minister. By 2009, the alliance was finished. Lalu was kept waiting for weeks, but the Congress leadership did not oblige—Rahul wanted to strike out on his own.

The experiment of going alone would prove disastrous. In the 2009 general elections, the Congress won just two seats in Bihar. In the 2010 assembly elections, the Congress won just four seats, the RJD (allied with Ram Vilas Paswan) twenty-five. The Nitish Kumar-led Janata Dal (United) JD(U)–BJP alliance was swept to power by a record margin. As Lalu Prasad wistfully remarked, *'Woh doob gaye, hamein bhi dooba diya!'* (The Congress drowned, and took us down with them).

The double blow of failure in UP and Bihar affected Rahul. The political confidence generated by the 2009 election win was ebbing away. 'I think the self-doubts that were always lurking in the shadows began to take over. He felt and looked like a loser, like someone who felt he wasn't really cut out for this. It almost seemed as if he had lost the appetite to fight back,' says a senior Congressman. Rahul withdrew into his shell and became almost risk-averse. He had promised to travel extensively through UP and rejuvenate the cadres. He did no such thing. At a time when the Congress was looking for leadership, the leader went missing.

~

Former Israeli prime minister Abba Eban once said, 'The Palestinians never miss an opportunity to miss an opportunity.' Much the same could be said of Rahul Gandhi in 2011 and 2012, two crucial years ahead of the 2014 elections. In 2011, an agitation led by social activist Anna Hazare, demanding the setting up of an anti-corruption ombudsman, called the Lok Pal, shook the nation. For two weeks in August, a seventy-four-year-old Gandhian from Maharashtra became a symbol of the growing public disgust with corruption. Hazare had vowed to go on a fast from 16 August if the Jan Lok Pal Bill was not passed. Sonia Gandhi had gone abroad for surgery for an undisclosed medical condition. Before leaving, she had set up a four-member committee to look after the daily affairs of the Congress. The committee had veteran leaders A.K. Antony, Ahmed Patel, Janardhan Dwivedi along with Rahul as its members. This was Rahul's moment to take charge. Instead, the committee did not meet even once. (See chapter 3.)

On 16 August, when negotiations on the Lok Pal failed to achieve a breakthrough, the government went ahead and arrested Anna Hazare as he was on his way to the fast site in the national capital. Rahul was informed about it only two hours later by fellow Congress MP Sandeep Dikshit, via a short email and SMS. 'As the East Delhi MP, I was very worried about Anna being arrested in a locality in my constituency. I knew it was a mistake and asked Rahul to intervene,' Dikshit told me later. Rahul, who was in Parliament, acted immediately, ringing up the home minister P. Chidambaram to have the arrest order revoked. The damage, though, had been done. Anna Hazare had been transformed from a relatively benign social activist into a heroic figure of national significance. Support for him began to swell as he shifted his fast site to the Ramlila Maidan. For the next thirteen days, Anna Hazare became a Mahatma Gandhi-like larger-than-life figure dominating television screens and the national discourse. The government was on the mat.

A week into the agitation, with no sign of a breakthrough, the government was getting increasingly desperate. A back-room negotiation team led by Pranab Mukherjee, which included Union minister Salman Khurshid and the Delhi MP Sandeep Dikshit, was attempting to broker a settlement with Team Anna. At one of the meetings between the two sides a suggestion was made—why doesn't Rahul Gandhi come to Ramlila Maidan, go on stage, meet Anna Hazare and offer him a glass of juice to break his fast? An assurance from Rahul that a Lok Pal legislation was to be enacted would be enough for Anna to end his fast. Rahul, the negotiators were assured by Team Anna, could take all the credit.

An excited Dikshit, who had played a key role in the negotiations because of his previous links with members of Anna's inner circle, promptly sent another email to Rahul detailing the possible compromise solution. Only this time he got no response. 'It could have been the biggest moment of Rahul's political career, when he could have claimed a major victory,' says Dikshit today, a touch wistfully. Adds another Congress leader, 'Think about it, the image of Rahul giving juice to Anna would have been plastered on every newspaper and television screen. It would have been the most enduring image of the times and would have established Rahul's credentials as an anti-establishment crusader.'

So why did Rahul not bite the bullet? Some Congress leaders claim that the idea of Rahul visiting Anna Hazare at Ramlila Maidan was fraught with risk. 'The atmosphere there was anti-Congress.

What if the crowd had turned hostile?' Another senior leader claims that Team Anna could not be trusted to keep their word. 'They had betrayed us on more than one occasion. How could we risk sending Rahul to Ram Lila Maidan with no guarantee of a final solution?' In the end, former Maharashtra chief minister Vilasrao Deshmukh was sent to end Anna's fast. Rahul stayed at home.

Rahul did speak in support of the Lok Pal in a Parliament debate on 26 August, calling for the entity to be given constitutional status similar to that of the Election Commission. 'Madam Speaker, why not elevate the debate and fortify the Lok Pal by making it a constitutional body accountable to Parliament like the Election Commission? I feel the time has come to seriously consider this idea,' he said. The Congress cheered, even called Rahul's 'idea' a 'game changer'. The reality was that the game had already changed. Rahul's brief intervention in a Parliament debate was lost in the din over corruption. At a time when the country was looking for visible and concrete action, Rahul was giving a sermon. Where he could have seized the moment, he was reduced to a bit player. Anna Hazare and his team, especially a short young man with a toothbrush moustache, had become the real stars of the show. Rahul's loss would be the gain of a certain Mr Arvind Kejriwal.

The Lok Pal Bill was finally passed in Parliament on 17 December 2013, just months ahead of the general elections. Congressmen cheered yet again, giving the credit to Rahul's commitment to weeding out corruption. No one really bought the claim. It was simply a case of too little, too late.

~

In December 2012, Rahul had another opportunity to position himself as a politician connected to the anxieties and aspirations of a young India. On 16 December, a young woman was brutally beaten and gang-raped on a moving bus in the heart of the national capital. Crimes against women are not unusual in Delhi. In fact, the city has acquired notoriety as a place where women are highly unsafe. Yet, the sheer gruesomeness of the rape appeared to shake the city from its stupor. The fact that it happened in close proximity to the headquarters of most national television channels gave it an instant profile as the big breaking news story of the moment. Silence was no longer an option. Rape could no longer be just a statistic.

Three days after the rape, as the girl battled bravely for her life in a hospital (she would die of her injuries thirteen days later), the anger spilled out onto the streets. A frenzied crowd, mainly youngsters, began marching along Rajpath towards Rashtrapati Bhavan demanding answers. Some of them even tried to climb the walls of North Block. A rattled police force used tear gas and water cannons to disperse the agitators. The crowds only grew. Gender justice campaigner Eve Ensler, on a visit to India for her One Billion Rising campaign, said she felt India was in the midst of a women's revolution.

I was at India Gate where hundreds of men and women, mainly college students, had assembled. The protests were peaceful. The demand was for justice, tougher laws and security for women. While interviewing people on the spot, someone in the gathering spoke out. 'Where is Rahul Gandhi, why doesn't he come here and talk to us? If he can go and meet farmers in Bhatta Parsaul, can he not come and meet us also?'

It appeared a perfectly legitimate question. After all, Rahul Gandhi had been projected by his party as a youth icon. He was meant to represent a generational shift in Indian politics. He himself had spoken out about the need to energize the youth and encourage new voices in public life. Here was an ideal opening for him to walk the talk—to embrace a spontaneous, public spirited movement for gender justice that was driven by a younger, impatient India hankering for change. But Rahul was nowhere to be found.

Congress spokespersons initially claimed that Rahul was out of the country when the story first surfaced. When he returned, he did meet a handful of agitators at 10, Janpath, but away from the glare of the camera. Apparently, a section of the party was keen that Rahul engage in a more direct manner, but he vetoed the idea. 'He was concerned, understood the emotions of the protestors, but didn't want to create a tamasha by going to India Gate to meet people,' was the explanation offered. A few days later, he quietly went and met the family of the Delhi braveheart. A few months later, Parliament passed a strong anti-rape legislation.

Should Rahul have been at India Gate expressing solidarity with the protestors? When I asked this question to the home minister Sushil Kumar Shinde in a live television programme, he controversially answered, 'You cannot expect us to go everywhere to meet protestors. Next you will ask the home minister to go to India Gate if Maoists are demonstrating there!' A more rational explanation was provided by Shinde's deputy, R.P.N. Singh, who was tasked with handling the crisis. 'I don't think we can reduce a serious issue to a photo op. If Rahul had met the agitators, news channels will get a photo op, but how will anything have changed on the ground?'

Ironically, in February 2014, when a young Arunachal student Nido Tania was beaten to death in mysterious circumstances in a Delhi marketplace, Rahul did go to Jantar Mantar to meet the protestors who were seeking greater security for north-east students. He promised to take up their cause. The incident took place just ahead of the Lok Sabha elections. Nido's father was a Congress legislator from Arunachal. The timing and context, it seems, were suddenly very different. Opportunistic, the critics alleged, not without justification.

Politics in India is often about symbolism. Indira Gandhi on elephant-back crossing floodwaters to reach the village of Belchi in Bihar, where Dalits had been attacked, became an enduring symbol of her fighting spirit that eventually catapulted her back into power after the Emergency. Had Rahul realized the power of political symbolism, he may well have won the perception war when it really mattered. Had he used either the Anna agitation or the anti-rape protests to mobilize public opinion, he might well have been seen as an intrepid young leader ready to break new ground. The anti-rape protests in Delhi were a defining moment for gender equality that cut across the political divide. The Anna agitation was equally an expression of rising public anger with corruption. Both movements had a strong connect with the youth, especially in urban India, a natural political constituency for Rahul to identify with. Yet, he chose to play safe. It was almost as if he was in power but still didn't know how to use it effectively. It was a tentative approach to politics that he needed to jettison if he wanted to be taken seriously as a leader.

~

On 19 January 2013, Rahul Gandhi was made the Congress vice president at a two-day Chintan Shivir (brainstorming) session organized in Jaipur. Congress workers were ecstatic. This was the moment for which they had been waiting for almost a decade—the official anointment of Rahul as the leader to take over the mantle from Sonia Gandhi. Large cut-outs of Rahul dotted the Jaipur skyline. '*Hamara Neta, Rahul Gandhi*' was the war cry. 'I can see Rajiv's dream being fulfilled today,' said an emotional Congressman, breaking down in front of the TV cameras. Asked whether this meant that Rahul would now be the Congress's prime ministerial candidate for the 2014 elections, the Congress spokesperson Janardhan Dwivedi quickly pressed the pause button. 'Any election- or campaign-related decisions will be taken at a later stage.'

The next day, Rahul made his maiden speech as Congress vice president. It was a passionate address. 'Last night each one of you congratulated me. My mother came to my room and she sat with me and she cried . . . because she understands that power so many people seek is actually a poison.' He added, 'My mother sees power as poison because she is not attached to it. The only antidote to this poison is for all of us to see what it really is and not become attached to it. We should not chase power for the attributes of power. We should only use it to empower the voices.'

The entire Congress leadership on stage and the party workers in the auditorium applauded. The '*ma–beta*' theme resonated strongly with a party of loyalists wedded to a family—the torch was being passed to another generation of Nehru–Gandhis. The speech, we were told, was spontaneous—this was Rahul Gandhi speaking from the heart. My own response as a political analyst in the studio was a shade sceptical. 'If power is poison, then why is Rahul Gandhi in politics which is ultimately the pursuit of power?' I asked.

The answer was given later that evening by Digivjaya Singh who had observed Rahul closely. 'Rahul is not like any other politician. He doesn't believe in power, he wants to fight injustice!' he claimed. I wasn't convinced. Politics is not about taking sanyas, it is about being a *grihasti*, it's about taking responsibility by leading from the front. Rahul's self-identity appears to be of someone who had entered electoral politics not out of choice but compulsion. The contrast with Narendra Modi, who wore his political ambition on his sleeve, could not have been starker.

~

Nine months after delivering his 'power is poison' speech, Rahul Gandhi showed why he was the second most powerful person in the country at the time. On 27 September 2013, he described an ordinance passed by the Union cabinet that would prevent the instant disqualification of convicted MPs as 'complete nonsense'. It was an open, blatantly direct and public criticism of the Congress-led Manmohan Singh government which had cleared the controversial ordinance just three days earlier. The prime minister was in Washington at a summit meeting with the US president Barack Obama. The moment he returned a week later, an emergency Cabinet meeting revoked the ordinance.

The 'nonsense' remark was made during a press conference at the Press Club of India in Delhi being addressed by the Congress's communication head and MP, Ajay Maken, who had come there to inaugurate a gymnasium. The press conference had just begun when our Congress beat reporter rang up the newsroom to say that Rahul Gandhi would be making an appearance. At first we thought it was a rumour. Then, mysteriously, Maken got up from the dais and said he had to attend an urgent phone call. Minutes later, Maken was back and smiled. 'Rahulji will come and address you now on the ordinance.'

Sure enough, Rahul strode in a little while later in his usual kurta–pyjama attire. Rolling up his sleeves, stroking his beard, he looked every inch the angry young man. 'My opinion about the ordinance is that it is complete nonsense. It should be torn up and thrown away.' Before the stunned journalists could seek a response, Rahul had walked away. It was a brief item number yet again—only here he was playing anti-establishment hero. Maken, who earlier had defended the ordinance, was clearly embarrassed but tried to put up a brave face. 'Now that the Congress vice president has made it clear, the line is very clear. The Congress party is supreme.'

Later, I asked Maken if the entire exercise had been choreographed in advance to project Rahul as an anti-corruption crusader. 'No, no, I had no idea that Rahul would make the statement. I was also caught unawares and was told about it just fifteen minutes before he made an appearance,' he claimed. But just a day earlier, one of Rahul's groupies, South Mumbai MP Milind Deora, had tweeted, 'Legalities aside, allowing convicted MPs/MLAs to retain seats in the midst of an appeal can endanger already eroding public faith in democracy.' Clearly, Team Rahul wanted to send out a message distancing themselves from the government decision.

The prime minister had been humiliated. Appearing on a TV programme that night, the prime minister's former media adviser Dr Sanjaya Baru told me, 'Enough is enough, Dr Singh should resign!' Sonia Gandhi reportedly rang up the prime minister and made suitably apologetic noises on Rahul's behalf. Rahul himself is believed to have admitted to Dr Singh that he should have framed his opposition to the ordinance in less combative terms. The prime minister wanted to step down but chose to keep the peace, yet again.

The sudden eruption in public reflected poorly on Rahul and the Congress party. His behaviour seemed brattish and disrespectful, hardly a sign of political maturity. It appears that his aides had convinced him at last that he needed to establish an independent identity ahead of the 2014 elections. He had to rid himself of the baggage of being part of the UPA-II's decision-making process. If, as a result, the prime minister and even Sonia Gandhi were left a trifle red-faced, then that was a small price to pay. What Rahul and his aides didn't realize in the autumn of 2013 was that their actions were not just undignified, but also once again a case of too little, too late. The narrative of UPA-II being a government that compromised with corruption had already been scripted. No one, not even Rahul Gandhi, could now alter the storyline in the popular imagination.

3

A Government in ICU

The Congress-led United Progressive Alliance probably lost Verdict 2014 on 1 June 2011, almost three years before judgement day. It was a searingly hot day in June when four Union ministers of the UPA government rushed to Delhi airport to receive yoga guru Baba Ramdev and urge him to call off his proposed fast against corruption and black money. The sight of the government prostrating itself before the controversial saffron-robed self-styled 'guru' as though he was a distinguished head of state said it all—the UPA government had lost its nerve and, perhaps, its self-esteem too.

The ministerial delegation to the airport was led by then finance minister Pranab Mukherjee and comprised telecom minister Kapil Sibal, parliamentary affairs minister Pawan Kumar Bansal and tourism minister Subodh Kant Sahay. Months later, I asked Mukherjee about the airport visit. Over several cups of lemon tea, Mukherjee admitted, 'It was a blunder, a big blunder. We should have never done it,' and, pointing to a photograph of Indira Gandhi on the wall behind him, added, 'We needed leaders like her to put these babas in their place.'

The Hardwar-based saffron-clad Ramdev was born Ramakrishna Yadav in a Haryana village. His yoga skills transformed him from a village boy to a highly successful businessman, running a chain of yoga training institutes across north India. He had even diversified into manufacturing herbal products. His critics accused him of being a land-grabber and selling fake herbal medicines, but his supporters saw him as a soldier of God (one of them had 'gifted' him an island near Scotland). He definitely was politically ambitious. 'I want to change India, Rajdeepji,' he told me, looking at me with his piercing eyes that seemed to hide many mysteries. Latching onto the anti-corruption bandwagon, he had set up an organization called Bharat Swabhimaan Andolan (Indian Self-respect Movement) with the backing of RSS affiliates. He was looking for his place at the high table. The UPA-II government, astonishingly, carried the banquet to him.

The attempt to placate Ramdev had actually begun weeks before the ill-fated airport visit. The yoga guru had declared he would go on an indefinite fast if the government didn't take steps to bring back black money stashed in illegal tax havens abroad. Worried about the black money issue catching national attention, finance ministry officials had begun secret negotiations with the yoga guru. A special plane was kept on standby to fly out to meet the baba in his ashram at short notice. Sibal had been told to cancel a scheduled foreign visit and lead a team to meet Ramdev. Mukherjee and the prime minister's office (PMO) were kept in the loop. And yet, no one will quite reveal who took the final decision to meet him at the airport, though the needle of suspicion points towards Mukherjee.

That morning, Mukherjee was scheduled to address the Editors' Guild of India at the India International Centre. His arrival was delayed because, we were told, his previous engagement had got extended. When he finally arrived close to noon, the gathering was already restive. Mukherjee was duly apologetic and promised to stay for lunch. He gave a brief speech and then prepared for a question-and-answer session. 'Ask me any question you want,' he said, sounding a little more relaxed. A few minutes later, his mood had changed. His assistant had whispered something in his ear and he now looked visibly agitated. 'Sorry, I have to leave, something urgent has come up,' he said. Forgoing the IIC's baked vegetables and ginger pudding, he hurried out. A few hours later, we realized the reason for the urgency. News channels had begun to flash the 'breaking news' on the Mukherjee–Ramdev meeting.

. Sibal told me later that the ministers eventually went to the airport not to 'receive' or 'negotiate' with Ramdev but to serve him an externment order from the national capital. 'We wanted to make it clear to him that he could not hold his proposed fast and start an anti-government gathering under the guise of a yoga camp. He agreed to our demand which is why he was allowed to enter the city,' he claimed.

And yet, three days later, the government's worst fears came true. Ramdev stormed into his proposed indefinite hunger strike on the black money issue at the Ramlila Maidan, charging the Congress and the UPA government with being corrupt and unconcerned about bringing back black money. His supporters began gathering in large numbers. A desperate government reiterated its appeal to him to call off the fast, with Sibal even making public a letter of Ramdev's aide assuring that the fast would be called off if a legislation was enacted on black money. An angry Ramdev accused the government of 'betrayal'. A battle of wits was being played out in the glare of television—a tough-talking, charismatic yoga guru with a vast following of common, devout folk, a god-man with nothing to lose, versus a mighty Union government whose credibility was on the line.

At midnight on a hot June night, as the devotees slept in crowded ranks at Ramlila Maidan, the Delhi police swooped down on the protestors, firing tear-gas shells and resorting to a lathi charge, forcing people out even as they were half asleep. Ramdev, who escaped disguised as a woman, was eventually detained and forced to leave the city. A few of his supporters were injured in the clashes with the police. One of them, Rajbala, was grievously hurt; she died in hospital weeks later. Ramdev had been dramatically transformed from controversial yoga guru into a heroic figure. The Government of India had been shown up as effete and insensitive. A sleeping congregation is not an unlawful assembly, the Supreme Court thundered a year later.

In a media interaction just ahead of the Lok Sabha results in 2014, then home minister P. Chidambaram said Ramdev had played a political game. 'He was not conducting a yoga camp. He was holding a political show. I think the way it was handled was right, except for that last misstep,' he argued. He even challenged those who called the yoga guru a 'baba'. 'He is no baba . . . he is no saint, just call him Mr Ramdev.'

And yet, in the summer of 2011, this same 'Mr Ramdev' had forced the government into an almost unprecedented panic mode. Intelligence sources claim the home ministry was worried that Ramdev had strong connections with the RSS and the entire Sangh Parivar, which is why there was a sense of fear of what could happen next.

The fact is, just weeks earlier, the government had faced a similar crisis when Anna Hazare's fast against corruption had led to massive protests. In the face of a seemingly gigantic mobilization against corruption, covered relentlessly on TV, the UPA had run terrified and cowered behind dithering officialese about media-manufactured movements. Seriously rattled, confronted by a ringing repudiation of its moral authority at its doorstep, clueless on how to gain the upper hand over disobedient crowds exploding from every TV set, the government certainly didn't want a repeat of the Anna paroxysm. In the end, the UPA got exactly what it didn't want—more public opprobrium. Anna first, and then Ramdev—2011 would turn out to be the UPA's annus horribilis, perhaps setting the agenda for a general election that was still three years away.

~

When Anna Hazare arrived in Delhi on 4 April 2011 to go on a fast against corruption, the country was caught up in cricket World Cup fever. Mahendra Singh Dhoni's Men in Blue had captured the hearts and minds of a nation. On 2 April, when Dhoni hit the six that lifted the trophy, the nation was euphoric and united. Television channels endlessly replayed images of Dhoni, Tendulkar, Yuvraj and the other heroes who had lit up the Mumbai skyline on that magical day. Even the politicians, led by Sonia Gandhi, were out on the streets waving the tricolour. Just three days later, the same Indian public had found an unlikely hero in a septuagenarian Gandhian activist from the small village of Ralegan Siddhi in Maharashtra. Television channels had a delicious new story to tell. Only, this time the politicians were on the wrong side of the divide in the face of pulsating citizen power.

If Dhoni had made winning the World Cup his goal, Anna came to Delhi with an equally focused mission. He said he was going on an indefinite hunger strike against corruption and demanded the implementation of the long-pending Lok Pal Bill that provided for the setting up of an anti-corruption ombudsman. The initial response was lukewarm. Very few in the national media were really aware of Hazare and his politics. He had spent most of his life in Maharashtra, taking on ministers accused of corruption, and had built a formidable reputation as an untiring crusader for public causes. At least three state ministers had been forced to resign because of his efforts. But in Delhi, the Gandhi topi of Hazare seemed like a museum piece from another era—he was seen as little more than a temporary distraction, just one of the many activists who populated Jantar Mantar through the year.

When Hazare began his fast on 5 April the story was just another headline. That day, Anna spoke out against the Union agriculture minister and Maharashtra strongman Sharad Pawar, questioning his credentials to be part of the group of ministers appointed to review the draft Lok Pal Bill. The attack on Pawar was sharp and hit home—the next day, Pawar resigned from the committee. Suddenly, the national media sat up and took note. Hazare was now a front-page story being played out across television channels. A fast which had begun with a few hundred supporters was now gaining momentum. Within seventy-two hours, it would strike a huge chord across the country.

I was at Jantar Mantar watching with amazement as the crowds kept growing. My teenage son Ishan had gone with his class friends on a Yamuna yatra to Uttarakhand. Suddenly, I spotted him at Jantar Mantar with schoolmates. 'We've come here to express our solidarity with Anna,' he said enthusiastically. He was not alone. A majority of the audience were middle-class Indians—government employees, housewives, shopkeepers, traders, all of whom had a story to tell about how corruption was affecting their lives. *'Annaji sahi kar rahe hain, woh hamari ladai lad rahe hai'* (Anna is doing the right thing, he is fighting our fight), was the overwhelming sentiment. Even one of the local policemen who had been charged with providing security for Hazare admitted quietly, *'Bande mein hai dum!'* (This man is strong.) Shades of Gandhi emanated subliminally from the image of Anna. A few years earlier the Bollywood hit *Lage Raho Munna Bhai* had popularized a pop icon Mahatma, a quaint throwback to the nostalgia-laden black-and-white era. Anna was clever enough to project himself as this New Age Mahatma, ideally suited for an urban public looking for a shortcut to reliving the heady atmosphere of the freedom struggle.

OB vans had now been permanently parked at the site. Live shows were being done from the venue by senior TV anchors, angry voices being magnified by the TV echo chamber in the studio. Just as Gandhi mugs and keychains had done good business after the *Munna Bhai* movie, now 'Anna caps' and tricolours were being sold at the venue like fairground delights. Candlelight marches were organized at India Gate and across several state capitals, while the social media buzzed with the Anna refrain through Facebook posts and Twitter trends.

In hindsight, it's easy to suggest we overplayed the Anna protests. A television anchor likened it to the 'second war of independence', while one channel created a permanent screen slug 'Anna is India'. News television has a tabloidish urge that thrives on conflict and controversy. The outrage at times is deliberately manufactured and I cannot claim to be indifferent to the temptation to join the chorus of indignantly aggressive voices. I remember anchoring a show from Jantar Mantar surrounded by Anna supporters. By the end of the programme, I was speaking a language which suggested I had become one of them! The popular Hindi news channels in particular, I suspect, were engaged in a class war—Anna, they felt, was storming the citadel of a corrupt and privileged anglicized ruling elite.

Not having experienced this kind of visible public protest, literally at the doorsteps of the state, the government, which had a communication strategy that oscillated between ambivalence and non-existence, pressed the alarm button. Ambika Soni, then information and broadcasting minister, called up to 'suggest' we 'tone down' our coverage. Unlike other information and broadcsting ministers, Soni was generally non-interfering. Not that day. 'Don't you have any other news to show but Anna?' she asked pointedly.

A section of the establishment was convinced that Anna's movement was an RSS-backed conspiracy designed to destabilize the UPA government. Images of Mother India on the stage, repeated chants of 'Bharat Mata ki Jai' and 'Vande Mataram' had persuaded some government ministers and officials to believe that the agitation was being propped up to target the central government politically. The presence of a few RSS leaders and volunteers on stage had only added to this suspicion. The strong presence of Sri Sri Ravi Shankar's Art of Living supporters had given what one government minister called a 'saffron edge' to the movement. 'Anna is only a prop—the real power is with the RSS,' Digvijaya Singh told me in an interview at the time.

He wasn't entirely off the mark. The RSS had decided to support the Anna agitation sensing an opportunity to embarrass the UPA government. Sri Sri's own role was suspicious as well. I had met the Art of Living guru for the first time during the Dharam Sansad at the Kumbh Mela in Allahabad in 2001. Then, along with other VHP-supported sants and sadhus, he had joined the demand for a Ram mandir in Ayodhya.

Since then, I had occasionally met 'Guruji' at the prodding of his followers, many of whom were wealthy and powerful women. 'He is truly a man of God,' is how one of his devotees described him. Dressed in signature white robes, long hair flying halo-like around his head, he appeared to exude calm. He once held my hand, looked in my eyes and asked, 'Are you happy, really happy?'

He may have been offering spiritual solace, but he was surely looking for a greater role for himself in public life. Be it Ayodhya, Kashmir or the Naxal issue, Sri Sri often tried to have his say. The anti-corruption movement offered him another chance. Sri Sri, according to some accounts, was to have been the original 'face' of the anti-corruption movement. 'He was very close to the Sangh Parivar and wanted us to negotiate with the BJP leaders. Once, when we refused, he flew into a rage,' recalls a Team Anna member.

But the Centre's reservations over the nature of the anti-corruption movement didn't stop it from initiating a dialogue with the Team Anna leadership. Here again, the UPA would stumble into a muddle. When Anna's fast took off, a decision was taken at a meeting in the PMO to forcibly lift him from the stage and hospitalize him. But in a parallel process, then law minister Veerappa Moily claimed he had got the go-ahead from Sonia Gandhi to negotiate with Team Anna. Moily initiated talks with Swami Agnivesh who was part of Hazare's group but also had an excellent relationship with the government. By 8 April, as the fast entered its fourth day, Moily drafted an agreement to set up a ten-member drafting committee to prepare a fresh Lok Pal Bill. The committee would have five ministers from the government and five representatives chosen by Hazare. It was seen as a compromise solution, but it was a bad compromise which only legitimized Hazare and his team as the official interlocutors on behalf of civil society. 'It was typical of our confused mind. The left hand did not know what the right hand was doing,' admits a former Cabinet minister.

Hazare called off his fast the next morning, but the government's limitations and weakness had been exposed. Three months later, the same government would be brought to its knees as a charged-up Hazare decided to take his agitation to another level by threatening to launch another fast if the Lok Pal Bill was not passed by 15 August. As the deadline approached, the confrontation worsened. On 13 August, Hazare wrote to the prime minister asking him 'to show courage' and instruct the Delhi police to allow him to go ahead with the proposed fast at JP Park in central Delhi. The prime minister declined to intervene.

Then something quite inexplicable happened. A US state department report appeared to back Hazare's agitation and called on the Indian government to exercise 'democratic restraint' in dealing with the anti-corruption protestors. It left ministers and Congress leaders fulminating. 'Who is Washington to talk to us like this, we must hit back,' said one minister.

A meeting of senior party and government leaders was called on the night of 13 August at the Congress war room in Gurudwara Rakabganj Road. Rahul Gandhi was yet to return from the US where Sonia was undergoing treatment. At the meeting, the consensus was: 'We must expose the Anna movement.' Congress spokesperson Manish Tewari, who had left for Mumbai to be with his ailing mother-in-law, was asked to come back immediately and hold a press conference.

The next day, Tewari followed instructions and lambasted Hazare, suggesting he was 'corrupt from head to toe'. It was an ill-chosen remark but one that had been officially sanctioned by the party. In his 15 August Independence Day address, Dr Singh was equally combative and said that the power to make laws rested only with Parliament. The battle between Hazare and the government had reached the point of no return.

But on the night of that very Independence Day, the Congress did another U-turn. Rahul had just returned from abroad and was angry with the criticism of Anna. 'Kindly issue a fresh statement and let us distance ourselves from what Tewari has said about Anna. We must respect him,' Rahul told chief Congress spokesperson Janardhan Dwivedi. 'I felt totally abandoned,' Tewari told me later. He had become the fall guy.

The confusion didn't end there. Next morning, as Anna was preparing to go to Rajghat to pay his respects at Mahatma Gandhi's *samadhi* before proceeding to the fast venue, the Delhi police landed up at his residence in east Delhi's Mayur Vihar area and arrested him.

I was on my morning walk when the story broke. Still in a T-shirt and track pants, I rushed, like so many other 24/7 journalists, to the television studio. Little did I know then that for the next thirteen days, the Anna Hazare story would consume the entire airtime of a nation, to the exclusion of all other news.

Who ordered the arrest of Hazare? While the finger of suspicion pointed at the home ministry, Chidambaram told me later that the original decision to 'detain' Anna was taken by the Cabinet Committee on Political Affairs in the presence of the prime minister and senior ministers. 'We never wanted to arrest him. We only told the Delhi police to detain him because he wasn't willing to accept our demand for a time-bound fast. It was the local magistrate who ordered his arrest,' Chidambaram claimed. By the time the magistrate's order was reversed (see also chapter 2), it was too late. Public opinion had turned firmly against the government.

Three days later, after intense negotiations, a triumphant Hazare emerged from Tihar jail, was lifted onto a truck and taken to the Ramlila Maidan where he had decided to continue with his fast. The motorcade from Tihar to Ramlila Maidan via Rajghat was another made-for-television moment. Thousands of delirious Hazare supporters cheered him along, showering him with petals and garlands. For the next week, Hazare would sit impassively on a special stage erected at the maidan, a life-size portrait of Mahatma Gandhi in the background. The eyes of an entire nation were riveted on one elderly man, now being projected as a modern-day Gandhi.

Meanwhile, an anxious government was forced to hold a special debate in the Lok Sabha on Hazare's proposed Lok Pal Bill. The House, after much sound and fury, virtually agreed to all of Hazare's conditions. On 28 August, Hazare broke his fast with a clenched fist and a 'Bharat Mata ki Jai' war cry. A social activist in the autumn of his life had been transformed into an iconic figure taking on the government of the world's largest democracy.

That wasn't the last act of Lok Pal-related errors committed by the UPA-II government in 2011. As the clock wound down to usher in another year, the government made another attempt to pass the contentious bill in Parliament. After being passed in the Lok Sabha, it was brought to the Rajya Sabha. There, amidst chaotic scenes, the bill was torn up by Rajniti Prasad, an MP from Lalu Prasad Yadav's RJD, even as the treasury benches looked on helplessly. Close to midnight, amidst the cacophony, Vice President Hamid Ansari, who was chairman of the Rajya Sabha, adjourned the House. The Opposition accused the government of stage-managing the show. The verdict of the analysts in the studio was unanimous—the UPA had committed political hara-kiri.

Why did the UPA get it all so horribly wrong? Why did canny experienced politicians like Mukherjee, Chidambaram, Khurshid, Sibal fail to deal with what was, after all, a fledgling movement being run by a curious mix of activists of varying backgrounds? Anna Hazare wasn't Mahatma Gandhi; he wasn't even Jayaprakash Narayan. His politics had been honed in a village panchayat where he had originally been an environmental activist. He could be stubborn, but he wasn't known to be unreasonable. And he wasn't above striking a 'deal' if necessary.

And yet, the nature of the UPA's response suggested that they were handling a national leader of great stature, a fakir-like figure who had intimidated them into submission. I remember meeting the late Vilasrao Deshmukh, the former Maharashtra chief minister, a few months after the noise had died down. Deshmukh was the one finally chosen to broker peace with Hazare. He told me, 'I wish they had entrusted me with the task from day one. I knew Anna from my Maharashtra days, I would have talked him out of the protests. But our Delhi leaders think they know everything!'

Of these Delhi leaders, Pranab Mukherjee and Chidambaram were the seniormost. Both were seasoned, intelligent politicians. If you wanted to understand how the government functioned, a visit to Pranabda's house post-11 p.m. was mandatory. He was an encyclopaedia on the Congress party and the Constitution. If you challenged him, he would immediately give you a historical reference. And yet, as the government's principal troubleshooter, you sensed he was tiring from the workload. 'I am not getting younger,' he would sometimes tell me.

Chidambaram was younger, with a cutting wit and a sharply sardonic tongue, a supremely knowledgeable intellectual powerhouse, but also someone with a trace of arrogance that made him much more difficult to deal with. If you got on his wrong side, there was no escaping his wrath. Once, during a studio discussion, we erred in putting his name in a list of 'tainted' ministers. He refused to speak to me for almost two years. 'Unless I get a public apology, I will not appear on your channel,' he said with his trademark frostiness. I don't think he was ready to forgive and forget even after we apologized on air.

It was no secret that Mukherjee and Chidambaram did not get along with each other. 'Leaked' reports would often surface that hinted at the two ministers sniping at each other. It didn't help the UPA-II government that the prime minister's two most able lieutenants didn't see eye to eye.

For Manmohan Singh, it was palace intrigue he could have done without in a moment of crisis. The Anna movement hit the credibility of his government by virtually questioning its legitimacy. It couldn't have come at a worse time for a government under siege. In 2010, the UPA was hobbled by a series of big-ticket corruption allegations. The Delhi Commonwealth Games saw the organizing committee chairperson and Congress MP Suresh Kalmadi being charged with fraud. He was arrested in April 2011, just as the Anna movement first exploded. I had known Kalmadi from my days as a reporter in Mumbai in the early 1990s. He would send us invites for his annual Ganesh celebrations in Pune. 'Come and enjoy, we will look after everything,' he would tell the media. I did partake of his hospitality once and then went on to write a slightly critical story. He was fuming. 'What is this, Rajdeep? We organize the food and drink, and then you turn against us!'

He clearly relished living king-size. The Commonwealth Games for him was not about making money (he had made enough)—it was primarily about power and stature. He was taken up with the idea of rubbing shoulders with British royalty, of being seen as the czar of Indian sport. He liked distributing largesse to friends. 'I want everyone to have a good time,' he said with a laugh. It was this 'sab chalta hai' brazen attitude that would lead to his downfall.

The bearded Kalmadi with his wicked-looking smile was pitched as the villain of the Commonwealth Games. I remember him asking me once why he was being singled out. 'My CWG budget is much less than the Delhi government, but still you only focus on me. What about Sheila Dikshit?' he asked. My answer was simple. 'Sir, life is about perception. When people see Sheilaji, they are reminded of their *dadima*. When they see you on television, they are convinced you must be a crook!' I am not sure my answer amused him.

Kalmadi wasn't the only Maharashtra politician in trouble. In November 2010, Maharashtra chief minister Ashok Chavan was made to resign over allegations that he had misused his power while allotting flats to the Adarsh cooperative society in Mumbai. That very month, the Union telecom minister A. Raja resigned over a report by the Comptroller and Auditor General (CAG) on 2G spectrum allocation.

Chavan, in fact, was made to resign even before an FIR could be filed in the case. When I met him just before he resigned, he had a forlorn look. 'I am not being given a chance to defend myself. The Adarsh flats were never meant for Kargil widows,' was his grouse. The truth is, even if he could make out a case, no one was ready to believe him. He was stuck with the label of a chief minister who had builders with questionable reputations hanging around his office all the time.

Frenzied headlines accompanied each scam, pushing the government even further on the defensive. 'We had become hyper-sensitive to public opinion and what was playing out in the media, especially prime-time television. Some of it was deliberately sensationalized, but we just didn't know how to counter it,' confessed a senior minister. In the public perception, the Centre was an inept, corrupt ancien régime, almost as unpopular as the British raj. The Anna movement latched on to this growing public outrage with great dexterity. TV images of swelling crowds only accentuated a crisis of confidence from which the UPA would never quite recover.

Significantly, Sonia Gandhi wasn't in the country when the Anna Hazare movement captured the national imagination in August 2011. The leadership vacuum created by her absence was never felt more strongly. Rahul Gandhi, meant to be the de facto leader of the Congress in her absence, was mostly absent as well. At a time when he was needed the most, to rally his forces, seize the political initiative, perhaps even defuse the Anna bomb by reaching out to the elderly campaigner, Rahul abdicated from his responsibilities.

And the prime minister, who should have taken charge, remained largely silent. Dr Singh had never been a great communicator. But in a crisis hour, the prolonged, almost stupefied silence of the man who was officially the chief executive of the Indian state was a recipe for disaster. 'Dr Singh had outsourced the entire Anna issue to the Congress party and key ministers—he just didn't want to get involved,' is how one minister put it to me later. It was almost as if the bureaucrat in Dr Singh had consumed his political being. Anna was a ticking-bomb file that he just didn't want to touch for fear that it would singe him. His leadership failure as prime minister in those turbulent days would significantly contribute to the eventual demise of the UPA-II government.

~

The first intimate meeting I had with Dr Manmohan Singh was on the eve of the 1999 general elections when he was made to contest a Lok Sabha election for the first time, from South Delhi. He had already built an impressive reputation as an economist who as finance minister had delivered the historic 1991 Union budget that had opened up the Indian economy like never before. But here he was being asked to garner votes, a completely different challenge. My assignment at NDTV was to spend a day with Dr Singh on the campaign trail. I was fascinated with the prospect of a middle-class professional academic-bureaucrat who had spent much of his life reading books and files now attempting to transform himself into a mass leader.

We started early in the morning, read a vast bundle of newspapers and went on a walk together. Dr Singh was filing his nomination that day, so he had to climb on a large truck encircled by muscular Sardars and the local Congress workers. His doughty wife Gursharan Kaur kept a safe distance, only ensuring that her 'Sardarji' had eaten a good breakfast and the kurta–pyjama was well starched. I remember asking him later in the evening what the most difficult thing was about trying to be an MP. His answer with a mild smile was, 'Being pushed around by so many people. Everyone, it seems, wants to shake your hand!'

My lasting memory of that day spent with Dr Singh came in our post-lunch shoot. Dr Singh wasn't the most spontaneous or voluble guest in front of the camera, so we were keenly looking for some 'colour' that would lift our programme. We found out that it was the birthday of one of his grandchildren and a small party had been organized on the lawns at the back of the house. Dr Singh, we were told, would spend some time with the children while the cake was being cut. 'Ideal TV image,' said my cameraperson enthusiastically. 'We can give a human touch to the show.' Unfortunately, the moment I broached the idea of filming the birthday party, both Dr Singh and wife shook their heads sternly in unison. 'The birthday is a private affair, no cameras please!' I tried to reason that as an aspiring MP, the lines between the private and the public were now blurred, but to no avail. The Singhs were determined to zealously guard their family life.

Dr Singh lost that South Delhi election to the BJP's Vijay Kumar Malhotra by a little over 29,000 votes. He never contested a Lok Sabha election again. And yet, by a remarkable quirk of fate, this intensely private, soft-spoken Sardar became prime minister five years later. A nation-building intellectual of the 1960s, Manmohan Singh was part of a generation that had been the frontiersmen of 'Nehruvian' modernity. Indira Gandhi had sought his counsel as well, and he was acknowledged as a highly competent scholar-bureaucrat. Sonia Gandhi had chosen him ahead of all other contenders because she trusted him and, equally importantly, respected him as a man of high personal integrity. Initially, the decision to anoint Dr Singh as prime minister appeared to catch everyone by surprise, except the renowned Oxford scholar and guru of psephology, Sir David Butler. Sir David had known Dr Singh since his Oxford days, and was in India to observe the elections. 'You know, he will make an ideal prime minister in a coalition government in India, the kind of man who will offend no one but will quietly get the job done,' was his sharp analysis.

In the first five years of the UPA government, it appeared that Sir David's assessment was near perfect. The 'accidental politician', as Dr Singh often described himself, proved to be an artful one too, cleverly negotiating the minefield of a government dependent on several allies. I sometimes met him in those early years in 7, Race Course Road, courtesy his proactive media adviser, Dr Sanjaya Baru. Dr Singh was unfailingly warm and polite. Power, it seemed, had not changed him a bit. Even the family, mercifully for an Indian politician, stayed away from the lure of office, exuding a no-nonsense feet-firmly-on-the-ground air.

When the Indo-US nuclear deal threatened to torpedo his government, with the left warning of a pull out, I was tipped off by a Congress source that the prime minister had talked tough and even offered his resignation to Sonia Gandhi. The breaking news story we did had several sceptics who were unconvinced the mild-mannered prime minister would dare Mrs Gandhi to remove him. The story, though, was later confirmed, and the gambit worked. Even as the left withdrew support, Sonia Gandhi and the party rallied around Dr Singh. Eventually, the Samajwadi Party bailed out his government. In the election that followed, the voter rewarded Dr Singh's clear-cut stand. UPA-II was created with a much stronger majority. And yet, in his moment of political success, Dr Singh would make his first major mistake as prime minister and reveal himself to be a political survivor who preferred compromise to conviction.

Dr Manmohan Singh was sworn in as India's prime minister for a second time, on 22 May 2009, along with nineteen ministers. Absent from the ceremony was a key UPA ally, the Tamil Nadu-based Dravida Munnetra Kazhagam (DMK). Their absence at the swearing-in became a major talking point. M. Karunanidhi, we were told, was incensed that he was not being allowed the ministers and portfolios of his choice. The prime minister's office had leaked the story that Dr Singh was unhappy with the performance of the DMK ministers in his first government, especially T.R. Baalu's and A. Raja's, both of whom were accused of corruption. 'The DMK wants "wet" ATM ministries!' was the joke in the corridors of power.

As the prime minister revealed a muscular refusal to bend, a worried Congress party decided to send senior leader Ghulam Nabi Azad and the national security adviser M.K. Narayanan to Chennai to negotiate with the DMK supremo. Karunanidhi was equally unrelenting. 'I must have the right to choose my ministers and portfolios. Raja comes from a Dalit family, we cannot remove him.' When the negotiators tried to broach the issue of corruption allegations, the DMK leader reportedly shot back, 'Who is the Congress to talk about corruption? You people even protected Ottavio Quattrocchi (a reference to the Italian businessman and Bofors accused who was close to the Gandhi family)!'

Keen not to lose a key ally, the Congress buckled. With Sonia Gandhi giving the go-ahead, the prime minister gave up. On 28 May, three Cabinet ministers of the DMK were sworn in. The list included Mr Raja who was given the prized telecom ministry once again, the very portfolio that the prime minister didn't want to give him. Dr Singh had conceded the fight. He would pay a heavy price for the concession.

Eighteen months later, Raja was forced to resign after a report of the CAG accused him of not distributing 2G spectrum in a transparent manner, resulting in an alleged loss of Rs 1.76 lakh crore to the exchequer. A few months later, he was arrested. Raja was a feisty character. A lawyer-politician from the Nilgiris, he exuded a certain political machismo. Days before he was arrested, I had a hearty south Indian breakfast with him, trying to convince him to do an interview. He sounded defiant, even as he munched on his dosa. 'If they arrest me, I will expose everyone. The prime minister, the finance minister—they all knew what was happening, why am I being singled out?' he asked angrily.

Till then, Manmohan Singh's calling card had been his spotless track record of personal probity. In his long career in public life, there had never been an accusation that the prime minister had engaged in, or winked at, corruption. The 2G case noticeably changed that. A series of letters emerged in the public domain suggesting that the prime minister was aware in 2008 itself that Raja was subverting the spectrum allocation process, possibly for personal benefit, but that Dr Singh had asked, in the words of one such communication, 'to be kept at arm's-length'.

PMO sources claimed that this was the reason why the prime minister had not wanted Raja in his Cabinet again. The fact, though, is that Raja continued as telecom minister for almost two years after the controversial 2G spectrum allocation. Dr Singh could have acted against him but chose the path of least resistance. He had failed to exercise prime ministerial authority and had revealed a weakness to place personal survival over principled politics. If the Indo-US nuclear deal had boosted his image, 2G undermined it, perhaps irretrievably. For the first time, Opposition benches trained their guns on the chief executive himself, crying out that Dr Singh's white kurta was stained with the taint of tolerating corruption. An entire Parliament session would be stalled over the issue.

Leading the charge against the government on 2G was Dr Subramanian Swamy, keen to resurrect his political career. Dr Swamy claimed to be a personal friend of Dr Singh, but had a visceral hatred for Sonia. Evil genius or brave crusader, he was not someone you wanted to make an enemy of. Once, when we cancelled him from a studio debate at the last minute, he warned me, 'Sonia Gandhi must have told you not to have me in the programme. I will expose you on Twitter!' A meticulous gatherer of allegedly incriminating material against his rivals, Dr Swamy took the 2G battle to the courts and made it even more difficult for the UPA-II government to try and distance itself from Raja.

It wasn't just Raja who became synonymous with corruption— there was also the figure of Rs 1.76 lakh crore that stuck in the public imagination. 'Ten zeroes' appeared to suggest that corruption had multiplied ten times, and led to a flurry of jokes on the Internet and social media. The figure seemed outlandish but the only minister ready to challenge the CAG's calculations was the newly appointed telecom minister Kapil Sibal. 'There can be nothing like "presumptive" loss. There is no loss at all, it is zero loss,' said Sibal in his interviews.

Sibal's charge was based on a complex legal–technical argument, claiming that the CAG's calculations had to be discounted because of various factors, including the maximizing of public welfare as a result of cheap mobile telephony. It may have been a persuasive argument in a courtroom, but Sibal was not a lead counsel appearing before a Supreme Court bench; he was a minister of the government appearing before the court of public opinion. And a disbelieving public found it incredible that a minister was using the word 'zero loss' when the CAG had pegged the loss at a whopping Rs 1.76 lakh crore.

'You people in the media were very unfair to us, very unfair,' Sibal would later tell me. 'I was never defending Raja. I always said that the criminal case will be handled by the CBI [Central Bureau of Investigation] without any government interference. I was only explaining why the notion of a presumptive loss was flawed.'

Flawed it may have been, but Sibal should have known that by then the public had made up its mind. He was fighting a losing battle. More so, because none of his ministerial colleagues, including the prime minister, were willing to speak up. In the age of a hyperactive media, the UPA's silence was interpreted as an admission of guilt.

The target of Sibal's ire was not just the media. It was also the CAG. If T.N. Seshan gave an identity to the office of the Chief Election Commissioner (CEC), Vinod Rai altered the profile of his post from dreary accountant to a robust auditor of policy. Rai, a Kerala cadre IAS officer, had gained a reputation for financial management before he was chosen by the UPA government for the CAG post. 'We scored a self-goal,' one UPA minister said later. 'We never thought someone like him would turn against us in such a public manner.'

Like Anna Hazare, Rai found himself becoming a popular symbol of the war against corruption. After he retired as CAG, I met the silver-haired Rai once on a flight and asked him about his newfound image as an anti-corruption crusader. 'I was only doing my job. I did not seek any media attention,' was his short reply.

Ironically, Rai, like the prime minister, was perceived to be an honest, industrious bureaucrat. Even more ironically, he had been Manmohan Singh's student at the Delhi School of Economics. It had taken one of his own to push Dr Singh's government to the brink. A hostile media, an unyielding judiciary, an empowered CAG—the prime minister was looking like an old man at sea besieged by rapidly rising waves. As the prime minister struggled to rescue his reputation, the one person who could have saved him with a supporting raft was also becoming less visible.

~

Between May 2004 and May 2014, Sonia Gandhi was the most powerful person in the country. Everyone within and outside the government, including the prime minister, acknowledged it. It was quite simply the nature of the ruling arrangement that had been created when Mrs Gandhi, citing her 'inner voice', declined to be the prime minister and chose Dr Singh instead. She was the chairperson, Dr Singh was her hand-picked Chief Executive Officer. It was an understanding based, above all else, on mutual trust and respect. It was also an agreement that suited both. Dr Singh, as the quintessential bureaucrat, was used to taking orders and handling the nitty-gritty of governance; Sonia was happy to wield power without the daily responsibilities of office.

Former Congressman Natwar Singh in his book *One Life Is*

Not Enough has claimed that Sonia's decision not to become prime minister was dictated by Rahul, who feared for her life. 'The inner voice theory is bunkum,' Natwar claimed in several interviews. Was it a conscience call? I had asked Sonia Gandhi this question during a private meeting, soon after she turned down the prime ministership. She had merely nodded her head enigmatically. It is likely that the decision was taken at the family high table in the presence of Rahul, Priyanka and a few close friends, but the final call was hers. The 'inner voice' theory may have been a convenient political spin—it did confer on her a moral halo of martyrdom. But then again, how many politicians will give up what can be so easily theirs?

I first met Sonia Gandhi in 1995 in Amethi when she had launched a veiled attack on then prime minister Narasimha Rao, accusing the government of 'going slow' in the Rajiv Gandhi assassination investigation. 'Are you joining politics?' we had asked her excitedly then. 'No, I am not. But I do believe that Rajivji's sacrifice must not be forgotten,' she had responded. The grieving widow in white seeking justice for her husband—Sonia's political profile seemed to be an extension of her private persona as a guardian of the family legacy, keeper of the Nehru–Gandhi flame. You didn't sense then that she was cut out for the rough and tumble of electoral politics.

And yet, three years later in 1998, she was Congress president, sparking off a furious debate over her foreign origins. She was probably prepared for the attack, but perhaps was not ready for just how personal it would get. I saw a flash of fury when I asked her the question soon after she took over the party leadership. 'I feel 100 per cent Indian,' she said. 'They are attacking me because they have nothing else to criticize me for.' The lonely and injured widow-of-Rajiv image came to the fore—Sonia played the victim card to perfection to outsmart senior leaders like Sharad Pawar who had raised the foreign origins issue.

While she could be gentle and genteel in private conversation (she liked to discuss art and culture), her political persona was marked by a ruthless streak. It was clear that she did not forget or forgive easily—she did not attend Rao's funeral nor did she allow his body to be brought to the Congress headquarters or a samadhi for him in Delhi. 'Sonia's world is divided into loyalists and those who are not with the family. Her political and even personal choices are determined by this,' is how a senior Congressman explained her behaviour. Dr Singh, as a docile, almost servile 'loyalist', was made for Sonia; a Rao or a Sharad Pawar would never be socially or politically acceptable to her as they simply did not pass the rigorous loyalty test to a family in which she had subsumed her entire being.

In December 2005, I did a fairly extensive interview with Mrs Gandhi, a rare occurrence since she generally refused to speak to the media. I had extracted a promise from her when I was setting up CNN-IBN that she would give us an interview in our launch phase. She kept her word. I asked her about whether she had any regrets about turning down the prime ministership. 'No, not at all,' she said with a quiet firmness. 'Manmohan Singh is doing a fine job as prime minister. I have full faith in him.' I asked her to respond to the charge that she was dictatorial and was remote-controlling the government. In a moment of candour, she smiled, 'Not dictatorial. In fact, sometimes I feel I am too democratic and seek too many opinions before taking a decision.'

The truth, as it often does, lies somewhere in between. Contrary to speculation, Sonia did not seek to intervene in the daily functioning of the government, but she did keep a close watch on key issues and appointments. Her policy involvement was driven through the National Advisory Council (NAC), a group explicitly set up to provide external inputs to the prime minister. It was Sonia's way of ensuring her stamp of authority over certain critical decisions. She had been deeply influenced by her mother-in-law's politics, and would tell her friends that the Congress was meant to fight poverty and communalism. In private conversation, she sounded a bit like Mother Teresa. 'India is a country of and for the poor!' she would often say.

The NAC was given a plush office in 2A Motilal Nehru Marg with a small staff. A gathering of ideologically like-minded left-of-centre individuals from civil society, the NAC would meet once a month between 9 a.m. and 1 p.m. to discuss various agenda papers. 'It was all very professional,' one NAC member told me. 'Sonia Gandhi is a very good listener—she would rarely interrupt and ensured that all deadlines for making presentations were kept.' The NAC, though, didn't have the final word. 'Soniaji made it clear to us—we should advise, but the final authority was that of the Cabinet,' says a member.

In UPA-I, the arrangement appeared to work, at least initially. The NAC assisted in the crafting of important legislation, including the Right to Information (RTI) Act, a landmark law in ensuring transparency in government. It helped that in UPA-I, the left was an ally and that many NAC members had strong links with the left. A standing joke in the NAC was, 'When in doubt, let's go and meet CPI(M)'s Sitaram Yechury, he'll be on our side!'

Mrs Gandhi's trusted bureaucrat Pulok Chatterjee was another bridge between the NAC and the PMO as a secretary in South Block, while Jairam Ramesh as an NAC member in UPA-I would push the envelope as well. 'We were all on the same page in UPA-I. There were regular UPA coordination meetings with a common minimum programme. In UPA-II, it was apparent that we were all operating on different agendas—no coordination and no common programme,' is how a member described the change. Sonia herself had to step away from the NAC in 2006 over the office-of-profit controversy when she was accused of violating a rule that as an MP, she could not hold another 'paid' post. She only returned in 2010. By then, the group had lost its sheen.

Not everyone in the government saw the NAC in benign terms. More than one minister told me there was no place for a 'super-Cabinet' in the Indian political system. 'It's only there to satisfy Sonia Gandhi's ego,' was one sharp criticism I heard often. Pawar, for example, felt that the NAC was, as he told a colleague, 'a group of busybodies who are undermining the Cabinet system'. Pawar, who had been in politics for close to five decades, was incensed when the NAC tried to fast-track the food security legislation during UPA-II. 'We must not do anything in a hurry like this,' he warned the prime minister, who was also worried about the financial costs in a period of economic slowdown. Pawar found support in deputy chairperson of the Planning Commission, Montek Singh Ahluwalia, whom the prime minister trusted implicitly. 'We tried to convince Soniaji but she was just not willing to listen,' Pawar told me later.

In the end, the Manmohan–Pawar–Montek combine had to yield ground to the authority of a Sonia-led initiative that aimed to provide subsidized foodgrains to approximately two-thirds of the country's 1.2 billion people. With Sonia holding firm, the bill was passed in September 2013. One estimate put the cost at Rs 125,000 crore. Even if the final figure was lower, there were still legitimate concerns over fiscal and inflationary pressures. 'You must understand Sonia Gandhi,' an aide told me later. 'She doesn't trust economists but goes by her political instincts, and her instincts told her that food security would be a political winner.' What she forgot was that many Opposition-ruled states had already initiated efficient foodgrain distribution programmes. At the fag end of its tenure, the Congress leadership was clutching at straws.

While the NAC was branded a civil society–state interface, Sonia had a more direct political involvement through a Friday evening 'core group' meeting at the prime minister's residence at 7, Race Course Road. This was meant to be the real power centre of the UPA government. The core group members included the prime minister, Pranab Mukherjee (before he became President), Chidambaram, A.K. Antony, Sushil Shinde and Ahmed Patel. None of them were vote-catching leaders—almost all of them owed their place to their proximity to the Congress's First Family.

Patel is an interesting character who exemplifies how the Congress has become a 'drawing room' party that relies on deal-making. A Rajya Sabha MP from Gujarat, he was a key power centre. A silent, almost shadowy figure rarely seen on camera, he was Sonia's political secretary, expected to handle the 'dirty business' of crisis management in politics. 'The rest of us work by day, Ahmed Patel works in the night,' was how one Congressman laughingly described Patel's modus operandi. For most journalists trying to penetrate the Congress's interlinked durbars, Patel was a gold mine—he gave us the '*andar ki khabar*', but never wanted to be quoted or come on camera.

The core group was meant to ensure greater coordination between the Congress party and the government. It was seen as a repository of all political wisdom. And yet, it was this very core group that created further headaches for both the party and the government. It mishandled the Anna agitation. It sent its ministers to meet Ramdev. It endorsed the breaking up of Andhra Pradesh. It even approved the ordinance that would give convicted lawmakers a reprieve.

The core group also could not stop the party and the government from speaking in different voices. The first sign of this came as early as July 2009, barely two months into the life of the new government. The prime minister had gone to Sharm el-Sheikh where, on the sidelines of the Non-Aligned Movement (NAM) summit, he had signed a joint statement with his Pakistani counterpart Yusuf Raza Gilani to cooperate on fighting terror. Born in Pakistan, Dr Singh had always been keen on breaking the ice with Islamabad. Empowered by a strong mandate in the elections, he thought this was the ideal moment to make a fresh effort at peace—it could even be a Nobel Prize-winning achievement.

Only, the timing went horribly wrong. The scars of the 26/11 terror attack in Mumbai had not healed and the Maharashtra assembly elections were just months away. The prime minister may have wanted a place in history; his party had an eye on the polls. Instead of backing him, they decided to criticize the move. Manish Tewari, who was Congress spokesperson at the time, recalled how he was sent an SMS from a senior party leader asking him to leave midway through a TV programme with former diplomats, and stop defending the government. Another spokesperson, Abhishek Singhvi, received similar orders.

'I think that's the moment the prime minister just switched off,' fears Tewari. If the party and Sonia would no longer back him to take tough decisions, then he felt it just wasn't worth it any longer. The same party leadership that had endorsed him on the Indo-US nuclear deal had now turned against him. Dr Singh had just had a major bypass surgery in January and his health was only gradually recovering—Sharm el-Sheikh set him back once again. He would never really recover. A senior member of the Congress Working Committee (CWC) confirmed to me that in his second term there were at least four separate occasions when Dr Singh offered to resign.

It was not just Sharm el-Sheikh. Whenever the government was in a crisis—be it the Anna agitation or the 2G scam—Dr Singh felt the party did not defend him vigorously enough. Sonia did make periodic statements in support of her chosen prime minister. For example, when the telecom scam broke, her first reaction was, 'It is shameful that a person of the integrity of the prime minister should be targeted in this manner. Everyone knows the prime minister is 100 per cent above board.' Somehow, though, her words lacked the confidence she had shown when she stood by him on the Indo-US nuclear deal.

Indeed, Sonia's own role in UPA-II's critical years between 2009 and 2011 is questionable. A good example of her political instincts failing her was the manner in which she dealt with the aftermath of the sudden death of Andhra Pradesh chief minister Y.S. Rajasekhar Reddy in September 2009 in a helicopter accident. A powerful regional satrap who had brought the Congress its largest basket of seats in a state in the 2009 general elections, Reddy had become a symbol of the Congress's electoral success. His death created a vacuum. His son Jaganmohan was keen to fill it and take over.

I had met Jagan just a few days before his father's tragic accident. Short but well built, he had the swagger of a mini Tollywood star. He wanted to make his Sakshi Television, he said, the largest regional television network in the country. 'It would be great if your channel can help me in this—we need your support,' he told me. I had heard about Jagan having become an extra-constitutional authority in Andhra—stories of alleged arm-twisting, vast riches and corruption were filtering through. I was keen to stay as far away as possible.

The accident changed all of Jagan's business plans. Now, he wanted to be chief minister. Only Sonia would not agree. At best, the party was ready to make him a minister of state at the Centre. A defiant Jagan decided to raise the stakes—he set off on an Odarpu (consolation) Yatra to grieve with the families of those who had self-immolated after his father's death. The yatra was his muscle-flexing moment, designed to convince the party high command that he was now Andhra's most popular leader.

Sonia, by all accounts, doesn't like being bullied. Jagan, she felt, was doing precisely that. At a meeting at 10, Janpath, with Jagan and his mother, Sonia drew a line—the Odarpu Yatra must be called off and no attempt must be made to destabilize the new chief minister of the state, the ageing K. Rosaiah.

The meeting went far worse than expected. When Sonia refused to meet Jagan's demands, his mother is reported to have hit back with, 'Would you have said the same thing if it was your son Rahul in Jagan's place? Why is my son being treated differently?' The duo were asked to leave at once. 'My mother and I were left feeling humiliated after all my father had done for the party,' Jagan later told me. Jagan decided there and then that he would form his own party, YSR Congress, taking with him a large chunk of Congress MLAs.

That wasn't the only Andhra blunder. More bizarrely, home minister Chidambaram made a sudden midnight announcement on a freezing winter day in December 2009 that 'the process of forming the state of Telangana was being initiated', an impulsive decision that would eventually mark the beginning of the end for the Congress in Andhra Pradesh.

Among the various theories mooted for the Telangana midnight announcement, two were particularly amusing—first, that some party loyalists wanted to give Sonia Gandhi, who had committed to Telangana in the election campaign, a 'birthday gift' (her birthday is on 9 December); second, that Rahul Gandhi had a fetish for small states and had drawn up a map of India which mirrored the United States with fifty states! The truth is that an Intelligence Bureau (IB) report claimed that there would be a possible 'bloodbath' in Hyderabad if Telangana was not announced. Pro-Telangana protestors, the IB report stated, had been infiltrated by Maoists who planned to march to the secretariat the next morning. The Centre, quite simply, panicked.

With that one midnight decision, the Congress lost control of the political situation in a critical state. Y.S. Rajasekhar Reddy had held the Congress together; without him at the helm, the party was falling apart and the Telangana decision mirrored a mind in turmoil. Andhra was lost, perhaps for good.

Some observers have attributed Sonia's relatively less dominating role in UPA-II to her health problems—she had to travel abroad frequently for a health condition that no one would confirm (we once put out a news flash that Mrs Gandhi had gone for treatment to Sloane Kettering, the world's oldest and largest private care cancer centre, only to be warned by Patel that we would be sued for putting out false information).

Others suggest that Sonia, like a doting Italian (or rather Indian) mother, was desperately keen to step aside so that Rahul could play a greater role and take control of the Congress party. The Congress was, after all, in her world view, a dynastical party whose past, present and future were tied to her family. Her critics say she was always a 'lucky' leader with limited political skills, and that her luck was always bound to run out one day.

The more logical explanation is that with the UPA government being buffeted by multiple crises, a sense of drift, fatigue and eventually, defeatism set in, and Sonia, like other members of the UPA, became a victim of it. As one core group member told me, 'We lost our desire to fight.'

~

By the time the summer of 2012 arrived, it was becoming obvious that the UPA-II government was a patient heading towards the intensive care unit with a lame-duck prime minister. Dr Singh always had two calling cards—his image as an honest politician and his track record as an economist. Now, both were coming under assault. In March that year, another CAG report, this time on coal block allocations, suggested a loss of Rs 1.86 lakh crore to the treasury. The opposition had fresh ammunition—but this time, it was directed at the prime minister personally.

Between 2006 and 2009, the prime minister was the coal minister. The CAG report claimed that as many as 134 coal blocks were given away in this period in an opaque manner without competitive bidding. Many of the beneficiaries had links to prominent politicians, especially of the ruling party. The government argued that the blocks were given out to enhance coal production at a time when the country was facing an energy crisis. The argument did not stick—a Supreme Court-supervised CBI probe was ordered. The Opposition had smelt blood. 'I had gently warned the prime minister that handling the coal portfolio was a bad idea. I don't think he realized what he was getting into,' recalls a former aide.

There was more bad news for the prime minister. The economy appeared to be on an irreversible downturn. Growth had slowed down, manufacturing was struggling, jobs had plateaued, the rupee was weakening, fiscal deficit was out of control, inflation was on the rise. Worried about an activist judiciary, ministers and bureaucrats had stopped taking decisions. Business confidence in particular was at a low ebb—a retrospective tax in the 2012 Union budget had infuriated industry. Several big-ticket projects had been stalled because of environmental concerns. The Eurozone crisis had already taken a heavy toll. In the second week of June, the global ratings agency Standard and Poor warned that India's investment grade rating could be downgraded to 'junk' status. A senior Cabinet minister would later admit to me that the period between 2009 and 2012 were the economy's 'lost years'. 'We had an economist prime minister but the government had lost control of the economy,' says the minister.

He was right. When Manmohan Singh became prime minister in 2004, his USP was his image as an honest man and his reputation as a politician who would manage the economy well. 2G and Coalgate cast a shadow on his integrity quotient. But it was the mistakes on the economic front that really shrank his stature. He won a re-election in 2009 because the economy was growing at a healthy 8 per cent over the five-year period. The 2008 global financial crisis forced the government to relax monetary policy and introduce a fiscal stimulus to boost domestic demand. But once the fiscal deficit began to balloon from 2009 and food inflation began to rise, Dr Singh was always on the back foot. P. Chidambaram offered me an interesting, and rather candid insight: 'If we'd got the economy on the right track, nothing else would have mattered in 2014. It wasn't corruption or scams, it was the economy which destroyed us in the general elections.'

Those who met the prime minister in that difficult period in the summer of 2012 said he was looking frail and troubled. 'He was clearly a worried man, very worried. He never spoke much in Cabinet meetings in any case, now he was almost totally silent,' confessed a Cabinet minister. Another minister told me, 'He just wanted to quit, but Sonia wouldn't let him.'

Whenever two ministers would disagree on an issue, the prime minister's reflex action would be to appoint a Group of Ministers to try and evolve a consensus. At one point, these ministerial groups had swelled to as many as sixty, many of them headed by Mukherjee. 'Pranabda was now the alternative centre of power in the government. Whenever we had an issue, we turned to him for advice,' confessed a minister to me. When Mukherjee, a product of the licence-permit raj, decided to announce the much-criticized retrospective tax in the 2012 budget, the prime minister disagreed but chose not to argue (see chapter 6). The path of least resistance was now a survival ticket.

The elections for a new President were held in the July of 2012. There was a buzz in Lutyens' Delhi that the Congress might consider Dr Singh for the post. The speculation was only partly true. No, Dr Singh was not being identified for a move to Rashtrapati Bhavan, but yes, it was an option that he himself was privately not ruling out. In fact, multiple sources have since confirmed to me that Dr Singh was very keen on being President. After all, he was now approaching his eightieth birthday—he had been prime minister for eight years. Only Jawaharlal Nehru and Indira Gandhi had enjoyed such an extended tenure. He had achieved everything possible in public life—Rashtrapati Bhavan would be a nice sinecure.

This is where the Congress made another big mistake. Moving Dr Singh to Rashtrapati Bhavan and having a new prime minister would have been just the tonic a party in crisis needed. But Sonia Gandhi is notoriously risk-averse. Her aides claim she was faced with the TINA (there is no alternative) factor. Rahul Gandhi had shown no keenness, A.K. Antony was seen as too weak and P. Chidambaram as unsuited to coalition politics. Yes, there was Pranabda, a veteran Congressman, and an able crisis manager with a wide network of friends across parties. But the fact is, Sonia Gandhi never trusted Mukherjee as someone who would protect the family legacy.

It was an old story dating back to the mid-1980s when Mukherjee fell out with Rajiv Gandhi over reports that he had tried to usurp the prime ministership after Indira Gandhi's assassination. Once over lunch, Mukherjee told us how he had been a victim of circumstances. 'It was all a big misunderstanding of what actually happened. I had chosen to chair a Cabinet meeting after the assassination as the seniormost minister. I wasn't aiming to be the prime minister myself, but people around Rajiv convinced him that I was plotting to get the top job,' he said ruefully.

Sonia, though, has a long memory, neatly dividing the world into those with the Gandhis and those against the family. Somehow, Mukherjee, who could well have proven to be an able prime minister, never quite made the cut. Though he would never accept it publicly, the fact is Mukherjee had also never fully reconciled to Dr Singh as his leader. 'He wanted to be prime minister but knew Sonia would never make him one,' a Union minister told me. Being pushed to Rashtrapati Bhavan as a near-consensus candidate was scant compensation.

That move also ended any chance Dr Singh may have had of easing himself out into a more comfortable environment. In any case, he had always been a great survivor. For the last two years of his political career, that's all he was—a survivor. In those two years, there was more dirt, more scandal, and more of his ministers had to resign. One of them, law minister Ashwani Kumar, had to resign amidst allegations that he had tried to 'protect' the prime minister by making changes in the status report of the CBI on the coal block allocations. Kumar was seen as a 'Manmohan man' and later insisted to me that he was made a scapegoat. Dr Singh's office was even accused of allowing crucial coal files to go missing. Through it all, Dr Singh hung on to the chair. But as one Opposition MP pointed out, 'Yes, the patient is breathing, but *yeh bhi koi jeena hai* [is this any way to live]!'

~

On 3 January 2014, just months before the general elections, Dr Singh announced at a press conference before the national media that he was 'retiring' from politics after the elections and he would not be in the race for prime minister. It was an unprecedented move—no Indian prime minister had publicly 'retired' before an election. Just months earlier, Rahul Gandhi had publicly snubbed the prime minister by rejecting the Cabinet's ordinance on criminal MPs. There were reports that Dr Singh had contemplated stepping down in protest and his family had suggested that he just walk away. When I later asked him about it, his response was, 'But the ordinance was a collective decision of the government, not just mine alone.' So was he angry with Rahul and had he ever thought of resigning at the time? He stayed silent and then urged me to have my coffee. We were alone in his room. The loneliness of a defeated man filled the air.

In fact, I have confirmed with a source close to Dr Singh that he did, indeed, once again offer to resign after Rahul tore up the government ordinance. Dr Singh told Sonia he'd had enough. 'Let me go now, madam. I don't think I can do this any longer—even my health is not good,' he pleaded. For one final time, Sonia chose to ignore his request to quit.

In his final press conference, Dr Singh was a little more voluble than usual while defending himself. 'I have served the country with utmost dedication and integrity,' he said. 'I do not believe that I have been a weak prime minister. I honestly believe that history will be kinder to me than the contemporary media or the Opposition in

Parliament. Given the political compulsions, I have done the best I could do. It is for history to judge what I have done or what I have not done.'

How would history judge the man with the most famous blue turban? Indians tend to be kind to their leaders. In an opinion poll CNN-IBN conducted on the sixtieth anniversary of Indian Independence, Indira Gandhi emerged as the most admired politician. It was almost as if the Emergency had never happened. Dr Singh is unlikely to be put on the same pedestal. As a self-made man who had built his career though hard work and scholarship, there is much to admire about him. The fact that neither he nor his family derived any monetary benefit from his prime ministership is not insignificant either. In an age where corruption and nepotism in politics happily coexist, Dr Singh was able to retain a certain decency and moral commitment in his private life. Outside India, global leaders saw him as a man of rare intellect.

And yet, the fact is, when asked to stand up to corruption in his own government, he chose to look the other way. There were enough opportunities for him to say 'enough is enough' and draw a *Lakshman-rekha* when faced with the compulsions of coalition politics. Rather than exercise prime ministerial authority, as he did with the Indo-US nuclear deal, he fell back into the safety of his original avatar—a bureaucrat happy to take orders and simply stay in office, almost by force of habit or second nature. Yes, he did offer to resign on more than one occasion, but not once did he take the more courageous option of just walking away.

He was never a mass leader or an orator. He had lost the only Lok Sabha election he had contested, and seemed to prefer the sanctuary of the Rajya Sabha after that. In happier times, it did not really matter. In the crisis-ridden second term in office, it became a cross that was too heavy for the government, party and eventually, the country, to bear. When the nation was looking for a strong, decisive leader who could take charge, Dr Singh went into silent mode. The joke that the only time he opened his mouth was when he had a dentist's appointment may have been cruel, but it reflected the exasperation of even his admirers who once saw him as a middle-class hero who had guided the economy through a critical period in the 1990s. Lamentably, the 'retirement' press conference was actually the first of its kind that he held since the onset of UPA-II.

Dr Singh's decision to quit politics was not unexpected. But in the build-up to the sixteenth general elections, it only highlighted the Congress's dilemma—a hapless prime minister ready to take sanyas and an untested young heir who appeared reluctant to take charge. The all-powerful *gaddi* of Delhi looked vacant. One man from Gujarat smelt his big chance.

4

I want to Be Prime Minister

Narendra Modi arrived in the national capital on 6 February 2013 looking every inch the muscular politician whose time had come. Delhi had seen many a conqueror aspire to its throne, and with news cameras tracking his every move, Modi gave the distinct impression he was ready to join the list. The sound of the Gujarat election triumph less than two months earlier was still resonating and Modi was keen to capitalize on the momentum. An *India Today* Mood of the Nation poll around Republic Day had suggested he was already the most preferred choice for prime minister—well ahead of the Congress troika of Rahul, Sonia and Manmohan—and he needed to capitalize on the enthusiasm.

The choice for his first public-speaking assignment was the Shri Ram College of Commerce (SRCC). The college was organizing a three-day business conclave and Modi was to deliver a memorial lecture as the grand finale. 'We took a poll among the students as to who they wanted to listen to. Modi came out on top, ahead of Ratan Tata,' says a member of SRCC's students' council. An invite was sent to Modi in mid-January, and his office responded in the affirmative in forty-eight hours. Interestingly, the students had also contacted half a dozen Union ministers from the Congress to come and speak at the conclave. All of them, including young leaders like Jyotiraditya Scindia and Sachin Pilot, refused. Some like Anand Sharma did not even reply.

Modi's decision to speak at SRCC was well considered. The leading college for economics and commerce in the country, SRCC boasted seemingly ridiculous cut-offs of 98 per cent. It had built an enviable reputation for attracting the best and brightest students. A number of BJP leaders from Delhi had been SRCC alumni, including Arun Jaitley, the leader of the Opposition in the Rajya Sabha and legal eagle. The topic—'Emerging Business Models in a Global Scenario'—was perfect as well. 'We were looking to launch Mr Modi in an environment which was not hostile and where he could speak to the young of India, not just as Gujarat chief minister but as a future CEO of India,' a key Modi aide told me.

The 'youth' factor was key. Team Modi had commissioned surveys which suggested that the mood for change was highest among the young, with the fear of lack of job opportunities in a weakening economy being a prime concern. There was a feeling that it was the young urban Indian whom the BJP had failed to attract in the 2009 elections, preferring as they did the youthful promise offered by a Rahul Gandhi to the tried and tested octogenarian L.K. Advani. 'We realized that the young voter, especially the first-time voter between eighteen and twenty-three, was waiting to be wooed. For that reason, SRCC as a college to which many young people aspired to gain admission was ideal for us,' said a Team Modi member.

Addressing a young, post-liberalization India had another advantage. The 3000-strong audience in the college's sports complex comprised mainly excited students who had not even entered their teens when the 2002 Gujarat riots took place. They were free, in a sense, of the images of the violence and criticism the Modi government had endured at the time. Six years earlier, Modi had come to Delhi for the *Hindustan Times* summit and found himself being asked uncomfortable questions on 2002. This time, he was taking no chances—it was a lecture where he could speak without having to take any questions. The media was present in large numbers, but this wasn't a press conference where they could try and corner the Gujarat chief minister. This time, they would simply have to listen, take notes and record the speech.

The event went off spectacularly well. Modi spoke for a little more than an hour, holding forth about governance, the economy and the Gujarat model of business. Speaking in Hindi without any notes or the slightest hesitation, Modi gave a masterful oration, peppered with one-liners: 'We have got swaraj, but after sixty years, we are still looking for *suraaj* (good governance); 'our youth are not snake charmers, they are changing the world with a mouse'; 'our biggest national resource are our people. Made in India must become our biggest brand.' Each statement echoed a sense of looking forward. In a climate of negativity and pessimism, it appeared to strike just the right chord for a young audience that frequently broke into applause.

There was also a fair amount of hyperbole, especially when 'selling' Gujarat. 'There must be no one in the audience who has chai without *doodh* from Gujarat in it. All the milk in Delhi is from Gujarat. Milk in Singapore is from Gujarat. Okra in Europe is from Gujarat. Tomatoes in Afghanistan are from Gujarat. The bhindi you eat is from Gujarat!' he claimed. Of course, what he conveniently did not mention was that it was a certain Dr Verghese Kurien and his Amul milk cooperative dream that ushered in Gujarat's White Revolution and not Mr Modi. The students did not seem to mind, though. Modi's public-speaking skills had won them over.

It wasn't just the students—the media also lapped up Modi's performance. All national and several regional channels carried Modi's speech 'live'. Next morning, every national newspaper had Modi as a front-page headline. 'Modi takes Delhi by storm,' declared the *Times of India*. The only paper not to carry Modi's speech on the front page was *The Hindu*; it was also the only paper to give equal coverage to anti-Modi protests organized by left students' groups outside SRCC. Its then editor Siddharth Varadarajan defended his decision by claiming that Modi, after all, was just another chief minister who had come to Delhi—why should it make a top headline? His was a lonely voice.

Modi and his team were thrilled by the response. They felt that the SRCC speech had not just captured the youth's focus but had also been able to reach out to thought leaders and the urban middle class through the power of live television. 'We realized that Modi was unbeatable in a town hall format. We had also managed to create just the right amount of buzz in the media and among opinion makers,' said a Modi strategist.

I spoke to Modi on the phone a few days after the SRCC speech (I would usually call him up late night or on a Sunday morning when he was relatively more relaxed). *'Kya feedback hai?'* he asked like a good politician. I confessed that his lecture had been most impressive and that he deserved a nine on ten. *'Kyon, dus nahi doge kya!'* he exclaimed. My response was, *'Sir, dus deta agar aap Kuriensaab ka bhi naam lete!'* (I would have given you a ten if you had mentioned Dr Kurien's name!)

Modi's supporters, though, had no such quibbles. A hit formula had been found—Modi speaking on governance-related issues to a captive audience, with millions watching on television. A pattern had been set which would transform Modi in the weeks and months ahead from just another chief minister into a national leader the country could relate to. In school in Vadnagar, Modi had been very fond of theatre; he loved the stage and had acted in several plays in the village. Now, in his adult life, the past training would serve him well. This was now his moment to shine as a solo performer in front of a national audience. At a time when the prime minister had slipped into a seemingly irreversible silent mode and Rahul was still a hesitant public speaker, Modi filled a vacuum in the public discourse. His skill as a natural orator made him a star attraction for an audience hankering for effective communication.

The aim was to establish Modi not just as a pan-Indian leader but, very importantly, as an urban hero. In the 2009 elections, the BJP had won just fifty of the 201 urban/semi-urban seats in the country. Team Modi's internal poll had shown that their leader was gaining strong traction in urban areas, except among the urban poor and women in the twenty-eight to thirty-five age group (young women reportedly found Modi's style 'abrasive'). 'If we had to win the 2014 elections, we knew we had to sweep urban India, which is why Modiji's initial focus was on the cities,' one of his aides told me later.

Between February and July 2013, Modi addressed several select gatherings in the town hall format that showcased him not just as a politician but as a trailblazer who had evolved, or rather reinvented himself, from demagogue to statesman, from divisive figure to governance guru, from a Hindu identity politician to a problem-solving 'ideas' man—the kind who would appeal to an increasingly urbanizing society.

He addressed the Indian diaspora via videoconference in March where he spoke passionately of how secularism for him meant 'India First'. At the *India Today* conclave in March, he spoke of the Gujarat model and his 'Namo Mantra'—how he had used technology to reduce inefficiency in government, and offered solutions to issues like power crisis and water management. When a journalist tried to ask a question on Gujarat 2002, Modi looked at him sternly and avoided a direct answer, pointing out that the SIT had cleared him. 'Looks like some people will not change,' was the terse response when the questioner persisted.

In April, he went down south to the Sivagiri Mutt in Kerala to address religious leaders there; the same week, he was flying north to Ramdev's Patanjali Yoga Peeth. But even while addressing the Sadhu Samaj at Ramdev's set-up, there was no trace of the majoritarian agenda of 2002. Instead, Modi spoke with telling effect on the need to blend spirituality with science and technology. As he referred to a benign and universal Hindu identity and consciousness, he sounded more like Vivekananda than a BJP politician.

Modi switched easily from one target audience to another. He spoke to NRIs across twenty cities in the US on Gujarat Foundation Day. He used Facebook to crowdsource ideas while speaking to Pune's Fergusson College students on the need to reform education. He addressed a book release function of RSS activist Vinay Sahasrabuddhe at the Bombay Stock Exchange where the gathering of traders and karyakartas was lectured on the Gandhi model of trusteeship and its links to good governance. At a Google+ Hangout, he spoke on politics and technology, and gave his formula for success: IT + IT = IT (Indian Talent plus Indian Technology equals India Tomorrow). The one-liners were headline grabbing even if there was a tendency to get the facts wrong at times—for example, Modi wrongly claimed that China had spent 20 per cent of its GDP on education. Each event played out live on television and the Internet. 'We just wanted to keep him in the news by getting him to share his ideas with different constituencies across urban India and even global audiences,' says a Team Modi member.

His energy was boundless. On 8 April, he spoke in the forenoon at the annual conference of the FICCI Ladies Organization, addressing elegant women from business families in a five-star hotel. He narrated to them the story of Jasuben's pizzas in Ahmedabad to make a case for women's empowerment. Jasuben, a Gujarati housewife, had started her own version of a pizza forty years ago. Now, her business has expanded to include six branches, with an average of 600 pizzas being sold every day in Ahmedabad. He even had a dig at Rahul Gandhi and his attempt to raise the issue of Vidarbha farm widows. 'Now, the media will think Jasuben is like Kalavati, and search for her. Let me just say that she died in Pune five years ago.' The FICCI ladies loved the free-flowing talk. 'He's just the kind of leader we need,' was the ecstatic verdict.

That same evening, Modi attended a Network 18 event which had been organized as part of a 'Think India' initiative of the network I worked for. The idea was a brainchild of Network 18 founder Raghav Bahl, who had already developed a fascination for Modi's thoughts, especially on markets and the economy. 'He is probably the only leader who is really committed to transforming the economy,' gushed Raghav. The original name for the programme was the 'Think Right' summit. I explained to Raghav that the name might send out the wrong message as we approached an election year, especially as Modi was the first speaker. Raghav was flexible—Think Right was changed to Think India. The topic for the interaction was 'Minimum Government, Maximum Governance', another pet Modi mantra.

Modi spoke passionately for an hour on a variety of issues, from speedier privatization to reducing red-tapism to reforming urban bodies: 'There is too much paperwork in government departments. Why can't this file culture be cut down?'; 'Open up the railways to the private sector'; 'We need to shift decision-making from Delhi to state capitals.' His 'can do' opinions were coming thick and fast. The entire interaction was telecast live on all the network channels (CNBC, CNN-IBN, IBN 7), including the ETV network that broadcast in half a dozen languages. The show was repeated at prime time, ensuring maximum eyeballs.

It was meant to be a 'soft focus' interaction. As it was winding down, I wanted to ask a question on crony capitalism and the charges that he was favouring select business groups. Modi saw my hand raised, politely ignored me and ended the session. Later, I was told Modi had been assured there would be no 'inconvenient' issues raised. He probably thought I would rewind to 2002. Clearly, there would be no 2002-related questions and no walkouts this time!

My enduring memory of that day was Modi's entry into the Taj Palace Hotel lobby. In his signature half-sleeved white kurta, he strode in with the self-confidence of a man who believed he had truly arrived. The BJP leaders at the venue—Smriti Irani, Meenakshi Lekhi, Piyush Goyal, Ravi Shankar Prasad, Kirit Somaiya—stood to attention, almost as if they were part of an army battalion whose general had just marched in. I tried to lighten the mood by asking Somaiya, a BJP MP from Mumbai, when he was planning to expose a CAG report on Gujarat, like he had done in Maharashtra. Modi glared at him and me. When Modi had departed the waiting room for the stage, Somaiya told me worriedly, *'Kya boss, marva daloge mujhe!'* (Boss, you will have me killed.) Modi was still not the BJP's prime ministerial candidate, but he was already acting like one. And party members were already both in awe and fear, already convinced that their leader was headed to victory.

~

The BJP national council in March 2013 at the Talkatora Stadium in Delhi was held against the backdrop of a mini crisis in the party. Just weeks earlier, Nitin Gadkari had been forced to resign as party president over allegations of financial impropriety. Gadkari claimed in private conversation that he had been done in by the BJP's 'Delhi leadership', a euphemism for the party's parliamentary wing. Rajnath Singh was brought back to head the BJP. The council was meant to ratify his appointment. It became instead an event that showcased the emerging star power of Modi.

At the two-day council meet, Modi became a Pied Piper. News cameras followed his every move, party cadres wanted to click selfies with him; every time his name was mentioned in any speech there were loud cheers, and he was given a standing ovation for a third successive win in Gujarat. 'I hadn't seen anything like this in the BJP,' confessed a veteran BJP watcher. 'The man's popularity within the rank and file was even greater than Vajpayeeji in his pomp.' Vajpayee, after all, was seen as a statesman in the Nehruvian mould; Modi was an ideologue who tapped into the BJP's natural Hindutva moorings. The groundswell of support to anoint him as the party's leader for the 2014 elections was rising.

Modi spoke on the second day of the meet. The speech was vintage Modi—he was addressing the party faithful, and the political aggression was back as he launched into the Gandhi family and the UPA government. 'Sacrificing national interest for the interest of one family is the tradition of the Congress,' thundered Mr Modi, going for the jugular. 'They appointed a nightwatchman by naming Manmohan Singh as prime minister . . . the prime minister is nothing but a puppet of the Gandhi family.' The 2000-strong cheering crowd chanted his name repeatedly. A political meet had become a show of strength.

That very day, Sushma Swaraj also spoke. Her speech, too, was powerful but stateswomanlike, as she reflected on the need to topple the UPA government. Her speech was applauded, with L.K. Advani even likening her oratory to Vajpayee. But while the television channels aired Modi's speech without any advertising breaks (it would become a familiar practice over the next twelve months, causing loss in revenues to news channels!), Sushma Swaraj's speech was shown only intermittently. In the TRP (television rating point) war, Modi was already the winner.

He also won another battle that day. Who amongst the BJP's Generation Next would succeed the Vajpayee–Advani duo as the face of the party—the issue had unsettled the BJP ever since Vajpayee had lost the 2004 elections. Vajpayee and Advani had, after all, dominated BJP politics for almost four decades, a unique partnership that was respectful and competitive at the same time. The battle to become their successor had left the BJP looking like a Hindu Divided Family.

Swaraj as leader of the party in the Lok Sabha had been one hopeful—with her blazing red sindoor and big bindi, she might have come straight out of a *saas–bahu* set. A terrific campaigner and forceful public speaker, she had the backing of Advani who had groomed her. There was also Jaitley, the suave lawyer and election strategist, who was leader of the party in the Rajya Sabha. He had a strong equation with Modi, having given the Gujarat chief minister sharp legal advice through his many battles with the judiciary. He had even got his Rajya Sabha entry from Gujarat.

Swaraj and Jaitley disliked each other and their 'camps' would often accuse the other of planting stories against the other. Once a photograph came out in the newspapers of Sushma 'blessing' the Reddy brothers of Karnataka after they had just been indicted in a mining scam. 'I know you have got this photo from Jaitley's office only to discredit me,' she told us.

A more charitable explanation of the Sushma–Jaitley cold war would be to call it 'sibling rivalry' between two individuals sharing a common space. Swaraj, in fact, once told me in half-jest, '*Arre, tum toh Arun ke dost ho* [You are Arun's friend], you go for a walk with him, you will only project him!'

Yes, Jaitley was part of our 'middle-aged' walking club in Delhi's picturesque Siri Fort forest park before he moved to the more upscale Lodi Gardens, but to be honest, he liked to talk as much as walk! The loquacious, extroverted Jaitley is a natural raconteur—from politics to cricket to just simple gossip, he has more than a story a day to offer. As brilliant a host as he is a lawyer, Jaitley is an aficionado of fine food, and his parties are examples of big-hearted Punjabi hospitality, though his taste in cholesterol-heavy Moti Mahal *burra* kebabs probably does not please his physician. I don't think I have met a politician with a wider circle of friends outside politics; within the power corridors, however, he was feared as much as admired. Feared because he never cloaked his fierce ambition in diplomacy, admired for his sophisticated and erudite debating skills. He was also totally wired into the media—if beat reporters of newspapers and channels had to vote for their favourite politician, Jaitley might win comfortably.

There was also Rajnath Singh, a former UP chief minister who liked to see himself as a consensus builder with friends across parties. As a proud Thakur from the Hindi heartland, he'd often been accused of strong caste loyalties and was not above low cunning, and sidelining his rivals. His personal astrologer had apparently told him 2014 would be a big year for him.

But for all their strengths, the triumvirate of Delhi-based leadership aspirants did not have a genuine mass base nor had they delivered election victories. The BJP was looking for a vote catcher and Modi in the spring of 2013 had the look and feel of one.

Three weeks after the national council meet, Modi was inducted into the BJP's parliamentary board, its highest decision-making body, the only BJP chief minister to get that honour. A few days later, I interviewed Rajnath Singh and asked him the obvious question—would Modi now be made the BJP's prime ministerial candidate? Singh, a smooth talker who had refined political diplomacy to a fine art, was evasive. 'Our party has many capable leaders. We are a democratic party and the parliamentary board will decide the leadership issue at the appropriate time.' I persisted, 'But isn't Modi the most popular BJP leader today?' Singh's answer was revealing. 'Yes, Narendrabhai is the most popular chief minister. *Logon mein unka jadoo toh hai* [There is Modi magic among people].' I had got my answer. Modi was no longer first among equals. He was THE BJP leader of the future. Only one man disagreed—the person who had once been seen, ironically, as a mentor of the Gujarat chief minister. As Modi's graph rose inexorably, a combative senior citizen readied for revolt.

~

Goa will always have a special place in the life and times of Modi. It was here that his political career was saved in the aftermath of the 2002 riots. And it was here in June 2013 that he was made the chairman of the BJP's election campaign committee, the first step towards making him the BJP's prime ministerial candidate. If he had to fight for his chief ministership in 2002, he also had to battle hard to lead the party in 2013. At the centre of both fights was the BJP patriarch and the man who had redefined the BJP, L.K. Advani.

Advani is one of the most complex characters in Indian politics. I had first met him during the 1990 Ayodhya rath yatra, a seminal moment in his political career. Till then, he was seen as an organizational man, not a mass leader. The yatra imbued him with a certain nationalist machismo and transformed him into the ideological mascot of militant Hindutva nationalism. And yet, he would often be discomfited with the description. In one interview he told me, 'I don't know why the media keeps referring to me as a Hindu militant. There is not a trace of militancy in me.' He then looked at his devoted wife Kamala and daughter Pratibha for endorsement. They both nodded in agreement.

Maybe Advani was the victim of an image trap, especially after the demolition of the Babri Masjid in 1992. Maybe he was simply having to live with the fact that while his yatra had consolidated a Hindu vote bank, it also led to communal riots. The divisive nature of that period in Indian politics meant that Advani could never become prime minister when the BJP first came to power in 1996, that honour going to Vajpayee instead. Vajpayee was seen as a statesman in the Nehruvian mould; Advani had been pigeonholed as a Hindutva ideologue.

And yet, the Karachi-born, Jesuit school-educated, English-speaking leader, who liked a Naipaul novel as much as he did a Hindi film, was always looking to evolve and reinvent himself. In 2005, he went to Pakistan and described Jinnah as 'secular' and an 'ambassador of Hindu–Muslim unity'. The remarks sparked off a controversy within the Sangh Parivar for whom Pakistan's founder is a hate figure. Advani had to eventually step down as BJP president. It was almost as if his roots in the RSS would prevent him from breaking free from his past.

It was Advani's ideological training in the Sangh that also, in a sense, defined his relationship with Modi. As a committed organization man, Advani had discovered similar skills in the young pracharak from Gujarat in the 1980s and had given him his first major break in the party. Advani believed in mentoring young people, and an entire generation of BJP leaders has been nurtured under his tutelage. Modi was one of them. That belief in Modi's abilities had even led him to strongly insist that the Gujarat chief minister be allowed to continue in office after the 2002 riots when Vajpayee had decided to remove him. 'Let's be clear, if there was no Advani, Modi would have lost his chief ministership at the Goa national executive in 2002,' one senior BJP leader affirms. 'Only Advani could have changed Vajpayee's mind that day.'

Now, the BJP's national executive was meeting again in 2013 at the very same Marriott Hotel along Panaji's Miramar Beach. Only this time, the party was preparing to announce Modi as campaign committee chairman for the 2014 elections. Advani's supporters claim he was informed about the plan just twenty-four hours before the executive was to begin. That's when he decided to stay away and boycott the meeting, citing ill health, and virtually forcing a confrontation. 'It wasn't a personal fight with Modi. Advaniji was just upset that as the seniormost BJP leader he hadn't been properly consulted before such a major decision was taken,' claims an Advani insider.

But the public nature of Advani's response suggested otherwise. A day after the Modi announcement was formally made in Goa, Advani announced his resignation from all party posts and shot off a three-paragraph letter to Rajnath Singh, claiming that the party had lost the 'idealism' of Syama Prasad Mookerjee, Deendayal Upadhyaya, Nanaji Deshmukh and Vajpayee. The letter stated: 'For some time I have been finding it difficult to reconcile with the current functioning of the party, or the direction in which it is going . . . Most leaders of ours are now just concerned with their personal agendas.' There was no mention of Modi in the letter, but it was obvious who the target of Advani's ire was.

The letter, leaked almost immediately to the media, embarrassed the BJP just when it was poised to announce its 2014 campaign strategy. It also reignited divisions within the party. A small group, which included Sushma Swaraj, appeared to back Advani. At the Goa meeting, Swaraj had suggested that any announcement on Modi as campaign chief be deferred because Advani was not present. She was overruled. Swaraj always saw Modi as authoritarian even as she had abiding affection for Advani. She also knew her great rival, Jaitley, was close to Modi and was worried the duo were plotting to marginalize her. Veteran leader Jaswant Singh, who had already been isolated within the party, also decided to stay away from the executive. But apart from the handful of veterans, the majority of the party was firmly with Modi.

A worried Rajnath Singh consulted the RSS top brass in Nagpur who advised him to stick to the original decision on Modi. But the Sangh leadership was also keen that he broker a truce with Advani. Gadkari, who enjoyed the full trust of the RSS, was assigned the task. The Nagpur-based leader kept shuttling between Advani and Rajnath Singh's residences. 'I lost a few kilos in the process,' he joked later. Modi called up Advani as well, and said he remained his 'guiding force'. Jaitley met Advani for two hours and told him that as the man who had built the modern-day BJP, his newfound image as a dissident was only doing him harm. After forty-eight hours of a family soap-like political drama, Advani had little choice but to take back his resignation.

So, why did the eighty-five-year-old Advani attempt to stall Modi's ascent? Critics suggest that the elderly leader had been driven by undiluted personal ambition, and that his family in particular was keen that he remain in the prime ministerial picture. 'Advani had not got over the disappointment of 2009 and could not accept the fact that the party had now moved onto a new leadership as represented by Modi,' says a BJP commentator. When a former political aide of Advani, Sudheendra Kulkarni, went on television calling Modi a 'dictator', it only seemed to confirm the belief that the Advani 'camp' had been spoiling for a fight. Kulkarni, though, denies drafting Advani's letter of resignation.

Advani's supporters say his actions were propelled by nothing more than a genuine concern over the party becoming a one-man show. 'Advani had observed Modi's style of functioning in Gujarat and was worried that he would bring in a similar brand of unilateral decision-making which was not part of the BJP's culture,' says an Advani loyalist. Advani also told BJP leaders who met him that he was convinced that if Modi became the face of the BJP campaign, it would lead to a Hindu–Muslim polarization and the core issue of governance and UPA misrule would be forgotten. 'We will not get allies and we will be stuck with 180 seats like in 1996,' he warned.

The truth is, Advani had never reconciled himself to the 2009 defeat under his helmsmanship. There were reports (denied, of course) that he would consult astrologers on when the Manmohan Singh government would fall. He even seemed to blame me for denying him his moment of ultimate glory, in an episode that revealed the darker side of our politics.

The cash-for-votes scandal had broken out during the nuclear deal vote in Parliament in 2008. There had been much speculation at the time that MPs were being offered bribes by both sides but we were not being given any evidence. CPI leader A.B. Bardhan had even claimed that Rs 25 crore was being offered to each MP for their vote. Our investigative reporter Siddharth Gautam had been attempting to get more details but had made no significant breakthrough. I was sitting in Parliament's central hall listening to the nuclear debate when Jaitley joined us. The BJP leader claimed some of his MPs had been contacted by the government to switch sides. 'We are planning to expose this in a sting operation,' he said. He agreed to allow our cameras to be a fly on the wall, watching MPs being 'purchased'.

That evening, we got a phone call from Jaitley, and sent Siddharth and a production unit to meet Sudheendra Kulkarni who was supervising the entire sting operation. The silver-haired Kulkarni, a former journalist, had worked in the Vajpayee PMO. He was now an Advani loyalist with an obsessive desire to see his leader as prime minister. Kulkarni had also played an important role in shaping Advani's contentious homage to Jinnah. Now, he was hoping that the sting would bring down the Manmohan Singh government. With Kulkarni were three BJP MPs, Ashok Argal, Faggan Singh Kulaste and Mahavir Bhagora, who had offered to be 'whistle-blowers'. None of us had met or heard of these MPs till that day.

The other key player in the sting was a more mysterious individual with a rather intriguing name—Sohail Hindustani. Our reporting team had no clue as to who Sohail really was. Dressed in a T-shirt, he was, by all accounts, one of those Delhi wheeler-dealers who liked to show off his alleged connections with powerful people. It was Hindustani who was trying to organize the actual money transaction.

Our investigating team was first taken to Hotel Meridien where we were told that Congress leaders, including Ahmed Patel, would be found striking a deal. But when the MPs who had been miked up with a hidden camera reached the hotel, they did not meet anyone. All we had were dark shots of people moving in and out of the hotel lobby. Something seemed wrong. Kulkarni was livid. 'Where are the Congress leaders you promised to get us?' he asked Hindustani.

An increasingly desperate Hindustani started making more phone calls virtually offering the BJP MPs 'for sale'. Late in the night, he finally got lucky. A Samajwadi Party MP, Reoti Raman Singh, landed up at the residence of the BJP MPs. Our team secretly filmed the conversations where the two sides talked of a potential money deal. Reoti Raman Singh asked the BJP MPs to meet his 'leader' the next morning to clinch the transaction. The presumption was that it was Amar Singh he was referring to. The MPs agreed. They went to Amar Singh's house in the morning in a Zen car with tinted glasses but crucially refused to take the hidden camera or mikes in with them. 'We don't want to get caught and take any risk. Amar Singh is a dangerous guy,' one of the MPs told Siddharth. We, however, did film the car entering the house.

But the real big breakthrough came an hour after the Amar Singh meeting. We had on camera someone called Sanjeev Saxena, ostensibly an aide of Amar Singh, meeting the MPs at their residence with a large bag of money. Kulkarni was delighted. 'We have nailed this now, the sting is done!' He even hugged our team and congratulated them. The cash was laid out on a table.

The tapes landed in the office around noon. Watching them, I knew we were onto potentially explosive stuff. The newsman in me was excited. 'This story is going to really create a splash,' was my gut reaction. Not all my senior editors were as convinced. 'This is a BJP-driven operation, surely we need to do some verification before we can go on air with it.' The more considered view that I eventually fell in line with was that the tapes on their own did not make a journalistically sound investigative report and the 'evidence' in them needed more examination. Remember, contrary to popular belief, we did not have Amar Singh or any Congress leader offering money on tape, either by way of audio or video.

Given the sensitive, even dramatic nature of the story, we decided to consult our lawyers. I also spoke to former solicitor general Harish Salve who advised restraint. 'The tapes will not stand legal scrutiny without due diligence and could be seen as unlawful entrapment,' was his expert opinion. After a long debate during our editorial meeting, we decided to hold off airing of the footage till we had done further investigation.

By now, it was 4 p.m. The BJP leaders who had organized the sting were getting increasingly impatient—they wanted us to telecast the tapes immediately while the vote was on. We said that a genuine, credible investigation meant there would have to be a process of cross-checking the information, especially as there were middlemen with questionable reputations involved. 'Give us a few days, we will put it all together,' I assured my BJP interlocutors.

The lawyer in Jaitley seemed to understand our predicament but not the others. The BJP was determined to block the nuclear deal vote. So, around 5 p.m. that evening, barely a few hours after we had caught the initial money exchange on camera, the BJP MPs went ahead to Parliament, displaying the bundle of notes in the Lok Sabha. By that one act, the BJP left us with no choice but to abort the investigation. Key players like Sanjeev Saxena just disappeared when we tried to track them down. I went to Parliament and met the Lok Sabha Speaker Somnath Chatterjee, and gave him a copy of the sting tapes. 'You have done the right thing. It is now for the Delhi police to investigate further,' he told me.

Three weeks later, we testified before a parliamentary committee on the cash-for-votes sting and placed all the tapes before them. Importantly, the very night of our testimony, we did telecast the tapes in a three-hour-long programme without editing out any relevant information. We also fully cooperated with the police investigation which was sadly slipshod (the police, for example, never sought the phone conversations of the MPs involved in the operation which were later obtained by *Tehelka* magazine). But, importantly, there was no cover-up—we were simply placing in the public domain whatever we had. No footage was ever hidden from any authority. Our investigating team's chief producer Rohit Khanna can vouch for this.

Advani and Kulkarni, though, were still fuming, convinced that we had held back the tapes under government pressure. The BJP even boycotted our channel for a few days. I tried to reason with Advani but knew I was fighting a losing battle. 'You have let us down under pressure from the Congress,' he said, incensed. 'You have betrayed us,' shouted Kulkarni.

The truth is, there was minimal external pressure not to show the sting. A worried Congress leader Prithviraj Chavan, who was a minister in the PMO, only called up to know if any Congressmen were on the tape and asked why we had done a 'deal' with the BJP. Others like Ahmed Patel, who had been closely involved in managing the numbers for the government during the vote, seemed just relieved to know that they weren't on any tape recording. *'Yeh BJP wale mujhe phasana chahate hain'* (The BJP wants to trap me), he claimed. Neither of them threatened me in any manner, contrary to some reports.

The only one who was really worried was Amar Singh. 'You are part of a conspiracy to destroy my career,' he told me. On the night we telecast the sting, he rang up and warned me, 'I will deal with you and Arun Jaitley for doing this to me.' Years later, at a book release function, he even accused me of being the journalist who sent him to jail. 'I will never forgive you for it,' he said angrily. I found myself in the strange situation of being condemned by everyone involved: the BJP accused me of protecting the government; the government blamed me for being hand in glove with the BJP; and Amar Singh believed I had sent him to jail.

Did I get the cash-for-votes sting horribly wrong? Should we have simply aired what we had right away without any journalistic checks? It's a tough one to answer. Maybe I should have gone along with my original instinct, which was to simply air whatever we had on tape and let all other issues be settled subsequently. We had strong circumstantial evidence against Amar Singh even though there were still plenty of holes in the overall story that needed rigorous cross-checking.

However, it is a golden rule of journalism that bigger the story, the greater the need for vigilance. 'The publish and be damned' theory cannot allow for an incomplete investigation to be aired. I am no votary of sting journalism. A sting must only be carried out when the public interest is so great that it necessitates the use of the hidden camera. The cash-for-votes scandal did qualify by this criteria—I am proud that we were able to point the searchlight on a seamier side of Indian politics and even the courts have praised our role. Where I badly erred was in not maintaining a sufficient firewall between the BJP politicians involved in the sting and our own reporting team. We had wilfully allowed ourselves to be used by a political party in their quest for power and my constant reporter's search, indeed hunger, for a big story.

The fact is, the decision when and how to telecast a sensitive story is an editorial prerogative based on sound legal and journalistic advice. Timelines cannot be decided by political parties. Political timelines and journalistic deadlines often do not, and should not, match. I know the sting operation damaged my credibility in the eyes of many BJP supporters, and I was the target of a sustained vilification campaign based on lies and abuse. Much of it was hurtful. I was even accused of taking money from the government and the likes of Amar Singh. Delhi can be a cruel city—even so-called friends here will look to find ways to bring you down. The cash-for-votes scandal left me scarred and shaken. I realized that in a surcharged political atmosphere, journalists are better off not getting entangled in murky dealings where the political stakes are blood-curdlingly high.

While I introspected, Advani thought that his chance to topple the government had come and gone. Now, his prime ministerial ambitions were being thwarted again, this time by one of his own. And yet, to suggest that Advani's rebellion was occasioned purely by envy towards Modi would be unfair to a leader who has devoted a lifetime to the party. Yes, he still felt he deserved to be prime minister, but Advani was also an instinctive democrat, someone who had vigorously opposed the Emergency in 1975. Perhaps he saw shades of an autocratic Indira in Modi's behaviour and was looking to warn the party of the negative consequences.

But the party he had once so effectively piloted now had little time for the tantrums or advice of the ageing neta. The new leadership represented by the Modi–Rajnath–Jaitley troika was in no mood to bend. Even the RSS, which had once been fiercely aligned to Advani, had now seen the writing on the wall.

~

The RSS has been often described as an extra-constitutional authority that lies at the apex of the Sangh Parivar, a 'brotherhood in saffron'. The RSS claims it is apolitical, that it only acts as an ideological guide to the BJP. The relationship between the RSS and the BJP, though, is often more intricate—the two are umbilically tied by their shared notion of cultural nationalism, and a cadre and leadership that work in close collaboration. The dual membership of the RSS and BJP (or Jan Sangh, as it was known then) had even contributed to the collapse of the non-Congress Janata Party government in the 1970s. The RSS may not be the BJP's daily remote control, as its critics suggest, but neither is it some voluntary organization solely devoted to social welfare. It is, at the end of the day, the final word within the saffron 'family'—the paterfamilias who has veto rights in the event of any internal dispute. In the build-up to the 2014 elections, the RSS had made its decision—Narendra Modi would be the BJP's prime ministerial candidate.

The backstory to the RSS's involvement in the 'Modi for PM' campaign began in the aftermath of the 2009 election debacle. If the 2004 election verdict had stunned the Sangh Parivar because of the surprise element, the 2009 result had left it despondent. The BJP, it seemed, was in terminal decline, the karyakartas were dispirited and the leadership was weak and fractious. The RSS, too, was facing the challenge of shrinking cadres, and a generational crisis was looming—a paradigm shift was called for. This is where Mohan Rao Bhagwat, the RSS *sarsanghchalak*(chief), decided to step in.

Bhagwat, a Maharashtrian Brahmin like many of his predecessors, was a third-generation RSS leader. With his walrus-like white moustache and wrestler-like physique (he was once the RSS's chief of physical training), he was not the kind of leader who would tolerate indiscipline. He became RSS chief in March 2009, just three months before the general elections, at the relatively young age of fifty-nine. The BJP was in disarray and Bhagwat was determined to correct it. 'He was angry and frustrated. He told us that either we change or it is all over for us. It is now or never!' says a BJP leader who attended an RSS–BJP meet.

One of his first tasks after taking over was to look for a new BJP president. Bhagwat wanted to bring in someone from outside Delhi for the post to reduce the friction. His first choice was Modi, but Modi wanted to focus on the 2012 Gujarat elections. He even considered Manohar Parrikar, but he, too, preferred to stay put in his home state of Goa. In the end, the mantle fell on Gadkari, the 'local' boy from Nagpur, the RSS's home turf. Gadkari had a warm relationship with Bhagwat—they sometimes dined together— and the explicit instruction was to unite the party. Voluble and expansive in more ways than one, Gadkari had tried and failed, like so many Maharashtra politicians before him, in taming north India. His business dealings came under the scanner as well—he is a businessman first, a politician much later, was a criticism within the party. The portly Gadkari is an interesting combination of bon vivant and *swayamsevak*. He'd invite you to lunch, declare he was on a diet and end up polishing off most of the meal! He also had a bagful of expletives, thrown at anyone who'd care to listen; he was the kind of individual who could abuse with a smile.

When the BJP lost badly in the UP elections in early 2012, Bhagwat knew time was running out for the party's revival. They needed someone who would galvanize the team, and do it quickly. When Modi scored a hat-trick in Gujarat in December that year, Bhagwat was assured that the quest for such a forceful leader had ended.

Bhagwat hadn't always been an admirer of Modi's style of functioning. In 2006, some BJP well-wishers had met the RSS leader and expressed their concern that the party wasn't using Modi effectively. Bhagwat heard them out and then expressed his reservations. 'The problem with Modi is that he argues all the time and you can never win an argument with him. Besides, once he becomes a national leader, he will want to be the sarsanghchalak next!'

That was then. Now, though, the situation was different. The BJP was in a crisis, Modi was just the man the party needed. A meeting was held in Nagpur in April 2013 where Modi was present along with the entire RSS hierarchy, including Bhaiyyaji Joshi and Suresh Soni, both key point persons for the Sangh in Delhi. The message was unambiguous—the Sangh would fully back Modi for prime ministership. There was no time to waste in organizing and mobilizing. As someone who had attended an RSS *shakha* at the age of eight, Modi knew the Sangh's commitment to the cause was complete. In the months ahead, RSS cadres would play an important role in door-to-door campaigns, especially in north India.

In November 2013, I got a chance to have a long and candid conversation with Bhagwat at Hedgewar Bhavan, the RSS headquarters in Nagpur. The meeting was organized by Nagpur's vibrant Rotarians. I had been putting off a visit for two years to address them. Finally I agreed, provided they arranged a meeting for me with the RSS chief, which they dutifully managed.

In a small room with limited furniture, and over chai, *chiwda* and *peda*s (most RSS leaders, I find, have a noticeable sweet tooth), we discussed the emerging political situation. I asked Bhagwat why the RSS, which claimed to be against a personality cult in politics, had chosen to put all its eggs in the Modi basket. 'It is not the RSS, it is the BJP workers and the people of the country who want a strong leader. It is the people who want Modi—why should we deny them what they desire,' was his response.

But what of the Sangh's ideological agenda? Article 370, common civil code, Ram mandir—had that been diluted in the pursuit of power? 'First, let us get a clear majority, then we can talk of implementing our agenda,' said Bhagwat, with a twinkle in his light eyes.

I also asked him why he had sidelined Advani, the seniormost leader in the BJP. Bhagwat then related a story he would later amplify while releasing a book on Advani's blogs in Delhi (which was reproduced in the *Indian Express*). 'In a village, once a housewife spat betel juice into a *havan kund*, only to discover that the spit had turned into a gold nugget. When her husband returned home, she narrated the episode. He told her not to let anyone else know. But word soon spread through the village, and everyone began spitting into havan kunds to find gold. All prospered except the woman and her husband. A year later, when they still had no gold, the unhappy woman told her husband that they should leave the village. He dithered but when she threatened to kill herself, he agreed. They left the village and soon reached a hillock. When they turned around, they saw the village burning and heard people screaming.'

The message, said Bhagwat, was clear—the party and the Parivar needed Advani to stay and guide them so that their 'village' did not burn. Advani was being asked to play a Bhishma-like role by the RSS because the lead actor for the Arjun-like hero had already been found.

~

By August 2013, it was apparent that it was only a matter of time before Narendra Modi was formally chosen the BJP's prime ministerial candidate. Modi's town hall meetings continued to attract a huge response. We had begun a series of 'election tracker' polls on CNN-IBN in partnership with Lokniti, the political research team at the CSDS. Our first tracker at the end of July was revealing— Narendra Modi was the preferred prime ministerial choice of 19 per cent of the respondents, Rahul Gandhi of 12 per cent. No other BJP leader was in double digits—L.K. Advani was preferred by just 2 per cent.

Modi, though, didn't want to take any chances. He wanted the announcement to be made as soon as possible and was looking for an occasion to drive home the point. In June, he had tried to use the Uttarakhand floods to make a pitch as the ideal crisis manager, parking himself in Dehradun for three days. A local BJP spokesperson had suggested that Modi had played a pivotal role in 'rescuing' as many as 15,000 stranded Gujaratis. The *Times of India* went a step further, likening Modi to Rambo, the all-powerful cinematic character. At a time when the nation was grieving, when the security forces were working round the clock on rescue missions, the self-publicity backfired. Modi was the butt of Rambo jokes.

Modi blamed the media for the controversy. While the Rambo remark was perhaps a typical journalistic exaggeration, my sources in the BJP said that the original 'great rescue' theme had been pushed by the chief minister's publicists. When I spoke to Modi about it, his response was predictably combative. *'Lagta hai aaj kal tum logon ko koi aur news nahi hai!'* (Looks like you people have no other news these days.)

Now Modi was looking for another big national event to boost his PM credentials. The 15th of August, Independence Day, provided Modi with just that special moment. The prime minister's Red Fort address is an Independence Day ritual. The country's VIPs gather to show off their privileges. The rest of us are meant to listen to the prime minister listing out his achievements and plans for the future. On a cloudy August morning, Dr Singh was delivering his tenth, and possibly final, Independence Day speech. The economist PM was, self-admittedly, not a great public speaker. He was, in fact, a pretty poor one. The 2013 speech was no different. Dr Singh droned on monotonously for about forty minutes about the UPA's track record over a decade in government—from RTI to NREGA to the proposed food security bill, he pressed all the usual buttons in a rather perfunctory manner. By 8.45 a.m., the speech was over; the VIPs began to disperse, and the news desk still struggled for a headline. We didn't have to wait long.

A day before, addressing a gathering of students in Bhuj in Kutch, Narendra Modi had boasted, 'Tomorrow the country will compare my speech with that of the prime minister. When we unfurl the tricolour, the message will also go to Lal Qila. The nation will want to know what was said there and what is said here.' Modi had thrown an unprecedented challenge. He may only have been the chief minister of Gujarat, he still hadn't been formally made the

BJP's prime ministerial candidate, but he was already acting and talking like one. It was typical Modi—cocky and arrogant, but also self-confident and daring.

Next morning, he lived up to his promise. A little after 9 a.m., soon after the prime minister's speech was over, Modi got up to speak in Bhuj. For almost an hour, he spoke almost as if he was participating in a public debate with the prime minister and the Government of India. This wasn't just an Independence Day address—this was an election speech. The audience wasn't Gujarat but the people of the country. He even had a mock Red Fort erected on the podium.

If the prime minister had sounded a bit mournful, like the Delhi weather that day, Modi exuded aggression in a direct attack on the Congress leadership. Sample this: 'You unfurled the tricolour so many times, Mr Prime Minister, but you raise the same issues that Pandit Nehru raised sixty years ago!'; 'You are so caught up in the bhakti of one family, you have forgotten all other issues'; 'The nation must be freed from nepotism, from the arrogance of those in power'; 'The country is in poverty and fed up of corruption. People want a new *soch* [thinking].' A police officer standing next to Modi fainted in the heat while the speech was on, but the chief minister just rolled on. Again, with no prepared text or notes.

India had never seen anything quite like it—a ceremonial Independence Day occasion, which is meant to exchange pleasantries, had been converted into an open, hostile bid for power. Predictably, the Congress was livid. Their spokespersons were all over television channels, accusing Modi of betraying the spirit and traditions of 15 August.

I telephoned Modi a few days later and asked him whether he had any regrets over confronting the prime minister on Independence Day. His response was typically unapologetic. '*Lagta hai een Congresswalon ko dar hai ki unki dukan bandh hone wali hai!*' (Looks like the Congress is upset that their shop is going to shut down.)

The strategy was clear—Modi was not here to play by the rules set by someone else; he wanted to create what Congress leader

Jairam Ramesh later described as his own version of bodyline where unconventional attack was the best form of defence. If that meant disrupting an institutionalized practice and using even an Independence Day ceremony for political benefit, then so be it. Modi had positioned himself as the anti-establishment challenger to the old order. He wanted to assert his prime ministerial qualification and use his oratory as a weapon.

The contrast between the soft-spoken, monosyllabic Manmohan Singh and the punchline-a-minute, hard-hitting Modi was unmistakable. A bit like a Pujara vs Gayle battle in a T20 match. As a Modi aide remarked, 'We were convinced that day that if we made this a presidential battle between a weak and a tough leader, then there could only be one winner.' Modi was still not the BJP's de jure prime ministerial candidate, but on 15 August, he became the de facto prime minister of his party, if not the country.

~

Modi was formally announced as the BJP's prime ministerial nominee for the 2014 elections on 13 September 2013 amidst garlands and crackers at the party headquarters in Delhi. Typically, the announcement was accompanied by more drama and controversy. Advani refused to attend the parliamentary board meeting where the decision was taken. Instead, he chose to dash off another letter to Rajnath Singh, expressing his 'anguish' over the party president's 'style of functioning'. At the board meeting, Sushma Swaraj expressed her note of dissent, saying she was accepting the decision 'under protest'.

The Advani–Sushma duo had a new rationale for their 'rebellion'. Assembly elections in four crucial states of north India were due in a few months and it would be best to hold off any announcement till the elections were over, was their argument. 'Why the hurry? Why mix issues before the assembly elections? Why take a risk at this stage?' Advani asked BJP leaders who met him. He tossed up another googly by suggesting that Modi was not the only 'successful' BJP chief minister. 'Look at Shivraj Singh Chauhan and Raman Singh. They, too, have been chief ministers for a decade—should their credentials as leaders be totally ignored?' was the question he raised.

Chauhan was almost, in fact, being pushed by the Advani camp as a more acceptable alternative to Modi. In a speech in Gwalior, Advani suggested that Chauhan's achievements in Madhya Pradesh were, to some extent, greater than Modi. 'He has turned a backward, BIMARU state into a developed one, Modi has inherited a healthy state,' he claimed. He even likened Chauhan's understated style to Vajpayee's.

Ever-smiling, self-effacing and courteous, the fifty-five-year-old Chauhan was a man with few enemies. If Modi had an aversion to an intrusive media, Chauhan went out of his way to cultivate journalists. Many journalists, including me, would often get invites to attend functions in Bhopal. 'We'll organize everything, *aap bas aa jaiye* [you just have to come],' he would promise. I did not avail of any such junket, but those who did tell me that Chauhan was the perfect host.

But if Chauhan had any prime ministerial ambitions, he had carefully masked them. I asked him once about Advani equating him with Vajpayee. '*Main toh Advaniji ko bahut adar karta hoon par mein toh ek sadharan karyakarta hoon*' (I respect Advaniji a lot, but at the end of the day, I am a humble worker), he said with his characteristic humility. And then reminded me once again that I must visit him in Bhopal soon.

But any attempt to drag in Chauhan as a prime ministerial option was never going to gain any traction. The leadership of the BJP and the RSS had made up its mind and wasn't going to concede an inch. The Modi decision was irreversible. 'Frankly, some of us were just tired of Advaniji's constant nitpicking. We even felt that if he wants to resign and leave the party, let him—we were done with his petulance,' a senior BJP leader told me.

Within the BJP, the Advani–Sushma group was now labelled the '160–180 club'—those who believed that the BJP could not cross a certain threshold in a general election. Their calculation was that with a maximum of 180 seats (the BJP's best-ever performance had been 182 seats in 1999 in the aftermath of the Kargil elections), a Modi-led BJP would not be able to get allies and the party would be forced to look for an alternative leadership.

The Modi camp had their own numerical counter. 'Mission 272-plus' became the new buzzword, signifying a desire to win a clear majority in the general elections. Modi is partial to sharp, catchy slogans. When his aides came up with Mission 272 as the goal for 2014, he added the 'plus' word. 'We must think positive. The more we aim for, the more we will get!' he told his team.

Some of his supporters were more modest, looking at 200 plus as their initial aim. 'Once we cross 200, we will get a rush of allies,' was Jaitley's view. The 272-plus number, though, had been pasted on the war room of Team Modi in Gandhinagar. The run chase was about to begin.

A key member of this Team Modi was Prashant Kishore, a young US-trained public health professional. I met the thirty-six-year-old Bihar-born Kishore to get under the skin of the Modi campaign. He told me he had been the head of a UN mission in Africa and was working on a UN project on malnutrition when he visited Gujarat for the first time for fieldwork in early 2011. 'I guess it was a case of instant attraction because the chief minister told me he wanted me in his team and I readily agreed,' he says.

Kishore was a policy strategist with a passion for technology and statistical data. His tasks were well defined—build a crack team of back-room boys who would take the Modi campaign to another level by staging high-profile events. The team's first major election event was the 3D campaign in the 2012 Gujarat assembly elections (see chapter 9 for more). The 2012 assembly elections, in fact, would serve as a trailer in many ways for the general election campaign to follow. 'We first commissioned detailed surveys for the Gujarat assembly elections in mid-2012 and then began to build for the general elections from January 2013 itself. We used the data collected to help shape the Modi campaign,' says Kishore.

The database built by the Modi team was truly formidable. On television, during our election programming, we would do national poll surveys with sample sizes in the range of around 15,000 to 20,000 respondents and feel satisfied. The Modi team had gone many steps beyond us. Its survey in January 2013, for example, had a sample size running into several lakhs and a detailed break-up of voting preferences, according to caste, community, age group. 'I won't reveal any secrets, but I promise you that our surveys would make your analysis look very limited,' claimed Kishore (of course, what he wouldn't say was just how expensive such exercises can be!).

I later found out that the BJP election surveys were supervised by a US-based agency, Penn Schoen Berland, one of the world's leading political campaign and market research groups that had also been involved in the Obama presidential election. This was perhaps the first time in the history of an Indian election that an American company was so deeply involved in poll surveys. 'It only proves the scale of our ambition. We wanted to get the best that money could buy,' is how a BJP leader described their choice of pollsters.

In June 2013, Kishore set up a formal group called Citizens for Accountable Governance (CAG) with an office in Gandhinagar. The group claimed to be non-partisan, but its objective was clear—widen Modi's appeal by showcasing him as a governance icon. Initially, it had just eight to ten full-time employees, but by the time the general elections campaign really kicked off in February 2014, the numbers had swollen to over 200 recruits, some of them working on short-term assignments. Many of the full-time employees at CAG were young, urban professionals who had given up secure jobs to work on the Modi campaign. Akhil Handa, a twenty-nine-year-old IIT Delhi alumnus, was typical. Bright and eager, Akhil had worked with JP Morgan as an investment banker in Hong Kong and was earning a salary running into a few crores, before chucking it all up in mid-2013 to join the Modi campaign. 'I was just tired of seeing my foreign peers be so down on India. I realized we needed change and felt Modi was the man to effect that change,' he told me.

Akhil was not alone. One of the striking features of Team Modi was how young many of them were. IIM and IIT graduates, lawyers and accountants—they symbolized the energies of a new, younger India. Conventional wisdom was that the educated young had become cynical of public life and had switched off from politics. The back-room team of Modi challenged that assumption.

Interestingly, Rahul, too, had tried to reach out to the educated young India while building his election team. But there was a crucial difference. Modi's young guns were not expected to involve themselves in micromanaging political strategy. Their task was to operate in more familiar territory—technology innovations, Internet, social media, made-for-TV events, statistical data interpretation. The nitty-gritty of election management—be it campaign planning, door-to-door campaigns or ticket distribution—was left to the full-time RSS and BJP political workers. In Rahul's case, his Ivy League 'boys' actually took over the task of running the election campaign instead of leaving that to the older, more experienced, Congress leaders.

Not surprisingly, a prime target group for CAG was the 'youth'. In June, CAG held a closed-door meeting on 'Youth and Leadership' in Ahmedabad where the guest speakers included former president A.P.J. Abdul Kalam and the HDFC group chairman Deepak Parekh. Modi sat in the audience through the day just listening to the speeches. In October, a one-day youth summit called Manthan was organized with the stated goal of setting the agenda for 'young India' in the 2014 elections. With an aggressive Facebook campaign, Manthan was able to attract lakhs of visitors to its site. 'We invited several leaders for the summit, even Rahul Gandhi, but he chose not to attend,' claims Kishore. Modi did come, speak and, predictably, was the showstopper. A journalist friend in the audience described the mood as akin to a rock concert.

It was clear by now that Modi had captured hearts and minds in urban India, especially among the young. A clever mix of town hall-type speaking engagements and well-planned rallies in the cities was making the difference. By September 2013, when Modi formally took over as the BJP prime ministerial candidate, a mini wave was already building up in his favour across urban India. The month of Modi's coronation as PM candidate was also the period when the rupee plunged to its lowest level to the dollar, and retail inflation was in double digits. The faltering economy had created an anti-UPA feeling in urban India in particular. Modi symbolized and channelized the anger against the government. 'He was the right man at the right place with the right rhetoric,' is how one senior UPA minister explained the rise of Modi in 2013.

But to win a general election and achieve 'Mission 272-plus', the magic needed to spread well beyond the bright lights of the metros. 'Yes, we had taken elements from a Barack Obama-style presidential campaign, but we needed to innovate and fine-tune it to a diverse country like India,' is how one Modi aide put it.

The findings of a nationwide survey done by Team Modi in the first half of 2013 had slightly worried them. The data showed that while Modi enjoyed instant recall and huge support in towns and cities, there wasn't an immediate connect when it came to rural India. Taking the Modi campaign buzz to rural India was the next big, and even more difficult, challenge for Team Modi. The November–December assembly elections in states with a large rural population like Rajasthan, Madhya Pradesh and Chhattisgarh would be a test case. 'We knew we had a hit film in the multiplexes. Now we needed to spread the message to single-screen cinemas in small towns and villages too,' says the Modi aide.

~

On 31 October 2013, Modi formally launched the 'Statue of Unity' programme—a project whose stated aim was to build the largest ever statue in the world, a 240-metre bronze statue of Sardar Patel, directly facing the Narmada Dam. The real target was to mobilize people from across India on a 'nationalistic' platform. Modi had been an unabashed admirer of the Sardar, Gujarat's tallest political leader during the freedom struggle. Mahatma Gandhi had always been a national icon; Sardar was seen as a rooted son of the soil, a farmers' leader who had evolved into the 'Iron Man of India' as the country's first home minister. There was also a parallel narrative, especially in Gujarat, that the Congress had been less than fair to Sardar Patel and that he, not Nehru, should have been India's first prime minister.

Appropriating Patel's legacy suited Modi. By taking on the mantle of the modern-day Sardar, he could take on the Gandhi–Nehru family and also boost his own image as a decisive leader. The fact that Patel had been a diehard Congressman (he was president of the Gujarat Congress for nearly three decades) or that he had banned the RSS after Gandhi's assassination in 1948 did not really matter. When there is an election to be won, history can be selective and expendable. Ironically, Modi's original icon Guru Golwalkar had been arrested in the aftermath of the Gandhi assassination. But Golwalkar was an RSS folk hero; Patel was a national figure. Golwalkar worked for Modi in his previous avatar as RSS pracharak; Patel fitted a prime minister-in-waiting. Modi's choice, then, was dictated by strategic pragmatism, not ideological affinity.

As was becoming typical, Modi came up with an innovative idea to bolster this strategy. He suggested that the Patel statue could be built by starting a donation drive across India, with a special focus on rural India. 'Villagers can give us iron in the form of used farm instruments. It will be a way of getting farmers to connect with us,' Modi told his aides. So, while 'Unity Run' marathons were organized in the cities, in rural India, there was a more direct campaign initiated to link Modi to the Sardar. A Loha Sangrahana Samiti was set up by the Sardar Vallabhai Ekta Trust to collect iron tools from across 7000 villages. Micromanaging the project would be the CAG team.

Modi was now in overdrive. The town-hall concept had served its purpose. The 'Modi for PM' presidential-style campaign had entered phase two and the need was to reach out to wider audiences. 'We knew the core Hindutva vote would stand with Modi because of his past reputation. What we needed was the "plus" vote, the incremental vote that can make all the difference in an election,' is how the strategy was explained to me by a Modi adviser.

Just days after being officially made the BJP's prime ministerial candidate, Modi addressed his first 'mega rally' in Haryana's Rewari.

The ex-servicemen were one constituency waiting to be tapped. Many of them were angry that the UPA had not delivered on its 'one rank, one pension' promise. Others were disappointed that the UPA hadn't taken a tough stand on Pakistan. Retired generals would often come on prime-time television shows calling for 'war' with Pakistan.

One of the organizers of the Rewari rally was General V.K. Singh, who had retired as army chief after getting into a public row with the Manmohan Singh government. General Singh had political ambitions (he would eventually contest the Lok Sabha polls on a BJP ticket, win by the second highest margin after Modi and become a minister). Modi wanted the support of the men in uniform. It was a perfect match. In a fiery speech, he claimed that the country's security problem was not on the borders, but in Delhi. 'Till we have an efficient, patriotic government in Delhi, it doesn't matter how capable our defence forces are!' he thundered. No, he didn't call for a war with Pakistan, and yes, he did conveniently forget the 1971 war under Indira Gandhi's leadership when referring to military achievements. But the assembled crowd was impressed. *'Dil se bol rahe hain'* (He is speaking from the heart), one of them told our reporter. If Modi was making a dent in Haryana, a state with a limited BJP base, then clearly there was a mood swing.

Over the next five months from September 2013 to February 2014, Modi addressed several such large rallies across the country, from Arunachal to Andhra Pradesh, from Mumbai to Meerut. In Hyderabad, he laced his speech with Telugu greetings; in Mumbai, with Marathi. Most of the speeches were on weekends, when television audiences are often at home. The standing joke in office was—if it is a Sunday afternoon, forget all other programming, there will always be a Modi rally to telecast live.

On weekdays, Modi was busy criss-crossing the battleground states which were going to the assembly polls—he did fifty-five rallies in four states in October and November alone. 'This was carpet-bombing, part one, a trailer for the general elections that were to follow,' says an aide. The stakes were high—in all the four election states, the BJP was in a direct contest with the Congress. If the BJP

Swant?

could sweep these states, it would be the ideal launch pad for the 2014 elections; the Congress, by contrast, would be demoralized by defeat.

The key state in the Modi game plan was Rajasthan. Madhya Pradesh and Chhattisgarh had strong BJP chief ministers in office—even in victory, the glory would have to be shared. Delhi had been complicated by the entry of the Aam Aadmi Party (AAP). Rajasthan, though, was a state that could serve as a laboratory to test Modi's appeal beyond Gujarat. Bordering Gujarat, it had a large tribal and rural population. 'If we could score a big win in Rajasthan, we would know we were on the right track and our campaign was making a dent beyond our traditional voters,' was how a Modi strategist described it.

It helped that the BJP's chief ministerial candidate for Rajasthan, Vasundhara Raje, was someone Modi got along with. Raje, like Modi, was a fierce individualist. She had endured her fair share of run-ins with the patriarchal male-dominated RSS leadership in the state and wouldn't be bullied into submission easily. Their private lives couldn't have been more different. Raje likes her occasional glass of wine, is often spotted at Page Three events, has even walked the ramp and celebrates her birthdays with much joie de vivre. Modi, of course, leads a more austere life, though he's partial to his designer kurtas, pens, watches and glasses, and even, I am told, shoes. And yet, the two of them made a good team. I once asked Raje what she liked about Modi. Her answer was breezily aristocratic. 'He is a man of action who doesn't bullshit around like the rest!'

It was in Rajasthan that Team Modi spent most of its energies in the 2013 elections. One of the campaign strategies here was to send 200 GPS-enabled mobile vans or digital raths with 50-inch LED screens across the state to reach out to far-flung villages where traditional media could not reach. The pick-up vans had images of Modi plastered all over them and the television set would play sixteen-minute videos of Modi's best speeches. Every day, the vans would touch fifteen to twenty villages, almost like a modern-day *jatra* enacting a slice of political theatre. Says the Modi aide, 'Our aim was to create excitement in the village around the theme *"Modi aanewala hai!"'* (Modi is coming.) (See chapter 5 for more.)

~

When the results of the assembly elections streamed through on 8 December 2013, the Modi campaign team was delighted. The victories in Madhya Pradesh and Chhattisgarh had run according to script. In Delhi, the BJP had emerged as the single largest party but a hung assembly had been thrown up. In Rajasthan, however, there was real reason to celebrate—not only had the BJP won, it had scored a historic three-fourths triumph. It had won a record 162 seats, with the Congress down to just twenty-one. Importantly, it had swept rural Rajasthan. Rajasthan, interestingly, was a state where the Congress and the Gandhi family had also invested heavily. Many of the party's pet social sector programmes—be it NREGA or a free medicine scheme—had been incubated there. Moditva versus Sonianomics—Rajasthan settled that debate conclusively. It also extinguished any whispers within the Advani–Sushma camp in the BJP that Modi was the wrong choice for prime minister. The anger against the Gehlot government in Rajasthan was palpable, but no one had expected such a tidal wave. The one state where Modi had campaigned most aggressively had yielded the most spectacular result.

'I think the scale of that win told us that we were onto something unique. This was a wave election in Rajasthan. If we could replicate the formula in other major states, Mission 272-plus was not a pipe dream,' is how a Modi team member summed up the post-Rajasthan feeling.

Mission 272-plus had been calculated keeping in mind that the BJP did not have an all-India base like the Congress but was largely focused on north, west and central India. 'A north-west monsoon seems to be building up in the BJP's favour,' is how I described on television the election mood after the assembly elections.

The belt from Maharashtra in the west to Bihar in the north had 314 seats across fourteen small and large states. In 2009, the

Congress had won 116 seats here, the BJP just eighty-nine. Now, the BJP needed to not just reverse that scoreline but virtually dominate this entire region and get a strike rate of at least 70 per cent of these seats, if not more. The key to fulfilling what seemed a highly ambitious target lay in the Indo-Gangetic plain, in the prized states of UP and Bihar. With 120 seats between them—UP with eighty and Bihar with forty—it was in these two states that Modi would now have to fight his biggest battle if he wanted to be India's next prime minister.

5

Battle for the Heartland

Every election campaign has a defining moment, an event which changes the course of the contest permanently. In the historic 1977 election, it was the day senior minister Jagjivan Ram left the Congress, signifying the beginning of the end of Indira Gandhi's government. In 2004, it was arguably a stampede over saris being handed out to poor women in Lucknow (where Vajpayee was the BJP candidate), which left twenty-one persons dead, raising the first big question over the Vajpayee government's India Shining campaign. The turning point in the 2014 battle was probably 27 October 2013 when serial blasts ripped through Patna's railway station and Gandhi Maidan where Narendra Modi was holding a massive rally, killing five and injuring more than eighty people.

The rally had been billed as Modi's grand arrival into 'enemy' territory. He had been kept out of Bihar for almost a decade at the chief minister Nitish Kumar's insistence. The BJP had been in an alliance government for eight years with Nitish, who had made it clear that Modi was not welcome in Bihar because of the taint of the Gujarat riots. When Modi was made the BJP's campaign committee chief in June 2013, Nitish had chosen to break the alliance. The war of personalities between Modi and Nitish was not just an ego

146

clash. Priding himself on uncompromising religious neutrality, rugged anti-Congress-ism and plebeian rootedness, Nitish had lost no opportunity after breaking with the BJP to heap veiled scorn on those relying on PR machines, media and advertisements to build their image. Nitish even seemed to be readying to set himself up as a national alternative to Modi, thumbing his nose at a BJP that he felt had betrayed his trust. The BJP was yearning for revenge.

The *hunkar* (a war cry) rally had been planned by the state BJP for months. All over Patna, large posters of Narendra Modi had come up at every vantage point—the city was dressed up to receive a special guest. The BJP had offered to take correspondents from Delhi to Patna for the rally. The CNN-IBN bureau chief in Patna, Prabhakar Kumar, was peeved and made his unhappiness clear. 'Why do you always need to send reporters from Delhi to cover a major event, sir? I am sure we can handle it on our own here,' he complained.

I tried to reason with him that this was a major news event. 'What if there is a bomb blast at the site, Prabhakar, what will we do then? Surely, we need a stronger team on the ground,' was my defence. Little did I or my Patna colleague know that the words would prove eerily prophetic.

The rally was scheduled for noon but being a Sunday, the crowds had begun to gather from early morning at the maidan. The BJP had organized buses to bring in people from neighbouring districts for a show of strength; the trains, too, were jam-packed. 'This will be the biggest ever rally in the history of Bihar,' the BJP spokesperson Rajiv Pratap Rudy told us.

'Big' in Bihar means gargantuan—the Biharis love their politics. In no state is the political discourse as animated as it can be in Bihar. Involvement in politics is almost a cottage industry for many Biharis. I had once attended a Lalu Prasad 'Lathi' rally in 2003 against George Bush's Iraq invasion. I never understood why nearly 2 lakh people would gather to protest against a war in a distant land, but they did. This time, Gandhi Maidan was poised for another massive show with some estimates suggesting an audience in excess of 2 lakhs.

The first blast went off in the toilet at platform ten of Patna junction at around 9.30 a.m. One person was injured. It sparked a scare but remained a news flash. The station, after all, was far away from the Gandhi Maidan. Two hours later, we knew we were dealing with a big breaking news story—between 11.40 a.m. and 12.15 p.m., four blasts ripped through areas in and around the maidan. A final blast took place while BJP leader Shahnawaz Hussain was speaking on stage. Hussain thought it was a 'cracker'. It wasn't. This was no longer just another incident on the campaign trail—it was now clearly a major, possibly terror, attack on a rally of the BJP's prime ministerial candidate.

Modi was just landing in Patna when the blasts occurred. BJP president Rajnath Singh and Arun Jaitley had already arrived. Jaitley was staying at the Maurya Hotel that overlooks the maidan. 'As a result, I reached the venue a little early,' recalled Jaitley. He was met by a senior officer of the Gujarat police who was handling Modi's security (the Centre still hadn't given him special Z category cover). 'Sir, we are asking Modiji to stay at the airport and not come to the venue. The rally will have to be cancelled,' the officer told Jaitley. The BJP leader consulted with Rajnath Singh and the duo decided to stay put. 'If we call off the rally, there will be total panic and people could die in a stampede,' was their fear.

The local Bihar police, which had clearly made inadequate security preparations, was asked to prepare for an emergency situation in case there was another blast near the stage. Four cars were lined up behind the main podium to whisk the top BJP leadership away in any such eventuality. Modi by now had arrived on the stage and the crowd began roaring his name out, almost oblivious to the crisis brewing around them. 'It was a bizarre situation. Serial blasts had taken place, but the crowd just wanted a glimpse of Modi,' remembers a senior police officer. 'I hadn't seen anything like this.'

Knowing the urgency of the situation, Jaitley completed his speech in just seven minutes. Rajnath Singh, who had promised to complete his address speedily too, took twenty minutes. The crowd was getting restive; the police increasingly worried. That's when Modi took over.

In a forty-five-minute speech, laced with phrases in the local Maithili and Bhojpuri dialects, Modi proceeded to tear into Nitish Kumar's government, calling the chief minister an 'opportunist' and a 'hypocrite'. 'Nitish Kumar has betrayed Bihar. He even betrayed his mentors Jayaprakash Narayan and Ram Manohar Lohia. How can anyone trust such a man!' he bellowed.

Modi emphasized his backward-caste credentials. 'Congress leaders don't know what poverty and hunger are. I used to sell tea on trains. I know how difficult it is to get onto trains and make a living. Even the railway minister doesn't have my experience of the problems one faces on trains.' He even reached out to Muslims. 'Our Muslim brothers in Bihar are so backward. In Gujarat, one of the fastest developing regions is Muslim dominated. Let Hindus and Muslims come together and work towards ending poverty. Our religion is India first. We have to maintain peace and harmony at any cost.'

He spoke of Bihar as the land of Buddha and Mahavira. He even got a bit carried away (not for the first time) with the historical references, wrongly claiming that Alexander was defeated by Biharis, and Taxila was in Bihar (when it is actually in Pakistan). But these were only blips in what was clearly a virtuoso performance once again.

Significantly, not once did he refer to the blasts in his speech, only asking people to go home safely at the very end of his address. A few hours later, he visited the injured in the hospital and expressed his solidarity with the victims. I asked Modi later whether he had ever considered calling off the rally. 'No, if we had called it off, there would have been an even bigger calamity,' he insisted.

This direct contact with a vast crowd is precious to Modi. Whether yelling 'Yes, we can' in Hyderabad, or exhorting an Ahmedabad crowd with chants of 'Vande Mataram' or extracting a laugh through colourful attacks on the Gandhis, the moment of contact with the public, the seizing of mass attention, is Modi's biggest prize, a legitimization of and a spur for his leadership.

That day in Patna was no different. Modi made a speech that

revealed a development-driven agenda—not divisive but potentially unifying. He had refrained from falling into the obvious trap—a BJP leader could easily have played victim and used the occasion to raise the familiar spectre of 'Islamic terrorism' even without waiting for the investigation into the serial blasts to begin (much later, the Ranchi module of the Indian Mujahideen would emerge a prime suspect). Most importantly, he had shown strong 'leadership'—staying calm and unflustered in the face of a major crisis unfolding around him.

The crowds at Gandhi Maidan and beyond had discovered a Modi trying to unshackle himself from a contentious past and evolve into the hope for the future. The chanting was almost frenzied—the crowd wanted more. A rally per se doesn't define an election campaign but Modi's Patna rally, with all the controversy swirling around it, was a landmark event. It gave the BJP the confidence that its leader could evoke a feverish response even in unfamiliar territory. 'Till that day, we were looking at the election from the point of view of conventional arithmetic. From that moment on, it was all about chemistry,' says Jaitley.

That very day, around the same time as the Modi rally, Rahul Gandhi addressed an election rally in Mangolpuri in Delhi. Most news channels kept it on mute, or ignored it altogether while focusing on Modi. There was to be only one obvious winner that day. Sitting at home and watching the events unfold, Nitish Kumar must have been a worried man. His government faced the serious charge of having provided lax security to his main political rival. A new hero had entered the Bihar drama. Post-blast emotionalism, surcharged TV debates on the threat to Modi's life and consequent disillusionment with administrative measures began to gather momentum. The battle for Bihar was about to be lost.

~

Some relationships are just not meant to be. The equation between Modi and Nitish Kumar is one such. I remember asking Nitish over dinner a few years ago what was it about Modi that enraged him so much. '*Isse kisi vyakti se mat jodiye . . . yeh **Kisi** vyakti vishesh nahi hai, yeh ek vichardhara ki ladai hai . . . Yeh desh secular hai aur secular rahega . . . kuch logon ko yeh pata hona chahiye . . .*' (Please don't link this to an individual, this is about an ideology. This is a secular country and will always remain one, some people must understand this), was his response. Typically, he did not refer to Modi by name; he would always refer to him in the third person.

But this was not just a simple 'secular' versus 'communal' divide, as Nitish would have us believe. When the 2002 Gujarat riots occurred, Nitish Kumar was a minister in the Vajpayee-led NDA government. Unlike Ram Vilas Paswan who resigned in protest, Nitish stayed on in the government. Nor did he call for Modi's removal. If he did protest, it was only in private. The public face of the NDA was Vajpayee, and Nitish appeared content with the prime minister's inclusive image. He even visited Gujarat as railway minister and shared a stage with Modi.

Nitish's formal break with Modi really began only in November 2005 when he formed a majority government for the first time. That's when he realized that his long-term political future hinged on reaching out to at least a section of the state's Muslims. He could not be a durable chief minister of a state with a Muslim population of 16 to 18 per cent by ignoring their concerns. One of those concerns was the nature of the Janata Dal (United)'s alliance government with the BJP. So, Nitish drew a Lakshman-rekha for his partners—his government would be guided by secular principles as defined by his socialist past. Protecting Muslim interests was an unwavering commitment. To that end, Bihar would be off limits for Modi. The BJP, as the junior partner, accepted the conditions.

Nitish had built a strong personal equation, in particular with Jaitley. Whenever he visited Delhi, he'd go to Jaitley's house for dinner. He also had a special connect with his deputy, Sushil Modi of the BJP, who had gone to university with him. With Bihar's Modi by his side, he believed he didn't need to worry about having to deal with a Modi in distant Gujarat.

Two events changed it all. The first occurred during the 2009 general election campaign. The NDA was holding a joint rally in Ludhiana as a grand show of strength under the leadership of their prime ministerial nominee, Advani. Nitish was reluctant to go, fearing Modi would also be present. Jaitley assured him that this was a personal invite from Advani and his presence was important. Nitish had grown to respect Advani; he agreed to make the trip.

No sooner had Nitish stepped onto the stage, Modi rushed to greet him, took his hand and held it aloft to the cheering crowd. It may not have been more than ten seconds, but the news channels had got their photo op, the newspapers a front-page picture. Nitish was left red-faced. He told his aides that the Ludhiana hand grab had been a breach of faith. 'You did not keep your word,' a fuming Nitish told Jaitley later. The BJP leader insisted that it wasn't a deliberate act.

Two years later, though, in June 2010, Modi did rather knowingly provoke Nitish. On the eve of the BJP national executive meeting in Patna, posters and hoardings were splashed across the city thanking Modi for his contribution to the Kosi flood victims—the Gujarat government had donated a sum of Rs 5 crore. The posters had been sponsored by local BJP leaders.

Nitish, who was travelling, had invited the BJP top brass to his house for dinner during the executive meet. Lavish arrangements had been made, with food being ordered from a local five-star hotel. But when Nitish returned to Patna, he was stunned by what he saw in the papers. Full-page advertisements of the *mahadaan* (great donation) by the Gujarat chief minister to the people of Bihar were in every major daily. The text was accompanied by the Ludhiana photograph of Nitish and Modi holding hands.

Nitish was infuriated. Modi, he felt, had deliberately publicized an act of charity to humiliate him. The dinner was cancelled, and the government was pushed to the brink. 'We can survive without them,' Nitish told an aide.

Modi, too, was angry. 'Why are you letting Nitish behave with me in this manner? We must pull out of the government,' he told BJP president Gadkari. 'That was the day when the Nitish–Modi battle took an ugly personal turn, and was no longer just about contrarian ideologies,' says Nitish's biographer, journalist Sankarshan Thakur.

Having just lost the 2009 general elections, though, the BJP chief didn't want to lose another state government. The party went into damage-control mode. Jaitley and Sushil Modi were once again put on the job of placating Nitish. The 2010 Bihar elections were just a year away and the alliance had every chance of returning to power. Both sides called a truce and in the elections that followed won by a record three-fourths majority.

By the middle of 2012, though, it was apparent that Modi was the rising star in the BJP. Nitish was anxious. He made a public statement calling for the BJP to declare its prime ministerial candidate for the 2014 elections by the end of the year. In an interview to the *Economic Times* he said the prime ministerial candidate must have 'secular' credentials. Clearly, Nitish was determined to revive his anti-Modi agenda. Only this time, the BJP wasn't willing to succumb—Nitish's deadline came and went.

By early 2013, Modi, having won the Gujarat elections for a third time, was being talked about as the most likely BJP candidate for the top job. Nitish decided to meet the BJP national leadership to get clarity. Advani reportedly assured him that no such decision had been taken. But when he went for his customary dinner to Jaitley's house, he sensed something amiss. *'Maine kai baar unko poochha, par seedha jawaab nahi mila'* (I asked the question many times, but did not get a straight answer), Nitish told me later. He knew then that the 'Modi for PM' plan of the BJP was now a fait accompli.

A few weeks later, as the BJP formally announced Modi as its campaign committee chief, Nitish decided to break the alliance and run a single-party government. I interviewed Nitish a few days later. On a hot summer day, Nitish seemed at peace with the choice he had made. He said, *'Ek vyakti ne party ko hijack kar diya hai, dictatorship karna chahte hain. Hamare saamne koi option hi nahi tha'* (One man has hijacked the party and is trying to be a dictator. I had no other option). Once again, he steadfastly refused to name

Modi even though I tried several times in an hour-long interview to get him to at least acknowledge the Gujarat chief minister.

That evening, on the flight back home, I had the 'Bihar Modi', Sushil Kumar, as my co-passenger. I like Sushil Modi—he strikes me as an honest, thoughtful politician. I asked him why he hadn't tried to prevent the BJP–JD(U) split this time. He, too, said, *'Koi option nahi tha!'* and then offered an anecdote to emphasize his point.

Apparently, the BJP had held a rally a few days earlier to protest against Nitish's decision. At the rally, a BJP worker chanted the names of different party leaders, including Advani and Sushma. The moment he shouted names other than Modi, the crowd began to heckle him: *'Bas Modi ka naam bolo!'* they said. 'Rajdeepji, I have never seen anything like this. *Logon mein Modi ka craze ho gaya hai!'* (There's a craze for Modi among the people), said Sushil Modi, almost apologetically.

It was a 'craze' that the BJP was determined to build on. From the day Nitish ended the alliance, the entire Sangh Parivar machinery was put on alert in Bihar. Winning Bihar became a prestige issue for Team Modi. 'If there was one north Indian state where Modiji was taking a daily personal interest, it was Bihar. It was almost as if he wanted to teach Nitish a lesson,' a BJP leader told me.

Angered by Nitish's public challenge, the upper castes had already firmly consolidated behind the BJP. The challenge was to break into Bihar's complex backward-caste matrix. When I pointed this out to Ravi Shankar Prasad, the BJP leader from Bihar, he smiled: 'Don't forget the biggest backward-caste leader in the country, Narendra Modi, is with us!' In every Bihar speech, Modi never missed an opportunity to stress his caste background.

Local BJP and RSS leaders had already organized caste-specific events in the state to break into the state's complex caste matrix—a convention for Dhanuks and Keots, a special programme for Koeris. There was a special push towards reaching out even to Yadavs, who, it was felt, were tiring of Lalu's brand of politics. The party roped in Upendra Kushwaha, a backward-caste leader who was once a Nitish aide. By February 2014, they would even have Dalit leader

Ram Vilas Paswan by their side. 'Except for Muslims, we had made inroads in all communities. You can call it a Hindu vote bank with a strong caste flavour,' is how one BJP leader described the party's Bihar strategy.

The Patna blasts only seemed to consolidate this 'Hindu' vote bank, with the needle of suspicion pointing at Islamic militant groups. Nitish was isolated and already appeared to wear a slightly defeated look when I met him for dinner in late 2013 at author-turned-JD(U) politician Pavan Varma's residence. With reports of a Modi mini wave blowing through Bihar and our election tracker showing him losing out, I asked him if he regretted breaking with the BJP. *'Kahan regret ki baat? Politics mein chunav hote rahte hain. Atma-samman bhi koi cheez hai ya nahin?'* (Elections keep happening in politics. Self-respect is more important), was his reply.

So, did Nitish make a mistake in making Modi's prime ministerial credentials a prestige issue? In pure electoral terms, he probably miscalculated. His own Kurmi caste was simply not large enough for him to be seen as a caste leader like a Lalu Prasad. He was hoping that the Muslims would 'reward' him for taking on Modi, but failed to realize that Muslims would rather back a leader like Lalu who they believed could actually defeat Modi. Nitish's original extremely backward and Mahadalit coalition was also eroded by the BJP's aggressive campaign.

In the end, Nitish perhaps just got a bit carried away by his own self-image as a defender of Lohiaite secularism and socialist values. Ironically, Nitish and Modi are not too dissimilar in several ways, a point I had emphasized in a column in June 2012 when the endgame was being played out. Both men have an authoritarian streak and keep an iron grip over their parties. Both are uncomfortable with dissent and have not allowed a second-line leadership to emerge in Gujarat or Bihar. Both also have a reputation for personal financial integrity.

They have similar family backgrounds. They had come up in life the hard way from mofussil towns—one from Vadnagar, the other from Bakhtiarpur. Both have kept their families firmly out of politics.

Modi had left his wife and family while still a teenager, while Nitish's wife stays away from him for extended periods. Both had cut their political teeth during the anti-Emergency agitation in the 1970s, but had taken very different ideological paths. One became an RSS pracharak and an eloquent defender of Hindu nationalism; the other is a passionate representative of socialist beliefs. Modi had publicly rejected Muslim headgear; Nitish was more than happy to wear an Islamic cap as a symbol of a plural heritage. Modi's economic model looks like a well-spun dream of market-driven growth and prosperity; the Nitish model is driven by a series of pro-poor schemes.

In 2014, like in any election, only one model and its leader could win. Modi, as an icon of change and hope, was that individual. Across Bihar, the RSS cadres contrasted Bihar's backwardness with images of Gujarat's prosperity in their door-to-door campaign. Perhaps in a state election where the chief ministership was at stake, Nitish might have been more of a factor. He had, after all, worked hard for the development of one of the most difficult states in the country to govern. His road-building projects in particular had been universally applauded. Patna was a safer city where women could finally walk freely after dark. *'Gujarat chalana aasan hai, Bihar ko sudharna bahut muskhil'* (It is easy to run Gujarat, to improve Bihar is very difficult), he told me once. But the 2014 elections were not a battle about who should rule in Patna but who was best placed to lead India. Modi in 2014 was a declared prime ministerial candidate; Nitish's horizons were limited by his state's boundaries.

'We had three weapons for Bihar,' a BJP strategist told me later. 'Modi as an OBC leader who could lead the nation, upper-caste anger against Nitish for ditching the BJP, and the promise of fast growth and jobs.' The strategy worked. A cross-caste Hindu consolidation was visible across a majority of the state's forty seats. Bihar had been conquered, but an even bigger challenge awaited Modi in neighbouring Uttar Pradesh.

~

The road to Delhi leads through Lucknow. Or so we have been led to believe for decades. Between 1947 and 1991, all of India's prime ministers came from the land of Awadh. The one exception was the Mumbai-based Gujarati Morarji Desai, whose ascent as the leader of the Janata Party government in 1977 was fortuitous. Less than two years later, he was replaced by another UP-ite, Chaudhary Charan Singh. Hindi–Hindu–Hindustan had defined the politics of the Jan Sangh and the BJP for years. The only BJP prime minister, Atal Bihari Vajpayee, had been the pride of Lucknow. In a sense, Narendra Modi was fighting history—not only had no sitting chief minister been prime minister, no BJP leader from outside the Indo-Gangetic plain had made it to the top.

No state had also witnessed the kind of tumult in the previous two decades as UP had. Stretching back to the demolition of the Babri Masjid in 1991 and the rise of Mulayam Singh and Mayawati, UP had been the cauldron in which the politics of caste and community were playing out in their most ugly form through this period. With a population of nearly 200 million—UP would have been the world's sixth largest country if it had been independent—poor, overpopulated, badly governed and riddled with socio-political conflict, it was a microcosm of the larger crisis confronting the Indian state. In the absence of large-scale industry and employment, politics remains UP's biggest *udyog* (industry). Every inch of that fertile Gangetic soil is intensely politicized.

As a journalist, I had a ringside view of politics as raw theatre in Uttar Pradesh. I had watched mikes being thrown by MLAs in the state assembly, a chief minister being sworn in for just a day at midnight, Mayawati being manhandled by Samajwadi Party MLAs (she later claimed they had wanted to rape and kill her), and heard gory stories of criminal MLAs taking *supari*s (contracts) to kill their rivals. For a political journalist, there was no place like UP to observe the turbulence of Indian politics (well, OK, Bihar under Lalu too!). As I would tell my school friends in distant south Mumbai, 'If you want to understand India and Indian politics, spend some time travelling through UP and Bihar.'

What had also become clear in this period of flux in UP was the decline of the national parties. The Congress had struggled to retain its relevance post-1989 when Rajiv Gandhi's government was defeated. 'You want to meet a real Congressman in UP? Look for a senior citizen who has been sleeping for the last twenty years!' was how one journalist once described the state of the party to me.

The BJP had built its cadres in UP on the back of the contentious Ram Janmabhoomi agitation, attempting to fill the vacuum left behind by the shrinking Congress. It seemed to work. But only for a short while. Soon, the 'Hindu' vote bank that the party had tried to consolidate realized that they were being taken for one giant ride. No mandir was going to come up in the near future. It was only an electoral ploy to garner votes. By contrast, sharpening caste identities—as represented by Mayawati's Dalit-dominated Bahujan Samaj Party and Mulayam's Samajwadi Party—appeared to have a more enduring appeal. Mandal had outlasted mandir in the electoral battlefield.

In the 2009 elections, the BJP won just ten of UP's eighty seats in the Lok Sabha, its worst performance in twenty years. In the 2012 assembly elections, things only got worse for the party. The BJP won just forty-seven of the 403 seats and got a mere 15 per cent of the vote share. I remember meeting a veteran BJP leader from UP after the assembly results who looked totally despondent. *Sab kuch khatam ho gaya. Ab bas Mulayam aur Mayawati ka khel chalega'* (It is all over for us. Only Mulayam and Mayawati will rule UP now), was his verdict.

Modi's own role in the 2012 UP elections had proved controversial. He refused to campaign in the state in protest against the party choosing his great rival Sanjay Joshi to handle the campaign. Joshi had been hand-picked by the BJP president Gadkari, with the RSS supporting the move. Modi would have none of it. I was privy to a phone conversation where Gadkari was literally pleading with Modi to at least address some rallies in UP since his absence was sending out the wrong message to the cadres. A defiant Modi refused to relent.

I remember telephoning Modi that night to find out why he was so insistent on not going to UP to campaign. I even 'advised' him that as a senior leader he was making a mistake by refusing to campaign in a crucial state. *'Jab tak woh aadmi wahan hai, mere campaign karne ka sawaal hee nahi uthta!'* (As long as that man [Joshi] is there, there is no question of my campaigning.)

Four months after the 2012 UP elections, Joshi was removed from the BJP national executive and almost banished from the party. I asked Gadkari why he had buckled so easily to Modi's determination to isolate Joshi. *'Arre, Rajdeepji, aap Modiji ka swabhaav jaante hai, unka mind badalna aasan nahi!'* (You know Modi's nature, getting him to change his mind is not easy.)

The Modi–Joshi feud has a chequered past but is highly revealing about the man who was now aspiring to be the next prime minister. Like Modi, Joshi, too, was an RSS pracharak but with a less dominating presence. Low-profile and soft-spoken, the Nagpur-born Joshi had worked with Modi in the party in Gujarat since 1989. When Modi was ousted from Gujarat in 1996 over a leadership battle, he was convinced that Joshi was behind his 'vanvas'. When he became chief minister in 2001, almost his first act was to have Joshi packed off from the state.

At the BJP's silver jubilee celebrations in Mumbai in 2005, a mysterious CD surfaced which allegedly showed Joshi in a compromising position with an unidentified woman. The buzz in the BJP was that the CD had been organized by the Gujarat police and distributed by leaders close to Modi. 'It is a well-planned conspiracy to malign me,' Joshi told me at the time. He was removed from all party posts and pushed into political exile. The UP elections were meant to signal his rehabilitation. Only, Modi would have none of it.

Modi by 2012 was poised to be the BJP's top-ranking leader, having been Gujarat chief minister for a decade. Joshi, by contrast, was struggling to revive his career. There was no comparison in power or stature between the two leaders. And yet, Modi was keen to exact revenge. 'It is not a question of who is a big or small leader,' Modi had told me in the phone conversation, 'it is a question of principle. *Woh aadmi achha nahi hai*' (He is not a good man).

What I realized that night was that Modi is an individual who does not forgive or forget easily—he has a long memory and bears grudges against those who he believed had harmed him. Dynamic, driven and energetic, he is convinced that he alone is the master of his destiny and must fight those who stand in his way. He may have become a national leader but at times he has a deeply insecure mindset of a provincial strongman constantly looking to settle scores. What was equally striking was the manner in which the BJP's central leadership seemed intimidated by Modi and did not want to alienate him in any manner.

But if in 2012, Modi did not even campaign in UP because of personal vendetta, he could not afford to think even remotely of any such move in 2014. Now, he needed to desperately turn around the BJP's fortunes in the state to achieve his prime ministerial ambition. And this time, he needed someone by his side who he could implicitly trust. There was only one such man in Modi's eyes.

~

The first time I met Amit Shah, the circumstances were rather unenviable, to say the least. I was covering the highly surcharged Gujarat 2002 assembly election campaign being held in the backdrop of the riots. My travels had brought me to Sarkhej on the outskirts of Ahmedabad where Shah was standing for re-election. Advani, who was the MP from Gandhinagar which encompassed the Sarkhej area, was to address a rally. I was attempting a live link with our Delhi studio when suddenly the crowd encircled me. '*Arre, yeh wahi Rajdeep Sardesai hai jisne Gujarat dangon mein hamare khilaaf prachar kiya. Isko hum nahin chodenge*' (This is the same Rajdeep who campaigned against us during the Gujarat riots. We must not let him get away). The next thing I knew I was being pushed and kicked by Shah supporters wearing saffron bandanas. A kind police officer stepped in and had to whisk us away to safety.

When the rally was over, I met Shah to complain. 'What kind

of behaviour is this, sir? You must rein in your supporters,' I told him. He was duly apologetic. '*Yeh galat hai, mein iski ninda karta hoon. Mein kabhi hinsa ke paksh mein nahi hoon*' (This is wrong, I condemn it. I would never support any kind of violence). And then, he smiled and delivered a parting shot, '*Rajdeepji, aapko bhi thoda apna khyal rakhna chahiye*' (You should also be careful). The words were said in a soft and gentle manner, but the underlying message, I feared, was a little more harsh.

That was then. In the decade that followed, much had changed in my life but also, more importantly, in the life of Shah. Then, he was seen as the local dada of Sarkhej, someone who enjoyed the unquestioned support of the BJP–VHP cadres. He had a reputation of winning elections by big margins—he won the 2002 elections by 158,000 votes; he won the 2007 elections by an even more impressive 235,000 votes. 'No one can touch Amitbhai in Sarkhej,' was the unanimous verdict. Sarkhej was typically new Ahmedabad—middle class, commercial, and with a strong Hindu religious identity.

Born in a Vaishnav Vania orthodox Hindu family (he still visits the Shrinathji temple in Rajasthan's Nathdwara at least twice a year), Shah had handled a successful family business in PVC pipes and had even dabbled in stockbroking like any financially sharp Gujarati. 'His blue-chip stock portfolio is pretty impressive,' one of Shah's friends told me. But while his mind may have been counting the money, his heart was really in the RSS. He joined the Sangh in the early 1980s while still a teenager. 'It was like my extended family,' he told me once. 'Being in the Sangh was the best thing that happened to me as a young man.'

Within the Sangh, Shah developed an image of an astute organizer and skilled election strategist. 'Then, whether it was a garba function during Navaratra, a charity drive or a political meeting, when we needed to organize something in the area, we always turned to Amitbhai and he was always there for us,' recalls an old colleague.

It was in the 1980s, while Shah was a Sangh activist, that he and Modi got to know each other. Modi, very much the senior leader, was impressed with Shah's organizational skills and total commitment to the Hindutva ideology. The Ayodhya movement had begun to bubble, the BJP was a party on the rise in Gujarat, and Modi as state secretary was looking for young men with desire and ambition. 'I think Modi liked the fact that Amitbhai was ready to do a lot of hard work silently without taking credit. He was not the kind who would challenge Modi's authority at any stage,' is how one Gujarati journalist explains the Shah–Modi chemistry. They both had strikingly similar looking beards as well!

When Modi was re-elected Gujarat chief minister in 2002, he gave Shah multiple portfolios, including the crucial home portfolio. The home ministry was critical because it gave Modi control over the police. In the backdrop of the riots and charges of conspiracy being made against the chief minister's office, Modi needed someone in the home ministry who would be totally faithful to him. Modi trusted very few individuals—Shah was the one politician he felt a certain comfort factor with. 'He was the eyes and ears of the chief minister,' is how one Gujarat bureaucrat describes Shah's role in that government.

It was during his tenure as home minister of Gujarat that Shah courted controversy. Between 2003 and 2007, there were a series of encounter killings in Gujarat in which several young Muslims were killed. Shah claimed they were 'terrorists', some of whom wanted to kill the chief minister, and that the killings were driven by a zero-tolerance policy towards terror. Human rights activists argued that many of the encounters were 'fake' and Shah was a 'Muslim killer'.

In 2010, Shah was arrested by the CBI and accused of killing a criminal, Sohrabuddin Sheikh, his wife Kauser Bi and their associate Tulsiram Prajapati, in a staged encounter. According to the CBI, Sheikh had been extorting money from marble traders in neighbouring Rajasthan. The traders complained to Shah, who reportedly got the state's Anti-Terrorism Squad to organize the killing. Several police officers were also arrested in the case.

Shah got bail three months after his arrest but was told he would have to leave Gujarat for fear that he would influence the investigation. For nearly two years, Shah stayed at Gujarat Bhavan in the national capital, away from his home state. 'What do you miss most?' I asked him. 'The khana,' he said with a hint of a smile. His wife had to come to live in Delhi with him to ensure that the *shudh* vegetarian Shah remained well fed—he liked his dal, *kadhi*, *khandwi* and Gujarati snacks.

Interestingly, on the day in September 2012 when Shah was finally allowed to return home, I was on the same flight with him, travelling to Ahmedabad. Dressed in his trademark kurta–pyjama and with a small bag in hand, he could have been mistaken for a small-time businessman. He was alone, no sidekicks by his side. But his spirit was undaunted.

I asked him about the serious charges he was facing. *'Sab saazish hai, bahut badi saazish hai'* (It is all a big conspiracy). I asked him who was behind the conspiracy. *'Poora Congress isme involved hai. Yeh chahte hain ki Modiji ko target karein aur mujhe isme phasaye'* (The whole Congress is involved. They want to target Modi and trap me), he said firmly. I sensed that adversity had brought Shah and Modi closer together. It was almost as if Shah was taking the bullets as a proxy for his 'saheb'. It was a 'sacrifice' that meant Modi was almost beholden to his junior minister. In an interview I did with Modi in 2012, I had asked him a question on Shah's legal travails. It was the one question he asked me to later edit out.

So, was Shah really the 'most dangerous man in Gujarat', as one police officer once described him to me? Was he, as one of the arrested police officers, D.G. Vanzara, claimed in a letter, an 'evil influence' on Modi? (Shah claims the letter was dictated by the Congress.) Or was he, as his supporters insisted, 'One of the most honest and straightforward persons you could wish to meet, an ace political mind'? The verdict was evenly split, depending on who you spoke to.

A former *Tehelka* journalist, Rana Ayyub, who had carried out a detailed investigation on Shah's alleged role in encounter killings, claims that the minister's men once tried to browbeat her. The magazine was pulled out of the news stands in Gujarat, and Ayyub got threatening calls. When nothing seemed to work, she received a courier package at her hotel in Ahmedabad with a wad of notes. 'I fear someone was trying to bribe me into getting off the story,' she says.

A local Gujarat journalist describes Shah as a karyakarta first, a political leader later. Apparently, when a local UP businessman offered to finance the BJP campaign, Shah did not entertain him for more than a few minutes. 'You must meet my district head first,' he told him. But when an RSS worker came to his office, he spent half an hour with him, trying to understand what was happening on the ground. 'He is the strong, silent type who likes his work to do the talking, he is not a *hawabaaz* [gasbag],' is how an old friend describes him.

My own sense is that Shah is a bit of a split personality. He could be warm and approachable in private conversation, with a sharp sense of humour. But he is also a ruthless politician who believes in a '*saam, daam, dand, bhed*' brand of politics where ends mattered more than the means adopted. Whether the ruthlessness extended to ordering extra-judicial killings, is a matter for the courts to decide; but clearly, the numerous controversies which have swirled around him suggest that Shah still has much explaining to do.

There is no doubt, though, that he's someone who relishes a political fight. Maybe it was this dogged determination to prove himself that made Shah the ideal person to take on the tough UP challenge. Within days of being made campaign committee chief in June 2013, Modi ensured that Shah was fully empowered as general secretary in charge of UP. The right-hand man who had been his 'eyes and ears' in Gujarat was now being asked to be his brain in the most crucial battle of 2014. UP offered the biggest prize of eighty seats. Most observers reckoned the BJP needed to win at least forty to fifty seats to have any chance of achieving Mission 272-plus. The odds were stacked against the man from Sarkhej. But they had also been against him when he had spent two months in Sabarmati jail. Now was redemption time.

When Shah arrived at the BJP office in Lucknow on 12 June 2013, he was aware of the magnitude of the task facing him. The state BJP

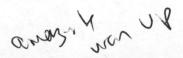

unit was totally demoralized—the party had been out of power in UP for seventeen years with little hope of a comeback. Its leadership was ageing and warring with each other. Some of the old guards saw Shah as an 'outsider' who was being thrust on them. UP politicians tend to have an exaggerated sense of self-importance and believe that no one knows their state like they do. '*Gujarat aur UP mein bahut fark hai, Amitji*' (There's a huge difference between Gujarat and UP), one of them openly told Shah. One of the new general secretary's first acts was to call day-long meetings, in small groups, of all the party MPs and MLAs who had won and lost elections. 'It's important to know why we were losing elections, why our voters had deserted us,' was his reasoning.

The legislators could not bluff Shah easily. He had already got detailed constituency-wise profiles of the state done and had used the Sangh Parivar network to identify just who were the MLAs, MPs and local leaders who were actually working on the ground. Interestingly, in the two years when he was forced to live in Delhi because of his bail conditions, he would travel to different parts of UP on weekends to familiarize himself with the environment. 'I think much before 2013, he had been given a sense that he was going to have to manage the UP elections for the BJP and was fully prepared for it,' says Sheela Bhatt, a senior journalist who has interviewed Shah on several occasions.

By contrast, Madhusudhan Mistry, the Congress's general secretary for Uttar Pradesh, who was also from Gujarat, did not even recognize some of the party's twenty-eight MLAs from the state. 'One of our MLAs once told Mistry in a party meeting that if you don't know who I am, how will you fight an election!' a senior Congress member told me. Mistry, with his jhola and faded kurtas, had been hand-picked by Rahul. Pitted against the dynamic Shah, neither he nor his party had a chance.

Shah knew that the key to success was in re-energizing the party workers. This is where his close ties with the RSS worked hugely in his favour. A core team of RSS pracharaks was deputed to work with him. From the moment he took charge in Lucknow, Shah tirelessly criss-crossed the state by road and rail, staying at the homes of party workers, often having simple meals of *saunf khichdi* and *chaas* (fennel rice and buttermilk) with them. By the beginning of 2014, he had already covered around seventy of UP's eighty Lok Sabha constituencies. By the time the elections were over in May, Shah had touched all eighty constituencies, spent 142 nights over a span of eight months in UP's villages and towns, and travelled more than 90,000 kilometres across the vast state. 'The idea was to awaken the dormant party worker, to make them realize that this was a do-or-die election battle,' says an aide.

Where Modi could easily relate to young English-speaking technocrats, Shah preferred to deal with loyal Sangh activists. Sunil Bansal, a forty-four-year-old ABVP (Akhil Bharatiya Vidya Parishad, the RSS's student wing) organizing secretary, was hand-picked by Shah to assist him in the UP campaign. The Hindi-speaking Bansal was from Rajasthan, did not have a foreign degree, but he had the common touch—he helped Shah set up a network of volunteers in Lucknow and every district headquarters. 'Amitbhai is very organized. He likes to ensure everything is planned in advance,' Bansal later told me.

A team of about 120 volunteers was ready by January 2014 to operate out of the party's Lucknow head office. These volunteers helped set up and coordinate with the booth-level committees that are so critical to any election. Some of the volunteers were IITians, lawyers, management professionals, but a majority of them were drawn from the RSS–ABVP ranks. These volunteers coordinated with anywhere between 80,000 and one lakh swayamsevaks engaged in a massive door-to-door campaign. 'Forget the technology, forget the media blitz, the 2014 election was ultimately a triumph of our foot soldiers who worked relentlessly on the ground in UP,' is how a BJP strategist captured the party's success story.

The RSS involvement was deep and intense. Each swayamsevak was referred to as a *panna pramukh* and made in charge of one page of a voter list (which has roughly around fifteen registered voters). Each booth has around 1200 votes, so eighty to ninety swayamsevaks were engaged in the campaign at every booth level. In a state with more than one lakh booths, this was election micromanagement being taken to a whole new level. 'Our mission statement was every vote counts. We believed in the power of one,' is how Bansal described the booth-centric approach.

The RSS campaign was divided into three phases. In the first phase, between Vijayadashmi in October 2013 and Republic Day in January 2014, the focus was on voter registration. In the second phase in February and March, the objective shifted to a door-to-door campaign aimed at around 6500 to 7000 villages in key districts. In the final stretch in April and May, the sole goal was to maximize voter turnout. 'I don't think that the RSS cadres have ever participated with such enthusiasm in any election since 1977. Even the Ayodhya election of 1991 was an emotional appeal to Hindutva. This time, we saw it as a fight to the finish. *Ek junoon tha worker mein*' (The workers were driven), is how a senior RSS leader from UP described the Sangh's involvement in the 2014 election.

The fact is, parties like the Congress simply don't have anything remotely matching the dedicated swayamsevak cadres. The Congress's frontal organizations like the Seva Dal have an antique look about them. Even the left has struggled to sustain its grass-roots network beyond Bengal and Kerala. Regional forces like the BSP and the Trinamool have been a shade more successful, but they, too, operate within a limited geography. To win elections, you need an organizational machine. And the RSS with its 45,000 shakhas and 5 million swayamsevaks across India provides the BJP with the feet on the ground, a cutting-edge advantage at election time.

Shah also turned his attention to the VHP which had been feeling isolated, convinced that their dream of a Ram mandir in Ayodhya would never be fulfilled. The VHP's sants and sadhus had already endorsed Modi at the Kumbh Mela in January 2013, hoping that he would revive their dwindling fortunes. In July, just a month after taking over, Shah paid a visit to the makeshift Ram temple in Ayodhya, offering prayers for Modi's *raj tilak* (coronation) and the Congress's vanvas. 'Ram and Ayodhya live in the hearts of millions of

Indians. I have prayed that everyone comes together for the building of a Ram temple,' he told the media. The VHP was enthused—finally, a BJP leader was speaking their language in unapologetic terms. A latent Hindu passion was being reawakened, as had been the case in the 1990s. Many VHP sadhus were now ready to join the 2014 campaign.

Perhaps this was easier to achieve with Modi at the helm. In the 2009 elections, the traditional Sangh Parivar workers had been disillusioned with Advani's attempt to recast himself as a more moderate Hindutva face. Vajpayee's inclusive politics didn't suit the more fiery VHP–RSS rabble-rousers. Modi was different. He could excite the saffron brotherhood because he was seen as one of their own. 'Modi may have become a national politician, but he is always a swayamsevak and pracharak first,' is how an RSS leader described Modi's appeal. Shah knew this, which is why it was that much easier to crack the whip and get the organization to go back to its roots. In every meeting, he would remind the local workers, 'This is our big chance, we must not squander it.'

But Shah knew that traditional Hindutva politics could only be one weapon—the real test was in piercing through UP's byzantine caste arithmetic. The Yadavs were loyal to the SP, Mayawati had cornered the Dalit vote (especially her own Jatav community's), and the Muslims would not trust the BJP. A new election paradigm was needed.

A massive drive was initiated to register young volunteers from across 13,000 colleges in the state. Around 800 full-time volunteers under the age of thirty were recruited and armed with mobiles with prepaid SIM cards; their prime target was the young voter. 'We felt that the young voter in UP was most likely to look beyond traditional caste politics. The slogan of parivartan was resonating with them most effectively,' says a BJP leader involved in planning the strategy.

I had a first-hand experience of this when I met an elderly Yadav in Gorakhpur who said he had been a life-long Mulayam voter but was shifting to the BJP this time. 'You see, my grandson in Noida is an engineer and he says Modi is the right person for India. *Ab pote ki baat toh sunni padegi!*' (I will have to listen to my grandson), he laughed.

Indeed, the demographic shift in UP's population—with a large and influential chunk of young voters—would eventually give the BJP an important incremental vote. Just as interesting was the role of economic migrants. Bansal claims that around 15,000 Purvanchalis (eastern UP-ites) based in Mumbai, Bangalore and Ahmedabad returned to UP for the election campaign and spread the 'Modi for PM' message among the locals. 'Even migrant workers from diamond factories in Surat came home and told their community members stories of how Gujarat was prospering under Modi,' says Bansal.

Not that Shah wasn't playing his own version of caste politics. In all booths, caste-based clusters were created based on the numerical strength of each caste, and volunteers chosen accordingly. More than eighty caste *sammelan*s (conferences) were held, especially to attract the non-Yadav OBCs and the non-Jatav Dalits. 'When in UP, do as UP-ites do. If caste matters, then we must play the caste game better than others,' was Shah's message to the booth-level workers.

I had a first-hand experience of Shah's caste calculations during the BJP's ticket distribution exercise. An office colleague came to me with a strange request. 'Sir, there is a friend of mine from UP. She is an MLA there and is very keen to meet you, she needs your help.'

An hour later, an astute young politician called Anupriya Patel, who was the sitting MLA from the Ruhaniya assembly seat of Varanasi, was in my cabin. She was from the Kurmi-dominated Apna Dal party which had been started by her late father, Sonelal Patel. 'Sir, I need a favour. Could you fix an appointment for me with Mr Shah? I wish to contest the elections in alliance with the BJP,' she said, with refreshing candour.

I wasn't quite sure how to react. As an editor, I had determinedly stayed out of the murky world of political wheeling and dealing. 'Look, I will request Amitbhai to meet you, but please understand, I am no great friend of his and I am not going to ask him to give you a ticket!' was my immediate response.

Hesitantly, I called up Shah. His reaction was instant: *'Please, aap unhe Gujarat Bhavan bhej do'* (Send her to Gujarat Bhavan). A few days later, I got a call from Ms Patel. 'Thank you so much, sir, my ticket is done. Our alliance with the BJP is sealed!' The Apna Dal was given two seats, both of which they would eventually win. I guess in my small way, almost unintentionally, I had contributed to the BJP success in UP!

I asked Shah later why he had decided to tie up with the Apna Dal, a party with a limited presence in a tiny pocket of eastern Uttar Pradesh. *'Isme chhote bade ki baat nahi hai, yahan har seat matter karti hai. Unke Kurmi samaj ka teen–char per cent vote hai'* (It's not a question of big or small. Every seat matters. The Kurmis have a 3 to 4 per cent vote in these areas), he claimed. The final BJP list for UP would include twenty-eight OBCs and seventeen non-Jatav Dalits.

Shah, with his astute planning, may have been the mind behind the UP campaign. But he still needed the 'face' of Modi to guarantee success. 'We wanted to project Modiji as the symbol of good governance and contrast the mess in UP with our development record in Gujarat,' is how Shah summed it up for me later.

Modi's mega rallies in UP were scheduled for each major zonal headquarter across the state, starting with Kanpur in October 2013. Booth workers were given Boleros (a status symbol in many parts of UP) and told to ensure that each rally in their area drew maximum attendance. 'The larger the crowd, the more the chance of creating Modi mania,' was the overarching philosophy.

But how was the message going to be sent out to every village across a vast state, many of which didn't even have proper electricity or access to media? Team Modi deployed 400 GPS-enabled digital raths—similar to the ones that had been used in Rajasthan in the assembly elections (see preceding chapter)—to reach out to what were described to me as 'media dark' villages. As many as 93,000 villages in UP across fifty-one gram panchayats (and around 39,000 villages in Bihar) were identified for video messaging. Some villages were literally small *kasba*s with just fifty voters but even they were not left out.

A sixteen-minute video with the '*Modi aanewala hai*' song and clips of Modi's speeches would be played on the TV screen on the rath, often taking up local issues like *bijli* and contrasting them with the promise of twenty-four-hour power supply as in Gujarat. The BJP/RSS volunteers who accompanied the video van would distribute Modi masks and caps to the children in the village. Every day, the journey of each rath would be monitored by a team of around a hundred IT professionals who would send a daily progress report to the nerve centre in Lucknow. 'We had done it in Rajasthan. Now we needed to scale it up in UP,' says a Team Shah member, sounding like a business executive.

It was becoming clearer by the day that the plump, bearded man from Gujarat had crafted a well-oiled election machine that was ready to roll across the banks of the Ganga. All he needed was one trigger that would sustain the early momentum. If, in Bihar, it was a terror attack, in UP it would be a tragic riot.

~

Muzaffarnagar is a ramshackle, crowded town in western UP, about 127 kilometres from the national capital. With its broken roads, unruly traffic and scores of young men just loitering around, Muzaffarnagar typifies the gradual decline of UP. It is also in the heart of the state's sugar belt and is a bit like the Wild West with a thriving business in unlicensed guns. A friend of mine who worked in a sugar company used to travel to his Muzaffarnagar factory with armed guards. 'You could take no chances, especially at night, in the town,' is what he told me.

Politically, this had been Chaudhary Charan Singh country. The former prime minister had built a social compact between his fellow landowning Jats and the local Muslims, many of whom were artisans and agricultural labourers. It had been a relationship based on shared economic interest which had endured for the most part. Travelling with Ajit Singh on the campaign trail in the 1990s, I was struck by the reverence people had for his father. '*Chaudhary sahib sabko saath lete hain, Jat ho ya Muslim'* (Chaudhury sahib takes everyone along with him, Jat or Muslim), was the near-unanimous refrain.

But in August 2013, that delicately woven social alliance collapsed. Jats and Muslims found themselves engaged in a bloody communal riot that lasted several days and left sixty-two persons dead, with more than 50,000 persons displaced. The riots, worryingly, engulfed Muzaffarnagar's villages which had been relatively immune to religious tension. No one is quite sure what sparked off the violence. The police FIR claimed there had been a bike accident which led to a fight in which two Hindus and one Muslim boy were killed. Others (mainly the Hindu Jats) claimed that there was an eve-teasing incident that triggered the conflict.

I must honestly confess that no national news channel gave the story adequate coverage, initially. Death in the age of breaking news can often be reduced to a statistic—three people killed in what appeared a localized clash didn't seem to shake the media into action. It was only in the first week of September, when the violence showed no sign of letting up, that the news antennae were aroused.

In my case, the violence literally hit home on 7 September when I was informed that Rajesh Verma, a stringer associated with IBN 7, the Hindi news network I was heading, had been shot dead while covering the clashes. A local photographer with him had also been beaten to death. At Rajesh's funeral the next day, the mood was one of sullen anger. Despite a curfew, hundreds had come out on the streets to protest. The administration has gone missing, was the universal complaint.

That night I rang up the UP chief minister, Akhilesh Yadav. He sounded suitably contrite, and promised full support to Rajesh's family. *'Hum unke family ko job aur compensation dono denge'* (We will give the family jobs and money), he assured me. I wasn't convinced. 'Akhileshji, this isn't just about money. People are being killed in Muzaffarnagar and your government is being blamed for mishandling the situation.' His answer was a classic case of passing the buck. *'Arre, aap media wale aur Opposition hamesha prashashan ko blame karte ho. Yeh danga to BJP walon ne karvaya hai'* (The

a lot of state
raid Modi shah 'Encounter 3 worldrenal,
kachi of
'Rict', in
2014: THE ELECTION THAT CHANGED INDIA   173 JP

media and Opposition always blame the administration. This riot has been stage-managed by the BJP).

The next morning, the army swung into action and an indefinite curfew was imposed. The violence slowly subsided. Not for the first time, the Indian state had woken up a tad too late. Too late to save the lives of innocent citizens caught in the crossfire.

The big question in the weeks and months that followed was—did the political parties of UP, especially the BJP, stoke the communal fires to derive political benefit? That BJP leaders were present at a 'maha' panchayat where a call was made to avenge the killings and to demand justice for Jat *bahu-beti*s is undeniable. That one of them, an MLA called Sangeet Som, put out a false video on Facebook showing an alleged lynching of Hindu boys is also true. At a Modi rally in Agra in November, the BJP leadership even felicitated its MLAs who had been charged with inciting violence. Two of its leaders named in the riot FIRs were given tickets, and one of them, Sanjeev Balyan, would eventually become a Union minister.

On the other side of the communal divide, it is a fact that local Muslim leaders from the Congress, SP and BSP, including the BSP MP Kadir Rana, were caught on tape delivering inflammatory speeches. Government officials who were pushing for an impartial inquiry were transferred. SP leader Azam Khan was later found in a sting operation to have asked the police to release the Muslims accused of rioting. To blame, therefore, only one community or party would be to camouflage the real tragedy of Muzaffarnagar—it represented the collective bankruptcy of a political class that was seeking votes over dead bodies.

In a way, this was the difference between the politics of religion in the early 1990s in Uttar Pradesh and what played out on the ground in 2013–14. During the Ayodhya movement, it was clear that the BJP was making an open and determined bid to stir the communal pot. Now, the communalization was more insidious. There was no blatant religious issue like the Ram mandir to incite trouble. Instead, a more silent divide was being created on the ground through a sustained whisper campaign that branded Muslims as untrustworthy and anti-national ('*Sab ISI agents hai*'). The response was an equally worrisome radicalization of Muslims, where the moderate voices in the community had given way to the extremist rhetoric of '*Islam khatre mein hai*' (Islam is in danger). Caught in the crossfire, the so-called secularists were much too enfeebled and compromised to be able to respond effectively.

Months later, I asked Shah about the allegations that he had taken political advantage of the religious polarization after the riots. His defence was, '*Dange humne nahi karvayen. Dange ek chhoti si ghatna se shuru huye. Agar sarkar prompt action leti, toh dange nahi hote. Yeh dange sarkar ki vote bank ki politics ki wajah se hue*' (We didn't start the riots. Riots started with a small incident. If the government had not played vote bank politics but taken prompt action instead, there would have been no riots).

Shah had a less convincing answer as to why tickets were given to MLAs who were charged with inciting the riots; he tamely claimed they had been 'defamed'. I also asked him about his controversial remark ahead of polling that UP's voters should exact 'revenge'. 'I was referring to the ballot box, not the gun. You media people are just trying to create trouble,' he insisted.

But the subtext of Shah's statement was apparent. It was obvious that post-Muzaffarnagar, a certain Hindu consolidation had taken place on the ground and Shah could reap its political advantage. In the six months after the riots, there were several minor communal flare-ups across western UP—stone throwing, local skirmishes, fights over loudspeakers—and with every instance, the religious divide widened. A senior UP police officer later told me that a pattern had been established as early as May 2012, soon after Akhilesh Yadav took over. 'Every week, we would get reports of communal tension from some district headquarters. It started in western UP, but spread to central and eastern UP,' he told me.

In October 2013, I travelled to Bareilly, a town that had seen a month-long bandh the previous year after riots broke out during Ramzan. A year had elapsed, but the divide on the ground was visible. In the Muslim mohallas, the Shah–Modi combine was seen as an 'evil' duo. *'Woh toh dange karvayenge, UP ko Gujarat banayenge!'* (They will incite riots, make UP into Gujarat), said a Muslim schoolteacher. Interestingly, in the Hindu bastis, too, there was a feeling that UP would become Gujarat if Modi became prime minister. *'Dekho, sir, Gujarat ne kitni tarakki ki hai, hum peechhe reh gaye!'* (See how Gujarat has progressed, we are left behind), a young graduate told me. It seemed that Modi was seen as a threat by the Muslims, but represented hope and opportunity to the Hindus.

The Muzaffarnagar riots drew the politically influential Jats into the BJP fold. But it wasn't just the Jats or upper castes alone—the Sangh Parivar made a deliberate attempt to woo Dalits as well, in an effort to cement an umbrella 'Hindu' identity. Mayawati was strangely muted in the aftermath of Muzaffarnagar, and the BJP sensed an opportunity. The RSS consciously wooed non-Jatav Dalit groups like the Pasis, even distributing pamphlets claiming that their ancestors were *rakshaks* (protectors) of the Hindu faith. Dalit families who were affected in the riots were promised protection. A news report suggested that in the first three months of 2014, more than 3000 Dalit youths who were once part of the BSP switched over as full-time BJP workers. 'We were able to take a large chunk of Mayawati's votes away from her in western UP,' claims a local BJP leader.

Just how successful the BJP was with this strategy was confirmed when we did a television programme from a Dalit-dominated village in Noida. The voices were vociferously pro-Modi. *'Hum Hindu samaj mein hain, Modiji hamare neta hain, iss baar unko hum chance denge'* (We are part of the Hindu community and Modi is our leader. We want to give him a chance). A subdued Mayawati didn't counter the RSS's propaganda machine (see chapter 6 for more).

But the even bigger political failure was that of the ruling SP. No major riot in India has taken place without some element of administrative complicity and/or incompetence, be it Delhi 1984 or Gujarat 2002. Muzaffarnagar 2013, in that sense, fitted in with a troubling pattern. As the leader of the party in power, Akhilesh Yadav has much to answer for the partisanship of the local administration. In the winter of 2011–12, he had been UP's great new hope; less than two years later, he was already becoming its worst nightmare.

~

The 2012 UP assembly elections was a 'wave' election—the Samajwadi Party was swept to power by an overwhelming majority. The star turn was that of Akhilesh Yadav who travelled the length and breadth of the state, often on a cycle. Though he bore an uncanny resemblance to father Mulayam, he promised a new face for the SP. He even denied a ticket to D.P. Yadav, the powerful politician with a long criminal record.

While travelling with Akhilesh on the campaign trail, I must confess to being impressed with his desire to change his party's image. *'Aap dekh lena, hum UP kee tasveer badal denge'* (Just you wait and see, we will change the face of UP). Young, fresh-faced, foreign educated and, importantly, with an ear to the ground, he appeared to have all the qualifications to become a symbol of hope and change.

I should have known better. At thirty-eight, Akhilesh was sworn in as UP's youngest chief minister. But the party he headed was much older. The SP had emerged from the womb of the original Socialist Party. On the wall at the residence of Mulayam Singh in Lucknow, there are portraits of all the great socialist leaders from Ram Manohar Lohia to George Fernandes to Madhu Limaye. Even those who disagreed with their political views could not but admire the simplicity in the lifestyles of these netas. I remember pointing out to Akhilesh that he should also have a picture of Madhu Dandavate, the former railway minister, on the wall. *'Haan, haan, aap kehte hain to unka bhi photo laga denge!'* (Yes, yes, if you say so, we will put his photo too.)

That was the problem with the modern-day Samajwadi Party— socialist values were reduced to cut-outs and lip service. Dandavate would have preferred to travel by train all his life; today's SP has got caught up in what can be best described as the *hawai jahaaz* (airline) culture.

It started, perhaps, with Amar Singh, a businessman-politician who was once Mulayam's Sancho Panza and who Akhilesh referred to politely as 'uncle'. Uncle Amar Singh was the de facto king of the Samajwadi Party till he was unceremoniously shown the door in 2010 over what was described as a 'family fight'.

Amar Singh is a fascinating political character. He is a neta by day, a party animal by night, a safari suit-clad friend of millionaires and film stars in a party of craggy, rural Lohiaites, who scoffs at being called a political 'fixer'. 'Boss, you can call me crony capitalist—my party sees me as socialist!' he once laughingly told me.

Amar Singh could have breakfast with corporate leaders like Anil Ambani, lunch with Mulayam and then dinner with the Bachchans. I once filmed him on the campaign trail in UP. We spent the day in the boondocks of Sonbhadra in eastern UP where he addressed a 'Thakur Sabha'. I told him I wanted to see the 'other side' of him by night. Within a few hours, he had organized a party at home. The guest list included actor Sridevi and husband Boney, industrialists and models. 'All my friends, they will do anything for me,' he said, his body oozing the latest perfume.

The Amar Singh culture of wheeling and dealing came to haunt the SP. Mulayam Singh had always been 'Netaji' to his colleagues, a political and real-life wrestler, born in a small village, who had started life as a schoolteacher. Amar Singh gave him a taste of the high life and he didn't want to let go. *'Party badal gayi, Netaji badal gaye, sabko paise ki lalach ho gayi'* (The party changed, Mulayam changed, everyone wanted to make money), said a veteran SP MP.

But the real decline in the SP's work culture was not catalysed by Amar Singh but by Mulayam's own family. Almost every relative was given a position within the party structure. Akhilesh's wife was an MP, an uncle was a minister, another uncle was a Rajya Sabha MP. *'Samajwaad parivarwaad ban gaya!'* (Socialism has become family raj), is how a senior UP journalist described it to me.

Family power can breed arrogance. No one was more arrogant than Shivpal Yadav, Mulayam's younger brother. The rough-talking Shivpal had acquired notoriety as a PWD minister who apparently had a 'rate card' for handing over government contracts. 'You want any work done in UP, you need to go to Shivpalji,' is what a UP bureaucrat told me once.

It was this work culture, then, that Akhilesh was inheriting, one which he needed to discard to be successful. I remember asking Akhilesh on the campaign trail how he would deal with his uncles once he became chief minister. *'Koi problem nahi hoga, hum saath kaam karenge!'* (No problem, we will all work together.)

His confidence was horribly misplaced. When the government came to power, the old order took over. Akhilesh for them was a *bachcha* (kid). UP's thriving transfer-posting business was back, as was a common practice by which Yadavs were given preference in government jobs. 'If you are a Yadav, you could get a police station of your choice,' is what a senior UP police officer told me.

Also marking a return was UP's 'goonda raj' in sharp contrast to Mayawati's tough-on-law-and-order image. Our office was in Noida in UP. When Mulayam Singh was chief minister in 2006, cars would routinely be stolen from outside the office premises. We complained but got no response. When Mayawati took charge a year later, we complained again. A police booth was set up just outside the office. The car thefts stopped.

Just as worrying was the fragile social peace. In the first year of Akhilesh's government, there were more than a hundred large and small communal riots. Akhilesh insisted that the riots were the brainchild of the BJP–VHP combine. *'Phayda to unhi ko hota hai dangon se'* (The BJP–VHP are the ones who benefit from riots), he claimed. The pattern of the riots was suspicious—any small incident could trigger a bandh call from saffron groups and spark off tension and violence. Local Sangh Parivar leaders, it seems, were spoiling for a fight.

And yet, the fact is the SP was also playing the politics of religious polarization. During the Ram Janmabhoomi movement in 1990,

Mulayam had ordered police firing on kar sevaks on their way to Ayodhya, to prevent them from reaching the disputed site. It was a controversial decision, but one that earned him the loyalty of the UP Muslims. It was the Muslim–Yadav base that had since sustained his politics.

But what started off as an attempt to maintain law and order eventually became a rather blatant policy of Muslim appeasement. From job reservations to promises to withdraw cases against Muslim youth accused of terror, the SP government became almost totally identified with the politics of the minorities. Matters reached a stage where the joke in UP's power circles was that if any politician with a topi and *dadhi* met Mulayam, he would be given ministerial rank and a lal-batti car. 'It had gone out of control, there was bound to be a backlash,' says senior Lucknow-based journalist Sharat Pradhan.

The Muzaffarnagar riots only exposed the fault lines further. In December 2013, I visited Muzaffarnagar along with an NGO to help in the relief and rehabilitation efforts. Many of the riot displaced were still living in tents in the bitter winter cold, too frightened to go back to their homes. Religious organizations and local madrasas had more or less taken over the relief camp, providing blankets and firewood. I had brought cricket kits for the children and we played a match. Adolescents who had seen their parents attacked or killed joined the game with an eager gaiety and free-spiritedness that brought tears to my eyes. 'I think this is the first time I have seen the children smile in weeks,' one of the NGO activists told me.

Just a week later, Mulayam Singh, who had not even visited Muzaffarnagar once since the riots broke out, termed those in the relief camps as 'agents of the Opposition parties'. Another SP leader said, 'Those in the relief camps are like professional beggars found in every community.'

A month later, even as the riot victims were still battling compensation claims and slow-moving FIRs, the Yadav clan held their traditional Saifai Mahotsav in their village. Images of film stars dancing in front of the ruling Yadavs were contrasted with those who were spending their nights in camps in an unforgiving UP winter. The news outrage industry was having a field day. I remember questioning Shivpal Yadav on the 9 p.m. news on the need for a grand celebration in Saifai so soon after the riots. He shouted at me, and then walked out. It was another dramatic 'TV moment' that only mirrored the moral and political decline of the Akhilesh government.

Akhilesh had clearly betrayed the mandate of 2012. Everywhere I travelled in UP during the elections, one encountered an overwhelming sense of frustration. '*Akhilesh sarkar nahi chala sakte*' (Akhilesh can't run the government), was a familiar cry of anguish. It was a sullen anger waiting for an outlet to gush out. Modi provided the voter that escape route—he promised them deliverance from doom and gloom. The discredited Yadavs versus Modi's promise of 'hope'—it was a no-contest. I remember meeting a young Yadav student leader in Meerut who said he was voting for Modi. 'Akhilesh has given us a laptop, but no bijli,' he told me. '*Modi aayenge, bijli layenge!*' (Modi will bring electricity.) UP's youth were ready to cross the caste Rubicon. If even the Yadavs were looking to vote for Modi, then UP's political earth was truly beginning to shake.

~

The erosion in support for Akhilesh's government was good news for Amit Shah. His UP strategy was working perfectly. SP down and out, Mayawati making no real headway, Rahul missing in action and his party in disarray—Shah's political rehabilitation seemed complete. Well, almost.

In the middle of November, while the country was mourning the retirement of Sachin Tendulkar, 'Snoopgate' hit the headlines. A scandal had broken out, with two websites, Cobrapost.com and Gulail.com, releasing audio tapes with telephone conversations that purportedly had Shah directing the illegal surveillance of a young woman at the behest of his 'saheb'. I was in Mumbai tracking the Sachin mania when the story broke. That evening, I got a call from Shah. His voice was as soft as ever but the message was less comfiting:

'Yeh kya headline story aap chala rahe ho. Thoda zara dekh lo na, hata do usko' (What is this story you are running, please do see and remove it).

I was used to politicians occasionally ringing up, asking for negative stories to be edited out. My standard approach was to say I didn't know what was airing on the channel and that I wasn't in the studio. The hope was always that the politician would forget about it and the sheer pace of a 24/7 news wheel would prevent anyone from trying to put pressure to censor content. Shah, though, seemed pretty insistent, but I wasn't going to be bullied easily. 'Don't worry, sir, you give your version too, story *ko to chalana padega* [I have to run the story],' I said, while asking our news team to be careful with the facts.

By next morning, the story had acquired a momentum of its own. The Congress had found a new stick with which to beat the Shah–Modi duo, this time one that they were hopeful would actually land a decisive political blow. The party's women MPs were summoned to Delhi by Rahul Gandhi's office and asked to hold a special press conference. Women's organizations were particularly irate and demanded Modi's resignation and Shah's prosecution. 'Why doesn't Amit Shah tell us who the "saheb" is on whose behalf he was snooping?' asked the National Commission for Women chairperson, Mamata Sharma. The Central government promised to appoint a judicial inquiry but didn't seem to make much progress. 'No judge was willing to take up a politically sensitive case,' a senior minister told me.

Worried about the fallout, the Shah–Modi duo acted swiftly. The Gujarat government appointed its own inquiry commission to look into the case. The young woman's father approached the Supreme Court and asked the court to restrain the Centre from ordering a parallel inquiry. The father even issued a statement, interestingly released from the BJP office, saying that it was he who had asked for security for his daughter. Whether that 'security' included an hourly update of her movements, including who she was having lunch with, is anybody's guess. The woman in question and her husband were reportedly flown out of Ahmedabad to Paris. When our reporter visited the family's flat in Ahmedabad, he found no one there. Later, a BJP source admitted to me, 'We were a little worried initially and had to go into damage control because this issue could have really blown up in our face.'

This wasn't the first I had heard of Snoopgate. In 2012, a senior police officer from Gujarat, Kuldeep Sharma, had met me for breakfast, claiming he had information that would gravely damage Modi and Shah. 'They have been illegally snooping on a woman,' he said. I asked for proof; he promised to get back.

Sharma was a decorated police officer who had now fallen foul of the Shah–Modi duo. He had approved the Sohrabuddin fake encounter report and had been also investigating a cooperative bank fraud in which Shah was allegedly involved. The Modi government hit back, he says, by putting his brother Pradeep Sharma, an IAS officer, in jail. Pradeep had been seen in the company of the woman who was now the subject of the Snoopgate controversy. Modi had reportedly met the woman who was a landscape architect, along with the IAS officer, while inaugurating a hill garden project in Bhuj in 2005 when Pradeep Sharma was district collector there. In his affidavit before the Supreme Court, Sharma claimed that Modi was besotted with the woman and had asked the home department to keep a tab on her. Gujarat government sources claimed that it was Pradeep Sharma who was actually in love with the woman. 'This is a complicated story, but *daal mein zaroor kuch kaala hai*,' was the response of a senior Gujarat bureaucrat when I had casually mentioned my conversation with Sharma. Now, the audio tapes had revived the story.

That the Snoopgate 'revelations' were met with some scepticism perhaps reflected the credibility crisis afflicting the ruling UPA government. In normal times, the audio tapes would have merited a detailed investigation, with tough questions being asked. But in the build-up to the elections, it was perceived as yet another 'hit job' on Modi and his man Friday. Had the Snoopgate story broken a year or two earlier, it might have resonated more strongly. The UPA had got its timing wrong—yet again.

As 2013 was winding down, Narendra Modi and Amit Shah were in a celebratory mood. Snoopgate hadn't taken off. The CNN-IBN election tracker was showing the BJP making steady progress and well ahead of the Congress nationwide. Modi's rallies were attracting a huge response, and the key states of UP and Bihar both seemed to be in control. Mission 272-plus was no longer unattainable.

But politics in India always has a surprise around the corner. Just as Shah and Modi were preparing to rejoice at a turnaround 2013, a new X factor emerged. Another pretender ready to challenge the front runners burst onto the scene. Arvind Kejriwal and his Aam Aadmi Party had just taken Delhi by storm. The battle for 2014 wasn't over just yet.

6

Kings, Queens and X Factors

It was a delightful Delhi winter afternoon in early January 2014, a light sun offering just the right dose of warmth. Senior BJP leader Arun Jaitley was holding his annual lunch at his 9, Ashoka Road residence, just next to the party office. The party's top leadership had gathered at the high table—food seemed to unite Advani, Jaitley, Sushma and Rajnath as they prepared for the start of the big election year. The spread was classic north Indian and there were even cooks flown in from Amritsar by a private caterer for the occasion. From *kulcha chole* to *bheja* masala to butter chicken, this was a lunch designed to break the cholesterol barrier.

The mood was upbeat with the party having done well in the December assembly elections in four states. Some BJP leaders were already being asked what portfolios they wanted in the next government at the Centre. I said to the BJP chief spokesperson Ravi Shankar Prasad that he could well be the next information and broadcasting minister once again. 'Why, you don't want me to get a promotion!' he laughed. I suggested he have another *kesar kulfi* for good luck.

The star attraction, though, was seated at one of the side tables. Amit Shah was back from Lucknow and was surrounded by journalists hanging on to his every word. Only, the talk wasn't so much about his UP adventure as it was about the newest sensation on the political stage. Arvind Kejriwal's AAP party had made a Sourav Ganguly-like debut by forming a government in Delhi just a few weeks earlier.

The AAP leader was splashed all over the media. He was CNN-IBN's Politician of the Year; the *Times of India* and *India Today* had chosen him as their Newsmaker of the Year. 'You media people have got carried away by Kejriwal, you think he is the only politician who has a simple lifestyle. Many of us also live simply, only we don't make a song and dance of it,' said Shah, polishing off the chole on his plate.

Since CNN-IBN had been one of the channels to honour Kejriwal, Shah turned to me with a smile. 'I believe you are getting an AAP ticket from South Mumbai to contest the general elections? If you do, I promise we will not get Narendrabhai to campaign against you!' I shot back, 'Amitbhai, I don't want to contest on an AAP ticket and lose. *Wave toh BJP ki hai.* If you give me a BJP ticket, I will be happy to contest!' The response was just as swift. '*Agar aapko BJP ki ticket milti hai, to main uska virodh karoonga!*' (If you get a BJP ticket, I will oppose it.) It was all light-humoured. We all had a good laugh.

As we prepared to leave, Shah called me to one side. 'Tell me, Rajdeepji, what is your honest feedback from the ground on AAP?' My view was that the AAP was a Delhi phenomenon whose success was unlikely to extend beyond the national capital. 'They don't have the organization to replicate their Delhi model elsewhere,' I said to Amit Shah. I even tried to console him with the figures of our election tracker which showed that almost 50 per cent of those who had voted for AAP in the Delhi election had said they would back Modi as prime minister in a general election.

Shah, however, appeared rather concerned. '*Nahi, hum unko lightly nahi le sakte. Desh ke sabhi urban areas mein unki popularity kaafi badh rahi hai. UP mein bhi log unke baare mein baat kar rahe hain*' (We cannot take them lightly, their popularity is rising across urban India. Even in UP, people are talking about them).

The BJP's treasurer Piyush Goyal had commissioned the leading global market research and polling agency, Penn Schoen Berland, to do a nationwide survey ahead of the December 2013 assembly elections. The survey showed that the BJP was well ahead of the Congress and was crossing 200 seats on its own. It confirmed that corruption and inflation were the dominant issues and that Modi's popularity was actually twenty points more than that of the BJP. But it also showed that there had been a surge of support for the AAP after its Delhi election success. Much of the gain was at the expense of the Congress, but the AAP was turning out to be an emerging third force.

From Shah's demeanour, it was obvious that Kejriwal's rise was troubling the BJP's strategists. Kejriwal had almost wiped Modi off the front pages, but even more importantly, had become a talking point amongst the youth and the urban middle class, the core target groups of the BJP's 'Modi for PM' campaign. A dark, short, slightly built moustachioed Hissar-born man who till a year ago had been seen as little more than a political gadfly was now threatening to take on the BJP's Goliath. It was lightweight versus super heavyweight, but Kejriwal had made a career out of punching above his weight.

~

I first met Kejriwal around 2003. He was then an IRS officer who had taken a sabbatical to start an NGO, Parivartan, which was involved in the RTI campaign. We were addressing a seminar together in Lucknow and I found him totally committed to the cause, with a vast knowledge on the subject. 'The media must partner us in spreading the RTI message,' he told me then. I guess he was always keenly aware of media power, but little did I foresee that the bright, energetic IITian in a white shirt, black trousers and chappals would one day become a national figure. Not even when he won a Magsaysay in 2006 for his RTI work.

We kept in touch—NGOs are a valuable source of stories. In February 2011, Kejriwal came to us with another story idea, this time along with IPS officer Dr Kiran Bedi. The duo were offering to be part of our citizen journalism show on CNN-IBN where we focused on corruption that affected people's daily lives. 'We are starting a signature campaign to push for a Jan Lok Pal and need your support,' said Kejriwal. We readily agreed to shoot a story with Kejriwal and Dr Bedi pitching for an anti-corruption ombudsman. But I had a note of caution. 'Please remember, television is a visual medium. Signature campaigns may not be effective on TV unless backed up by a story that catches the eye.'

Dr Bedi said they had just come back from Mumbai and noted social activist Anna Hazare had agreed to fast outside the Maharashtra assembly for the cause of a Lok Pal. 'You can interview Anna too,' she suggested helpfully.

That's when I offered a final piece of gratuitous advice, as editors are often prone to do. Tahrir Square had just happened in Egypt and the sight of thousands of citizens marching on Cairo's streets had captured global eyeballs. 'Let me be honest, Arvind and Kiranji. If you really want people to sit up and notice your Lok Pal campaign, you need to create your own Tahrir Square-like moment here in India. Only then will the system awaken! And if you want the national TV channels to focus on your cause, then bring Anna to Delhi. In Mumbai, it will remain a local story.'

Little did I know then that a casual conversation over a television programme would transform into a volcanic nationwide eruption over corruption just a few months later. Forget signature campaigns, this was about to become the biggest story of 2011.

If Anna Hazare became the face of the Lok Pal movement, Kejriwal became its heartbeat. He planned, organized and micromanaged the entire campaign, tirelessly working eighteen hours a day to ensure its success. 'I am Anna's Hanuman,' is how he described himself. Once, sitting with Anna at Maharashtra Sadan, I asked him about his equation with Kejriwal. '*Arre, main toh ek chote gaon ka fakir hoon, Arvind jaanta hai ki bade shahar mein kya karna chahiye*' (I am a fakir from a small village, Arvind knows what you need to do in the big city).

The IITian and the Gandhian; the tech-savvy mobilizer and the crowd-pulling ascetic; the urban activist and a rural folk hero—Kejriwal and Anna forged a unique partnership that, by August 2011, had the mighty Indian state bending before it. Ironically, a little over a year later, the duo had parted ways. Those who know Anna and Kejriwal were not surprised. Anna was a nomad with his roots in rural Maharashtra; he often moved from one agitation to another. He relished the national limelight for a while but eventually was more comfortable in his home environment in Ralegan Siddhi. He may have been perceived as anti-politician, but truthfully, he had friends in all political parties.

Kejriwal, by contrast, was the archetypal angry young rebel, looking for a cause. There was a single-minded, almost manic, determination that seemed to guide his moves. '*Unme ek desh ke liye kuch karne ka paagalpan hai* [He is obsessed with doing something for the country], which is his strength and his weakness,' is how an admirer described Kejriwal to me. An old-time NGO associate, though, insisted that a highly ambitious Kejriwal had a habit of using people and then discarding them. 'Anna is only a stepping stone in Arvind's own journey,' is how he described the relationship. My own sense was that Kejriwal and Anna were both headstrong individuals—a clash was inevitable once the original fervour of the Lok Pal movement died down.

Salman Khurshid, the former Union minister who negotiated with Team Anna during the Lok Pal movement, says the differences in the team were apparent right from the beginning. 'You spoke to Kiran Bedi and she would say one thing; you spoke to Arvind, he would say something else. And rarely did they have a nice word to say about each other,' he claims.

In July 2012, the government had begun backchannel talks with Anna through friendly politicians and businessmen in Pune. Khurshid met Anna and convinced him that the government would support the Lok Pal in Parliament. 'He even agreed to campaign for the Congress as part of the deal,' says Khurshid. A letter was drafted by the prime minister's office to thank Anna and put a stamp on the agreement. But then in a last-minute twist, the letter meant for Anna was dispatched to Kejriwal's residence by mistake. Or so the government claimed. Kejriwal was furious. He had been taking on the Congress and here was Anna striking a deal with them. Anna was embarrassed as well. He apparently called up Kejriwal that evening, saying, 'We must teach the Congress a lesson, they are practising the politics of divide and rule!'

Anna decided to go on another fast, this time calling for an FIR to be registered against fifteen UPA ministers. On day nine of the fast, he made a public appeal to Kejriwal to form a political party. Kejriwal, who had realized that the politics of fasts and dharnas was subject to diminishing returns, was excited at the prospect. Two days later, Anna backed out of the proposal, leading to complete confusion in the ranks. 'We had made all the plans and then Anna ditched us,' is how one Kejriwal aide described it.

Why did Anna not eventually support Kejriwal's political party? My sense is that Kejriwal was itching to change the scope of his movement and coerced Anna initially into endorsing the idea of a political party. Anna relished the attention being showered on him but he was clever enough to know that he derived his power from staying away from formal politics. Kejriwal, though, was always a man in a tearing hurry.

A few weeks later, Kejriwal decided to gherao the homes of Sonia Gandhi and Nitin Gadkari, alleging a Congress–BJP collusion in the coal scam. 'But when we went to seek Dr Bedi's support, she refused to endorse the move to protest at the BJP president's house. She wanted us to only target the Congress,' Kejriwal later told me. Bedi countered, 'The movement was losing focus. We could not equate the Congress and the BJP all the time.' A break was now inevitable in the original Team Anna.

On 24 November 2012, the Aam Aadmi Party was formed by Team Kejriwal. Anna decided to keep out, as did Dr Bedi. A fledgling party created without their mascot Anna and with limited resources, Kejriwal's political experiment was given hardly any chance of succeeding by people. I was among the sceptics. When my friend and political scientist Yogendra Yadav, who used to do our election programming at CNN-IBN, told me of his decision to join the new party, I gently suggested he might be making a big mistake. 'Politics is a different cup of tea, Yogendra, this won't work. Why do you want to give up the studio for the street?' I asked. The next twelve months would prove all of us sceptics very wrong.

~

The spectacular rise of the AAP from neophyte party to the ruling power in Delhi rewrote all the rules of electoral politics. Instant success in politics is rare. N.T. Rama Rao's Telugu Desam won its debut election in 1983 riding on the cinematic charisma of their leader and a strong regional appeal; the Assam Gana Parishad also won its first election in 1985, but it was an extension of a six-year-long popular students' agitation.

AAP, on the other hand, did not have a film legend to lead it, no long history of agitational politics, limited funding and no strong organizational base. What it did have, though, was the infectious energy and ideas of a young, highly motivated team. And yes, it had an issue which felt urgent at the time—public anger against political corruption.

Kejriwal crafted his political strategy for Delhi brilliantly. The symbolism of the aam aadmi in a Gandhi topi with a *jhadu* (broom) in hand taking on Delhi's entrenched VIP culture was too powerful to ignore. 'I wanted the man on the street to identify with us. The Gandhi topi which we had used during the Anna movement and a jhadu gave us that identity,' he told me later.

I visited the AAP headquarters once and was struck by how young and enthusiastic everyone was. It felt to me that the spirit of idealism and voluntarism, which seemed to have disappeared from politics, had been revived here. A merchant banker who had quit his job to join the AAP told me, 'When I was making money at the bank, I didn't really know who I was making it for. Now, when I am collecting funds for AAP, I know I am involved in nation building.'

The AAP's tactics were almost guerrilla-like, a 'hit-and-run' politics designed to create a constant made-for-TV drama. I remember when Manish Sisodia, Kejriwal's man Friday and a former journalist, came to see us seeking media support for their campaign against inflated power bills. 'Arvindji will be going on a fast on the issue, please do cover it well,' he requested. I must confess a certain weariness had developed over Kejriwal's perpetual dharna politics, and the newsroom wasn't too excited.

The dharna was on a Sunday, usually a slow news day. Kejriwal had most likely chosen the day for this very reason. But he wasn't going to make this a routine news event. He asked the gathered crowds to burn their electricity bills and then climbed up an electricity pole himself. Pandemonium broke out, the police rushed in, water cannons had to be used. Kejriwal had got his breaking news TV moment .

Right through 2012–13, there were several such moments when Kejriwal simply outsmarted his more experienced political rivals. When the municipal authorities tore down AAP posters and banners, he got auto rickshaws to carry his political message or volunteers to hold up banners at traffic signals and flyovers. When the Delhi gang rape in December 2012 led to street protests, Kejriwal was the first politician to join the protestors and call for the Delhi police commissioner's removal. The AAP got 10 lakh citizen letters protesting the inflated power and water bills, and handed them over to chief minister Sheila Dikshit. Kejriwal set the agenda; the national parties were forced to follow in his wake.

The aim was always to create the kind of news which would excite the national media and keep the AAP visible at all times. An SMS joke ran as follows: The Congress and BJP tell Kejriwal, 'We have money, muscle, men, what do you have?' Kejriwal replies, *'Mere paas media hai!'* (I have the media with me.)

A good example of how the party operated was the AAP 'exposé' on Robert Vadra, Sonia Gandhi's son-in-law. An *Economic Times* report had mentioned Vadra's land deals in 2011 but the story had been quickly buried. An investigative journalist had taken the documents to a senior BJP leader, asking him to take it up in Parliament. But the documents never saw the light of day. Tired of waiting, the journalist took the papers to Kejriwal and lawyer-activist Prashant Bhushan. They held a press conference almost right away and got mileage across the media. A few weeks later, in an attempt to appear even-handed, they did another 'exposé', this time on Gadkari's alleged links with an irrigation scam.

Kejriwal was conscious of using the media as an ally. Like Modi, Kejriwal was at ease in front of a camera and never short of a strong sound bite. Some of the AAP leader's closest advisers were journalists. One of my own colleagues, Ashutosh, who edited our Hindi channel IBN 7, joined AAP. 'He is the cleverest politician since Mahatma Gandhi!' claimed Ashutosh, sounding like a complete fanboy.

Ashutosh eventually contested the Lok Sabha elections on an AAP ticket, one of quite a few journalists to take the bait. Kejriwal had, as Amit Shah had suggested at Jaitley's lunch, once offered me the lure of a ticket. 'We need good people in politics, you must join us,' he said earnestly. This was not the first time a political party had suggested that I make the switch. My response each time was much the same. 'Thank you, but no thank you. Happy to observe politics from a distance.' I loved journalism too much to lose my independence. Besides, I didn't have the thick skin that *netagiri* required and was far from endorsing the Kejriwal brand of non-stop agitational politics.

Despite the rising support for his party, I never did believe Kejriwal would form the next government in Delhi. The day before the Delhi assembly election results, I was moderating a session at the *Hindustan Times* Leadership Summit with Pakistan cricket captain-turned-politician, Imran Khan. Before we went on stage, I told Imran that he was a bit like the Arvind Kejriwal of Pakistan. 'How come?' he asked. 'Well, you both have a huge fan base among the young, are very popular on TV and the social media, but you both would probably do better in cyberspace than at the ballot box!' Imran was only faintly amused.

The next day, I was proven wrong. Kejriwal won twenty-eight

of the seventy seats in the Delhi assembly while the Congress was decimated with just eight seats and the BJP fell short of a majority with thirty-two seats. Kejriwal held the balance of power. In an interview on 10 December 2013, the day after the results, he told me he would never take Congress support to form a government. A little over a fortnight later, he appeared to conveniently change his mind.

The Congress decision to support Kejriwal was reportedly orchestrated by Rahul Gandhi. Apparently, Rahul was impressed with Kejriwal's style of politics based on youth power and voluntarism. Maybe he liked the idea of an NGO activist transforming himself into an idealistic politician. Or maybe, as some Congressmen suggested to me, he saw Kejriwal as a potential ally in the future battle against a Modi-led BJP.

Arvind Kejriwal was sworn in as Delhi's chief minister on 28 December before a rapturous crowd at the Ramlila Maidan. He spoke with great passion, as always. 'If 1.5 crore Delhiites can get together, we can root out corruption. Let us swear we will never take or receive a bribe.' He even sang songs that had the audience cheering him along. For those few hours at least, it appeared that Narendra Modi was not the only magnetic politician who could connect with the masses. He now had real competition. But Kejriwal would soon learn that there is a big difference between being a populist streetfighter and occupying a seat of responsibility.

~

From a newsman's perspective, there is only one word to describe the forty-nine days Kejriwal was in power in Delhi—chaotic. Not a single day passed without Kejriwal or some member of the AAP party giving us a news break. For a while it seemed that tracking Kejriwal had become a media obsession. In one of our Sunday phone conversations, Modi seemed to lose his poise, *'Tumhare Dilli media ko Kejriwal ke aage kuch dikhta hai ya nahi. Baaki chief ministers ko tum nahi dikhate aur Kejriwal ko tumne national leader bana diya!'* (Your Delhi media does not seem to see anything beyond Kejriwal.

You don't show any other chief minister and you have made Kejriwal a national leader). Clearly, in the run-up to the general elections, the AAP leader was getting under the skin of his bigger rivals.

Modi, though, had a point. My defence was the 'tyranny of distance'. The phrase comes from the landmark Australian book (with the same title) by historian Geoffrey Blainey which argued how Australia's geographical remoteness had shaped its history. Geographical proximities, sadly, define news priorities in the so-called 'national' Indian media. Since Kejriwal was operating in and around Delhi within a few kilometres of most TV studio headquarters (Noida near Delhi has the highest media density in India), he was easily accessible. It was so much easier to park an OB van outside the Delhi secretariat than in the heart of Bastar or Kokrajhar.

It's a dilemma I have wrestled with for years. Most news channels have dozens of reporters in Delhi but just one for the entire seven states of the north-east. In states like Jharkhand and Chhattisgarh, we rely on a stringer network. Naturally, news becomes metro-centric, with vast areas of the country going uncovered. On any given day, stories from Delhi occupy more than half the news space. We cover Ranchi when Dhoni reaches home; only a major Naxal attack takes us to a Raipur. The business model of modern television is our lamentable excuse. We are simply not willing to invest in building a strong national network.

The media-savvy Kejriwal knew this and exploited the situation to the hilt. Everything he said or did became a live news event. When he attempted a Janata Durbar (public hearing), there was a near stampede. When he decided to provide free water and subsidized power to specific income groups, it set off a raging debate. When he invited people to 'sting' government officials, it generated even more controversy. And when a minister in his government, Somnath Bharti, went on a midnight raid at the homes of African nationals accused of drug and sex trafficking, he was accused of 'racism'.

The first major turning point was Kejriwal's decision to go on a dharna at Rajpath just outside the Union home ministry, demanding the suspension of five Delhi police officers. At a thirty-two-hour street protest at the venue where the Republic Day parade was to take place in a few days, Kejriwal appeared less like a chief minister and more like a self-styled anarchist. 'Yes, I am an anarchist,' he told his supporters, urging them to reach Rajpath. It was an ill-considered remark. For once, his attempt at clever political choreography had let him down. With the images of an elected government clashing with its own police on the streets splashing across the media, Kejriwal's confrontational politics now signalled political immaturity. Former judge Santosh Hegde termed it 'pure and simple arrogance of power'.

Slowly, the goodwill began to dissipate and middle-class disenchantment with the AAP leader set in. The television studio, which had once been his ally, became a double-edged sword, subjecting his government to an almost unprecedented scrutiny. If the coverage of the AAP during the assembly election campaign bordered on the euphoric, it was now openly hostile in some news networks. 'Hashtag aggression'—an euphemism for agenda-driven 'supari' journalism—saw Kejriwal being targeted with tags like #AAPAnarchy, #AAPDrama, #AAPIntolerant, #AAPMobocracy on Twitter. Kejriwal was convinced that the 'corporate' media under Modi's instructions was behind the campaign. When we did a critical story around the Rajpath dharna, I got a call from one of Kejriwal's aides who said, 'Looks like Modi has bought you guys too!' Paranoia had now set in.

The BJP was delighted that Kejriwal had pressed the self-destruct button. Party leaders like Subramanian Swamy were 'assigned' to find anything they could to undermine the AAP leader's credibility. 'I will expose this corrupt guy,' Swamy told me with relish. He had apparently been promised a Lok Sabha ticket for his efforts. The promise would not be met. Nor would Kejriwal's 'corruption' be revealed.

The underclass in the slums and jhuggis who had voted for AAP were still firmly with Kejriwal. I remember a street vendor telling me that for the first time the constables were scared of taking hafta for fear of being 'stung'. But the middle class and the opinion makers who had been swayed by AAP's rhetoric were now losing faith. It was only a matter of time before AAP scripted its own obituary.

I was in Mumbai attending an award function on Valentine's Day morning when the rumours began to swirl that Kejriwal was about to resign because the Opposition in the Delhi assembly wasn't going to support his Jan Lokpal bill. My hosts asked me why I wasn't in the studio to anchor the impending breaking news. I rather cynically replied, 'Don't worry, Kejriwal won't resign in the morning, he will only step down, if he does, in prime time!'

Sure enough, around 6 p.m., the story began to gather momentum. A meeting of the AAP's political affairs core group had been called to take a decision on whether to step out of the government. I was still in Mumbai and rang up Yogendra Yadav to find out more. 'I am just entering the committee meeting. No decision has been taken yet, but I think we should go back to our voters and seek another referendum on the road ahead,' he said. The idea of a 'referendum' was a unique AAP concept, designed to give a sense that the party was practising 'true democracy' by constantly talking to the citizens.

I was, as always, more cynical. 'Well, whatever you do, I don't see the need to resign when you have been in power for just a few weeks. You need to prove yourself to the people of Delhi still,' I said, more worried that a sudden resignation would mean a long evening in the studio.

Yogendra seemed in agreement. 'Yes, I agree with you. Best not to do anything in haste. That is exactly what I intend to tell Arvind.' A few minutes later, our correspondent who was covering the AAP wanted to flash the news. 'Sir, my sources inside AAP tell me that Arvind has already resigned.' I told her of my conversation with Yogendra and how the issue was still not decided. My correspondent was insistent. She would be proven right. An hour later, close to 8 p.m., Kejriwal confirmed his resignation. It was prime time on TV!

I later learnt that Kejriwal came to the party meeting and, without consulting his colleagues, went ahead and resigned before the waiting media. 'This lack of consultation bothered some of us. The high command culture had entered AAP too, where decisions were taken by an individual on a whim,' says one senior AAP member. Kejriwal denies this, insisting that the party had been taken into confidence. 'We all thought that the Jan Lokpal was part of our core belief system. We should not be sticking to a chair if we could not get it passed. It was a matter of principle for us,' he later claimed to me.

I was less sure of the principle involved in resigning over a legislation which needed oversight from the Central government. It seemed to me that Kejriwal, after just seven weeks in power, was looking for an exit strategy. The power discoms were threatening a blackout in the summer and the AAP would have to bear the brunt of public anger. A snap poll was perhaps the best way out.

Though he denies it, my view (with which many others would concur) is that Kejriwal was aware the countdown had begun for the general elections, and he wanted to offer himself as a national alternative. Carried away by his Delhi success, his impetuosity got the better of him. The AAP, with no national organization, suddenly announced it would contest more than 400 seats. 'We thought this was the best time to make an impact. Even if we could get thirty to forty seats, we could become the third largest party in the country,' a Kejriwal aide told me. The resignation was to prove a big blunder, driven as much by hubris as naivety.

Weeks later, Kejriwal would admit to me in an interview that resigning as Delhi chief minister was a 'mistake', but he called it a failure to communicate to the people the reasons for the resignation. Maybe he had slowly realized that politics is a game of patience. Maybe he had finally recognized the changing public mood. I certainly could sense it. We were recording an election programme in Delhi's Chandni Chowk, and in a number of middle-class colonies, the typical response we got was, 'Kejriwal, arre voh toh bhagoda hai!' (Kejriwal is a politician who runs away.)

I continue to believe that if Kejriwal had remained in office, focusing the energies of his administration into making Delhi a corruption-free city, he would have forged an administrative track record for his party and a possible 'Delhi model of governance' to offer to a future electorate, just as in this election Modi had so successfully held up his Gujarat model. Kejriwal's rise, like that of Modi, had been the direct fallout of the wave of public anger against the Congress-led UPA government. India was looking for leaders who could shake up the system and challenge the ruling establishment, but do it through effective governance, not just through rhetoric.

The AAP's abdication from governmental responsibility caused widespread disillusionment. The March election tracker we did showed a drastic fall in Kejriwal's popularity in Delhi and beyond. The poll also showed AAP would get less than ten seats in the general elections. Narendra Modi and Amit Shah could afford to breathe easily again. It was almost as if the fall of the AAP gave a fresh momentum to the NaMo wave. But there were others, just as powerful, who were still feeling the heat.

~

On 11 February, just three days before resigning, Kejriwal ordered FIRs to be filed against India's richest man Mukesh Ambani, the present and former petroleum ministers, Veerappa Moily and Murli Deora, and senior government officials, accusing them of wrongfully increasing natural gas prices in the country. In a press conference, which was carried live across the media, he claimed that the Centre's decision to raise gas prices had led to a windfall profit of Rs 54,000 crores for Reliance Industries Limited.

This was not the first time that Kejriwal had openly targeted the Ambanis. In late 2012, Kejriwal had addressed two press conferences accusing Mukesh Ambani of holding black money in Swiss bank accounts and artificially lowering production in its gas wells in the Krishna–Godavari basin to blackmail the government into raising gas prices.

A central figure in those press meets and in the attack on the Ambanis was Prashant Bhushan, a Supreme Court lawyer and senior member of the AAP. A fierce activist, Bhushan was a pugnacious lawyer, always itching for a fight. He was known to pick up seemingly unpopular causes. He had appeared in defence of Naxal sympathizers, Kashmiri separatists and anti-Narmada Dam activists. He had even been physically assaulted by fringe Hindu right-wing groups for his remarks calling for a plebiscite in Kashmir. He also seemed to have an almost pathological dislike for big business, which he was convinced was steeped in cronyism and corruption. It was Bhushan who had taken up the gas price issue against the Ambanis in a PIL that had been filed in the court. Now, wearing his AAP cap, Bhushan was preparing to convert the legal battle into a political war. 'The attack on the Ambanis was originally Prashant's idea,' claims a senior AAP member.

The move suited Kejriwal perfectly. Clearly eyeing the general elections, he was looking for a headline-grabbing issue that would position him as an alternative to both the Congress and the BJP. Kejriwal wanted to show that the Congress and the BJP were two sides of the same coin in the war on corruption. The Ambanis and gas prices became his entry point into the 2014 Lok Sabha battle. 'Why are Rahul Gandhi and Narendra Modi silent on gas prices?' asked Kejriwal.

When the allegations were first made in 2012, the Ambanis were rattled. All the channels which telecast the press conference live received legal notices for defamation. Many channels blacked out the AAP, fearing the wrath of Reliance. At Network 18, a meeting was called and we decided to refrain from going 'live' with a press conference or speech where personal allegations were being made, without getting a proper response from the other side.

We had reason to be cautious. In January 2012, Reliance Industries had made a large investment in Network 18. To be fair, Reliance had not interfered in the editorial content of the channels. They were truly, as our promoter Raghav Bahl kept reassuring us, being kept at arm's-length.

The build-up to campaign 2014 changed all that. In every public meeting, Kejriwal would single out the Ambanis as his prime target. Raghav asked me to look to my 'conscience' and exercise due diligence. 'Why do we need to show everything Kejriwal does in such detail?' he asked me. I promised to be careful in not giving disproportionate coverage, but made it clear that any boycott of Kejriwal in an election year was journalistically unsound.

In April, we did a Google+ Hangout with Kejriwal, one amongst several we had planned with top politicians. About an hour before the programme was to be recorded, we got a restraint notice from Reliance's lawyers, warning us not to go ahead with the interview. Our in-house legal team was flustered by the notice. 'Can we please drop the programme? Why do we need to pick a fight with Reliance?' they asked. I refused. 'Look, we are not taking a *panga* with anyone, just doing a professional job.' We had been promoting the interview since the morning on the channel and withdrawing it at the last moment was just not an option. Google backed our stand. 'Look, we are aware of the sensibilities involved here and will not allow anything to be aired that is potentially defamatory,' I assured our legal team. A few minutes before the programme went on air, I got another mail from the Reliance lawyers, urging us to back off. We went ahead and aired the programme that night but ensured we edited out any personal attacks.

A few days later, a well-networked banker friend called up from Mumbai. 'Mukeshbhai is very angry with you. Why are you guys giving this Kejriwal any airtime at all?' he asked. The unfriendly tone of the conversation surprised me. I had met Mukeshbhai on a few occasions in connection with an annual event, *Real Heroes*, which we did in partnership with Reliance. The event showcased stories of hope and courage shown by anonymous Indians and had become a big success. We had built a reasonable personal equation, or so I presumed. Whenever we met, he was always sharply insightful about India's problems, bubbling with ideas and spoke with an almost obsessive vision of 'Brand India' and how he wanted to contribute to the India growth story.

I tried to explain to my banker friend that we had done almost a dozen Google+ Hangouts with BJP and Congress politicians. Kejriwal was just one more voice. 'It's your call, Rajdeep, but be prepared for a rough time from Reliance from now on,' was the parting shot. Little did I know then that the moment the elections were over, Reliance would formally take over Network 18, a move that would eventually spur my resignation from the channels I had helped create.

The Ambanis' disquiet with Kejriwal may have been driven by the sharply accusatory nature of the AAP leader's campaign, but it was also symptomatic of a growing belief within corporate India that they were now under siege. In any social gathering, it was almost routine to hear an industrialist take off on the policies of the Manmohan Singh government. Jairam Ramesh, in his avatar as environment minister, was often singled out by the captains of industry. 'He is responsible for at least a 1 or 2 per cent dip in our GDP,' one of them told me. 'Because of him so many of our projects are stuck.'

Jairam was equally strident. 'There are three types of environment ministers. Those who just give a stamp to every project without even looking at it; those who are ATM ministers and want money for each approval; and those who implement the laws of the land. Business houses don't like me because I reminded them of their environment violations,' he told me in response to these accusations.

Jairam's successor as environment minister, Jayanthi Natarajan, proved equally controversial. If Jairam would strike down projects, Jayanthi was accused of sitting on files. Her detracto in the power corridors alleged that she was a 'rent-seeking' minister who had to be bribed for clearances, with her OSD (officer on special duty) Gayatri Devi being the supposed go-between (Modi in a campaign speech would later refer to a 'Jayanthi tax'). When I asked her for a response to the charges on a television programme, she had angrily dismissed it as 'a tissue of lies'.

On 21 December 2013, hours before Rahul Gandhi was to address a FICCI audience, Jayanthi was removed as the environment minister. Publicly, the fourth-generation Congresswoman from Tamil Nadu (her grandfather had been chief minister) kept silent on her removal. Privately, she was seething. Interestingly, Jayanthi had been close to Rajiv Gandhi. She had been in Sriperumbudur when the former prime minister was assassinated. But with Rahul, the equation was different. She was once pulled up by a Rahul aide and asked to change her Kanjivaram sari on a TV programme because it had a lotus symbol along the border!

Jairam and Jayanthi, though, were sideshows. Corporate India's greater disenchantment was with the prime minister himself. Manmohan Singh, after all, had always been much admired by India Inc. since his path-breaking budget of 1991. They had once been his biggest cheerleaders. Now, they wanted him out. And soon. 'Our financial bottom lines were bleeding and yet the government was happy to keep announcing large-scale subsidies. Manmohanomics was over, and we were dealing with Sonianomics,' said one corporate leader to me. Another lamented, 'Surely, when Pranab Mukherjee brought in the retrospective tax in the 2012 budget, the prime minister knew it would send the wrong signal to business. Yet, he just kept quiet.'

The retrospective tax, in particular, was seen to symbolize corporate India's discomfiture with the UPA government. It had been introduced in the 2012 budget to virtually force the UK-based telecom giant Vodafone to pay Rs 11,000 crore in tax for acquiring the India business of another telecom company, Hutchison, in 2007. The Supreme Court had ruled that Vodafone was not liable to pay the tax but now the government was seeking to amend tax laws retrospectively to bring Vodafone-like deals in the tax net. When an industry delegation met the prime minister to raise the issue, Dr Singh seemed helpless. 'I will try and speak to Pranabda and see what is possible,' was the weak assurance. Delayed land clearances, contentious tax amendments, FIRs against leading industrialists, high expenditure on social welfare programmes in a period of low growth—bombarded with such negatives, corporate India was desperately looking for their white knight. When Modi began speaking of less government, more governance, it was just what they wanted to hear. 'He speaks our language. Five more years of the UPA and the India story is finished,' is how a corporate leader explained his unstinted support for Modi.

Businessmen are usually careful in articulating their political preferences. At any post-budget show, the men in suits tend to give the finance minister eight or nine out of ten. But ahead of the elections, the reticence was slowly disappearing. At a closed-door meeting in Mumbai called by a prominent business leader to garner support for Modi in early 2014, there was virtually a full house.

The one industrialist who was seen to be firmly in the Modi camp was Gujarat-based entrepreneur Gautam Adani. Like Ambani, Adani, too, had been in the cross hairs of the AAP attack. AAP leaders had questioned Modi's proximity to Adani and accused the Gujarat chief minister of 'gifting' him land at the Mundra port site at well below market rates and by disregarding environment norms.

That Modi and Adani shared a 'special relationship' is beyond doubt. In the aftermath of the 2002 riots, when Modi was confronted by senior industry voices at a CII conference, Adani had stood by him and set up a parallel body of Gujarati businessmen, 'The Resurgent Group of Gujarat' (see chapter 1). News reports claimed that in the decade of Modi's rule in Gujarat, Adani's assets had grown twelve-fold to over Rs 35,000 crore, with interests in ports, power, coal and edible oil. At Adani's son's marriage, Modi had attended almost all the ceremonies, including flying down to Goa for the celebrations.

While the Ambanis had responded with legal notices, the Adanis had stayed mostly silent. 'Gautambhai doesn't want to get into a blame game with anyone,' is what I was told. Which is why I was a little surprised when in April 2014, while the campaign was picking up steam, I got a call from a London-based businessman that Gautambhai was keen to do an interview. The reason for his anxiety was obvious. Now, it was no longer Kejriwal pointing fingers; even Congress leader Rahul Gandhi was attacking the Modi–Adani 'nexus' on land deals.

'Can you fly down to Ahmedabad urgently tomorrow? We want to show you our port and then do an interview,' I was told. I said it would not be possible since I was shooting elsewhere. I sent our national bureau chief, Bhupendra Chaubey, instead. Adani vigorously defended himself in the interview, saying he had got a clean chit from the courts and had received no special favours from Modi; he insisted that he was charging the BJP's prime ministerial candidate 'commercial rates' for use of the aircraft. 'I am not the BJP's or Modiji's ATM machine—I have friends in all parties,' said Gautambhai, in his heavily Gujarati-accented Hindi.

We thought we had an exclusive interview. As it turned out, Gautambhai gave nearly half a dozen interviews over the next forty-eight hours. For a self-confessed low-profile individual, the PR overdrive betrayed his anxiety at being caught in the midst of a political battle.

What is true, though, is that like all upwardly mobile business leaders, Gautambhai had struck friendships with politicians from different parties. He kept a steady equation with Congress leaders in Gujarat and beyond (a photograph of him with Robert Vadra at the Mundra port site also made it to the papers). Perhaps his closest friend in politics was NCP leader and UPA minister, Sharad Pawar. When a journalist friend went to interview Pawar once, he saw a relaxed Adani watching television with Pawar's family in the adjoining room. The two would often dine at each other's houses, and had reportedly even gone on a holiday together once. 'People seem to forget that Gautambhai has as many business interests in Maharashtra as he does in Gujarat,' an NCP leader told me. A senior Congressman from Maharashtra even claimed that the Adanis had ensured that Modi did not campaign aggressively or put up a tough candidate against Pawar's daughter Supriya or the NCP's high-profile minister Praful Patel.

Indeed, most corporates at election time prefer keeping their options open while funding political parties. In 2014, though, the balance of power had clearly shifted. No one wanted to divulge exact numbers, but one industrialist summed it up for me. 'If in 2009, we gave sixty paise to the Congress and forty paise to the BJP, this time, it's eighty paise to the BJP and twenty to the Congress.' The 2014 election was perhaps the first time in Indian electoral history that the Opposition was getting more funding than the ruling party.

When a businesswoman met Sonia Gandhi at the height of the 2014 campaign in April, the Congress president looked troubled. 'I don't think something like this has ever happened to the Congress party in any election,' she said. 'We are struggling to raise money.'

Motilal Vora, the octogenarian treasurer of the Congress party, was getting desperate. The Congress's cash cow state in 2009 had been Andhra Pradesh, but its main fundraiser Y.S. Rajasekhar Reddy was now dead. In Maharashtra, Prithviraj Chavan didn't have the rugged ability of his predecessors to get the state's powerful builder lobby to contribute to the party. Haryana and Karnataka were the only Congress-ruled states that could be tapped for funds. 'Even individual Congress leaders who had acquired large personal wealth weren't willing to help,' claims one Congress office-bearer, adding, 'the public was knocking us for being corrupt, but even this so-called corrupt party was short of cash.'

In fact, one senior Congress minister who had contested several elections rang up Vora seeking funding for his campaign. 'But you are such a wealthy man, why do you need money?' the beleaguered treasurer asked. 'Well, every rupee counts!' was the unashamed answer.

Ahmed Patel, who had handled the party's funding for years, then stepped in. He rang up several top industrialists. One of them told him, 'Yes, sir, we will definitely give money, but you know how business is at the moment.' Another corporate leader who had felt unfairly drawn into a legal tangle by the CBI was more direct. 'When I needed you, no one helped me. Now, how can you expect me to bail you out?' One Congress MP jocularly remarked, 'Even those who wanted to help would see the opinion poll figures and rush back home with the money. No one wants to waste cash on losers!'

By contrast, a senior BJP leader was receiving so much money that bundles of 1000-rupee notes were lined up along the walls at his house. There was so much cash floating around for the BJP that not only did it fund several candidates, some of it was eventually returned to the party coffers. 'I had never seen anything like it. Not a single high net worth individual or corporate we contacted said no to us,' the leader told me later. It wasn't just the big corporates; even several small- and medium-size enterprises were willing to give the

BJP around Rs 10 to 20 crore each. Also, all corporates with large investments in Gujarat lined up firmly behind Modi. They included groups like the Ruias of Essar who had found themselves under the legal scanner in the 2G scam. Non-resident Indians, especially non-resident Gujaratis, were also willing to pump money into the BJP campaign.

Did the contrasting financial positions of the two main parties make a difference in the campaign? Yes, to some extent. Generally, parties like the Congress and the BJP have a 'graded' system— 'winnable' candidates are provided a sum of around Rs 2 crore from the party funds, while the next category gets Rs 1 crore. The balance amount is expected to be raised by the candidates, with Rs 5 to 10 crore being the average cost for fighting an election (in states like Andhra and Maharashtra, it can go up to Rs 15 to 20 crore, but is less in north and east India; while urban seats are more expensive than rural ones).

'We had to rely on our individual connections more than ever before to raise money,' a defeated Congress MP told me. In contrast, the BJP told their candidates that any fund crunch would be compensated by the party. They would also not have to spend a single paisa on any Modi campaign in their constituency—the leader had a sufficient war chest to manage his entire campaign blitz.

With the campaign stretching over several months—remember, Modi was on the road for almost nine months—the ready availability of cash meant that there was no let-up in the intensity of the BJP campaign. The Congress funding began to dry up as the campaign wore on. By the last stage, it had become a one-way street as the BJP campaign reached a crescendo and the Congress became practically invisible.

So, how much did the two main parties actually spend? When I put this question to the two party treasurers, they would not reveal any figure—Piyush Goyal of the BJP at least laughed at the figures I threw at him; Vora of the Congress just stared blankly at me. Election expenses remain notoriously opaque. Only a few business houses have set up official electoral trusts to give money by cheque. Most

of the election money is generated through cash-rich businesses like
real estate, liquor, stockbroking and mining.

At a rate of around Rs 8 to 10 crore per 'winnable' constituency
plus other campaign expenses, the BJP had raised anywhere between
Rs 4000 to 5000 crore—at least that's my hunch, though Goyal
insists it was much less. The Congress was probably a few thousand
crores behind in the race this time. Given the mood in the country,
the Congress would have almost certainly still lost badly. Money
talks—but it can't influence a wave election like that of 2014, it can
only provide additional momentum. A few years ago, a prominent
Congress politician from Andhra is believed to have spent more
than Rs 70 crore on a by-election and still lost! As one corporate
leader told me, 'We didn't decide this election, we only backed the
right horse!'

I got a sense of the mood in the business community when in
February I made a presentation on likely election scenarios to a
group of foreign investors in Mumbai, and placed a clear Modi win
as the top possibility. The prospect seemed to enthuse the gathering.
'If Modi wins, the India story lives,' said one of them effusively.

One of the investors, though, still seemed troubled. 'Please tell
me, is there any chance of another hung Parliament and a third-front
prime minister after the elections?' Mamata Banerjee had once again
announced her intention to forge a federal front of non-Congress,
non-BJP parties. And Jayalalithaa, too, had said she was in the prime
ministerial race. If there was a prospect more nightmarish than
Kejriwal for the business world, it was the revival of a khichdi sarkar.

~

Teen Deviyan is a 1965 Bollywood film where Dev Anand, the hero,
courts three women—Nanda, Simi Garewal and Kalpana. In early
2014, Lutyens' Delhi would joke of how the next prime minister
needed the support of at least two of three women leaders—Mamata,
Jayalalithaa and Mayawati—to form a government. All three were
expected to get between twenty and thirty seats, so any party or

pre-poll alliance that crossed 200 seats but was short of the 272-seat majority would need their support. 'Just think of it, the prime minister will go crazy having to deal with them!' a senior bureaucrat laughed.

Mamata, Jayalalithaa and Mayawati—women who have endured a brutally patriarchal world of Indian politics and have survived to play and to win. Scarred by their battles, what seems to unite them is a stern authoritarianism in their leadership styles, and being the centre of a personality cult that commands the reverence of their male cadres. The ladies are doughty, intolerant fighters, yet trapped in a way by the family honorifics of Didi, Amma and Behenji.

Of the troika, I know Mamata best. For some reason, Didi appeared to have a soft corner for me. She would call me over for tea, give me lengthy interviews and had offered me a Rajya Sabha seat, which I politely declined. She even cooked a Bengali meal for me once. The sight of the Bengal chief minister in the kitchen, her crumpled sari tied in a no-nonsense knot, sweat pouring from her brow, rushing between steaming pots of Bengali delicacies was, I must confess, more than a little disconcerting. The food—*macher jhol, aloo poshto* and *kosha mangsho*—was fit for a Durga Puja banquet. When we left that evening, she made a Trinamool leader (who was also mayor of Kolkata!), carry large packets of ice cream into the car. 'Give it to the children, they will like it,' she said. She wasn't an easy person to say no to!

And yet, she was mercurial and moody, appearing almost bipolar at times. She could be warm and caring (every Puja she sends me a kurta), but also ferocious and short-tempered. In 2012, she agreed to do a show with us in Kolkata's Town Hall on the completion of one year of the Trinamool Congress government. Our deputy editor at CNN-IBN, Sagarika Ghose, was anchoring the programme. When we began recording, Mamata's mood appeared to be cheery. Barely ten minutes into the show, her attitude swung dramatically. A student asked her about her handling of the Park Street rape. It was enough for Mamata to flip. 'You are a Maoist, this audience is full of Maoists,' she shouted in a manic manner and walked out, with Sagarika struggling to hold her back.

A year before, I had an even more bizarre experience when we chose Mamata as the CNN-IBN Politician of the Year for her stunning achievement in dismantling the left citadel in Bengal. Just a day before the function, Mamata rang me up to say that she would not attend. 'I will not share a stage with Anna Hazare,' she said emphatically. Anna had been chosen as the Indian of the Year for being the mascot of the anti-corruption movement. I pleaded with Mamata and promised her we would give away her award first so that she wouldn't have to encounter Anna. She relented.

The next evening, she entered the Taj Palace Durbar Hall with a large contingent of Trinamool MPs. She seemed happy at all the attention being showered on her. We had tried to keep Anna away from her in a room next to the hall but couldn't hold him there for long. The moment he entered and their paths crossed, Mamata blew a fuse. 'You have not kept your promise, Rajdeep—I am leaving,' she hollered. Dressed in my bandhgala, I ran after her right across the lobby of the five-star hotel, pleading with her to come back. Finally, as she was driving off in her blue Maruti, at the gate, I almost physically pulled her out. With a little help from Trinamool MP, Dinesh Trivedi, we escorted her back to the award ceremony. She received the award, gave a brief speech, smiled for the cameras and left. I don't think the Taj has ever seen a scene quite like that.

Ironically, in February 2014, Mamata and Anna addressed a press conference together where Anna promised to support the Trinamool leader in the general elections. 'She is an honest politician, I like her simplicity,' gushed Anna. 'Annaji is like a father figure to us,' Mamata said with equal feeling. Obviously, Taj Palace, December 2011, had been forgotten!

The 'alliance' between the 'simple woman' and the Gandhian lasted less than a month. A rally at Ramlila Maidan, hyped as Mamata's grand entry onto the national stage, was a flop show, attracting only a few thousand people. Anna himself stayed away, citing ill health. When I went to see him in Maharashtra Sadan, he claimed to be on a soup diet. A few minutes earlier, former army chief, General V.K. Singh, who had just joined the BJP, had met him. The buzz was that Singh had gently 'persuaded' Anna to keep away from the Mamata rally.

The fiasco with Anna virtually ended Mamata's 2014 dream of playing a greater role in Delhi. She, like many regional leaders, had been hoping to forge a post-election 'Federal Front', a coalition of non-Congress, non-BJP chief ministers. My own view is that Mamata, a shrewd politician, knew that a broader, national-level third front was always going to prove difficult. Her real concern was that the enemy number one—the left—was trying to cement a similar national alliance of its own. 'The left will be left out,' is how she once put it to me.

Mamata hated the left. It was a visceral hatred that stemmed from years of fighting a lonely battle as the Opposition in Bengal. She could do business with anyone but them. It appeared a limited political world view. She didn't really care beyond a point who became prime minister as long as the bhadralok of Kolkata's Alimuddin Street were kept at bay. 'You don't know, Rajdeepji, these leftists want to kill me,' she told me once.

To isolate the left further, Mamata even reached out to Tamil Nadu chief minister Jayalalithaa and spoke to her about future alignments. If Mamata was mercurial, then Jayalalithaa could be fire on ice. While Mamata would display her tantrums in public, Jayalalithaa maintained a steely demeanour at all official engagements. If Mamata was the quintessential streetfighter, Jayalalithaa was imperious in her style. 'She just had to look at you without saying a word and you would be intimidated,' is how a bureaucrat explained Jaya power to me once.

I had met Jayalalithaa once in Chennai, soon after her remarkable comeback win in Tamil Nadu in 2011. I had taken a Ruskin Bond book as a gift because I was told he was one of her favourite authors. She was polite and gracious, thanked me for the book, and then said, 'I will now have very little time to read. The DMK has left behind a mess, I will have to clean it up.' With her perfect convent-school

English accent, she sounded as though she meant every word. I didn't dare counter-question her.

In fact, taking on Jayalalithaa in any form could be a hazardous business. I experienced it first-hand when we got a criminal defamation notice from her office for our highly popular weekly comic programme, *The Week That Wasn't*. Stand-up comedians Cyrus Broacha and Kunal Vijayakar would every week lampoon political figures—Sonia, Rahul, Modi, Mamata. No one was spared (except Bal Thackeray because we feared the Shiv Sena would then attack our Mumbai office!).

Then we made the mistake of showing a Jayalalithaa-like character, with a fun gag on her wealth and relationship with one-time close friend Sasikala. It was all meant to be good-humoured, but Jayalalithaa clearly didn't see the funny side. We had a legal battle on our hands. I asked a Chennai-based lawyer to help. 'Whatever you do, never mess with Jayalalithaa,' was his friendly advice (incidentally, the case is still being fought in a Chennai court with our efforts at an out-of-court settlement not having succeeded).

It's a lesson many politicians and even well-wishers of the AIADMK leader have learnt over the years. Cho Ramaswamy, the satirist and editor, was among the few who had some access to Jayalalithaa. But when I visited him at the office of his magazine *Tughlaq* in February 2014, he claimed Jayalalithaa wasn't meeting him any longer. 'She is angry with me because I am supporting Modi for prime minister. She wants me to support her instead!' he said with an exasperated look.

Mamata had never claimed she wanted to be prime minister. Her heart and head were firmly located in the by-lanes of Kolkata. Not so Jayalalithaa. She did have a lurking ambition to be prime minister one day. Ironically, while Mamata spoke out openly against Modi, Jayalalithaa actually was one of the few state leaders who shared a special equation with the Gujarat chief minister. She had even attended his swearing-in as chief minister in 2012. But two years later, she wasn't willing to endorse Modi for prime minister. Instead, the AIADMK 'supremo' wanted to be the Supreme Leader herself, and her party had made a public declaration of the intent.

I asked Cho if he felt Jayalalithaa was really serious about moving to Delhi. 'I think she feels she has the capability to be the prime minister. And that Modi must also accept her leadership!' he said. My own understanding was that Jayalalithaa's prime ministerial ambition in this election was a smokescreen. Of course, she wanted to be prime minister, but she wasn't going to be a roadblock for Modi. She only wanted to tap into Tamil regional pride by playing the 'Jaya for PM' card. If she could maximize her seats in Tamil Nadu, then she would be a national player. The DMK had been in every central government since 1999 and had extracted a heavy price for their support. Jayalalithaa was hoping for a similar deal. If she could win thirty seats in Tamil Nadu, then in a hung Parliament she would have a decisive role to play in any ruling dispensation in Delhi. It was, therefore, a limited election strategy, not any long-term battle plan for the future.

Political expediency was guiding Mayawati as well. Like Jayalalithaa, she nurtures dreams of occupying 7, Race Course Road one day. But she probably knew that 2014 was not her moment. The BSP leader had been routed in the 2012 Uttar Pradesh assembly elections and hadn't fully recovered from the defeat. She was also tangled in a string of corruption cases that were still being heard in the Supreme Court. She needed to regroup and stay a little under the radar.

I had first met Mayawati around 1994. I had just moved to Delhi and had been researching the writings of Dr Babasaheb Ambedkar. Kanshi Ram, the founder of the BSP, was a great admirer of the Dalit icon. We'd spent many afternoons together sharing thoughts on Ambedkar's legacy. Dressed in a loose, white bush shirt, towel wrapped around his neck, and ill-fitting trousers, Kanshi Ram was a straight-talking politician. 'Ambedkar has been reduced to a statue in Maharashtra—it is we in UP who are taking his legacy forward,' he once told me.

Serving us tea at their Humayun Road residence would be Mayawati, already the leader of the party in UP but playing hostess to Kanshi Ram in Delhi. I never asked Kanshi Ram about his relationship with her, but it was apparent that he saw her as his obvious successor. 'She is much stronger than me. *Woh ek din raaj karengi!*' (One day she will rule.)

He was bang on. I was in Lucknow when Mayawati was sworn in as the country's first Dalit woman chief minister in June 1995. It was a news event I shall not forget. Just a day earlier, Mayawati, who had withdrawn support to the Mulayam Singh government, had been attacked by SP workers in what was infamously described as the 'state guest house' incident. We didn't have a twenty-four-hour news network at the time, but the images were frightening—MLAs of the Samajwadi Party chasing Mayawati and her men through the corridors of the building while the police remained mute spectators. Fearing for her life, Mayawati had to lock herself in a room. I interviewed her a few days later and she claimed that the incident had changed her forever. '*Yeh mera murder karna chahte thhe. Inko mein kabhi nahin chodoongi, inko sabak seekhana padega*' (They wanted to kill me, I will teach them all a lesson).

Over the next two decades, Mayawati did teach her opponents a fearsome lesson. Her politics was ruthlessly unforgiving. making and breaking governments. It was her style to keep her political opponents guessing, a lesson she had learnt from Kanshi Ram who believed that political power was the 'master key' that would eventually open the door to Dalit liberation. She was tough on law and order, but was also accused, like Jayalalithaa, of massive corruption. A UP businessman once told me, 'It's a straight deal in UP. Pay Mayawati money, get your work done. No middlemen needed.'

Like Jayalalithaa, she, too, could be a daunting presence. She would rarely meet the media, but I did meet her once in her rather opulent residence in Lucknow. A few weeks earlier, BSP supporters had broken our OB van and almost bashed up the driver over a story we had done on Mayawati's undeclared wealth. She offered me Limca and a plate of cashews, and then proceeded to lash out at the media. '*Aap logon ko sharam aani chahiye, kuch bhi dikhate ho!*' (You people should be ashamed, you telecast anything you want.) There wasn't even a hint of apology for the havoc her cadres had caused. Through our meeting, the fearful senior bureaucrats remained standing, none of them even daring to catch her eye.

Mayawati had clearly come a long way from the quiet hostess serving us tea at Kanshi Ram's house. Every day on my way to office in Noida, I would pass the Ambedkar Park, dotted with large statues of Ambedkar, Kanshi Ram and Mayawati herself, and think of Kanshi Ram's furious indictment of the 'statue culture'. A party that had initiated robust Dalit political empowerment was now in danger of becoming a caricature of the very politics it had once despised.

In January 2014, Mayawati's past seemed to catch up with her again. The Supreme Court decided to revive the disproportionate assets case against her. The case filed by the CBI in 2002 investigated Mayawati's vast riches. Her 2012 election affidavit placed her assets at Rs 111 crore and she had many properties in Delhi. Mayawati claimed the money had come in the form of gifts from her supporters. 'That case petrified her,' a Mayawati aide told me. 'She was worried that one day she would go to jail.' There were reports that the BSP leader was negotiating a deal with the Congress in return for protection from the CBI. Some Congressmen claim that it was Rahul Gandhi who nixed any attempt at a BSP–Congress alliance. What was clear, though, was that both sides were desperate—one for political survival, the other for personal immunity from the law. The deal eventually never happened as Mayawati perhaps realized that the Congress was a sinking ship.

During the election campaign, Amit Shah told me that Mayawati had dropped out of the race in the final stretch. *'Iss baar BSP baith gayi hai, chunav ladh hi nahi rahi'* (BSP is not really fighting the elections this time). He was right. In the twenty years of tracking the BSP, I hadn't seen such a listless campaign by the party. No logical explanation has been offered for Mayawati's relative silence in the run-up to the 2014 elections. She had started early by announcing several candidates in 2013 itself. But gradually, she began to witness the erosion of her *sarvajan* social engineering experiment that had successfully brought together Dalits, Muslims and upper castes on one platform in the 2007 assembly elections. This time, a Dalit–Muslim conflict in places like Muzaffarnagar made her position precarious. The Brahmins in any case had returned to a Modi-led BJP and the Dalit vote had splintered as well. As a result, she was left rudderless, an anomalous situation for a party with the most entrenched vote bank.

With defeat staring her in the face, by the end of the campaign it almost seemed as if Mayawati had decided to save her war chest for the UP assembly elections of 2017. Maybe, at fifty-eight, she felt she still had time on her side to fight another election.

~

Time was certainly not what another prime ministerial hopeful had in 2014. At seventy-four and a cancer survivor, Sharad Pawar knew his moment had perhaps come and gone. Every interview with the Maharashtra leader included a question about his prime ministerial aspirations. Pawar's answer was equally routine. 'How can I think of becoming prime minister when I have hardly ten MPs. I am a practical man, I have no such dream.'

The truth is, Pawar has lived the prime ministerial dream for years, having first become Maharashtra chief minister at the age of just thirty-eight. He even blamed me once for preventing him from becoming prime minister. It's a story that goes back to 1991. I was a young Mumbai-based journalist in the *Times of India*. Rajiv Gandhi had just been assassinated in the midst of the general election campaign and speculation was mounting about who would succeed him as the leader of the Congress. Sitting in faraway Mumbai, we could only guess what was happening in the Delhi durbar.

Then, on a Saturday morning, a few days after Rajiv's death, we went to see Vilasrao Deshmukh, then a state minister, later to become Maharashtra chief minister. Deshmukh told my *Maharashtra Times* colleague Prakash Akolkar and myself how Pawar, with the backing of a few senior Congress leaders, planned to make a bid for the top job. Apparently, a meeting had been held in a south Delhi hotel where Pawar had promised to financially support potential Congress MPs in their election campaign in return for endorsing him as the party's prime ministerial candidate. 'The strategy is all in place. Pawar is ready for the final push,' Deshmukh said.

We rushed to the office to file the story. It was a slow news day. The news editor decided to carry it as a bottom spread on the front page of the *Times of India*. Delhi's power brokers were thrown into a tizzy when the story broke the next morning. Sitting in Mumbai, we had no idea our story would change political equations in Delhi. At midnight, I got a call from Pawar himself. 'How could you print such a story? Do you know the damage it has caused me?' he said angrily. And before I could calm him down, came the punchline. 'Don't you want to see a Maharashtrian as prime minister?!'

A few weeks later, Pawar was edged out in his attempt to be prime minister by P.V. Narasimha Rao. The Congress's old order had united to stall Pawar's hopes. Though the NCP leader is not the kind of politician to bear grudges for long, I don't think he ever forgave me. It only convinced me just how desperate Pawar was to move, as one Maharashtra journalist once put it, 'from the Sahyadris to the Himalayas'.

Pawar did try again to conquer Delhi, a task which had eluded the Marathas since the defeat in the third battle of Panipat in 1761. He took on Sonia Gandhi over her foreign origins in 1999. It was a period when Pawar as the party's Lok Sabha leader sensed a vacuum in the Congress and was itching to take control. Sonia had been party president for less than a year and was vulnerable to an internal rebellion. Just ahead of his 'revolt' against Sonia, he had met a few of us and hinted that the Congress needed a new leadership. 'We need mass-based leaders to get the Congress back on track,' he claimed. But he had miscalculated the Congress's loyalty quotient for the Gandhi family. Most of the top leaders in the party chose to stand by Sonia. He later claimed that he was not against Sonia as Congress president but only as a potential prime ministerial candidate. He sounded like a defeated rebel. Interestingly, when Vajpayee's BJP government collapsed in February 1999, Pawar had reportedly tried to strike a deal with the BJP too. 'He wanted to be prime minister with outside support of the BJP much in the manner that the Congress had once supported Chandrashekhar as PM in 1990,' a BJP leader who was privy to the discussions told me. Again, things had never quite worked out. Pawar appeared destined to miss out each time.

Now, in 2014, things were even more difficult. Rahul Gandhi was set to take over the Congress and Pawar had made it clear he would not serve in any government led by Rahul. 'How can I serve under someone who is my daughter's age?' he confided to a friend. On record he told me that Rahul still needed to prove himself. He even decided to opt out by not contesting the Lok Sabha elections, preferring instead the Rajya Sabha route.

And yet, Pawar hasn't entirely 'retired" from politics. He has friends in all parties, including the BJP. BJP sources confirmed to me that Pawar was in touch with fellow Maharashtrian, Gadkari. If the BJP got less than 200 seats and no pre-poll alliance was in a position to form a government, then Pawar and Gadkari had reportedly agreed to try and stitch up a non-Congress government.

When I asked Pawar about any back-room deal, he rejected it outright. 'Where do you get all this news from? You media people will speculate on anything and everything!' Journalists were clearly not high up on Pawar's list of favourite people. Only months earlier, Pawar's nephew, Ajit Pawar, had been targeted in a series of exposés for his alleged role in an irrigation scam in Maharashtra. Ajit's shockingly insensitive statement during a drought asking 'if there is no water in dams, should we urinate to create water?' had been ripped apart across the media. Other NCP ministers, too, had found themselves being unmasked in corruption scandals. Pawar's name had often popped up in controversial land deals as well. Clearly, in the age of a hyperactive media, Pawar was on the wrong side of the divide. And he didn't like it one bit. The positive takeaway, though, was that you could criticize Pawar and he would still give you an interview. Like many old-style politicians, he really did have the hide of a rhinoceros!

If Pawar was constantly looking for ways to capture power in Delhi, another regional chieftain Naveen Patnaik seemed happy in his 'den' in Odisha. Naveenbabu is a fascinating politician whose life can be divided into two distinct halves. Before joining politics, he had enjoyed the high life—he had partied with Jackie Kennedy and Gore Vidal, he had written books on herbs and gardens, and his plush Aurangzeb Road residence was home to many wine-and-cheese evenings. And then in 1998, the Doon School-educated Naveen suddenly plunged into politics after the death of his father, the redoubtable Biju Patnaik. In 2000, he became Odisha chief minister from the Biju Janata Dal (BJD), carrying forward a family inheritance. He could barely speak Oriya at the time and had hardly lived in Bhubaneshwar. And yet, this denizen of metropolitan India, who loved his Scotch and his caviar, transformed himself into a tough local politician. The man who would once zip in and out of London made his first foreign trip as chief minister only in 2012.

So what was his secret formula that ensured repeated electoral success? 'Among all the senior politicians in Odisha, he stands out as honest and earnest,' claims a BJD MP. He could be gentle in private conversation, ruthless in his political dealings—he had split with the BJP just ahead of the 2009 elections and had removed close aides who he thought were conspiring against him. Most importantly, he had stayed the course. In the 2014 elections, he told me he wanted to remain equidistant from the BJP and the Congress. 'We will not support anyone, neither Modi nor Rahul, after the elections,' was his public position. He would be true to his word.

Perhaps his success offers hope to Rahul and the other elite children of dynastical privilege. The lesson is simple—even 'disconnected' Macaulay *putra*s can triumph in politics if they are ready to actually work at it with relentless focus. If only Rahul had made Lucknow his karmabhoomi like Naveen had Bhubaneshwar, who knows, the Congress leader might actually have emerged a battle-hardened politician.

~

A vexed relationship with the media is common to all the political contenders described in this chapter. Kejriwal had realized, to his cost, that a movement which had received oxygen in television studios could just as easily be snuffed out by a hostile camera. Mamata and the Bengali media are often locked in bitter conflict. Jayalalithaa has almost stopped giving interviews and only issues the occasional press statement or sound bite. Mayawati treats the media with similar contempt, her press conferences totally scripted, with no questions being allowed. Pawar after his throat surgery is barely audible and, quite simply, un-telegenic. Naveen, too, prefers to keep the media at bay and has perfected the art of monosyllabic responses to any tough questions.

The two top contestants for prime minister were also a study in contrast. Rahul Gandhi still seemed hesitant to open himself to media scrutiny. In comparison, Narendra Modi was preparing to launch the biggest ever media blitz in the history of Indian elections. The divergence was glaring, and in the final analysis, would prove decisive.

7

Multimedia Is the Message

Two battles were fought in the elections of 2014. One was the traditional battle across the heat and dust of a vast country, in basti and maidan, in street corner and chai shop; the other on a television screen near you. Election 2014 was India's first general election where television became the defining arena of the contest.

In 1989—the first election I covered as a journalist—only Doordarshan was on air. In 2004, there were half a dozen major 'national channels' and about a dozen regional channels. By 2014, the information and broadcasting ministry list suggested that there were almost 400 24/7 news and current affairs channels beaming out of India, a crazy number, way more than any other country in the world. It was a mini revolution that was changing the way Indians consumed and communicated news. Television defined politics, politics was played for television. The TV top story often engulfed the political class. Every evening as channels stampeded towards the prime-time headline, netas and commentators were at hand as the ever-ready chorus.

In the 2004 elections, when I broke the story of Sonia Gandhi opting out of the prime ministerial race, I was, for at least a couple of hours, onto a genuine 'exclusive'. I was actually able to stand outside

10, Janpath, and broadcast my report without being bothered by a forest of other cameras. By 2014, the idea of a news 'exclusive' was lost. Within minutes, every channel would be onto the story. Often, several channels would flash the same newsbreak or interview as an 'exclusive'.

The idea of breaking news, in particular, has 'broken down'—even a piece of trivia is now breaking news. The new newsroom mantra is to keep the screen 'buzzing' at all times, almost as if it is a flight schedule monitor at the airport. Breathless urgency is our stock-in-trade, crises and triumphs only as durable as the thirty-minute news bulletin that rolls out every hour. When I joined television in 1994, I got a full week to do my first story for *The World This Week*. Now, a reporter is expected to deliver a story in a couple of hours. A certain frenetic mindlessness has crept in, driven perhaps by what I call the demands of a 'sound bite society'.

In this manic environment, there is still the hunger for being 'first' on air. In particular, who would get the first interviews with the two main actors of the election—Narendra Modi and Rahul Gandhi. The Rahul battle was won, fairly and squarely, by my former colleague at NDTV and now editor in chief of Times Now, Arnab Goswami. Arnab and I go back a fairly long way. I remember a slim, floppy-haired, bespectacled youngster visiting my home in the early 1990s to inquire about TV opportunities. I had then been a mentor of sorts to him. We worked together for almost a decade and had even co-anchored a show. But television news can be maddeningly competitive, and a personal relationship based on mutual respect can easily descend into a slightly troubled professional equation revolving around constant one-upmanship. Arnab's 'nation wants to know' rumbustious style of anchoring had won him a lot of fans; I found it, at times, disturbingly chaotic and sensationalist.

The backstory of the Rahul interview reflects some of the cross currents in modern-day TV journalism. Several news channels had been hounding Rahul's office with requests for an interview. Barkha Dutt, another star anchor and also a former colleague at NDTV, had been promised the first interview. She had met Rahul and Priyanka in December 2013 and an 'agreement' had been reached. NDTV is seen as occupying a politically left-liberal space—a channel that perhaps the Congress leader felt comfortable talking to. A date, 12 January, was also fixed for the interview. The channel's producers even went to the location—Jawahar Bhavan, home to the Rajiv Gandhi Foundation—and worked on the lights and camera positioning.

By now, the news had spread in the TV industry that NDTV was poised to get the first Rahul interview. But as D-Day approached, Rahul's office suddenly changed their plan. The All India Congress Committee (AICC) session was on 17 January and Rahul's team felt that they'd rather wait till his big speech on the occasion before giving interviews. NDTV was promised that the interview would be done on the 18th, the day after the AICC session.

Arnab sensed an opening. He wrote a long mail to Rahul's office pointing out that Times Now's TRPs were much higher than NDTV's and of other competition in the English news space. 'We gave them charts with details of our viewership and even told them how in the US presidential elections, the first interview normally goes to the channel with the highest rating,' Arnab later told me. The TRP system in India is highly skewed and contentious. A few thousand television meters are expected to calculate viewership in a country with over a hundred million cable and satellite homes. But it was also the only available measurement to gauge a channel's or show's popularity.

Rahul's office bit the bait. The NDTV interview was again cancelled at the last minute, and Times Now was given the first interview, on 25 January. Arnab was met by Priyanka herself and Rahul's staff before the Congress leader walked in. It was meant to be a forty-five-minute interview. It lasted all of eighty minutes. 'Rahul did not ask for any questions in advance—he said he was ready to answer anything thrown at him,' says Arnab. Contrary to speculation, he claims neither Priyanka nor any other Congressman was actually present in the room during the recording. An M.F. Husain painting was the sole witness.

The interview was aired on the 27th night at 9 p.m. after incessant promos on the channel. When it began, Rahul appeared to show some flashes of promise, with a look of earnestness and well-meaning intent. By the end, it was clear to any viewer who was watching that Rahul was, in fact, completely out of his depth and had no clear answers or big idea or message. Arnab had come to the interview well prepared; Rahul, by contrast, appeared woolly-headed, ill-informed and hopelessly unprepared for tough questioning.

He tried to appear confident, often speaking of himself in the third person, saying things like, 'I will give you an insight into what Rahul Gandhi thinks.' But when asked a direct question of whether he was ready for the Modi challenge, Rahul would veer off and say, 'What Rahul Gandhi wants to do is to empower the women in this country—he wants to unleash the power of these women.'

In fact, women's empowerment, RTI and 'system change' were recurring themes that were repeatedly mentioned by Rahul through the interview, often irrespective of the question being asked. Even a specific question on the 2002 Gujarat riots led to Rahul speaking loftily of strengthening RTI, women's empowerment and democracy. It was as though he was speaking from another planet.

His political naivety was also exposed when Arnab grilled him on the Congress's role in the 1984 anti-Sikh riots and contrasted it with the party's stand on the 2002 Gujarat riots. Rahul tried to claim, rather foolishly, that the Congress government in 1984 had tried to stop the violence while the BJP had actively abetted them in 2002. Strangely, rather than offer an unequivocal apology for 1984, of the kind that prime minister Manmohan Singh had already issued, Rahul schoolboyishly pussyfooted around it, saying, 'Firstly, I wasn't involved in the riots. I wasn't part of it. I was not in operation of the Congress party.'

To blame Modi for 2002 was one thing; to absolve the Congress of responsibility for the massacre in 1984 was quite another. All Rahul needed to do was sound genuinely contrite, perhaps even offer a heartfelt apology, promise complete support to the legal process and even point out that the Congress had appointed a Sikh prime minister subsequently. He did none of it. Not surprisingly, his prevarication provided an opportunity for Sikh groups the very next day to protest against the Congress. The year 1984 was back on the front pages. In the eyes of the Sikh protestors, Rahul, far from being the youth leader promising a new era, had taken his place among the same old Congress double-talkers on 1984. Their disillusionment burst forth in howls of rage.

The interview was a smash hit in TRPs. It also got more than 2 million views on YouTube. But even more tellingly, it sparked off a slew of videos and tweets that lampooned and ridiculed Rahul. For example: 'Arnab is looking to London, Rahul is talking to Tokyo'; 'Arnab qs: What if aliens invade India? Rahul ans: I want to say our government brought in RTI'; 'Arnab qs: What is the capital of China? Rahul ans: Women's Empowerment!'; 'Charlie Chaplin died again yesterday laughing in his grave after watching the interview'; 'After Comedy Nights with Kapil, we must now have Comedy Nights with Rahul!'; 'Rahul walks into a bar and lowers it!' It just went on and on. Amul even had a hoarding: 'Najawab Rahul'.

Till that interview, Rahul Gandhi (or RaGa, as he is referred to in cyberspace) was targeted by his critics as 'pappu', suggesting he was just a novice, a kid in comparison to Modi (or NaMo). The Congress claimed the criticism was unjustified and Rahul was just waiting for the right moment to prove himself as a leader of substance. But now, the interview only confirmed the caricature of him as a babe in the political woods. In most urban, English-speaking middle-class homes in particular, RaGa was now really a pappu, unfit to be prime minister of the country, woefully short of the muscularity and dynamism that the voter seemed to crave.

The next morning, I telephoned Rahul's key aide Kanishka Singh to remind him of my long-pending interview request. 'Now that you've done one, I'm sure you can do more,' I pleaded. 'Of course, we will do more and am sure you'll get one. By the way, how do you think the interview went?' he asked. I didn't really know what to say. If I was brutally honest, I'd probably lose a chance to interview Rahul. If I lied, I wouldn't be professional. So, I played the diplomat, saying, 'It was good to see Rahul take all questions, but maybe he could have prepared himself better.' Kanishka assured me he would.

Sadly, he didn't need to. The adverse fallout of the interview meant that Rahul went back into his shell, as did his entire team. He did a couple more interviews during the campaign in Hindi, but they were all soft focus and singularly undistinguished. I would send mails to his office every week but did not even get the courtesy of a response. NDTV's plight was even worse. They were promised an interview for a third time soon after the Times Now interview, only to have it cancelled again, at 3 the night before. 'It was all very unfortunate and, frankly, unprofessional, if you ask me,' Barkha told me later.

I later asked a Congress media manager why it went so horribly wrong. He said, 'Well, you see we thought that if we gave an interview to a tough interviewer like Arnab and got full coverage across the Times of India group which is the largest in the country, then we would establish Rahul as a politician who was open to public scrutiny unlike Modi who walked out of interviews. I guess we just didn't know how badly Rahul would end up looking.'

Yes, Rahul had botched up big time. When he should have come out looking firm, candid and wise, he had ended up looking unsure and inexperienced, a bit like a nervous batsman on his debut. As the advertisement jingle went, 'Pappu paas nahi hua!' It was now time for Modi to show his young rival how it was done.

~

Ever since he walked out of a CNN-IBN interview in October 2007, Modi had been very careful of his public interactions. My Gujarati journalist friends in Ahmedabad would often complain, 'Modi treats us like crap. Baat hi nahi karta!' (He doesn't talk to us.) Though he did a few interviews during the 2009 and 2012 election campaigns (including the one on a bus with me), he had been circumspect in picking and choosing his moments. He had done an interview with Reuters in July 2013, which had stirred a fresh controversy. Asked whether he regretted the Gujarat 2002 violence, he had said it was how one would feel if a puppy came under a car wheel. The 'puppy' analogy led to his critics accusing him of gross insensitivity. Modi insisted his comments had been distorted. It made him even more wary of interviews.

The wariness stemmed from the hostile media reaction Modi had encountered in the aftermath of the Gujarat riots. Till then, Modi had assiduously courted the media and, as party general secretary in the 1990s, he was always willing to appear on television debates (see chapter 1). The year 2002 changed the Modi–media equation. He now felt hounded and chose to play 'victim'. He would often say in private conversation, *'Kuch logon ne mann bana liya hai ki Modi gunahgaar hai!'* (Some people have made up their mind that I am guilty.) He especially felt this way towards the mainstream English-language media. In his eyes, the English-language journalistic club along with civil society NGOs were determined to malign his reputation. For Modi, the media is important yet untrustworthy, an ally for publicity, an adversary on issues. It is his intimate enemy—he grudgingly relies on it for feedback but scorns it when it acts as a mirror or sounding board. If he was to open up ahead of the biggest election in his life, it would be to someone he fully trusted.

Rajat Sharma was one such individual. Rajat was one of the original print journalists to switch to television in the early 1990s. He had built his reputation through the programme *Aap ki Adalat* on Zee TV. Designed in a courtroom format, the programme had Rajat play prosecutor with the guest being placed in the confession box before a judge and an audience. By 2004, Rajat had started his own Hindi television channel, India TV, and had become a successful entrepreneur. His channel was now housed in a rather Bollywood-style palatial three-floor building on the Noida highway.

Before plunging into journalism, Rajat had been an activist of the ABVP, the students' wing of the BJP, in the 1970s. He had even been arrested for eleven months in the anti-Emergency movement. That's when he got to know Modi who was then a young RSS pracharak. Their common friend was Jaitley, another rising star in the student politics of the 1970s. Jaitley would become president of the Delhi University students' union; Sharma became general secretary.

The Modi–Rajat bond would survive the test of time. 'Modi would come to our house for simple vegetarian food when he was in Delhi in the 1990s. I guess we hit it off well right from the beginning,' reminisces Rajat. When Modi was sworn in as Gujarat chief minister in December 2002 after the riots, he invited Rajat to be his special guest. 'I was reluctant as a journalist to be seen on stage with Modi, but he was insistent. He said that I was being invited as a friend, not as a journalist,' he told me.

Rajat was fondly referred to as 'Panditji' by Modi. So when he approached Modi for an interview soon after he became the BJP's prime ministerial candidate in September 2013, the response was positive. 'I will do it, I promise, Panditji, but let us wait for the right time,' he'd told Rajat.

The 'right time' was originally meant to be just before the election campaign really took off in March. But caught in the whirl of ticket distribution and rallies across the country, Modi kept delaying the interview. Finally, 12 April 2014 was fixed as the date. It was perfect timing. The first two rounds of the voting were just over, and the election was about to enter the critical phases across much of north India. *Aap ki Adalat* was the ideal platform. It was Hindi news TV's longest running show, with a loyal viewership. And the host was someone with whom Modi had a high degree of comfort.

The interview almost didn't happen on the day. Modi had been relentlessly campaigning that day across Bihar and Bengal, and had addressed half a dozen rallies. He had promised Rajat he would fly down to Delhi after the rallies were over and drive straight to the India TV studios, at least a ninety-minute drive from the airport. When Modi finally arrived, it was 10.45 p.m. and he was totally exhausted. His throat was hurting and he was struggling to speak. 'We told him to rest a bit, hoping that he would feel better. We even offered him some food but he said he was observing Navaratra so would only drink water,' recalls Rajat. For the next hour, Modi rested with a flask of warm water by his side. '*Panditji, programme karte hain, lekin fifteen to twenty minutes ke liye, usse zyada karna muskhil hoga'* (I will do the programme, but only for fifteen to twenty minutes—more than that will be tough), a tired Modi told Rajat.

All that changed the moment Modi entered the studio in his blue jacket kurta. As soon as Rajat called out his name, the studio audience went wild. They began chanting his name in a crazed manner. One of the girls even shouted, 'Modi, I love you!', at which the prime ministerial candidate burst out laughing. Says Rajat, 'I had done hundreds of *Aap ki Adalat*s but had never seen anything remotely like this. Even film stars like Salman and Shahrukh had not got this kind of a frenzied response.'

The audience was predominantly north Indian urban middle class—housewives and college students, government clerks and traders. It was just the kind of urban constituency that was driving the Modi juggernaut. 'We had asked all our staff members to bring their friends and relatives because we knew the programme would start late and we needed the audience to stay till it was over,' says Rajat.

Modi was transformed once the cameras turned on. The palpable adulation of the audience was his tonic and the long day on the campaign trail was forgotten. He was now Modi, the consummate stage performer, acting before an adoring audience. This is what he had learnt in his early days of theatre in Vadnagar—gauging the mood of the audience, knowing when to raise them to a fever pitch, when to dissolve them into laughter. Modi understands all this well and plays an audience like a conductor leads an orchestra.

He was serious and witty in equal measure. The one-liners just kept coming. When Rajat asked why he didn't wear a topi offered to him by a Muslim religious leader, Modi shot back, 'Have you ever seen Gandhi and Sardar wear a topi?' When asked about his anti-minority image, he claimed, 'I want Muslims to have a Koran in one hand and a computer in another.' When told that Azam Khan, the SP leader, had called him the 'elder brother of puppies', he replied, 'I say thank you very much because the loyalty of dogs is unparalleled.'

Every answer was met with rapturous applause and loud cries of 'Modi, Modi!' For a viewer, it seemed as though one had been transported to a BJP rally. This was a master communicator in total command, pulling off yet another virtuoso solo act. The recording went on for almost ninety minutes, finishing after 1.15 a.m. The entire crew and audience now wanted 'selfies' with their hero!

Next Thursday, the TRP figures were out. Modi's show, aired on a Saturday night at 10 p.m., was by far the number one show, getting almost 70 per cent audience share. 'We were stunned with the numbers. It was by far the highest we had got for any *Aap Ki Adalat* programme,' says Rajat.

At the same time the Modi programme was playing out, Aaj Tak, the leading Hindi news channel, was airing a Rahul Gandhi interview. It barely registered on the TRP meter. The Modi interview had 7 million views on YouTube by the time the elections were over. It was repeated seven times (often just before a major election day) and the viewership kept soaring.

And yet, there was a question mark over whether the interview had been stage-managed. Rajat insists that he asked Modi all the hard questions and the audience wasn't tutored to cheer for the BJP's prime ministerial nominee. 'The fact is Modi is simply the finest political communicator I have seen since Vajpayee. He knew how to reach out to an audience, it was all spontaneous,' he says.

But the India TV editorial director Qamar Waheed Naqvi did not agree. The morning after the show was telecast, he resigned. 'The entire programme was part of the Modi propaganda machine. No hard questions were asked and the audience was full of Modi *bhakt*s who were only there to cheer for him,' he told me later.

Rajat denies the accusations, saying Naqvi was fully aware of the programme content and had actually praised it after it was recorded. 'I think the AAP members got to Naqvi and forced him to resign, and tried to make a political issue out of it,' he claims. Rajat's proximity to Modi meant that his neutrality would always be questioned by his critics. But it's also true that lines are often crossed when a journalist gets too close to a politician.

Whatever the truth, the fact is the interview was a blockbuster. If the Rahul interview forced the Congress leader to retreat, Modi's India TV programme only added to the aura around him. Over the next twenty-eight days—between 12 April and 10 May—Modi did almost fifty print and television interviews. It was almost as if he now felt 'liberated' from the self-imposed cage in which he had locked himself over the last five years.

The media blitz was well choreographed. Modi would do his interviews almost in tune with the election calendar. So, for example, he did an interview with the news agency ANI just a day before the crucial phase five of the elections. Campaigning had ended in 121 seats in twelve states, but Modi knew the interview would be carried across all the channels which subscribed to the agency just ahead of the polling. When Tamil Nadu was going to the polls, he spoke to Tamil channels; when Bengal was going to elections, the preference was for regional Bengali channels; and when his home state of Gujarat was polling, Gujarati news channels were targeted. 'Narendrabhai knew the power of regional networks and actually told us he would prefer speaking to them,' is how a Team Modi member put it to me.

His energy was boundless. He would do the interviews at his Gandhinagar residence either before he set off on the campaign trail at 9 a.m. or after he had returned well past 10 p.m. Modi had always loved the camera; now he wanted to make up, it appears, for the lost years, when he had consciously stayed away from it.

The scheduling of the interviews was left to a small group of officials, mainly from the Gujarat government. Modi didn't have, contrary to popular belief, a highly qualified team of external professional media advisers. His PRO, Jagdish Thakkar, for example, was from the state information department and had been with the Gujarat chief minister's office since 1989 (he would later move with Modi to the PMO). Whenever I'd phone Jagdishbhai seeking time for an interview, he'd talk to me about my father's batting instead. 'Oh, what a batsman Dilip Sardesai was!' he'd say, fobbing me off. I told him that much as I liked hearing praise of my father's cricketing skills, I'd feel even better once I had got my Modi interview.

I did not get the interview, though Modi had promised me one and had even said no questions were taboo ('*Arre, tumse koi dushmani nahi, Rajdeep*'—I have no enmity with you), but at least my network did get more than one. The only major news network that wasn't given an interview was NDTV. Modi, it seems, still hadn't forgiven or forgotten the reporting done by the NDTV channels (yours truly included) during the Gujarat riots and its aftermath. In fact, during a Network 18 event in 2013, Modi made a snide remark that NDTV's 'Save the Tiger' effort got sponsorship because 'the tiger was secular and maybe the lion was seen as communal'. The BJP members in the audience laughed; I thought the remark was in rather poor taste.

Indeed, some things did not change even as Modi tried to appear more conciliatory towards the media. Whenever an interviewer asked a tough question (but very few did), you sensed a certain frostiness return to Modi's eyes. It happened when he was asked a question about his wife Jasodhaben and when an interviewer tried to push him once again on the riots. He chose to describe any criticism as being the handiwork of 'news traders', a rather unfortunate and ominous term that sadly no interviewer dared challenge. It was as if Modi had mentally divided journalists into camps and was urging his supporters to see any criticism of him as 'paid media', another regrettable term designed to put even professional journalists on the defensive.

The truth is, Modi was in full control. He was setting the terms of engagement with the news media and relishing the challenge. Most journalists were just grateful for the limited access and happy to be co-opted. A charismatic speaker, Modi knows what will 'sell' with the viewers and what won't. His ear for a good slogan or a line rarely fails him. While a Rahul Gandhi dithered after his initial faux pas, Modi was on a roll. Body language is also a potent communicator. A burly swagger compared with cutesy hand-waving became the default TV split screen for the Modi–Rahul personality clash. Modi on stage is a domineering figure with not a trace of tentativeness; Rahul, by contrast, looks like a shy schoolboy pushed into a dramatics class.

As one political observer put it, 'A doctorate in communication was being pitted against someone still in kindergarten!' It was a no contest. The prime-time battle had been settled.

~

Every night on television screens across the country, you have a live courtroom drama with news anchors sometimes playing judge, jury and prosecutor, and 'guilty till proven innocent' being the presiding mantra. Familiar talking heads pop out of every debate, often swiftly moving from one channel to another. Studio 'talk' is cheap; solid ground reporting needs deep pockets. Journalistic laziness and a warped business model have ensured that loud and highly opinionated court martials have become a staple diet on news channels. It is often rather inane, high on noise and low on substance, but it is a rough democracy of opinion. The debate is robust, if not always constructive, and can nevertheless be entertaining.

Election time is no different. Every political party has to line up party spokespersons to defend their position. Here again, the battle was unequal. The BJP had a strong line-up of articulate, TV-savvy leaders; the Congress's best did not want to go out and face the bouncers being thrown at them by aggressive anchors.

In June 2013, Ajay Maken was put in charge of the Congress's communication department. Maken had proved to be an enthusiastic sports minister, and the party was hoping he would bring some of that energy to this key post ahead of the elections. His predecessor, Janardhan Dwivedi, was an old-world neta who preferred poetry to sound bites. I got the feeling that he was part of that frustrated group within the Congress who actually derived vicarious pleasure from seeing the government embarrassed. Congress gossip was that Dwivedi had been given the job because he had taught Hindi to Sonia Gandhi!

Maken's first task was to try and ensure that the Congress got its most eloquent voices to speak up for the party. His team prepared an exhaustive list of leaders to appear on television. But as a Maken aide put it, 'It was a thankless task. None of our major leaders who were now ministers wanted to come on TV debates.' I asked one of the ministers what the reason was. He said, 'Why should we come on a cockfight on television and make a fool of ourselves!'

Some Congress ministers like Anand Sharma made it clear to Maken that they would only appear in occasional one-on-one interviews. 'You don't expect us to be on the same debate as some junior spokesperson of the BJP,' Sharma said, somewhat dismissively. Even Manish Tewari, who was once their main pugilist on television, was now an information and broadcasting minister. 'I am now part of the government, so I can't speak freely on every issue,' was his explanation.

It was a familiar excuse. The UPA government wasn't short of effective speakers. Individuals like Chidambaram, Kapil Sibal, Jyotiraditya Scindia and Sachin Pilot would have made a formidable communication team. But they shunned the media like wounded lions, with barely concealed rage, believing that 24/7 news was responsible for most of the UPA's misfortunes. Till 2010, Chidambaram, easily the government's most cerebral politician, would even offer to come to the studio. Now, neither he nor any potentially credible voice was ready to get into the hurly-burly of 'noise' television. It almost seemed as if the cacophony over the Anna agitation and the string of scams had forced the government's key interlocutors to surrender a crucial public space. In 2009, many of them had led the Congress charge; now they had gone missing in action. Their silence only added to the cloud of doom and gloom hanging over the party.

By contrast, the BJP had packed its ranks with Smriti Irani, Piyush Goyal, Ravi Shankar Prasad, Nirmala Sitharaman, Meenakshi Lekhi, even Arun Jaitley, each a doughty fighter for the cause. The party was well prepared for the war on television. As an Opposition party, it was perhaps a shade easier to be aggressive. The BJP had a standard operating media drill in place for the election. Every morning at around 10.30, there would be a tele-conference of all the BJP spokespersons to decide the official stance on an issue. By

3 p.m., the party would have decided which spokesperson would be assigned to which news channel.

Under Maken's watch, the Congress belatedly attempted a similar media plan, only their cupboard appeared bare in contrast. Unlike the BJP, many senior Congress spokespersons were contesting the elections and were not available in Delhi. In desperation, the Congress rehabilitated Dr Abhishek Singhvi, its long-serving lawyer-spokesperson. Singhvi had been out in the cold for over a year after being caught on tape in a sex CD. The party also turned to the urbane Shashi Tharoor, aware that he might lend some gravitas to their side in debates. But Tharoor, too, was often tied up in his own election battle in Thiruvananthapuram. 'Too many news channels, too few credible faces,' is how a member of the party's media cell summed up the Congress problem.

The Congress's plight was exemplified by one of its newer spokespersons, Sanjay Jha. I had met Jha almost a decade ago when he was involved in a cricket website. He struck me as a nice, regular Mumbai guy. He ran a successful leadership training business, was a member of all the right clubs, liked his sport and did the occasional writing.

Suddenly in 2012, I found Jha appearing on television channels as a founder of a website, HamaraCongress.com, designed, he says, to change the Congress's negligible presence on the Internet. A year later, he was made an official spokesperson of the Congress. Soon, he was speaking on three or even four channels on a single night. It seemed a spectacular rise for someone who had never fought even a local election. 'Doing multiple shows in a single day can be exacting, but I had the passion for a fight and strongly believed that the Congress is part of India's DNA, its ethos,' he told me.

Jha made a valiant attempt, but he often seemed to be a lamb to the slaughter. He had debating skills but on many occasions, he just didn't have the political weight to take on his more influential counterparts. Do nightly television debates make a difference to the voter? Maybe not. News television, especially English news TV, occupies a very small space in the overall TV universe. But it does add to the surround sound during an elections and has acquired an almost monstrously larger-than-life image in the lives of opinion makers. It can, importantly, set the news agenda. In 2009, I would hear the chattering classes gush over how the Congress had come out looking so strong in the Indo-US nuclear debate on TV. In 2014, the talk was all about how the Congress spokespersons were defending the indefensible, be it 2G or inflation. A senior Congress leader admitted to me, 'You know, every time Renuka Chaudhary tries to shout and filibuster her way through a debate, we lose another 100 votes!'

But in the media clash of 2014, television had competition too— the war in cyberspace, especially social media, was about to change the rules of old-style debates and political jousts. It was to prove, in many ways, the ultimate triumph of not just an individual, but the idea of 'Team Modi'.

~

Narendra Modi joined Facebook and Twitter in late 2009. It wasn't the kind of spectacular big-bang entry that the BJP leader normally likes. For the first two years, Modi didn't set the popular social networking sites on fire. In 2011, he still had barely 6 lakh followers on his Facebook page. His Twitter following, too, was well behind that of someone like Shashi Tharoor's, who was really the first Indian politician to join the Twitterati.

By the time the elections were over in May, Modi had a staggering 1.5 million 'likes' on his Facebook page, second only to US President Obama in terms of his fan following. Through 2014, Modi had, according to a Facebook spokesperson, the fastest growing page of any politician worldwide. 'Facebook was our mother site which drove our social media campaign,' says a Modi aide. Several individuals set up their own Modi Facebook pages—for example, a volunteer called Vikas Pandey set up an 'I support Modi' page, another had a 'NaMo for PM' page, all of which became aggregators to the Modi social media machine.

On Twitter, too, the Modi base kept increasing. By the time the elections were done and dusted, Modi had 4.27 million Twitter followers. According to Twitter India, five of the top ten election tweets had been sent from Modi's account. They included a selfie with his mother and a victory tweet.

Contrast it with Rahul Gandhi. The Congress's 'youth' talisman wasn't even on the world's two most popular sites for youth interactivity. I asked a Congress social media cell member why. 'You know, Rahulji doesn't like impersonal communication. If he is to get on Twitter, he would like to handle his account himself and, frankly, he doesn't have the time for it,' was the explanation I was given.

Modi didn't handle his own Twitter and Facebook page. That was done by a team of hired professionals based out of Ahmedabad, Gandhinagar and other smaller centres. Leading them was Hiren Joshi, a computer science lecturer in a college in Bhilwara, Rajasthan, who had been assigned as OSD to Modi. It was this team that ensured a constant engagement on Twitter. Joshi first met Modi when he attended a function for computer engineers which had been organized by the Gujarat government in 2009. Apparently, a technical glitch developed at the meeting which Joshi solved instantaneously. Modi was impressed enough to recruit Joshi to lead his social media outreach—one more evidence of his talent-spotting skills. It was Joshi who would provide Modi a daily late-night update on his Twitter messages, supervise all Twitter interactions, and help translate Modi's Twitter account into half a dozen regional languages.

'We had a clear goal—don't allow the buzz around Modiji to drop through the election, keep our leader and what he says and does trending all the time,' says a Modi social media team member.

Statistically, it was as one-sided as it could get. According to Twitter India, during the elections a total of 56 million election-related tweets were sent out. Modi was mentioned in 11.1 million tweets, almost 20 per cent of the total traffic. Arvind Kejriwal was next with 5 million (9 per cent) and Rahul Gandhi well behind with just 1.2 million tweets (or 2 per cent).

Kejriwal was at least giving Modi a fight on the social media meter. A small team working out of the party headquarters in Delhi and wired to NRI supporters would work tirelessly to take on the BJP media machine or raise funds for the party through crowdsourcing. 'We found social media a relatively cheap and effective way to take our message forward,' is how Kejriwal put it to me.

That a party which was just a year old was scoring better than the Congress on the social media meter reflects just how ill prepared Rahul's team was. In the 'pappu' (Rahul) versus 'feku' (Modi) hashtag war, there was again only one clear leader. Every time, Rahul spoke, BJP supporters would swarm all over the social media and start trending 'pappu' to ridicule him. The Congress then hit back by labelling Modi a 'feku' (braggart), but it was more of a reactive move.

'The BJP had a head start over us and started well before the Gujarat election campaign of 2012. We really focused on social media only at the end of 2013,' concedes Congress MP Deeepinder Hooda who was in charge of the party's social media cell, while also fighting his own election from Rohtak.

Hooda says while the BJP successfully 'personalized' their social media campaign around Modi, the Congress strategy was to make it about the organization instead. 'One big learning for us is that individuals invariably draw more traction than organizations on the social media,' is how he put it. Admits another Congress media cell member, 'We treated this as some kind of a mechanical exercise without attempting any kind of real innovation to engage with more people.'

The BJP's social media team, by contrast, was innovating all the time. On every voting day, they would send out personalized messages on Twitter encouraging people to go out and vote. 'We used Facebook and Twitter to make micro messaging part of our election strategy, a bit like what Obama did in the US,' is how a Team Modi member described it.

Social media collapsed the distance between voter and politician. The personal connect worked. For example, just ahead of a rally in Hyderabad, a Modi follower tweeted how his elderly mother was a great fan of the BJP leader and wanted to meet him. The local BJP unit was asked to contact the woman—she was brought on stage and Modi sought her blessings. 'It was just the kind of human touch we were looking for,' says a Modi aide.

The Modi selfie when he went out to vote was another good example. 'A prime ministerial candidate putting out a selfie—what could be a better symbol of a tech-friendly leader? It was bound to be a super-hit,' says the aide. The selfie with the black-and-white lotus had another function. By holding up the election symbol designed to look exactly the way it looked on the EVM (in black and white and not saffron) and by associating his face with it (for those voters keen to vote for Modi, if not the BJP), Modi had put into the public space an image both viral-worthy and politically communicative (in fact, Modi would use the black-and-white lotus symbol as a lapel on his kurta in all public interactions from 7 April 2014, the first day of polling, if only to reinforce the party's logo in the eyes of potential voters).

Modi has always liked technology as much as he likes wearing designer kurtas. He had started his website back in 2002 when few politicians even glanced at the Internet. An old Modi associate recalls how the seasoned politician was almost childlike when he was gifted an electronic diary once. 'He just likes to play around with some new tech device. He may not have the time to learn it always, but he just likes to be seen with it,' is how the friend describes Modi's tech-savvy avatar.

Modi was also aware of what was being tweeted about him. Once during a phone conversation, he suddenly said, '*Arre, tum aur tumhari biwi aaj kal bahut Twitter pe ho!*' (You and your wife are on Twitter a lot). Sagarika had just tweeted about how Modi should have acknowledged his wife Jasodhaben much earlier. Without mentioning the specific tweet, Modi had sent out the message he wanted to.

Even if Modi didn't look closely at his tweets, his team and followers certainly did. If the Gandhi family had their political chamchas, Modi had his 'Internet Hindus' (or bhakts, as I called them). I often found myself facing the ire of what appeared as an organized, systematic campaign of hate and abuse against anyone who didn't follow the prescribed narrative. Their social media profile usually was 'Proud Hindu nationalist. Want Namo for PM.' Internet Hindus are highly organized and motivated, and demolishing the narratives and reputations of mainstream media practitioners is their avowed objective.

My worst moment with this group came when I tweeted, 'While NaMo travels the country, my Nemo needs to be taken for a walk in the park. Different folks, different priorities!' It was an innocuous, if perhaps ill-advised attempt at wordplay—my beagle Nemo had been named after my daughter Tarini's favourite movie, *Finding Nemo*. The bhakts were unimpressed and let off a volley of abuse on social media. A few hours later, I got a threatening phone call. 'You have likened our leader to a dog. You and your family will pay for this. We will cut you into pieces.'

I was tempted to call the police but decided not to in the end. I had complained to Modi once about the abuse. *'Galat hai,'* he said, *'lekin mein har vyakti ko kaise rok sakta hoon'* (It is wrong, but how do I stop everyone who speaks). I found it difficult to accept that a politician who had such overwhelming control over his party faithful could be so helpless. Maybe it was just a crank call, but it reflected just how a robust medium of communication could just as easily become a rather noxious chamber of nastiness.

Were these anonymous Twitter trolls hand in glove with the BJP party machinery? A BJP insider admitted to me that there was a 'media watch' group of party volunteers who were tasked to 'take down' Modi's critics. Whether they were 'paid' volunteers is unclear (a Cobrapost sting operation had shown how IT companies could be used to artificially hype up a politician's image or malign his opponents). Some of the most abusive Twitter activists seemed to be linked to either pro-BJP websites or even individual party members. But Arvind Gupta, who headed the BJP's IT cell, strongly denied the linkages. 'No question about it, we would never support such behaviour,' he insisted.

I wasn't convinced. The campaign was much too organized for it not to have at least some level of endorsement from the leadership. The 'HDL', or Hindu Defence League, on Twitter was like a swarm of bees that would sting anyone who questioned their political beliefs. This wasn't healthy debate—it was vile abuse being spewed under the cloak of anonymity. One of my perennial Internet Hindu abusers even rang me up once and invited me for a conference on Hinduism. I was tempted to attend, if only for a bit of fun, but eventually backed off. It isn't as if parties like the Congress and AAP don't have their fair share of Internet trolls, it's just that they aren't as mobilized on social media.

And yet, trolling cannot detract from the more positive aspects of the BJP's well-structured social media campaign in 2014. Gupta spoke passionately about it over lunch at the India Habitat Centre. He struck me as the kind of focused professional the Congress lacked. An IITian, with a doctoral degree from the US, he had worked in Silicon Valley before he got a *bulawa* (call) to return to India. A long-time BJP supporter, he first approached the BJP leadership in 2010 with the idea of setting up a digital strategy for the party. 'I was able to convince the party that this was going to be a crucial piece in future elections,' he says. In July 2013, he formally set up the rather impressive sounding National Digital Operations Centre (NDOC) at the party's headquarters in Delhi with a single point agenda— how to use digital technology to help win the 2014 election. 'This wasn't a one-day affair—we went through many quarter-finals and semi-finals to get ourselves prepared for the big match,' is how he described the planning that went into the BJP's 'Mission 272-plus'.

Three things stood out from my conversation with Gupta. One was the constant urge for innovation among his team, some of it simple as much as it was brilliant. For example, his team created a 'missed call' system as early as in 2011—you give a missed call to a designated BJP number and a party worker would get back to you and feed you details of the Modi campaign or you could even volunteer to join it. The BJP got 1.3 million volunteers through this. Another dial-in number allowed you to listen to a Modi rally live.

Gupta even started Yuva TV, an Internet channel that would webcast the BJP's campaign. 'Our motto was—organize online for success offline,' says Gupta. The aim was to use technology to make Modi available to every Indian across every platform.

The second was the genuine team approach. Their leader may have been a fierce individualist when it came to his politics, but he had built a crack team when it came to technology. In Delhi, Gupta was supervising the NDOC which handled the BJP's Internet and mobile planning. But he was not alone.

One of the key members of the technology outreach was Mumbai-based Rajesh Jain, a successful Internet entrepreneur, who in 1999 had sold his Indiaworld.com venture for Rs 499 crore. Jain was running a mobile data solutions company, Netcom Solutions, when BJP treasurer Piyush Goyal met him in January 2009, seeking a better rate for sending out bulk SMSs for the general elections. 'I was impressed with his strong "nationalist" desire to see the Congress being replaced by the BJP,' recalls Goyal. The two met for dinner with like-minded friends a few days later and their discussions led to the setting up of an advocacy group, Friends of BJP, with Jain as the convenor.

In May 2011, Jain wrote a remarkably prescient blog which caught the attention of Modi. 'The BJP's approach needs to be to work towards creating a wave in 2014, across the country and especially in the 330–350 seats where the BJP is competitive. Switch focus from maximizing allies to maximizing seats for 2014 . . . the party must change its approach from winning 175 seats to winning 250 to 275 seats.'

For the 2014 elections, Jain created a digital software system that was truly revolutionary. It would create a voter identity database right down to the booth level. 'We could track the smallest of households and use the data to build a volunteer base at the booth level which is critical in an election,' a Team Modi member told me. If anyone wished to volunteer for the Modi campaign, all they needed to do was dial 7820078200 and punch in their voter ID card number. The NaMo volunteer programme was kick-started in September 2013 soon after Modi was declared the BJP's prime ministerial candidate. 'It was Rajesh who pushed for the "Power of One" voter registration and the NaMo volunteer programme first, and he did it all with his own money,' says a BJP leader admiringly. Along with another IT professional, Bangalore-based B.G. Mahesh, Jain also created the India272.com portal, a site aimed at further widening the volunteer base for Modi's campaign. He also set up the pro-Modi right-wing website Niticentral.com. The low-profile Jain didn't want to speak on record, but a BJP leader described him as a 'real rock star'.

The third key takeaway was the complete 360-degree approach to the election campaign. When journalists tracking the BJP's manifesto arrived at the party headquarters in early April, they were given a pen drive with a film and the contents of the manifesto. The manifesto release was not just live on television, it was also playing out on the party websites, YouTube, Twitter, Facebook, mobile dial-ins and WhatsApp. From thirty seconds to thirty minutes, separate videos were created depending on the platform. 'This was multimedia carpet-bombing,' Gupta told me.

Fascinated by the power of the Internet, Modi would sometimes attend the meetings of the technology team. 'He's a great listener. He'd see the presentations, give us his inputs and then leave us to execute,' is how one Team Modi member described the exercise. There was, they insist, very little attempt made by the BJP's prime ministerial candidate to micromanage the campaign at any stage.

As in the case with television, it would be an exaggeration to suggest the digital offensive won Modi the 2014 election. It was, at best, a force multiplier. Several parts of rural India in particular still aren't connected to the Net revolution. But when you look at the millions who now use smartphones—the Internet and mobile association claims that mobile Internet users had touched 185 million by mid-2014—there is little doubt that digital media can no longer be ignored in any future election campaign plan.

Indeed, the Internet blitz was another crucial piece in the reinvention of Modi. For example, by building a large and devout

Twitter following, Modi was able to challenge the monopoly of the traditional media on opinion making. Modi was always convinced that a large section of the English-language media would never make him forget the 2002 riots. Now, thousands of handles on Twitter systematically attacked any narrative that challenged Modi in particular and the BJP in general. Journalists increasingly tend to follow Twitter like a wire service and watching social media trends has become part of a reporter's duties. Thus, by sheer force of numbers, Team Modi wielded social media's power over mainstream media's news priorities. On Facebook, too, he was able to connect to a wide urban audience that was looking for a leader they could engage with. It became another vital platform to spread his ideas effectively (13 million people made 75 million Modi-related interactions during the two election months on Facebook).

Most importantly, the technology push enabled Modi to consolidate his new image as a modern technocrat-administrator. This was not a pracharak with a closed shakha mindset, but a leader with an eye to the future. Tech geeks can be ideologically rigid and illiberal, but technology also symbolizes an egalitarian spirit based on merit and opportunity. Modi may have been twenty years older than Rahul, but technology helped him look and feel much younger. No surprise then that his highest ratings were often in the below-thirty age group.

The BJP has often been stereotyped as an ageing Hindu revivalist party which takes up potentially divisive issues like Ram mandir. The technology drive gave it a dramatically new avatar as a party that was holding out the dream of a 'digital democracy'—a nation of mouse, and not snake, charmers, as Modi put it. For a younger, aspirational India, this was just the kind of message of hope they wanted to hear from their leadership.

It was now a message that needed to be taken beyond the digital world. The advertising and media planners were ready to take Brand Modi to the next level.

~

In the first week of February 2014, the advertising agency Ogilvy and Mather's (O&M) executive chairman and national creative director Piyush Pandey got a call that Narendra Modi wanted to meet him urgently. Pandey knew Modi from his 2010 Gujarat tourism advertising campaign which had featured Amitabh Bachchan and had been a huge success. He flew down to Gandhinagar for the meeting. Modi had a simple request: 'I want you to handle my advertising campaign. Only you can do this for me.'

Pandey, with his field marshal-style moustache was an iconic figure in the advertising industry, having won numerous awards. Modi's plea put him in in a slightly awkward position. He had turned down numerous offers to do political advertising in the past, including from Modi in the 2012 Gujarat elections and from the Congress as well. David Ogilvy, his guru, had advised against doing work for political parties in his seminal book on advertising. Modi, though, wasn't going to take no for an answer. 'He was extremely persuasive. Besides, I liked him, felt he was good for India and wanted him to win. I just couldn't say no this time!'

When Pandey returned home to Mumbai, Piyush Goyal, the BJP's treasurer, who was emerging as a key point person in the media strategy, was waiting for him with the contract. Two hours later, the deal was done.

Pandey would design and oversee the campaign but in his personal capacity. Soho Square, a subsidiary of O&M, would handle the BJP account. Madison, headed by another advertising world powerhouse, Sam Balsara, would do the media buying and planning. For the next three months—from February to May—this crack team, assisted by BJP party leaders, well-wishers and professionals, would put together an advertising campaign of the kind an Indian election had never seen. There would be eighteen-hour days and long nights, but there was a single-minded obsession—to make Brand Modi simply unassailable.

When the creative team began planning the strategy, they had three clear goals in mind. First, position Modi as a credible, decisive leader; second, swing public sentiment among fence sitters; and third, create a wave that would push the BJP beyond 272. The approach would be two-fold—target the public anger against the UPA-II government, and then create a sense of hope that Modi would usher in change. Anger and hope would become the twin planks of the advertising assault.

By the third week of February, Pandey's team was ready with its presentation. The BJP had set up a war room in Delhi at 1, Lodhi Estate, a cosy Lutyens bungalow near the busy Khan Market which had been assigned to its Goa MP, Shripad Naik. The power elite of the BJP gathered to watch the ad pitch. Jaitley, Swaraj, Shah, Goyal, Nirmala Sitharaman were joined by pro-Modi business executives like Sunil Alagh, right-leaning columnists Swapan Dasgupta and Ashok Malik, and new BJP entrants M.J. Akbar and Hardeep Puri.

With so many influential voices in one room, there was bound to be some disagreement. Should the campaign slogan be, as the ad agency was suggesting, 'Abki Baar Modi Sarkar', or should it be 'Abki Baar Bhajpa Sarkar'? Sushma Swaraj preferred the latter slogan because she felt that the party must be kept ahead of any personality cult. She was overruled by the Shah–Jaitley duo (some insiders even credit Shah with the original Abki Baar Modi Sarkar idea). Jaitley pulled out surveys which showed Modi's popularity well above that of the BJP. 'This election is presidential, let's keep it that way,' was the overall consensus.

Three weeks later, party president Rajnath Singh went ahead and tweeted, 'Time for Change, Time for BJP, Bahut Hui Mehngai ki Maar, Abki Baar BJP Sarkar.' Within minutes, he had withdrawn the tweet, and twitted 'time for Modi'. In 2014, there was no escaping the Modi factor. The man, in a sense, was the message, artfully packaged. His face would dominate every creative.

The overarching campaign tag line had been clinched. Pandey and team now got down to preparing the creatives. The first outdoor hoarding came up on 7 March at 5.30 a.m. on Delhi's Mint Road. The copy was simple—'Janata Maaf Nahi Karegi. Bahut Hua Bhrastachar, Abki Baar Modi Sarkar!' (The voter will not forgive. Enough of corruption, time for Modi government.) 'Mehngai' (inflation) and 'Bhrastachar' (corruption) would be recurring themes to reflect public disgust against UPA 2.

The first week of March, was, as Pandey puts it, 'crazily exhausting'. A 100 television commercial spots—ten each in different languages—were shot in a span of ten days. 'We shot them as black-and-white commercials with "real" people speaking in their local language. We wanted the idea that the average man on the street was angry to resonate,' says Pandey. Phase one of the campaign had been unleashed on the nation.

Then came a real brainwave. The World T20 was starting in Bangladesh on 16 March through to 6 April. Pandey was a cricket addict, having played Ranji Trophy for Rajasthan. Jaitley had been involved in cricket administration for years. 'Why don't we create a political campaign around cricket and push it on Star Sports while the Cup is on,' was Pandey's suggestion. In a cricket-crazy country, it was the perfect pitch.

Pandey's team got to work again. This time, they came up with a series of animation commercials that linked politics to cricket. The first one was a classic. An umpire goes for the toss with the captains, only to find one captain is missing. The punchline is 'Bina kaptan ki team khai maar, abki baar Modi Sarkar' (A team without a captain loses, this time vote for a Modi government). 'I don't think anyone has used animation in a political campaign. People just loved it. It showed that voting for Modi was a "cool" thing to do!' Pandey told me. Seventeen animation films were done—often four or five in a night—and plastered right through the T20 and IPL season.

The cricket ads were only a bridge before the final assault on the eve of elections in April. If the first phase of creatives in the build-up had been about anger, round two would be about 'hope'. Another simple message to communicate the idea of 'Modi = Hope' was needed. The concept 'Achhe Din Aanewale Hain' (Good days are coming) was born, the line and song attributable to Soho Square's creative head, Anurag Khandelwal.

When the presentation was made to the BJP team at 1 Lodhi Estate, opinion was divided. Some BJP leaders were worried that the 'acche din' focus could become another India Shining, the 2004 BJP campaign that had gone so terribly wrong. 'Should we be raising hopes of people so soon?' was the query. This time, Jaitley and Sushma, for once, were on the same side. The country was steeped in negativism, Modi was offering a shift in mood—the 'acche din' idea was approved. The line would stick in the minds of millions.

In a telephone conversation with my son Ishan who is studying medicine in Manipal in Karnataka, I asked him what the election buzz was on campus. *'Dad, achche din aanewale hain!'* he replied. Clearly, the BJP was onto another winner.

The backstory of the BJP's ad campaign reveals much of how passionately the party fought and won the 2014 campaign. For one, there is every reason to believe that Modi empowered his team fully. There was minimal interference from the leadership which ensured quick decision-making, so crucial in a frenetic election campaign. When a new ad was ready, it would often be sent via WhatsApp, sometimes late in the night, to Modi's office. His assistant, O.P. Singh, would show it to the Gujarat chief minister, who would revert almost instantaneously.

Pandey says that Modi intervened just twice. First, when there was a view that the advertising campaign should emphasize *'Dus Saal Se Bhura Haal'* (Ten years of bad governance). 'I went to tell him that we didn't think it worked, he just said, "*Piyushji, aage badhiye* [carry on],"' recalls Pandey. On another occasion, he was shown a creative with a green line running through at the bottom of every Modi poster. Modi looked at it and changed it to a diagonal line. 'It was actually better than the original,' laughs Pandey.

The campaign highlights once again the centrality of 'Team Modi' and its business-like approach to the campaign. Political campaigns can be notoriously unstructured—king-size egos and internal battles can often be a recipe for chaos. The BJP managed to bring in a strong professional element to their communications strategy and worked in unison.

Manoj Ladwa, a London-born, UK-based lawyer whom Modi trusted implicitly, was in charge of the in-house media research team and had to ensure that all the messaging went out smoothly. The forty-one-year-old Ladwa had met Modi through the Gujarati NRI network in the 1990s, and despite the age difference, had struck an instant rapport. He had also lobbied for Modi with the British government after the 2002 riots. Another Modi man from Gujarat, Vijay Chauthaiwale, who was a molecular biologist and an ABVP activist, handled the back-room operations and coordinated between the Delhi and Gandhinagar war rooms. Ajay Singh, who had worked closely on the India Shining campaign with Pramod Mahajan in 2004, was a key figure in the media buying and planning. Piyush Goyal was the man for all seasons, a crisis manager and the one who controlled the money flow. Shah was the political ideas man. Jaitley was the final word on the creatives.

'We soon realized that we were not dealing with any other political party, but one that was following a professional work ethic that even most corporates could not match,' says Sam Balsara, chairman and managing director of Madison. The respect is mutual. Goyal gives Madison 'eleven out of ten' for the media plan.

But the third, and most remarkable, factor was the sheer intensity of the BJP campaign. In the space of about nine weeks, Soho Square created about 200 unique TV commercials, 300 radio spots and over 1000 press and outdoor creatives. Madison's media plan involved taking more than 130,000 ad spots across 226 channels, 9000 insertions in 295 publications and sixteen languages, and 150,000 ads on websites.

On every voting day, the newspapers of the region going to the polls would be splashed with Modi advertisements in the local language. Every regional channel—news or general entertainment—would have a Modi ad roadblock at 9 on the night before a poll. 'We probably prepared about 500 TV commercials in the end because we weren't sure what the Election Commission would approve. One Election Commission official even told us, *"Ab aur kitna dikhaoge!"* [How much more will you show],' says a member of the ad team.

The 'localization' was, in fact, a distinctive feature of the Modi campaign. Ad films and songs were even made in local dialects like Bhojpuri and Maithili to target the Bihar voter. Separate ad campaigns were created for the five regions of Uttar Pradesh. More BJP ads were done in Urdu than ever before, including one in the Kashmir Valley with the message—'*Jannat Yahan, Tarakki Kahan*' (This Is Heaven, but Where Is the Progress). Spots were taken on FM channels in all small towns. If the ad in Bengal highlighted the chit fund scam, the one in Uttarakhand would focus on the lack of flood relief. 'I think this micro-level messaging was the big difference between 2004 and 2014. This time, we took no chances,' says Ajay Singh.

There was a party anthem as well, composed by lyricist and ad man Prasoon Joshi and sung by Sukhwinder. It had a high-pitched, almost jingoistic flavour to it—*Saugandh mujhe iss mitti ki, mein desh nahi mitne doonga* (I swear on Mother Earth, I will not allow this country to be destroyed). Personally, I didn't find the song striking the right notes, but Modi loved the words so much, he used them in a speech. Modi himself appears in the song with a clenched fist. The song was played on the entertainment channels because, as a media planner puts it, 'that's where the real viewership is'. It was even translated into Punjabi for the audience in that state.

Two instances highlight the sheer energy of the Modi advertising blitz. The first was when Modi in mid-April went to file his nomination from Varanasi amidst massive crowds. The television images of the motorcade suggested a surge of support for him. Almost overnight, a fresh commercial with visuals from Varanasi and Modi's '*Ma Ganga ne bulaya hai*' sound bite was created. 'It was a powerful scene that had great recall value. The viewer could connect "achche din" to the euphoria around Modi,' is how a brand strategist describes it to me.

Pandey has an even better story to share. In early May, Modi took a sudden decision to hold a rally in Amethi, the bastion of the Gandhi family. Just two days before the rally, Pandey got a call from Goyal, saying Modi was keen that a film be created around Amethi's neglect. Pandey was in Goa with his ailing mother-in-law and said it would be difficult to get away. 'Please, Piyush, you have to do this for us. I will be forever obliged to you and I will owe your wife big time,' said Goyal. Within hours, the two Piyushes were flying off to Ahmedabad.

For the next twenty-four hours, Pandey and his creative partner from O&M, Rajkumar Jha, worked on putting together an Amethi film from a small studio in Ahmedabad. A camera team was sent to Amethi to get pictures of crater-like roads, and shanties. The pictures were uploaded via computer from Lucknow, a ninety-minute drive from Amethi. 'It was almost unreal. We were scripting, editing and recording in Ahmedabad, even as someone was shooting in Amethi and sending pictures from Lucknow!' says Pandey.

At 8 the next morning, a few hours before the evening rally, an eight-minute film was ready and flown off to Lucknow. The title of the film was *Amethi: Congress ke Liye Vote kee Peti* (Amethi: A Vote Bank for the Congress), and it was shown at the rally. 'It was the craziest twenty-four hours in my advertising career, but I loved it and felt twenty-five all over again!' says the fifty-nine-year-old with a glint in the eye.

The energy levels didn't drop till the last day of the campaign. Denied permission to hold a rally in Varanasi by the district administration, Modi embarked on a successful roadshow through the city's streets on 8 May. Buoyed by the response, the BJP's media team sensed an opportunity for a fresh campaign film. Within twenty-four hours, a film with shots of Modi in Varanasi was readied—it was fine-tuned at least a couple of times—and aired continuously till the moment the campaign officially ended.

It is this intensity which was missing in the Congress advertising campaign. I had seen shades of it in 2004 when Jairam Ramesh and a small team had developed the 'Aam Aadmi' slogan. Then, perhaps, the Congress had nothing to lose. I had witnessed it again in 2009 when the Congress successfully stuck to its 'aam aadmi' theme. In 2014, the Congress didn't have a big idea nor the hunger to execute it.

The 'aam aadmi' patent was no longer with the Congress. Kejriwal's party had usurped, almost 'stolen' it, and built their own political model around it. Moreover, with price rise hurting the common man, the 'aam aadmi' tag was never going to win hearts. 'We needed something different, a concept that would stand out in comparison with the competition,' is how one Congress leader puts it.

The BJP campaign was Modi-centric. The Congress decided early enough that while Rahul would be the face of the campaign, the slogans would suggest that a party and the country were above any individual. The Congress theme tried to capture the idea of an 'inclusive' India. That's how the original tag lines were conceived— 'Main Nahin, Hum' (Not Me, Us), 'Tode Nahi, Jode' (Unite, not Divide) and the umbrella concept of 'Har Haath Shakti, Har Haath Tarakki' (Strength and Progress for All). The posters had Rahul in the middle, surrounded by anonymous faces, dressed so as to denote ethnic origins—Muslim girl in a headscarf, Sikh boy in a turban, an Adivasi in a dhoti. It clearly lacked originality. 'We wanted to show that the BJP was about a divisive personality cult, while we stood for every Indian,' is how Jairam Ramesh describes it.

One of those Indians featured in a Congress advertisement was a young party activist from Goa, Hasiba Amin. The president of the Goa unit of the NSUI, she was the face of a Congress ad which said, 'Kattar Soch Nahi, Yuva Josh' (Not Fanaticism, but Youthfulness). A young Muslim leader from the Congress, Hasiba became the soft target for a slanderous campaign on social media, initiated by Internet Hindus. She was accused of being involved in a Rs 300 crore scam and having served a jail term. When I checked with my Goa correspondent, he said the reports were 'totally bogus'. I felt sorry for her—no one deserved to be abused in this manner—and rang her and expressed my sympathy. She thanked me in a tweet. The next thing I knew I was being accused of being a 'Congress agent'! In a highly charged election climate, this vitriol was not surprising.

The Hasiba episode, though, raises questions over the Congress ad strategy. Surely, if the party wanted to showcase its commitment to the youth, it didn't need a testimonial from one of its own. It should have gone out and got college students with no party affiliations to vouch for it. 'We shot sixty ads with party workers in different parts of the country because the party saw it as one way to enthuse its cadres,' says an ad executive involved in the campaign.

The Congress campaign was handled by Dentsu. The agency insists that phase one didn't go off too badly. 'We were getting good traction in January, but then the Rahul interview happened, and everything went downhill from there,' is how one of the agency executives described it to me. The leader had been shown up as a political novice on television—demoralization gradually set in.

Till January, the agency had been dealing mainly with Jairam Ramesh, Pradeep Kaul (a former adman and friend of the Gandhi family) and Suman Dubey (journalist and another friend of the Gandhis), with Priyanka Gandhi also, interestingly, being shown all the creatives. Suddenly, in February, a new face called Manoj Bhargava, an NRI entrepreneur from the US, landed up. Bhargava had reportedly run a successful energy drink business in the US and had impressed Rahul with a presentation on brand marketing. 'The guy started ordering us around and dropping Rahul Gandhi's name. He wanted a complete shift in the strategy,' I was told by a member of the ad team.

There was complete confusion. Multiple power centres, typical of the Congress, were emerging. Dentsu threw up its hands; finally, the party's media team took up the matter with Sonia. Manoj was packed off back to America. 'In all the confusion, we lost valuable time. It was a completely unnecessary distraction,' admits a Dentsu team member. By the time the agency was ready with its second phase of the campaign, it was too late.

One big difference between the two campaigns was that the BJP's had simple and clear messaging; the Congress campaign was tangled in jargon and tended to use long-winded words, especially in Hindi. For example, its ads used words like *arajakta* (anarchy), *kaajniti* (work policy) and *sashaktikaran* (empowerment). 'Who the hell uses such bureaucratic language today? This was the worst form of language used by Doordarshan in another era!' is how one advertising professional describes the Congress campaign's failure.

There was also a lack of clarity on the Congress's target audience.

Suddenly, in March, the agency was told that the new focus was to be the so-called 'sandwich class'—not rich, not middle class, not BPL (abbreviated to NRMB). Rahul's adviser, Mohan Gopal, had pointed out that about 700 million Indians, mainly from the unorganized sector, live in this income group and the party needed to shine a light on this group which had derived maximum benefit from UPA-II's policy initiatives. Decoding NRMB may have been an interesting talking point in a seminar, but how would the image be captured in an election advertising campaign? A new ad line was coined: '*Bharat ke Mazboot Haath, Hum Sab Hain Ek Saath.*' (India's Strong Hands, We Are All One.) 'The voter wanted answers to questions of corruption and inflation, and we were giving them some upbeat stuff—it was never going to work,' is the candid admission from Dentsu. Gopal counters, 'The ad agency just didn't understand what the unorganized sector was all about and how to reach out to them.' Many Congressmen insist that it was the sheer money power of the BJP that gave them an added edge. 'The Congress is a poor party with rich individuals; the BJP in 2014 was a rich party with wealthy individuals,' is how Ramesh describes it. A BJP insider insists that the final ad campaign bill was around Rs 385 crore (their opponents insist it was more like Rs 600 crore). The Congress claims to have spent around Rs 300 crore ('We didn't have money left by April,' is what one party leader told me).

Yet the money game is only a slice of the story. The fact is, the BJP played it much smarter. While the Congress ad campaign began as early as January, the BJP put all its might into the final critical phase just ahead of the voting. They also, reportedly, managed to squeeze the television channels for better rates. 'Our plan was to completely take over the media space in the crucial one week before polling—that's when the voter is most influenced,' is how a BJP leader describes the media plan.

Indeed, it wasn't as if the ruling alliance didn't have money during its period in government. In the three years between 2011 and 2014, the ruling UPA spent more than Rs 400 crores on its flagship Bharat Nirman programme's publicity campaign; and

Rs 187 crore were spent in its last year in office alone. The final thrust was planned by Tewari, who had become the information and broadcasting minister in October 2012, perhaps as a reward for his tireless attempts at defending the government on television as party spokesperson.

When the Bharat Nirman campaign was to be unveiled in May 2013, Tewari called some of us for a special screening. A slick short film had been prepared by Pradeep Sarkar, director of the film *Parineeta* and there was a song composed by Rajya Sabha MP and lyricist Javed Akhtar—*Meelon hum aye hain, meelon hamein jaana hai* (We have come a long way, we have a long way to go). The film radiated a feel-good factor—happy farmers, smiling youth, empowered women, along with a list of UPA achievements. 'So what do you think?' asked Tewari, anxiously. I didn't reply but muttered to myself, 'India Shining, Part 2!'

The fact is, for all its claims, the dominant narrative of the UPA-II government had been set—a weak leadership, corruption scandals, slow growth and inflation. No amount of glossy advertising was ever going to fundamentally change the storyline. Credibility was the issue and the UPA had already lost the perception battle. A spotty past record versus the promise of a shining future—the Congress versus BJP war had already been settled in the minds of the voters. And no one in the Congress hierarchy had the appetite to challenge it.

Ramesh later conceded to me, 'Look, the BJP had an idea of hope that revolved around an individual, Narendra Modi; we had an idea of inclusion that was based on issues like right to food. Their idea won. In an election, someone wins and the other person has to lose—why blame advertising for it?' Pandey, too, admits, 'In the end, every successful ad campaign needs a great product to sell. In Modi, we had a terrific Made in India product!'

On 16 May, when the results were announced, Pandey's team had a small party in Delhi's Taj Vivanta (formerly Ambassador Hotel) that is located close to the BJP's 1, Lodhi Estate war room. Three rooms in the hotel had been permanently booked for the advertising executives through the election period. Now was the time to celebrate. As the drinks flowed, there was a banner put up on the makeshift bar. It said, quite simply, 'Abki Baar'!

~

In early June, a few weeks after the election verdict, the Mumbai Press Club held a debate on 'Did the media create the Modi wave?' The self-introspection was occasioned by a growing belief that the media had acted as cheerleaders for the cult of Modi. 'You people have sold out to Modi mania,' was a criticism I heard throughout the campaign.

The Centre for Media Studies (CMS) claimed in a survey of the election coverage of five news channels (three Hindi and two English) that Modi occupied a little more than a third of the total airtime (33.21 per cent). The next highest was Kejriwal with just over 10 per cent of the news space, followed by Rahul Gandhi with just 4.33 per cent. Regional leaders like Mulayam Singh, Mamata, Naveen Patnaik and Jayalalithaa barely registered on the chart.

In an interview to the media watchdog website, The Hoot, AAP leader Yogendra Yadav complained that the incessant coverage of Modi did give him an incremental vote. 'I would say if the BJP had finished 5 per cent down, they would have lost around eighty seats. Roughly speaking, this is the effect you can attribute to the media,' was his conclusion.

Unlike Yogendra, I am not a numbers man. Nor will I hold up the CMS figures as indicative of a pro-Modi bias in the media. The fact is, Modi did become the central figure and the main talking point in this election. The BJP's great success was in making the 2014 elections truly presidential, thereby enabling Modi to set the pace and the agenda. The media was, to that extent, only mirroring a reality that existed in large parts of the country. He got disproportionate coverage because he was, after all, the newsmaker number one. And don't forget, the BJP also did remarkably well in states like Jharkhand and Chattisgarh where media penetration is much less.

256   RAJDEEP SARDESAI

What is true, though, is that the media, especially television, lost its capacity to seriously interrogate the BJP's prime ministerial candidate's leadership credentials. Modi's Gujarat model, which he offered through the election as a symbol of his success, was almost never tested on the ground. Modi said it, we believed it. As a result, we forgot a cardinal journalistic principle—the truth often nestles in shades of grey.

While Modi reaped the benefits of the media's fascination in this election, we must not forget that the TV camera's love affair with the Gandhi family was once perhaps almost as intense. For years, we tended to treat the Gandhi family with exaggerated deference, almost never seriously questioning their prolonged silence and unwillingness to open up on contentious issues, be it their relations with Bofors-accused Quattrocchi, their sources of wealth or their feudal style of decision-making. Sonia Gandhi has been in politics for almost two decades now—how many times have we really been able to quiz her? When I interviewed her in 2005, she almost walked out over a question I raised on dynasty politics. Modi has at least been subject to intense scrutiny for his role in the 2002 riots.

But in 2014, the equation dramatically changed. The same media that had once been hostile to Modi was now effectively co-opted to his side. His every virtue was extolled, the criticism was muted. By contrast, the UPA leadership had to contend with an openly adversarial media from 2009. The Gandhis were subject to searching analysis, and found wanting. The UPA-II government had no place to hide. Much of the opprobrium was deserved, some of it was hyped. The CAG said the country had lost Rs 1.76 lakh crore in spectrum allocation; we believed it, almost uncritically. We screamed 'scam' every time the Opposition told us there was one. Maybe this is an inevitable fallout of a media ecosystem where noise replaces news and sensation takes over from sense.

Or maybe it's just the nature of the beast that is twenty-four-hour news TV which simply gets carried away by the surround sound. Nearly every rally or public event of Modi got live coverage, in a manner that smacked of the herd mentality which bedevils contemporary news TV. One channel would air it, the rest would quickly follow. We even dropped advertising breaks for a Modi rally. ~~amusing~~ On one particular day, Modi had four rallies. We had shown two of them live. I suggested that we need not air the third because it was getting repetitive. Five minutes later, I saw the rally was being telecast. 'Sir, everyone is showing it, we should be showing it too,' was the response in the newsroom. A colleague was even more direct. 'Modi is TRP boss!'

Just how far we were willing to play along with the Modi agenda was reflected in the controversy over the release of the BJP manifesto. The manifesto release coincided with the first day of polling when parts of the north-east, including Assam, were voting. The BJP officially insists they did not deliberately target a voting day but that the manifesto exercise was 'delayed' because Modi was unhappy with the lengthy booklet originally prepared by a team headed by senior leader Murli Manohar Joshi.

Twenty-four hours before the release, there had been an intense debate amongst news channel heads whether we should be telecasting the manifesto release live while voting was on, since it might be seen as a violation of the election code. 'Can you please check this for us?' Shazi Zaman, the head of the News Broadcasters Association, asked me.

I rang up the Chief Election Commissioner (CEC), V.S. Sampath, to get an official view. He promised to get back after seeking legal opinion. A little after 11 p.m., he rang up to say that 'The manifesto release could be shown in all parts of India, except those where voting was taking place.' I pointed out that as national news channels, our telecast was being beamed across India. 'Well, then I leave it to your judgement as to how to ensure the law is not violated,' was his parting shot.

I rang up Shazi, summarizing the gist of my conversation with the CEC. My suggestion was that, 'Whatever decision we take should be a collective one.' Frankly, I didn't want to risk being isolated on the issue.

The next morning, every news channel showed the telecast live even though I think we were all aware we were flirting with the election law. Our public defence—this was a news-worthy event that had to be telecast in viewer and national interest. Our private admission—we know it violates the law, but hey, let's take a chance, especially as the Election Commission hasn't sent us anything specific in writing.

The same philosophy applied again when Modi was filing his nomination from Varanasi on 24 April. It was a really big polling day—117 seats were polling across twelve states. Did a live roadshow of Modi in Varanasi while polling was on in other places constitute an election law violation? It was an open question. Maybe it did or maybe the law itself was outdated in a multi-phase election where every event is in any case being played out on the Internet. The Election Commission's Model Code of Conduct over a nine-phase election violates the Code of Common Sense, fulminated voices on Twitter.

But even if it was legal, was it morally right? Sadly, none of us wanted to even consider raising the troubling ethical questions. Modi was on an impressive march of victory; he was box office—the man the country wanted to see and listen to. We were happy to simply allow the TV studio to be a loudspeaker for his voice, and almost wilfully participate in the propaganda offensive. Cumbersome election laws be damned. Our moral compass as journalists had shifted, almost irreversibly, in the race for TRPs.

On TV, Modi was the dramatic binary contrast to Manmohan Singh and Rahul, the Bharatiya, even 'Dabang' action man, compared to the disconnected Luytensland dynasty. Starved of drama and communication by the uncommunicative UPA and silent Manmohan, the TV camera veered thirstily to Modi for the continuous theatrics and hard-hitting sound bites that emanated from him. In the process did we become participants rather than disconnected observers? Perhaps the media did become part of the Modi propaganda machine, the camera transfixed by the unfailingly sharply dressed PM candidate (apparently, he did not repeat an outfit through the campaign), who seemed to dash between multiple locations with not a hair out of place.

There was no denying the massive viewer interest every time Modi was on air, the sheer size of the rallies, the social media popularity of Modi which became a crucial guide to TV coverage, or the cascading effect of every outlet beaming out Modi, thus perhaps creating a self-perpetuating cycle of constant coverage. The TV camera, I have always believed, is an amoral technology—it covers both good and bad, and it simply goes where the action is. Nirbhaya protests or Ramdev's rallies, Anna Hazare's or Kejriwal's dharnas, in the 24/7 cycle, the camera is invariably drawn to the maximum possible action. Modi was the man who created the action, and inevitably the camera became his constant companion.

In the final analysis, neither sanctimoniousness or self-flagellation is necessary. To suggest the media 'created' the Modi wave is to give ourselves undeserved self-importance. And it is also disrespectful to the mandate given to Modi by millions of Indians who have reposed faith in him. At the Mumbai Press Club debate, ad whizz Piyush Pandey got it right—'Media didn't create the wave, it simply rode on it.'

8

The Making of a Wave

Rahul Gandhi entered what was potentially the most decisive year of his political life by being absent from the country. The young leader's foreign trips were the subject of much speculation within the media and even the Congress party. The bazaar gossip was that he was either in Dubai or London. 'He always spends New Year somewhere out, even Rajivji used to do it,' is how a Congressperson put it to me, rather defensively.

The Delhi that Rahul returned to in the first week of January 2014 was in the grip of a cold wave. What was also slowly becoming apparent was that in this general election year, the Congress party could soon be left out in the cold. The party had just been swept out in the four state assembly elections in December. The CNN-IBN January election tracker brought more bad news—the NDA was now crossing the 230-seat mark; more significantly, the BJP alone was winning around 210 seats. The UPA was way behind, with around 120 seats; the Congress on its own was just below the three-figure mark. Price rise was still hurting, with retail inflation hovering around the double-digit mark. It was the number one public concern, according to our poll. The voters were still very angry with the UPA. The poll even showed that a majority believed that the prime minister had allowed, or had been unable to rein in, high-level corruption.

The other noteworthy statistic from the poll survey was the leadership battle between Rahul and Modi. When asked a straight question on who should be prime minister, 52 per cent preferred Modi, just 16 per cent wanted Rahul. The gap widened when the question was posed in north and west India. The only state where Rahul was ahead was in Kerala. The situation from a Congress perspective was grim.

Digvijaya Singh, the senior Congress leader, was a very worried man. Like many Congressmen, he could see the writing on the wall. But unlike several Congress leaders, at least he had relatively direct access to Rahul. Digvijaya had, so far, been against the idea of making this election Rahul versus Modi. Now, he felt that it was important that the young Gandhi at least send out a message to the party cadres that he was ready to lead. 'The workers need to be energized, Rahulji, they need you to give them a sense of direction, a feeling that we can win this election. You need to lead us from the front,' he said. Rahul nodded attentively. 'Yes, yes, I know, Digivjayaji. When the time comes, we will be ready!'

But time was running out. The AICC session was scheduled for 17 January at Talkatora Stadium in the capital. Hundreds of party delegates from across India had gathered to listen to their leadership. Manmohan Singh, who had just announced his retirement from politics, spoke in the morning. Sonia Gandhi had also spoken before lunch. The crowd, though, was getting restive. *'Rahul Gandhi aage badho, hum tumhare saath hai'* (Come forward, we are with you), was the predictable chant. A resolution was passed that the party would fight the 2014 elections under his leadership.

Rahul finally spoke around 3.30 p.m. A year earlier, he had addressed a similar conclave in Jaipur and delivered his famous 'power is poison' speech. This time, there could be no emotional message of self-renunciation. The party was looking to win an election and needed their leader to take the battle to the enemy. For once, Rahul did not let them down.

In an hour-long speech that alternated between Hindi and English, Rahul displayed an aggression which had been missing so far. He repeatedly targeted Narendra Modi, without naming him. The one-liners came thick and fast: 'Democracy is not rule by one man; democracy is rule by the elected representatives of the people'; 'The Opposition are very good marketeers, they sing, they dance, they can sell combs to the bald. Do not be swayed by their big talk.'

If the party had been looking to revive its fighting spirit, Rahul gave them ample reason for hope. 'No matter how dark the night, India teaches you to fight on. We will go into this battle as warriors, with every single thing we have,' he thundered. The audience of loyal Gandhi family supporters, for the moment at least, was electrified.

He stopped short of pronouncing himself as the party's prime ministerial candidate, saying the Congress was a democratic party and the elected MPs would choose their leader. But there were enough hints that he had finally decided to shed his reluctance to take the plunge. 'I am your soldier, I will do whatever you tell me,' he said, as a rapturous audience cheered him on.

And if there was any doubt that a change in guard had been effected, it came when Rahul turned to the prime minister on the stage and almost 'demanded' of him, 'Mr Prime Minister, nine subsidized LPG cylinders are not enough. This country's women want twelve cylinders every year.' Two weeks later, the UPA government tamely raised the quota of subsidized cooking gas cylinders from nine to twelve per household.

In the studio, we analysed the speech and felt that Rahul had finally come of age. The attack on Modi had been blistering, the kind you expect at election time. His stance and posture were of a man who saw himself as the Supreme Commander of his forces at last. Even the Hindi had noticeably improved, and was near flawless. Most analysts gave the performance eight on ten.

Had the election turned, we asked ourselves. Television likes instant judgements, and a bit of hyperbole—our verdict was that the speech could be a turning point in the fortunes of the Congress party. This, after all, was a party which was umbilically tied to one family. Finally, their yuvraj was showing some signs of stirring and taking charge.

It didn't take long for the bubble to burst. That very morning at the party session, Mani Shankar Aiyar had given a sound bite to the news agency ANI, lashing out at Narendra Modi. Aiyar had a visceral hatred for Modi. In our studio discussions, almost foaming at the mouth, he would liken the BJP's prime ministerial candidate to Hitler, and the RSS to the Nazis. Now, asked for his views on Modi, Aiyar shot back, 'He can never be the prime minister of India, never. However, if he wants, we could arrange a tea stall for him here.'

When I interviewed Mani that night, he refused to accept the charge that he had called Modi a 'chaiwallah'. 'You have a bad habit of distorting everything I say, Rajdeep. You and your channel are past masters at this,' and then almost ripped off his mike.

Mani's political journey had been full of ups and downs. A former IFS officer and a senior of Rajiv Gandhi at Doon and Cambridge, he had joined politics in the 1980s, enamoured by Rajiv's fresh-faced zest to build a new kind of politics. The dream had died a long time ago, but Mani remained a family loyalist, a self-described Nehruvian 'secular fundamentalist'. Labelled a sycophant by his critics, he had seen his own political career drift into near oblivion. He had made panchayati raj his calling card, but this was never going to be enough to sustain his politics, especially as he was from Tamil Nadu, a state where the Congress was a marginal player. He had been removed as petroleum minister, allegedly because he wouldn't bend before the Ambanis; as sports minister, because he detested the Commonwealth Games chief Suresh Kalmadi. He was now a Rajya Sabha backbencher, a nominated MP, courtesy Sonia Gandhi.

His pungent humour made him an entertainer on television; his acerbic tongue meant he had few friends left in politics. At times, it seemed he had never grown out of a debating fraternity in Doon School and St Stephens College, a still too-clever-by-half septuagenarian brat. But this was not a school or college debate where you could throw punches and then share a few laughs. This was a real-life political *akhara*, the jousting being played out on live television. You can be critical of an opponent in politics, but being disrespectful and socially contemptuous is fraught with danger.

I had seen both sides of Mani. He could be a wonderfully convivial host, generous with his food, drink and intellect. But he could also get vicious and personal in debates on TV. 'I don't ever want to come on your channel again—you have no clue what you are saying,' he spat at me once during a nightly slugfest. Next morning, in Parliament, he was happily inviting me for a Track 2 dialogue with Pakistan, another pet subject of his.

Now, he was accusing me and other channels of falsifying his remarks on Modi. The fact is, we hadn't distorted Mani's derisive comment. The reference to the 'tea stall' was as direct as it could get. During his election campaign, Modi had often spoken of how he had started life as a young boy selling tea at the railway station in Vadnagar. It was his way of distinguishing himself from the privileged upbringing of the Gandhi family, and in his speeches he projected himself very much as a pulled-up-by-my-own-bootstraps achiever compared with silver spoon-sucking bungalow babies. Now, an elite Congressman, who identified himself completely with the Gandhis, was mocking his tea boy origins. This was too good a chance to miss.

Prime time on the night of Rahul's best public speech should have been dominated by the Congress leader's 'coming of age' moment. Instead, the BJP got an opportunity to hijack the debate by targeting Aiyar's insulting remark about their leader. A new narrative snaked out to cut the ground from under Rahul's feet—Rahul, the *shehzada* (prince) versus Modi, the *chaiwallah* (tea boy). In an aspirational, highly socially competitive India where there is growing rage against elite and entitled privilege and where sensitivities on 'westernized' condescension towards desi mores run high, Mani had just scored another self-goal for his beleaguered party.

~

'Where did the idea of "*Chai pe Charcha*" come from?' I asked several BJP strategists. No one gave me a clear answer. 'Good ideas always come from the leader,' a Team Modi member put it diplomatically.

There was a distinct Modi touch to the concept. Right from the time I had first met him during the Ayodhya rath yatra, I could see he was a shrewd event manager. I would often joke in the office, 'If Modi loses the election, we should hire him as our chief marketing officer!' He fancied the idea of branding any occasion that he felt would resonate with the voter. 'Chai pe Charcha' was one such occasion.

'The idea was to create a *nukkad* [street corner] Parliament,' is how Prashant Kishore of Citizens for Accountable Governance (CAG) which executed the Chai pe Charcha concept describes it. A chai stall is, after all, omnipresent across the country. From a small village to a sprawling metropolis, having a cup of tea was a universal Indian experience. Now, Modi would be identified with it.

There was also another, less obvious, reason behind the idea. In early February, the Aam Aadmi Party's popularity had peaked. The AAP was making the headlines across the country by taking its politics to the street and directly communicating with the voter. The AAP had also launched a sustained attack on Modi's proximity to corporate India, suggesting that he was a *'khaas* aadmi' who was disconnected with the 'real India', an attack potentially far more damaging to Modi than the Congress trotting out shopworn secularism shibboleths. 'We were acutely aware of what the AAP was doing and needed our own bit of street theatre to combat the AAP's communication strategy,' says a BJP leader.

Chai pe Charcha was the perfect answer to correct any impression that Modi was not an 'aam aadmi'. A tea stall where a potential prime minister sits with his fellow citizens drinking chai—what could be a greater equalizer? There was always, of course, the subtext of Modi having grown up in poverty that would also play out. Team Modi, it appeared, had hit upon another winning formula. Mani Shankar Aiyar's unwise snobbery had been superbly marketed to win public sympathy for the so-called social pariah.

Ironically, on the many occasions I had chatted with Modi, I had never heard him speak about selling tea at a railway station. In fact, in all his political campaigns as Gujarat chief minister, Modi had never referred to his early years in Vadnagar. His politics had always been fashioned around the present and the future, not about his past. A senior Gujarat journalist told me the tea story was, in fact, bogus. '*Sab jhoot hai, unhone koi chai nahi bechi*' (It's all a lie, he never sold any tea), he told me confidently.

But Modi's younger brother Prahlad insists that the brothers did help their father who ran a tea stall near the Vadnagar railway station. 'Our school was next to the railway station, so whenever we got a break, we would go and help my father,' Prahlad told me. Later, as a teenager, Modi worked with his uncle Babubhai who had a canteen-cum-tea shop near Ahmedabad's bus station. 'Narendrabhai would get up at 4.30 a.m., make hot pakoras and chai and sell them at the bus stand,' claims Prahlad. Congress leader Ahmed Patel says Modi would only sit at the billing counter of his uncle's canteen. 'From what I have found out, he never actually sold tea,' Patel claims. It seemed to me a case of nitpicking. Modi had, all said and done, endured a tough childhood.

Maybe some of the hardships had been dramatized over the years. Ambedkar decried India's hero-worshipping culture and indeed we Indians quickly make legends of our leaders. Many apocryphal stories are spun and admiringly retold about a larger-than-life figure. In Vadnagar, I was told that Modi as a child had swum across the lake braving crocodiles!

Fact or fiction, the chaiwallah story had acquired a life of its own. As always with Modi's campaign, the choreography and use of technology was brilliant. The first Chai pe Charcha event took place on 12 February 2014 from the Iskcon tea stall in Ahmedabad. It was relayed live in 1000 tea stalls in 300 cities, all connected by video conference. Modi would appear on a giant screen at each stall with a cup of a tea in hand, taking selected questions from the CAG website. 'We created a truly multi-media event that played out on television, Internet, mobile and DTH,' says Kishore.

The theme for the first 'charcha' was Modi's favourite subject—

good governance. In March, on International Women's Day, Modi's second discussion over 'chai' was on women's safety and empowerment. Modi sat in a tea stall in Delhi, a city which in the aftermath of the anti-rape protests was a perfect location for the subject. The third and final charcha was at the end of March, from Vidarbha in Maharashtra, where the conversation was on farmmer's suicides in a region where agrarian distress was a major concern. 'The locations, the topics, all were chosen with an eye on what makes news,' says a Team Modi member. Using satellite technology, the three Chai pe Charcha events touched 500 cities and 4000 locations—the messaging had been scaled up in typical Modi style. Interestingly, one of the country's largest corporates, Videocon, loaned their field staff to set up the infrastructure for the Chai pe Charcha events. This again was quintessential Team Modi—plan in-house and then get an outside vendor with expertise to execute the project.

I didn't find the content of the charchas particularly news worthy. The questions asked had been carefully vetted. Most of the time, Modi would give lengthy answers, and no cross-questions were posed. As a journalistic exercise or an exercise in democratic questioning of a politician, it didn't really work. As a public relations ploy, though, it was a cracking success. Modi, the humble 'chaiwallah', was aspiring to be the country's prime minister—it was a classic poverty-to-power script that even Salim–Javed couldn't have bettered.

I realized just how effective Chai pe Charcha had been while covering the elections in south Bangalore. I was trying to get the usual vox pop on the street, asking people what they thought of Modi. At a local restaurant, a group of young men smiled at me and said, 'We are all with Modi,' and then holding up cups of tea, they exulted, 'Time for Chai pe Charcha!' If, in the heart of south Indian coffee country, tea was the flavour of the season, you knew something unique was happening.

~

On 5 March, the Election Commission sounded the bugle for the sixteenth general elections. A nine-phase poll would be held from 7 April to 10 May, with the counting scheduled for 16 May. We had commissioned another election tracker in the week leading up to the announcement—once again, it showed the NDA steadily inching up, now crossing the 240-seat mark. The UPA was in danger of falling further behind. A Modi-led government now seemed inevitable. The only question raised in the television studio was whether Modi would have enough allies to form a coalition government, or would he be isolated like Vajpayee was in 1996, because of his 'communal' tag. On our expert panel, P. Sainath, the distinguished journalist, made a memorable remark. 'Rajdeep, once the BJP crosses 220 seats, it will become a secular party for everyone!'

Prophetic words. Just a week before the big election announcement, Ram Vilas Paswan joined the NDA. It was a psychologically important moment. Paswan, after all, had left the NDA in 2002 over the Gujarat riots, demanding Modi's resignation. Now, the Dalit leader from Bihar was sharing a stage with the man whom he once accused of 'dividing' the country.

The backstory to Paswan's re-entry into the NDA fold is indicative of how the die was being cast. For months, Paswan had been trying to forge a grand 'secular' alliance in Bihar with Lalu Prasad and the Congress. Lalu wouldn't take his calls, the Congress was undecided. Then, one evening, Paswan met Bihar BJP leader Shahnawaz Hussain on a flight. 'Why don't you consider joining the NDA—we may be able to give you a better deal,' Hussain told him.

Paswan prevaricated at first but his son Chirag grabbed at the idea. The dashing young man had tried his hand at Hindi films, failed, and was now looking for a break in the family business of politics. 'Modi is winning the elections,' Chirag told his father. 'Let's just join the right side this time.' When I interviewed Paswan for a programme, it was his son who did all the talking. The pro-Modi generation gap was showing here as well!

Getting Paswan on board suited the RSS too. Part of the Sangh's strategy was to woo as many Dalit leaders as possible to their side—Udit Raj in Delhi, Ramdas Athawale in Maharashtra were all brought on board. 'We wanted to create a sense of a pan-Hindu identity without saying so openly,' admits a BJP strategist.

More allies quickly followed. From Maharashtra came an important farmer leader, Raju Shetty. Just weeks earlier, Shetty had come to see me and said he had an offer to join the AAP. I later asked him why he had switched to the Modi camp. 'In rural Maharashtra, there is no AAP. The only person the rural youth want to listen to is Modi!' he said. The deal was stitched by the Maharashtra BJP leader Gopinath Munde.

The BJP also tried to strike a secret deal with the Maharashtra Navnirman Sena (MNS) leader Raj Thackeray. In the 2009 elections, Raj's presence had cost the BJP–Sena alliance around eight seats because he split their vote. Gadkari was assigned the task of wooing Raj. The meeting was fixed in a five-star hotel in central Mumbai. 'The only problem was that as we entered the hotel lift, a journalist saw us. The meeting was no longer secret,' Raj told me later. The Shiv Sena, which was engaged in a family war with the MNS, wouldn't allow the deal to go through. But an agreement was still reached— Raj would at least support the idea of Modi as prime minister.

Raj, unlike his cousin, the very earnest-looking Udhav, was charismatic. He had modelled himself on his uncle, Shiv Sena founder Bal Thackeray. Like Balasaheb, Raj enjoyed the good things of life—beer, cigars and an enviable DVD library of old movies; he also had an impressively large collection of aftershaves. The Great Dane which guarded his residence seemed to trumpet his tough style. We had common friends, most notably Sachin Tendulkar. Raj loved play-acting before the camera. He would be warm and friendly in conversation, but the moment the camera was switched on, he would become openly hostile. In an interview we did during the elections, he kept asking me to 'keep quiet', 'sit back' and 'behave yourself'. The moment the interview was over, he laughed, 'Arre, Rajdeep, did you like my style, *maza aya*? I am sure you will get huge TRPs for this interview!' It was, as they would say in Mumbai, 'full-on drama'.

That every seat mattered for the BJP was confirmed when the

party decided to allow its former Karnataka chief minister B.S. Yeddyurappa to return to the fold. For months, Yeddyurappa, who had been tangled in corruption charges, had been kept waiting. Advani was against allowing him back into the BJP. Modi had no such compunctions. 'If Yeddyurappa can get us even one or two extra seats in Karnataka, it's worth it,' was the verdict. He was, after all, still the party's most powerful Lingayat face and mass leader.

Yeddyurappa, his forehead perpetually adorned with sandalwood and fingers crowded with rings, like so many Indian politicians, is a great believer in astrologers and gurus. During one meeting, he introduced me to a gent who looked a bit like one of the less pleasant creatures from Tolkein's *Lord of the Rings*. 'This man can predict your future,' he assured me. It was a bit surreal. I had gone to interview a powerful politician but was instead given a discourse in palmistry and planetary perambulations.

Perhaps the political stars were with Modi in 2014 and the netas could foresee the future. Smaller parties from the north-east also joined the NDA. But the big prize came from Andhra Pradesh when Chandrababu Naidu, another former chief minister, formally shook hands with the BJP. This alliance had been in the making for months. Naidu, we were told, was desperate because he was running out of cash in a state where money plays a major role at election time. His great rival, Jagan Reddy, by contrast, was flush with funds. Naidu needed Modi for his political survival.

The journey of Naidu reflects how no one can be written off in Indian politics easily. Between 1999 and 2004, Naidu, the bearded, trim, industry-friendly, tech-savvy creator of 'cyber' Hyderabad, was one of the most powerful politicians in the country and a crucial ally for the Vajpayee-led NDA. The business dailies gushed over him as the CEO of Andhra Pradesh, a man who was driving Hyderabad's IT superpower dream. He had virtually forced the NDA to call an early election in 2004, a move that proved fatal for him. The moment he lost the election, the world suddenly turned against him. When he was in power, we would all queue up to interview him; out of power, he was ignored. Whenever he'd call to say, 'Let's meet,' I, too, found myself making excuses. Political Delhi is a ruthless city and an out-of-office Naidu just didn't make news.

But I did meet him in early 2014 while he was negotiating an alliance with the BJP. 'Modi is a very far-sighted leader,' he told me. 'We need to come together to defeat the Congress which has divided my state.' I asked him whether his claim to be a 'secular' politician would take a knock if he joined a Modi-led NDA. 'At the moment, the challenge before us is to save Andhra Pradesh,' was the response. Modi's past was being quietly buried by his one-time political adversaries.

At one stage, Modi had hoped that Jayalalithaa, too, would join his team, but she wanted to be the captain herself. With limited options, the BJP plumped for actor-turned-politician Vijayakanth as the chief prop for an alliance in Tamil Nadu. Vijayakanth's Desiya Murpokku Dravida Kazhagam (DMDK) was a typical example of a New Age small regional party, available, we were told, to the highest bidder. These parties are often one-person shows with small but well-defined pockets of influence that enable them to bargain with larger parties from a position of relative strength. Vijayakanth, for example, had won around 10 per cent votes in the 2009 Lok Sabha elections, enough to make him a potential 'swing' factor. 'He will negotiate with everyone and then will go with whoever gives him the best money deal,' is how one Tamil journalist explained Vijayakanth's politics.

The BJP was a minor force in Tamil Nadu. It had won just seven seats from the state in fifteen previous Lok Sabha elections. But that didn't stop Modi from addressing major rallies in Chennai. Or from meeting Tamil superstar Rajinikanth in April 2014, just ahead of polling in the state. The meeting was projected as a courtesy call but was obviously much more than that. Rajinikanth described Modi as a 'strong leader' and a 'good friend'. 'The Rajini–Modi photo op may not have given us extra votes in Tamil Nadu, but we were able to send out a message across the country that even the most popular face of south India was effectively endorsing him,' claims a BJP strategist.

The pan-India appeal was what Modi was constantly seeking. Speaking to him a few days after the Tamil Nadu alliance was sealed, I sensed that he saw an enlarged NDA as crucial to his self-image as a genuine 'national' leader. *'Yeh political punditon ko lagta tha ki koi hamein join nahin karega . . . ki Modi untouchable hai. Ab yeh kya kahenge?'* (Political pundits thought no one would join us, that Modi is an untouchable. Now, what will they say?), he said to me on one of our calls. Modi will not concede it, but he had been anguished by his years of political 'isolation'; now, he finally felt politically 'acceptable' and his rehabilitation was tinged with pique.

This search for wider acceptability even led Modi to reach out to Muslims. Our election surveys were consistently showing that Muslims still remained very wary of the BJP prime ministerial candidate. Zafar Sareshwala, Modi's gnome-like, media-friendly Muslim face from Gujarat, was assigned the task. Zafar has a strong bond with Hindi film writer Salim Khan and his actor son Salman. Salim had been in touch with Modi since 2009 and the two had struck a friendship. Salman, Hindi cinema's box office king, was more wary. 'I am not politically inclined at all,' the actor had once told me. We had double-dated together once in college; while I had grown old and grey, the six-pack star remained the eternal eighteen-year-old.

It was Salim who persuaded Salman to make the trip to Ahmedabad. Salman's film *Jai Ho* was releasing on 24 January and the actor was on a punishing promotional campaign. Modi suggested 14 January, the date of Gujarat's famous Uttarayan kite-flying festival, for a meeting. The moment he arrived in Gujarat, Salman was treated like an honoured state guest. The astute political salesman, ever alert for a headline-grabbing opportunity, Modi took Salman on a kite-flying outing. Salman in a Being Human T-shirt flying a kite next to Modi—it was the ideal photo op the BJP leader craved for, even if Salman stopped short of endorsing him as prime minister. 'To have a popular icon like Salman standing next to Modi helped us a lot when we were trying to convince Muslims to give Modi a chance,' claims Sareshwala. The kite-flying happened in a

Hindu-dominated area of Ghatlodia (no Muslim comes here, claimed Zafar). The photo op was now being projected as a momentary breaking of the infamous invisible 'borders' that divide many of Gujarat's towns between Hindu and Muslim quarters.

In February, Sareshwala organized a trade exhibition to showcase Muslim-owned businesses in Gujarat where Modi was the star attraction. 'You must come and see what Modi is doing for the Muslims. You can even sit next to him on stage as a special invitee,' he told me. I attended the function but preferred not to be on stage. In his brief speech, Modi spoke glowingly of Gujarat's Kutch Muslim artisans and the community's work ethos. 'My government is here for you,' he claimed. The audience, though, was dominated by wealthy property developers, restaurant owners and car dealers. The average Muslim, it seems, still saw Modi through the prism of 2002. He would clearly need to do much more than well-crafted photo ops to win their trust.

Modi, though, wasn't too concerned that his pitch to the Muslim community had made only a limited headway. With small and large parties by his side, he was now heading a robust twenty-party-plus NDA alliance. The Congress, by contrast, was in danger of either gaining no new friends, or, in some instances, losing even its sitting MPs.

Jagdambika Pal, its senior UP MP and spokesperson, quit on the eve of the elections. The off-record reason he gave some journalists on the Congress beat for switching sides reflected poorly on the party. Apparently, he had been seeking an appointment with Rahul for weeks. 'Every time I tried, some operator in his office would keep me waiting on the phone. I finally got tired of waiting!' he claimed. He, like many Congress MPs, did not have direct access to Rahul nor his mobile number. But the truth is, Jagdambika, like so many others, just wanted to be on the winning side. The saying in UP, after all, is 'Ugta suraj ko sab namaksar karte hain' (All salute the rising sun).

The only new ally the Congress got was Lalu Prasad in Bihar, and even that was not without controversy. Rahul did not like Lalu. The RJD leader, he felt, represented an old-style politics of caste and corruption that discomfited him. When he had spoken out against the ordinance that provided a reprieve to convicted MPs, it was leaders like Lalu who had been Rahul's target. In the 2009 Lok Sabha and 2012 assembly elections in Bihar, Rahul had resisted a Congress–RJD tie-up. This time, too, he kept Lalu waiting.

Meeting Lalu at his Delhi residence as he waited for a nod from the Congress, I could sense his growing frustration. I said I wanted to interview him. *'Arre, interview toh theek hai, par pehle bolne ko kuch hona chahiye'* (I can do an interview, but at least I should have something to say). I asked him what the problem was. *'Arre, hamein kyon poochte ho, Rahul Gandhiji se poochiye'* (Why ask me, go and ask Rahul Gandhi). Lalu eventually waited for almost a month to seal the deal when he should have been out in the battlefield of Bihar.

The uneasy Rahul–Lalu equation summed up the Congress leader's limited world view. For Rahul, Lalu was the village idiot, not a potential ally to do business with. Rahul failed to realize that under the cloak of the clown ticked a very sharp political brain. I had met Lalu for the first time in the early 1990s—a meeting of an English-educated south Bombay boy with a rustic Bihari. Our interview was fixed for 11 o'clock. I arrived at 11 a.m., only to be told that Lalu had meant 11 p.m. We set up for the interview in his official residence, only to be told that it would take place not in the house but in the cowshed in order to broadcast the right 'effect'! The spitting, bellowing cowherd's send-up of elite politics was part reality and part highly strategic performance. Interview over, Lalu tried to teach me how to milk a cow. *'Tum angrezi logon ko yeh sab seekhna chahiye'* (You anglicized folk should learn how to do these things), he told me with barely concealed contempt at my failed attempts.

Lalu had built his political reputation as a saviour of the minorities by arresting Advani during the 1990 rath yatra. And the source of his political appeal lay beyond just Muslims and his fellow Yadavs. In 1995, when he scored a big win in Bihar, he invited me to a late-night celebration. The garden at the chief minister's bungalow had been converted into a song and dance soirée—the drink, too, was flowing. Sitting in a corner was an old man in a slightly torn shirt.

I went up to him and asked him what he was doing there. 'I am a street vendor. Laluji has given an open invitation to all of us to come and celebrate here tonight,' he told me. Then he said, tellingly, *'Pehle toh hum chief minister bangle ko bahar se bhi dekh nahi sakte thhe, aaj Laluji ne toh hamein izzat di'* (Earlier, we couldn't even see the chief minister's house, now Lalu has given us respect).

Yet, Laloo's drive for empowering backward castes quickly descended into a dark pit of corruption, criminality and family raj. I remember interviewing Rabri Devi the day she was sworn in as chief minister, with Lalu constantly prompting her from the sidelines. One sensed his time was up and the revolution he once championed had devoured him. And yet, one couldn't help but admire his principled stand against majoritarian communalism through good times and bad. Call it my fondness for the underdog (or lovable crook), but Lalu for me was sui generis.

Rahul obviously didn't share my affection for Lalu. But while he dithered on even this one alliance, Modi and the BJP pushed ahead with the ticket distribution. In a meeting with RSS leaders, the BJP strategists had made it clear—this time, winnability was the defining criteria, emotions had to be set aside. Predictably, the old order in the BJP made one last attempt to have its way. L.K. Advani, for example, wanted to move from his Gandhinagar seat and contest from Bhopal instead. He was worried, he told friends, that Modi would sabotage him in Gujarat, and preferred the 'safety' of Madhya Pradesh. The new BJP leadership held firm, calling it a bogus argument. 'Advaniji was again trying to create a false conflict between Modi and Shivraj Chauhan—we would have none of it, ' a senior BJP leader told me. Advani had to stay put in Gandhinagar.

Another veteran BJP leader, Jaswant Singh, had even less luck. He was keen to contest from his hometown of Barmer in Rajasthan. The party had reluctantly agreed but Rajasthan Chief Minister Vasundhara Raje put her foot down. 'His wife once filed an FIR against me, he has spoken ill of me. He cannot be given the ticket,' she insisted.

Jaswant was always a bit of an odd man out in the BJP. A

former armyman who loved his Scotch and literature, he was a
reminder—with his clipped British major accent delivered in his
fruity baritone—almost a caricature, of a bygone colonial era. He
had been forced out of the BJP in 2009 after writing a book which
suggested that Jinnah, the founder of modern Pakistan, had been
unfairly demonized. Even after he returned to the party, he had few
friends left in the BJP. His only real ally, Vajpayee, was now too
infirm to help him. At seventy-six, he was now part of the BJP's
past; Vasundhara was its present. His ticket was denied, which led
him to leave the party. In the midst of his revolt, Jaswant gave me
a notable sound bite, worthy of a redoubtable Rajput. 'They think
I am a fossil, but I am a proud fossil!'

'If he had stayed in the party, we could have considered him for
governor or even as ambassador to the US,' a senior BJP leader
later told me. The Jaswant episode highlights that, contrary to
speculation, it wasn't Modi who was unilaterally taking decisions on
ticket distribution. In a collective exercise, state leaders were given a
much greater say. But there were a few seats, especially in Gujarat,
where Modi had veto power. One such seat was Ahmedabad east.
A seven-time MP, the silver-tongued Harin Pathak represented one
of the safest BJP seats in the country. But Modi was convinced that
Pathak, who was close to Advani, was part of a group in Gujarat
that had tried to undermine his authority. 'I have given my life for
this party when we were nothing in Gujarat, but you know how
Modi is. He can be very vindictive,' Pathak later told me ruefully.
The seat was given instead to film star Paresh Rawal, whose dialogue
delivery, many said, had a striking resemblance to that of Modi.

While the BJP had a surfeit of ticket aspirants, the Congress had
a very different problem—in some states like Bengal, it wasn't even
finding enough candidates to contest. 'If you know anyone who
speaks good Bengali, let us know!' one Congress leader told me
jokingly. Worse, some of its sitting MPs, including Union ministers
like Manish Tewari, didn't even want to contest. While the tickets
were being decided, Tewari was admitted to hospital complaining
of chest pain. The official reason he gave us was, 'I don't think I can

stand up to the pace of an election campaign.' While his health was a concern, Manish was also upset that the party hadn't allowed him to contest from his preferred Chandigarh seat. With the Congress left with no allies in Tamil Nadu, finance minister Chidambaram also dropped out, pitching for his son to contest instead. 'Mr Chidambaram isn't sacrificing his seat—he is sacrificing his son instead,' was the joke in the Congress headquarters.

Rahul, meanwhile, had pitched his own 'novel' idea to the party at its AICC session—a system of US-style primaries to select candidates in fifteen specific constituencies. 'We must empower our grass-roots workers. Give them a say in who they want as their candidates,' he told the AICC. In principle, it seemed like a bold innovation, designed to 'open up' the political system. In practice, it was a disaster—some sitting MPs objected to their constituencies being chosen for this, and there were familiar charges of bogus voting and infighting. 'Of all the daft things we did, this was one of the stupidest. Instead of fighting an election, we were fighting amongst ourselves,' a senior Congress leader later told me. He was right. India is not the US, and if a political experiment is to be attempted, it can't be done on the eve of a crucial national election. The primaries were held in February and March even as the campaign was kicking off. Not even one out of the fifteen candidates chosen through the primary system won their election—the naivety of Rahul's team was cruelly exposed yet again.

The 'primary' concept also exposed the widening gulf between Rahul and the old guard in the Congress. Ticket distribution in the Congress is a complex exercise aimed at faction management—the party distributes the tickets to various groups based on a traditional patron–client system. It was perhaps an archaic way of functioning, but many Congressmen felt it was the only system which worked. 'In previous elections, Ahmedbhai [Ahmed Patel, Sonia's political secretary] managed it all and we had clarity. But with Rahul, we were always second-guessing what he was planning to do next,' a senior Congressman told me. Another veteran Congressman was more caustic. 'When you fight an election, you give tickets based on "winnability"—Rahul seemed to be handing out character certificates.' Even here, there was no consistency. Ashok Chavan was given a ticket even though he hadn't recovered from the Adarsh scam taint but Suresh Kalmadi was frozen out.

A senior political commentator met Rahul in early February while he was preparing for the election campaign. He came out of the two-hour-long meeting convinced that Rahul was 'totally out of it'. 'It was just one long crib session. He kept telling me how he is just a cog in the wheel, and how difficult the UPA-II government had made life for the Congress, how he was having difficulty finding the right people for the party,' the analyst recalls. Rahul apparently even felt that 'inflation' wouldn't hurt the Congress chances because only the rich complained about price rise, the poor had food security. 'I really don't know which planet Rahul is living on,' the analyst told me.

Interestingly, Rahul had spoken a very different language after the party's debacle in the December 2013 assembly elections. Then, he had strode defiantly to the Congress headquarters and told the waiting media, 'I am going to transform the Congress organization and I will do it in ways you cannot even imagine.' Now, just two months later, he was claiming to be just a 'cog in the wheel'. Far from being transformed, the Congress and its leadership was already looking battle weary.

When we broadcast our final election tracker towards the end of March, the NDA figure was pushing towards the 260-seat mark—272-plus was now firmly in sight. The Congress was in total disarray, slipping further to under eighty seats. Aware that this election was theirs to be won, the BJP decided to go for the kill. The perfume of victory was in the air.

~

After offering prayers at the Vaishno Devi shrine, Narendra Modi began his final march towards Delhi with a Bharat Vijay rally in Jammu on 26 March. Modi had already addressed more than 200 rallies since becoming BJP's prime ministerial candidate in September.

Now, with the first voting day less than two weeks away, Modi decided to take his campaign to another level. Over the next seven weeks, he would address as many as 185 rallies spread across 295 constituencies, often doing four, at times even six, in a single day. An *India Today* report claimed that by the end, Modi would have travelled 300,000 kilometres, or seven times the Earth's equatorial circumference.

Organizing the logistics for the rallies was a team of about fifty people at the party's headquarters in Delhi, led by party MP Mukhtar Abbas Naqvi. It was a gargantuan exercise, ensuring, for example, that the BJP's privately hired multi-camera teams were present at each major location to uplink a feed that could be carried by all news channels. The camera teams were told to ensure plenty of close-ups of Modi and crowd shots that would effectively project the vastness of the rally.

There was even a small research team at the BJP party headquarters which would monitor all the media to check on what the Opposition was saying about Modi and ensure that their leader could respond quickly if required. 'We created a system of instant feedback, apart from providing all the background of a constituency Modi was visiting,' says Naqvi. The information would then be sent to the chief minister's office where it was filtered by Prateek Doshi, an OSD to the chief minister, who had originally joined the Modi secretariat as an intern on a fellowship programme. As with so many members of Team Modi, Prateek was young, bright and professional (he had done a management degree from Singapore).

But the real heavy lifting was done by Modi himself. Starting his day at 5 a.m., he would go to bed well past by midnight. Meditation, a light breakfast, a pre-fixed interview. By 8.30 a.m. (sometimes even earlier, if he was flying to the north-east), Modi would be ready to take off. Travelling with him was his ever-faithful personal assistant, O.P. Singh, while two others, Dinesh Thakur and Tanmay Mehta, would hold the fort at the chief minister's office. All three had been drawn through the RSS pool.

As he criss-crossed the country giving one speech after another, he would drink warm water to protect his throat. He kept his food simple—dal, roti and *sabzi* that the local rally organizers would prepare. 'We only told them to put less oil and salt, and keep it very basic,' a Modi aide told me. On long flights, he would catch a little sleep but mostly worked on his speeches and Gujarat government files. He would almost always come back to Gandhinagar every night, primarily because he didn't want to bear the additional parking costs of the private plane hired from the Adanis, he said.

He was inexhaustible. 'Earlier, the aim was to just target winning areas, but by the end, almost every candidate wanted Modiji to address at least one rally in their area,' Naqvi told me later. North, central and western India had been the BJP's primary catchment area for Mission 272-plus, and this is where Modi's original travel plan had been focused. But carried away by the large crowds, Team Modi was now seeing the possibility of extra seats in non-traditional areas like Bengal and Odisha. '*Odisha aur Bengal mein to chamatkar ho sakta hai*' (There could be a miracle in Odisha and Bengal), Modi told me once, excitedly. He even ventured into small states like Arunachal and Manipur. 'Every seat counts,' was his mantra.

I asked Modi in one phone conversation what kept him going. '*Yeh toh ab ek mission hai, ek junoon hai. Mehnat karne se aadmi kabhi nahi thakta!*' (This is now a mission, a craze. No one gets tired from doing hard work). I sensed that the early years of discipline in the shakha as an RSS pracharak were now an asset for life.

Much has been said about Modi's oratorical flourish. A close aide told me that their leader had a knack of being able to deliver a speech with minimal preparation. 'All we did was provide him a few bullet points detailing some local issues—the rest was all his mind.' One of his great skills was to convert an abstract idea into popular idiom. So, when some of his strategists in the last phase of the campaign suggested that the BJP should push for a stable government, Modi went to Himachal and delivered a simple slogan, '*Yeh Dil Maange More!*', referring to the famous words of Param Vir Chakra winner and Kargil hero, Captain Vikram Batra. When the Congress challenged his 'idea of India', Modi countered by unveiling his *indradhanush* (rainbow) of ideas by quoting from the Upanishads and the Rig Veda.

Vajpayee had been the BJP's supreme political orator. I remember Advani once almost enviously confessing, 'We used to be awestruck just listening to Atalji speak.' Vajpayee's style was that of the poet-politician—lyrical and emotional, he could sway an audience with the *jadoo* (magic) of the Hindi language. Even his long pauses were redolent with meaning. He could leave you teary-eyed as he did me when I heard him speak during the 1999 Lahore bus yatra. Modi is different. His style is that of the pugnacious streetfighter, full of machismo. He can captivate you with his energetic presence and rapid-fire one-liners, but he doesn't tug at your heart.

Modi's speeches at the rallies had a set pattern. He would begin by applauding the audience while slowly raising the pitch. A few words in the local language would enthuse the crowds. While raising a local issue, he would often contrast the situation in that state with what he claimed was 'development' in the BJP-ruled states. And then would come the final promise. 'Give me sixty months, I will bring change!' Interestingly, Team Modi had ensured that trained cadres would mix with the crowds, both to gauge the response and to try and enthuse the crowd at the right moments.

I attended one Modi rally during the campaign. It was in Meerut in February 2014, a rally that was taking place against the backdrop of the riots in the neighbouring district of Muzaffarnagar. The crowds were massive. People from the entire western UP belt had come by the truckloads to listen to Modi; some had even climbed up electric poles. For at least sixty seconds before he spoke, the crowds kept chanting his name and blowing conch shells (the rally had been branded Vijay Shanknad Rally). When Modi contrasted a 'powerless' UP with a fully electrified Gujarat, there were wild cheers.

Sonia Gandhi had just attacked Modi for sowing what she described as '*zehar ki kheti*' (fields of poison). Modi now hit back, accusing the Congress of spreading the poison of communal division. Rahul had always been dismissively referred to as 'shehzada' by Modi. Sonia was usually given a little more respect, though in the

2002 campaign he had dubbed her the 'lady from Italy'. Now, the gloves were off again as Modi called for a '*Congress Mukt Bharat*'. 'The poison of vote bank politics has been spread by the Congress and a family which has ruled the country for most of the years since independence,' he said, rousing the crowd into a frenzy.

The direct attack on the Gandhis was deliberate. Good governance was the overarching theme of Modi's campaign, with the idea of drawing in new voters to the BJP; but Modi was also keen to make 'dynasty' an issue—it was 'us' versus 'them', son-of-the-soil karyakarta versus the born-to-rule First Family. Non-Congress leaders have often been accused of being a little intimidated by the Nehru–Gandhis; now, Modi was actually calling for dismantling the edifice of the Congress party.

When Modi first called Rahul a shehzada, I had asked him about it, suggesting that the tone and words sounded politically incorrect. Modi was characteristically defiant. '*Kya galat kaha hai? Woh to shehzada hi toh hai*' (What is wrong, he is a prince). Other BJP leaders admitted to me privately that Modi's language could at times be coarse, but as one of them reminded me, 'Elections aren't a place for politeness!'

Sniffing victory, Modi became even more belligerent. He would fine-tune his speech to suit the location. In Bihar and UP, the thrust remained on governance and the Gujarat model, but in Assam and Bengal, he did raise the more communally charged issue of Bangladeshi migrants. 'You don't expect him to talk of bullet trains in Assam,' said one BJP leader to me sarcastically. It was classic *rajneeti* (politics).

Earlier, he had been careful about attacking regional leaders. Now in this final phase of campaigning, it was 'Modi versus all'. In Bengal, he attacked Mamata Banerjee for her alleged role in the chit fund scam and even questioned the sale of her paintings. In Odisha, Naveen Patnaik was upbraided for underdevelopment; in Maharashtra, it was the Pawars who were targeted. Even his old friend Jayalalithaa was not spared. 'These are my political adversaries, not my enemies,' he would say later.

The Modi offensive rattled his opponents. Mamata said she would have put the BJP leader in jail if she was in power in Delhi. Her spokesperson Derek O'Brien went a step further by tweeting, 'The butcher of Gujarat who could not take care of his own wife, how will he take care of the nation.' This was, by all accounts, a low blow. Appearing on my programme that night, Derek, a TV quiz host-turned-politician, was unrepentant. 'Read my lips, Rajdeep, Modi is the butcher of Gujarat!' he said with a showman-like elan. As those words echoed on TV I felt quite sure that while the Trinamool seemed to be pandering to its Muslim vote in Bengal, a few more fence-sitter votes might just have been lost nationally.

The story of Modi's wife, Jasodhaben, which Derek raked up, is worth reflecting upon. That Modi had a child marriage and a wife tucked away in the village was one of the worst kept secrets of Gujarat politics. I had tried to meet Jasodhaben once during the 2007 Gujarat assembly elections, only to be advised by a local friend to avoid bringing up the issue. 'Modi is very sensitive about it. Best not to interview her and only worsen relations with the chief minister,' was the advice I was given. I took the hint, choosing not to pursue it as it seemed like a private matter between two individuals.

But was it really a 'private' issue? Modi acknowledged Jasodhaben for the first time only while filing his nomination from the Vadodara seat for the 2014 elections. Till then, he had kept his marital status column blank because Election Commission rules do not make it mandatory to reveal it. But did it require a statutory change in election documents for Modi to publicly accept that he had a wife?

Yes, it may have been a forced marriage for the teenager who had left home soon after to join the RSS. Yes, it should not have any impact on his credentials as an able administrator. But should he not have at least acknowledged Jasodhaben's existence, or else annulled the marriage and given her 'freedom'? In an interview in the *Indian Express*, Jasodhaben hinted at her long years of loneliness as a schoolteacher who had never remarried, living in her brother's home. While Modi worked towards political glory, did he ever spare a thought for the girl he married when they were adolescents?

It's a question I would have ideally liked to ask Modi, but never did. Or dared to, even in private conversation. I don't think he would have answered it. Perhaps, like the chaiwallah story, the single-man image was designed to dress up his politics—the ideal *brahmachari* (bachelor) politician who had devoted his life to nation building was also part of the Modi myth-making factory. The 'bachelor' CM's appeal among Gujarati women voters was well known and his identity as the family-less *karmayogi* was subliminally projected in all advertising and political campaigns. Jasodhaben's identity was, tragically, almost expendable.

And yet, the shrillness of the attack on Modi by some of his critics was equally jarring. One of the worst offenders was the SP leader Azam Khan. In one rally, he said, 'Modi's hands are coloured with the blood of innocents'; in another, he spoke of how 'Kargil's peaks were conquered by Muslim, not Hindu, soldiers'. This was spiteful hate speech, designed to divide communities, the kind that deserved more than just an Election Commission ban.

Frankly, I was not surprised with Azam Khan's behaviour. I had a run-in with Khan first in 2006 when we had done an exposé on his alleged land-grabbing in his bastion of Rampur. *'Main aapko jail mein daaloonga'* (I'll put you in jail), he had threatened then. A year later, as UP Speaker, he wanted me to appear before the state assembly for doing a sting operation that showed UP's politicians ready to trade in drugs for cash. He could speak flowery Urdu but could also be abusive. He represented that breed of dangerous politicians who saw themselves in pure religious terms, a politician who was a 'defender of the faith'.

Khan's anti-Modi rhetoric was predictable. The Congress, by contrast, seemed rather confused. When Modi's ascent first began in 2013, some Congressmen were unwilling to see him as an equal to their leadership. 'He is only another chief minister—why give him so much importance,' was the official party line. Others, though, could not stop taking him on. Kapil Sibal challenged Modi to a face-to-face debate. Salman Khurshid called him a 'frog', Jairam

Ramesh referred to him as a fascist and Bhasmasur (a mythological character who had destroyed his creator).

That muddled approach seemed to influence Rahul too. He had avoided direct references to Modi in many of his public interactions. But in election season, he suddenly stepped up the heat. Modi was now Hitler, and worse. I attended a Rahul rally in Ghaziabad where he lashed out at his BJP rival. The Congress candidate here was the charismatic actor-politician Raj Babbar. If, at Modi's Meerut rally, the crowd had a desi rock concert feel to it, here there seemed to be an almost surreal silence. The noisy excitement, such an integral part of a festive occasion like an Indian election, was missing. It was almost as if the audience couldn't relate to what the leader was saying.

Rahul spoke of Modi's 'toffee model' of development. He claimed that the BJP leader had sold valuable land at just Re 1 to the Adanis, while farmers and the poor were neglected. 'Where once there was a partnership between Vajpayee and Advani, now Modi and Adani are business partners,' was Rahul's charge. There were a few, almost forced, handclaps.

Kejriwal had already challenged Modi's business links—Rahul looked like a copycat. If Rahul had wanted to seriously interrogate Modi's Gujarat model, then he should have done it much earlier. The 2012 Gujarat assembly elections would have perhaps been a good time. A Team Modi member admitted to me, 'We were far more vulnerable then. That was the big missed opportunity for the Congress.' Now, it seemed almost like an afterthought. In the decade after 2002, the Congress's principal attack on Modi had been his handling of the riots. He was for the party, as Sonia Gandhi had described him, a '*maut ka saudagar*'. The gambit hadn't worked. The trenchant criticism only allowed Modi to play victim. Where the Congress failed to challenge the Modi narrative was in his claims to be solely responsible for the Gujarat growth story. 'Modi makes Gujarat seem like a land of milk and honey and he as the only development-oriented leader. We never did enough to puncture holes in his storyline,' a Congress strategist confessed later.

The list of mistakes didn't end just there. At a rally in Indore, Rahul claimed that Pakistan's intelligence agency, ISI, had contacted some Muzaffarnagar Muslim families who had been affected by the riots. It gave Modi just the opening he was looking for. 'Rahul should name the families, else apologize to all Muslim youth,' was Modi's riposte.

The truth is that an Intelligence Bureau (IB) report had pointed to possible ISI links in western UP. But the report, like many IB reports, was short on specifics. 'You don't make IB reports the subject of a political debate in this manner,' a senior IB official told me. If Rahul was drawing attention to a national security concern, then he should have addressed it differently. By going public with a sensitive issue, he had angered local Muslims who felt they were being stereotyped as potential terrorists, and confirmed the worst fears of Hindus who were already feeling they were under siege. It was a unique role reversal. Modi was now talking the language of communal amity, Rahul of polarization.

Out of curiosity, I tried to find out who was Rahul's speech-writer. Typically, I was given no clear answer. 'He has a team to help him,' I was told. So who was in this 'team'? 'Well, Jairam Ramesh used to be involved, now it's Mohan Gopal; Sam Pitroda provides inputs, so do Kanishka and Sachin Rao, and so does Priyanka. It all depends on the subject at hand,' was the best response I could get. It sounded a bit like a pig's breakfast!

Even Jairam, who could have played the lead role in Rahul's speech-writing team, appeared to be slowly edged out from the inner circle. I recall ringing him up and suggesting that we could do a youth-centric show with Rahul where he could take questions from IIT/IIM students. 'Good idea, will share it with Rahul,' Jairam told me. A few weeks later when I asked Jairam whether there was any progress, he simply shrugged his shoulders and pleaded helplessness. Rahul's one-time political 'guru' Digvijaya Singh's son-in-law, Paranjayadityasinh Parmar, scion of the royal family of Santrampur in Gujarat, who had been pushing for a ticket from Gujarat, was also struck off the final list. It was almost as if the spectre of looming defeat had pushed Rahul into a self-imposed cocoon of aloofness where he trusted very few people. 'We are told that leadership demands that when the going gets tough, the tough get going—here just the opposite was happening,' is how a Congress MP summed up Rahul's plight.

Senior journalist Coomi Kapoor relates a delightful story which perhaps exemplifies the widening gap between Rahul and the party. Apparently, Rahul had come to campaign in Devgarh Baria in the tribal-dominated Dahod constituency of southern Gujarat. The party candidate, Prabha Taviad, was prevented from sitting on the stage when Rahul was speaking by the SPG even though she tried to explain to them that she was, after all, the local Congress candidate. Rally over, Rahul shook a few hands and rushed to the helicopter. The candidate was desperate to have a word with her leader. *'Bhaag, Mummy, bhaag!'* her children implored her. She ran after Rahul, only to find that he was already sitting in the helicopter and on his way to another rally.

As the campaign wore on, it was obvious that Team Rahul was still groping in the dark for a big idea to counter the BJP. When Modi embarked on his Chai pe Charcha, they were again forced to react in an attempt to recapture at least the 'aam aadmi' space. Rahul had spoken of an 'open manifesto', one that would be shaped by interacting with Congress workers, civil society groups and people working in the unorganized sector. Mohan Gopal was assigned the task.

Several meetings were organized with prominent NGOs as well as informal sector groups like railway porters, fisherfolk, rickshaw pullers, stonecutters, street vendors and anganwadi workers. 'It was a unique exercise in the history of Indian politics. For the first time, a leader was engaging with those who had been marginal to decision-making. Through this one gesture, we could activate hundreds of NGOs and gain enormous goodwill,' Gopal later told me.

In theory, he may have had a point. In reality, high inflation and low growth meant that Team Rahul's target audience—those who were just above the poverty line and yet not quite middle class—was also feeling the squeeze. Modi's promise of a return to a high-growth economy was attractive to this social group. 'We were offering them a New Deal based on legal rights; Modi was using this aspirational class for a fascist takeover,' is how Gopal tries to draw a contrast between Rahul and Modi's approach.

The fact is, the Congress needed to make a strong comeback in an election in which they were trailing. The Rahul interview had been a disaster and the party was trying to desperately reposition their leader. Every time Rahul carried out a public interaction, a hapless member of the Congress media cell would call us and plead, 'Please cut live—it will be very interesting.' Sadly, it wasn't.

The interactions were somehow wooden and scripted, an attempt by Rahul to do an Aamir Khan in *Satyamev Jayate* by talking to 'real India', but defeated by his own self-consciousness. Aamir's show worked because of its clever positioning as an alternative to regular television entertainment shows. The viewer had tired of soaps and reality shows, and was looking for something different. Rahul's addas didn't catch the eye because he was sermonizing and theorizing at a time when the nation wanted answers to the burning issues of the day—from price rise to corruption.

Yes, there was the odd lively exchange. For example, Rahul had a passionate debate with railway coolies. But it was all too brief and clearly wasn't enough to alter the course of the political debate. Rahul's own epiphanies about India, whether on caste identity or gender rights or decentralization of power, felt like college seminars, hardly the shooting-from-the-hip, directly communicative speeches voters could connect to.

Modi's Chai pe Charcha had drawn attention because it was excellently packaged, even if the content was unexceptional. Rahul's town hall-like programmes didn't work because they had neither glossy marketing nor a well-defined message. 'To be honest, we needed to take the battle to the enemy camp. Instead, our leader was still acting like a jholawalla engaged in the discovery of India's poor through group discussions!' is how one frustrated Congressman summed it up for me.

Through March and April, as I travelled around the country for a series of on-the-ground reports, I could see which way the political wind was blowing. In south Bangalore, where former Infosys posterboy Nandan Nilekani was contesting, I met a group of techies. 'We'd love to vote for Nandan, but he is the right man in the wrong party. *Abki Baar Modi Sarkar*!' they shouted in unison.

Already something of an icon among educated youth, Nandan had joined the government in 2009 and initiated the ambitious Aadhar citizen identification project. As a lateral entrant into politics, he offered hope to many private-sector professionals who wanted to shift to public service. In a normal election, Nandan might have had an edge over an Ananth Kumar, a five-time BJP MP accused of doing precious little for the city. But this was no longer a 'normal' election. At Mavalli Tiffin Room (MTR), Bangalore's most famous south Indian eatery, I asked an old man why he was still voting for Ananth Kumar if he was a failed MP. 'This election is about Modi, not Ananth Kumar,' he told me as he poured the ghee over his dosa.

In south Mumbai, Milind Deora was considered a certain winner for the Congress. But I knew he was in trouble when I met an old school friend who said he was going to vote for the Shiv Sena for the first time. 'I strongly disapprove of the Sena's brand of politics, but I want to see Modi as our prime minister,' he rationalized.

In Chandni Chowk, my former journalist colleague Ashutosh was contesting on an AAP ticket. There was still some goodwill for AAP, but this wasn't a Delhi assembly election but a national referendum. The local shopkeepers verdict was emphatic—'We tried Congress, we tried AAP, now only Modi for India!'

Ironically, the only city where I noticed a slightly divided opinion was Amritsar in Punjab where Modi confidant Arun Jaitley was contesting a Lok Sabha election for the first time, against former Punjab chief minister Amarinder Singh. Jaitley could have stood from a Delhi constituency but the fear of the AAP had led him to look for a 'safe' seat. Akali MP Naresh Gujral convinced him that Amristar, with the backing of the Badal family, was the right choice. Jaitley's wide circle of high-powered friends had all descended from Delhi to express solidarity with their *yaar*. It almost seemed like a *baraat* for a *shaadi*, with Jaitley as the *dulha*. While covering the constituency, I would often bump into someone from Delhi. 'We all hope Arun wins, he's such a nice guy,' was a shared feeling. I wondered, though, how their presence was really helping his campaign since a number of them seemed more intent on discovering Amritsar's best kulcha chole joints! By contrast, driving in convoy with his turbaned posse in the city of the Harmandir Sahib, Amarinder Singh looked every inch the Sikh-of-the-soil.

Indeed, on the ground in Punjab, it was apparent that the Modi wave had hit a bit of a wall. At a popular dhaba in the heart of Amritsar, I drank a cool glass of excellent lassi with a group of morning walkers. The dominant sentiment was anti-Akali more than pro-Modi. The local leaders, I was told, were disgustingly corrupt. 'Yes, we want Modi as prime minister. Jaitley is also good, but first we need to teach the Badal government a lesson,' was a common refrain. The Akalis were accused of promoting the worst form of family raj where their relatives monopolized all state resources. It was another telling reminder that the Indian voter cannot be taken for granted. Jaitley may have moved to Amritsar from Delhi to escape the AAP factor, but it was in Punjab that the AAP's anti-corruption plank would resonate most tellingly—the party eventually won all its four Lok Sabha seats from Punjab.

Amritsar, though, was just one out of 543 seats in the country. The overwhelming feedback elsewhere was of a rising Modi wave. A desperate Congress was in a state of utter despair. An attempt was made to get Sonia Gandhi to campaign a bit more aggressively. Sonia had, perhaps consciously, chosen to take a backseat in the election build-up. This, after all, was supposed to be Rahul's moment in the political sun. Her long-serving aides like Ahmed Patel and Ghulam Nabi Azad were already feeling sidelined by Team Rahul. Patel had direct access to Sonia and could virtually walk in and out of 10, Janpath. 12, Tughlaq Lane, Rahul's office-cum-residence, was different. Here, Patel had to ask for time and was kept out of key elements of the campaign strategy. When I asked him about it, he denied having differences with Rahul. 'He is our leader,' was the cryptic response. Truth is, there was an acute generation gap. Patel and Azad, both veteran crisis managers for the party, had been contemporaries of Rajiv. There was a communication issue too—one sensed that Rahul was more comfortable with the English-speaking politicians who shared his political beliefs. 'I think he has a disdain for a particular type of Congress politician. Maybe he sees them as oily dealmakers,' is how someone who knows Rahul well described his attitude to the party's old guard.

Aware that Rahul was not being able to challenge Modi on his own, Sonia decided to step up her assault on the BJP leader. She probably still had more spunk left in her than her son. 'She is the only real politician left in the party,' is how a Sonia loyalist put it to me. One April evening, just as I was going into the 9 p.m. bulletin, my Congress correspondent Pallavi Ghosh sent me an SMS. 'Sonia is going to make an address to the nation on TV shortly. It could be important.' On the face of it, it seemed a bit odd—nationally televised addresses are normally made only by the prime minister or the president of India, not by the Congress president. Would Sonia make a dramatic announcement that she, and not Rahul, would now lead the Congress charge in the final phase?

Our rising excitement at a potentially big news break didn't match the end product. The Congress put up a short video on its website of Sonia addressing the country and warning that the BJP would destroy the 'Bharatiyata', the 'Hindustaniyat' of the country if it came to power. Looking a little weary and speaking in halting Hindi, Sonia with this short intervention was never going to be enough to halt Modi's march.

The Gandhi family brand had plummeted in recent months. With her accented Hindi increasingly met with howls of derision, Sonia's weak harking to the Congress version of Bharatiyata sounded only like the wail of a rotten old order, far removed from the restless dynamism of the times. Just days before her Bharatiyata statement, Sonia had secretly met Syed Ahmed Bukhari, the Shahi Imam of Jama Masjid. The Shahi Imam had appealed to Muslim voters to stand with the Congress and stay away from the 'communal' Modi. That a discredited cleric was being used to woo the minorities only reflected the bankruptcy of the Congress's tattered secular vision. The country had moved well beyond the fear that a Modi-led government would create a divided India. Her instinctive aversion to Hindutva politics notwithstanding, Sonia appeared to be caught in a time warp. This election was being fought on who offered a better governance vision and, importantly, on who could revive the economy, not by stirring past memories of a Hindu–Muslim conflict.

To this day, I maintain that the Congress just failed to understand the Modi phenomenon, failed to grasp that he had presented himself as perhaps India's first true post-liberalization politician. The social changes set in motion after the great economic transformation of 1991 (ironically, kick-started by the Congress) created generations of Indians for whom wealth creation and upward mobility became the fundamental markers of the good life, even as their licence-permit era parents' and grandparents' ambitions may have centred on government jobs and academic qualifications. A new India had bounded into existence—restless, aspirational, with access to the information superhighway, the silicon economies, multinationals and global opportunities. The explosion of purchasing power, the shopping mall culture, the booming service industry, new industries in leisure and tourism . . . all contributed to a society where the consumer marched one step ahead of the citizen. This new Indian wanted efficiency, good services and the ability to get rich fast (and yes, a nice smartphone!).

Culturally, globalization even spurred a return-to-roots faddishness, a nationalism born from anxieties about westernization. This unique historical moment where consumer culture and fascination with wealth sat alongside nationalism and a desire to see India as a First World economy created conditions for the Modi phenomenon. He promised wealth, uber-nationalism and access to quality public goods for those he liked to describe as the 'neo-middle class'. This 'neo-middle class' was, in a sense, Modi's answer to the Congress's aam aadmi, and captured the vaulting aspirations of a rapidly changing India, from a taxi driver to a call centre operator and from a pizza delivery boy to a hair stylist in a small town. In this new India, within a fiercely competitive political environment, Sonia Gandhi seemed like a neta from another era; a younger, restless, aspirational India had no time for history lessons in Bharatiyata.

By early April, the whispers in the Congress corridors were getting louder: 'If Rahul can't deliver, if Sonia can't revive us, can Priyanka save us?'

9

The Big Fight: Amethi and Varanasi

Like her mother, Priyanka Gandhi Vadra has always been an enigma. She carries the allure of the family surname, yet remains intensely private. Her dressing style is delightfully schizophrenic—she is sometimes seen in international-style designer wear at Delhi parties, and at other times goes native in handloom saris in Amethi and Rae Bareli. Charismatic, charming, good-looking and intelligent, she is a media favourite, an effortless occupant of newspaper front pages and TV headlines.

I first met Priyanka during the 1999 general elections. She was in Amethi, supervising Sonia Gandhi's debut foray into electoral politics. We had a programme on NDTV called *Follow the Leader* and the consensus in the newsroom was that Priyanka would be an ideal choice for it. I telephoned Sushil Kumar Shinde, the senior Maharashtra leader who was then the party's point person for Amethi, and asked if he could help arrange an interview. 'I don't know for sure, Rajdeep. Why don't you come to Amethi and take a chance?' he suggested helpfully.

When we reached Amethi, the security presence around the Gandhis was intimidating. Nor could we find a decent place to stay. I spent the night in a tiny dingy room with Shinde as my room-mate.

'Let's go early morning to Priyankaji's place. There is less security then. If she sees you, she might agree,' Shinde advised.

So, at 6 the next morning, anxious for my interview, I parked myself outside the Munshiganj guest house where the Gandhis were staying. I needn't have worried. The moment Priyanka arrived, she appeared to recognize me (television does have its advantages!) and offered us a cup of chai. I mentioned that we wanted to spend the day travelling with her on the campaign trail. She readily agreed and almost instantly got miked up for her first media interview.

For the next twelve hours, the young woman was pure television box office. She was wonderfully effervescent and spontaneous as she handled party workers and excited crowds with ease. She was able to strike an instant rapport with women in particular. Many of them would say, *'Beti, aap toh bilkul Indiraji kee tarah dikhti hai!'* (You look a lot like Indira Gandhi.)

I must confess I was bowled over. We even had lunch in the middle of a field in Amethi with Shinde lovingly serving us parathas and achar, all of it captured on camera. A few years later when Shinde became Maharashtra chief minister, I teased him that it was his lunch service in Amethi that did the trick!

I asked Priyanka whether she would enter politics. 'No, no. I am only here to help my mother. Otherwise, I am happy being away from it all,' she said with a smile. It's a refrain I would hear almost constantly for the next fifteen years. In 2004, when I returned to Amethi, she was there again, only this time she was helping her brother and mother who had now shifted to the neighbouring Rae Bareli constituency.

I kept in touch with Priyanka. She had kindly given me her mobile number, would always reply to an SMS and was helpful in fixing the odd meeting with Sonia. Occasionally, we'd bump into each other at a private gathering where she would be unfailingly gracious. The one time the equation seemed to sour was in 2012 when Kejriwal first raised the issue of her husband Robert Vadra's land deals. I asked if she or Robert would like to respond.

Her response was terse. 'Why don't you journalists leave us alone?

Do you know what impact all of this is having on my children?' I had read stories of how Priyanka was a devoted mother who often attended her children's sports events in school. She also strongly denied the Delhi gossip that she and Robert had separated. 'Where do you guys get all these stories from?' She sounded genuinely hurt and angry. I backed off a bit.

Till 2014, it was clear that Priyanka had drawn a Lakshman-rekha on her involvement in politics. Whenever a Congressman publicly implored her to contest elections, her office issued a strong denial. 'If I decide to enter politics, I won't do it in some secretive manner,' she would tell me. The 2009 election victory appeared to settle any doubts as to who would take forward the family legacy. A doting sister, Priyanka seemed content to remain in Rahul's shadow, their us-versus-the-rest relationship most famously captured in the photograph of the siblings arm in arm in mutual consolation after the UP defeat in 2012.

The year 2014, though, was different. The Congress was in serious trouble and Rahul's leadership was under the scanner. Priyanka was still unwilling to play a formal role in the party's decision-making, but it was clear that her involvement was growing beyond Amethi. She would be spotted visiting Rahul's house while strategy meetings were on and she had been involved with the Congress advertisement campaign with every creative being shown to her. 'She may not have been hands-on, but she certainly wasn't hands off,' is how a Congress insider describes her presence.

From early April, Priyanka was in Amethi and Rae Bareli. Her brother and mother were the party's main campaigners elsewhere; she was needed to keep the family turf secure. Amethi was no longer a safe constituency—in the 2012 assembly elections, the SP had won three of the five segments, the Congress just two (they had lost all the Rae Bareli seats too). Rahul had done some good work in the area—most notably, a women's self-help group project—but UP's perennial issues, especially bijli, sadak, pani and shiksha troubled the residents here as well. 'Sir, yahan toh andhera hi andhera hai' (There is darkness everywhere),' is how one Amethi resident put it to me.

In fact, one could sense a growing frustration amongst the people about Amethi's stagnant condition. At more than one 'Nukkad Sabha' that Priyanka addressed, she would have to listen to irate villagers speaking out: *'Priyankaji, dus saal ho gaye, Rahulji ke aane se kuch nahin badla'* (Ten years have passed, nothing has changed with Rahulji coming here). The Indian voter is still attracted by the family name; the Nehru–Gandhi brand has a magnetic appeal in their bastion. But voters in Amethi are no different to their peers elsewhere and they can no longer be taken for granted by promises without delivery.

I never quite understood why UP's VIP constituencies like Amethi and Rae Bareli haven't seen greater progress. One only has to look towards the Pawar bastion of Baramati in Maharashtra to see what a VIP constituency can look like. In sharp contrast to Amethi, the Pawars had turned a sleepy village into a dynamic agro-industrial hub. The Gandhis clearly hadn't shown the entrepreneurial vision of the Pawars in transforming lives in a backward region.

Perhaps there was just something in the air of the Gangetic plain that retarded growth. It was almost as though the sharply polarized politics here had placed caste and community above vikas. Or maybe there were just well-entrenched interests and mafias committed to keeping the industry of backwardness alive and thriving. Certainly, the adversarial relationship between the state and Central governments didn't help. My own view is that the Gandhis, like many feudal politicians, were trapped in a *mai–baap* culture and that the odd public sector project can never be a substitute for long-term infrastructure (Amethi's roads are designed to rupture the backbone).

The BJP had sensed that the breeze of parivartan that was blowing through UP could, if not sweep, then certainly challenge, the Gandhi family dominance in this eastern UP pocket. For years, the Opposition had been accused of giving the Gandhis a soft landing in their pocket borough. Narendra Modi and Amit Shah were determined to change that perception.

Which is why the party dramatically announced the candidature of Smriti Irani from Amethi. A television soap star-turned-neta, the feisty and fearless Smriti was ready for a new role. Smriti had once spoken out against Modi on the Gujarat riots but then quite successfully (and uniquely, I might add) had been able to win him over. Modi liked Smriti's unflinching spirit and communication skills (I rather think he also saw her modern woman in a sari–sindoor image as a potential long-term counter to Sushma Swaraj whom he did not like). On prime-time television, we journalists appreciated Smriti's willingness for a fiery joust—she always came to shows well prepared and spoiling for a good fight. As a Rajya Sabha MP taking on Rahul, she had nothing to lose. 'I am going to Amethi to win—it's not a token fight,' she told me.

Also fighting from Amethi was the AAP, which put up Kumar Vishwas, another TV-savvy neta. Unlike Smriti who saw Amethi as another step up the political ladder, Vishwas was looking for his fifteen minutes of fame. A Hindi poet, he was a great favourite on Hindi news TV because of his quick wit and sharp one-liners. I told him once in an interview that he was being seen as a 'joker in the pack' in Amethi. Pat came the reply: *'Circus mein sabkee nigahein joker par hee toh hotee hai!'* (In a circus, all eyes are on the joker.)

Rahul and Priyanka versus Smriti versus Vishwas—Amethi had suddenly become a made-for-TV high-profile contest. Priyanka knew she was in a contest this time, which is why she decided to raise the pitch. The moment she stepped out to address rallies, she became the Pied Piper of Amethi. Cameras would follow her everywhere. It became a media circus. The message to the newsroom was that one reporter must track Priyanka all the time—you never know what she would say where. Chasing Priyanka wasn't easy for the swarm of journalists. They had to fight not just the heat but the SPG as well.

My former colleague Shreya Dhoundial was assigned the task of trailing Priyanka. She describes to me a typical day. 9 a.m.: stand outside the Munshiganj guest house; 10.30 a.m.: thrust your mike at the car window as Priyanka's car leaves the gate but with no luck; 10.35: start chasing the car with around fifty other crew and OB vans, with the SPG fleet as an immovable barrier in the middle; 11 a.m.: Priyanka stops to meet people, so you stop, try and shoulder your way through the circle of towering AK-47-wielding commandos, get your mike as far forward as you can towards her, she just smiles and drives away. 'Finally, we struck a deal. If Priyanka spoke to us once every morning for even thirty seconds, then we would leave her alone for the rest of the day,' Shreya told me later.

I remember asking Priyanka's secretary Preeti Sahai whether it was worth my coming to Amethi and seeking an interview. 'For now, no interviews. She will only give sound bites while on the campaign,' I was firmly told. 2014 was no 1999. Then, there were just a handful of cameras. Now, with hundreds of news channels around, getting an exclusive with Priyanka was that much more difficult.

The sound bites, too, were well choreographed, designed to create just enough news to keep the hungry bite-soldiers (as we referred to our reporters) feeling happy and also to take potshots at the BJP leadership: 'You don't need a 56-inch chest to run India but a big heart!' 'How can a person who snoops on other women respect the Indian woman!' Her best Indira Gandhi-style regally dismissive remark about the BJP was that they were 'running around like panic-stricken rats'. For news channels, these sound bites made perfect headlines. Priyanka Gandhi taking on Modi became an almost regular sideshow for about a fortnight in the larger electoral battleground.

Priyanka's punchy remarks seemed to get under Modi's skin. He hit back and, unsurprisingly, Robert Vadra was the Achilles heel he targeted. 'The UPA model of governance is RSVP (Rahul, Sonia, Vadra, Priyanka). How did one person multiply his earnings from one lakh to 400 crores in five years?' he asked. The BJP's media department even prepared a video detailing Vadra's land transactions.

Right through her campaign, Priyanka did not take any direct questions on her husband—a dismissive gesture with the hand and a suggestion that this was a 'bunch of lies by panic-stricken people' was all that she was willing to say. I got the sense that one reason she didn't want to do a lengthy interview was the fear that the Vadra question would inevitably crop up.

I had briefly encountered Vadra at a couple of social events but never really spoken to him. Often dressed in black, with a tight belt, manicured moustache and a well-toned body, he looked more like a trendy dance show contestant in an *India's Got Talent* show than a businessman (I am told Priyanka was swayed by his dancing charms when she first met him!). Robert had sent rejoinders to the media, but the charges just wouldn't go away. The fact that many of his windfall profits had been acquired from deals in Congress-ruled states like Haryana and Rajasthan was a reality he could not escape from. He simply needed to answer more searching questions. Till he is willing to do so, Vadra will remain a cross that Priyanka will have to live with if she ever enters electoral politics. Already, his name painted on every security-exemption list at airports had enraged the aam janata as a symbol of undeserving VIP privilege.

The Priyanka factor meant that, for a few days at least of the election campaign, the media gaze appeared to shift from Modi. When I interviewed Amit Shah later, he caustically remarked, 'Priyanka may be good for your TRPs, she will have no impact on this election.'

On 2 May, Shah made a sudden visit to Amethi to review the campaign. The feedback he got astounded him. Smriti, with her oratory and boundless energy, was making rapid gains. The general feeling was that the party had a real chance to cause a big upset in the constituency. 'We really felt it was a *kaante ki takkar* [tough fight],' says Sudhanshu Mittal, one of the BJP leaders who had based himself in Amethi.

An excited Shah rang up Modi. 'I think you should do one rally in Amethi also. It could be just what we need to spring a surprise.' Amethi had not been on Modi's original itinerary—there had been a tacit understanding among the Opposition to avoid a direct conflict with the Gandhis. Modi, though, was itching for a fight.

The 5th of May was the last day for campaigning in Amethi. That was the day Modi decided to make his late charge into Rahul's turf by cancelling another scheduled public meeting. Almost overnight, an ad film detailing Amethi's woes was prepared (see chapter 7). Shah asked the RSS–VHP–BJP local leaders to galvanize the cadres from the neighbouring areas. On the ground, Smriti's workers reached out to as many villages as possible. Trucks and Boleros were loaded with expectant crowds. 'Let's give it our best shot—we have nothing to lose,' Shah told his team.

Modi's speech in Amethi was probably his fiercest attack ever on the Gandhi parivar. Each line dripped with anger and sarcasm. 'For forty years, one family has destroyed the dreams of three generations of Indians. I will ensure your dreams are fulfilled'; 'I can go back to selling tea if I don't become PM, what will Rahul do?'; 'My *choti behen* Smriti can give you the names of 100 villages of Amethi, the Gandhis won't be able to give the names of more than ten.' Never before had any politician dared to take on the Gandhis with such a frontal assault, that too in their family fortress. A BJP leader summed it up for me rather well. 'It was a bit like Sehwag hitting Shoaib for a six in Pakistan!"

The Modi onslaught forced Priyanka to react. She accused Modi of dragging her late father Rajiv Gandhi into the election battle and claimed the BJP leader was engaging in '*neech* rajniti' (low-level politics). It was an unfortunate expression to use, especially in a part of UP where the word 'neech' was a derogatory reference to the lower castes. Priyanka to be fair hadn't made the reference in caste terms, but it was enough for Modi to seize upon. Affirming his OBC status, Modi accused Priyanka of insulting his caste identity. This was typical Modi-style 'rajniti'—ingenious spin doctoring, seizing the words of the opponent to turn the tables on them and capture the political advantage in a flash. For Priyanka, it may have been a wake-up call.

Before leaving Amethi on the last day of the campaign, Priyanka thanked the journalists who had been chasing her for a fortnight for their support. Most of them had been swayed by her charm and candour. For one last time she was asked if she would take the political leap. She replied, 'I have to drop my son off to school.

Doon has strict rules. When you come from a family like mine that has seen personal loss, your priorities are different. Your family is everything.'

Perhaps, that one remark signifies the dilemma of the new generation of Nehru–Gandhis. For Motilal and Jawaharlal, the freedom movement was a magnet that pulled them away from the luxury of Anand Bhawan towards street agitations. Indira Gandhi learnt her politics by the side of her father, even if her style may have been dramatically different. Sonia, too, to some extent benefitted from constantly observing her mother-in-law.

Priyanka and Rahul, by contrast, had lived a sheltered existence—family tragedy and perhaps personal choices had made them wary of the daily hardships of politics. Priyanka, for example, was married at twenty-five and became a mother two years later. Politics in the twenty-first century demands a near-complete blurring of the lines between your private and political life. The need for privacy is an obstruction for an individual seeking to win the unrelenting battle to capture hearts and minds, and in the end family concerns invariably give way to political ambition. Modi, Mamata, Mayawati, Jayalalithaa, Naveen, Nitish are all good examples of the modern neta—single men and women for whom politics is all-consuming.

While Priyanka focused on her children, the BJP's priorities were very different. The party had achieved what it had set out to do—send out a message that no seat anywhere in UP, not even Amethi, was unwinnable in 2014. But there was one even bigger battle that the Modi–Shah duo had their eyes firmly focused on—the battle for Varanasi.

~

Varanasi, Kashi, Banaras—many names for one of the most ancient and complex cities in the world, nestled on the banks of the great river Ganga. A city of poets and pandits; of sages and mafia; of philosophers and politicians. Ancient Hindu texts describe Varanasi as heaven on earth; a modern-day traveller is more likely to associate this corner of eastern UP with the idea of a living hell.

The Ganga feels holy at dawn, by dusk it resembles a sewer. Banarasi saris look gorgeous at weddings, but the weavers who make them work out of tiny, powerless tenements. You feel a sense of tranquillity at the ghats during the Ganga *aarti*, but your stress levels will rise while dodging the city's outrageous traffic. The Banaras Hindu University (BHU) once produced scholar-statesmen; now it is trapped in sloth and decay. You can live here in awe of the city's intellect but also in fear of the gun-toting gangs. And yes, you can worship the cow, but how do you deal with the piles of dung on the streets?

A city of a million stories, in 2014 Varanasi was preparing to script an epic political battle. Narendra Modi had been named the BJP candidate from here, a decision that had spurred the AAP leader Arvind Kejriwal to also announce his candidature from the city. The Congress had put up a local strongman (*bahubali* as they call them in eastern UP) and a sitting MLA, Ajay Rai (a section of the UP Congress was hoping Priyanka would stand from Varanasi, but she had no such intention). It was billed as the 'mother of all battles'.

The decision to field Modi from Varanasi was taken as far back as August 2013 even before he was formally made the party's prime ministerial candidate. In a meeting with the RSS, Amit Shah had suggested that Varanasi was the ideal location for Modi to make a pitch as a true national leader. 'Modiji will of course contest from Gujarat, but contesting from Varanasi is even more important,' Shah told the RSS leaders.

The Sangh readily embraced the idea. Varanasi, after all, was the ultimate repository of Hindu civilization. As Diana Eck says in her classic account of Varanasi, *Banaras: City of Lights*, 'Here all the Hindu gods have emerged from the shadows into bold relief, as people have come to understand them, have seen their faces and created their multi-form images.' If Modi was indeed a Hindu Hriday Samrat, then Varanasi was a natural choice as the capital of his kingdom.

Shah had another, more pragmatic political reason for the decision. In his analysis of UP, it was Purvanchal or eastern UP that worried him the most. Of the twenty-five seats in the region, the BJP had won just four in 2009. The SP and BSP had become the dominant forces here. If Mission 272-plus was to be achieved, a dramatic shift was needed in Purvanchal and the adjoining Bhojpur belt in Bihar. What better way than to get the BJP's mascot to contest from the region? 'I was convinced this would enthuse our workers and send out a strong message to the voter,' Shah later told me.

Kejriwal, too, saw political benefit in contesting from Varanasi. Having suddenly, and mistakenly, resigned as Delhi chief minister in mid-February, the AAP leader was in danger of isolating himself. His decision to contest over 450 Lok Sabha seats hadn't really taken off and AAP workers appeared to be in a state of drift. Kejriwal was looking to position himself as the principal challenger to Modi; he also needed to seize the media mindspace once again. Varanasi was the place to do so. This would be another David versus Goliath fight—Kejriwal was convinced he had nothing to lose.

Kejriwal's entry upset Shah's calculations once again. He had been hoping for an easy ride for Modi; now Varanasi was becoming a more complicated seat than originally anticipated. Shah's first problem was within the party. The sitting Varanasi MP was Dr Murli Manohar Joshi, the veteran BJP leader who saw himself next only to Vajpayee and Advani in the party hierarchy. Dr Joshi's loyalists would often tell me, 'He has all the credentials to be the party's prime ministerial candidate. You people must project him better.'

Few others within the BJP, though, seemed to share Dr Joshi's opinion of his own capabilities. His self-image may have been of a scholarly voice with a doctorate in nuclear physics from Allahabad University, but on the ground, he had no real support base. In Varanasi, where he had won the 2009 elections by just 17,000 votes, the anger against Dr Joshi was palpable. 'He should spend less time talking about WTO and more time here in Varanasi dealing with our local problems,' they told me. When Dr Joshi was denied re-election from Varanasi, he initially sulked but then realized he was better off in moving to Kanpur.

Shah's other difficulty in Varanasi lay in the sheer demographics of the constituency. With a population of nearly 3 lakhs, Muslims comprised nearly 15 per cent of the voters. OBCs and Dalits made up sizeable chunks too. The upper castes were the backbone of the BJP, but Shah needed to make a dent in the other social groups to offset the likely Muslim consolidation. A tie-up with the local Kurmi-dominated Apna Dal, which has a strong base in and around Varanasi, was only the first step (see chapter 5). But Shah knew he needed something bigger to set the Ganga on fire. It was time for a Big Bang event.

~

The nomination filing process in an Indian election is a customary show of strength. Candidates rustle up their supporters, hire jeeps and crowds, and move in a cavalcade to the collector's office amidst a shower of garlands and petals. The *mahaul* (climate) of victory has to be created is the underlying assumption. But what happened in Varanasi on 24 April was not just any other roadshow—it was the mightiest ever display of political power during any nomination journey in Indian elections.

The planning for Modi's nomination began almost a week to ten days before D-Day. 'We had a series of meetings and did several trial runs to ensure absolute perfection,' says Nalin Kohli, who was the BJP's media coordinator in Varanasi. High-end platforms were set up at vantage points along the road for the large media contingent to use. A mobile van equipped with cameras and satellite equipment would be placed in front of Modi's open truck so that frontal images of the leader waving to the crowds could be constantly beamed live. All local BJP leaders were told to ensure that their supporters congregated in large numbers. The entire journey was mapped to ensure both maximum crowds and maximum security.

In an effort to give the event an 'inclusive' appeal, the BJP even tried to get Varanasi's Bharat Ratna, shehnai maestro Ustad Bismillah Khan's son, Zamin Hussain Bismillah, as one of the proposers for Modi's nomination. He refused. 'We have been a Congress family for years. Besides, my father's music was always above politics,' he told me later. It was perhaps the only misstep in the BJP's preparations.

Even the chosen date appeared to have been carefully calculated. The 24th of April happened to be the sixth phase of polling, with 117 seats at stake across twelve states and union territories. Central UP, too, was polling that day, apart from the whole of Tamil Nadu, Mumbai and parts of Rajasthan, MP and Bihar. 'We knew that if we created a mega television event, the cameras would focus on Modi and we could capture eyeballs even while the voting was on,' confessed a senior BJP leader to me. The other reason, of course, was to make sure that eastern UP knew that Varanasi was now the new political capital of the country. And Modi its putative emperor.

Modi landed at Varanasi's Lal Bahadur Shastri airport a little before 11 a.m. He was taken by chopper to the BHU campus, then driven to the statue of Pandit Madan Mohan Malaviya, Varanasi's most revered freedom fighter. After the garlanding of the statue, the chopper took him to the Kashi Vidyapeeth where he garlanded a statue of Sardar Patel, and then set off in an open truck towards the collector's office. On a normal day, the journey would not have taken more than half an hour. That day, it took almost four hours. BJP leader Ravi Shankar Prasad, who was accompanying Modi in the truck with Shah, says it brought back memories of the anti-Indira JP andolan in the 1970s. 'I had never seen this kind of frenzied enthusiasm during an election, never,' he later told me.

My colleague Bhupendra Chaubey was on the ground while I was in the studio. In the studio, we were a little sceptical—we thought the crowds may have been hired. But Bhupendra had a different take. 'This was not a paid janata. The atmosphere was festive, people had come because they just wanted to catch a glimpse of Modi. I met someone who had taken a six-hour bus journey from Bihar just so that he could take a photo of Modi!' he said in astonishment.

Rose petals were showered on the truck, youngsters sported saffron caps and Modi T-shirts and masks, thousands lined every street corner. It was a political Maha Kumbh. And it was being played out live on television. The news agency ANI had as many as seven 3G satellite units along the route just to ensure that no image was missed. In the studio, my producer kept asking me if we should move away and show pictures of voting taking place in other parts of India that day. 'Shahrukh Khan has come to vote in Mumbai—should we cut to him?' she asked. I thought about it for a moment, and then sighed, 'I guess the real Bollywood show is being played out in Varanasi today with a star who has become even bigger than Shahrukh!'

Like Shahrukh, Modi once again revealed himself as a master of the TV moment, never short of a memorable sound bite or a bit of political theatre. Having filed his nomination, he provided yet another quotable quote. *'Mera mann kehta hai mein aya nahi hoon, mujhe bheja bhi nahi hai. Mujhe Ma Ganga ne bulaya hai!'* (My mind tells me I have not come, nor been sent, Ma Ganga has called me here.)

But the final punchline of the day was reserved for the less voluble Shah. 'The Modi wave has now become a tsunami,' he told the throng of journalists. The Congress hit back, pointing out that the tsunami which hit the Tamil Nadu coast in December 2004 had only brought death, destruction and grief. But this could no longer be a debate over semantics. The fact is, the political earth of India had begun to shake and there was a tectonic shift taking place on the ground. The Modi nomination had been another masterful act of political choreography, but this was no longer just a manufactured 'wave'. The spontaneous upsurge of support was unmissable. The camera was not lying.

What explains this craze for Modi? He was, after all, at the start of 2013 just another chief minister, that too from a state with a relatively small pool of MPs. Within eighteen months, he was the most sought-after national figure. No state leader has ever been able to make the transition so quickly and effectively. Yes, there was a leadership vacuum in Delhi, and the invisibility of the prime minister and Rahul's immaturity had led to a desperate longing for change. The economy was in a downward spiral and big-ticket corruption had alienated the middle class. The UPA's demise was certain.

But why was Modi preferred to any other prime ministerial aspirant? My belief is Modi's USP was his staunch promise to shatter the status quo—his undiluted aggression appealed to a new India. In the 1970s, Amitabh Bachchan's angry young man persona was suited to a film-going public tiring of chocolate-box heroes. In 2014, Modi's image as a robust 'man of action' gave him a decisive edge with voters who were sick and tired of being told by a slow-moving government that 'money doesn't grow on trees'. As the man who had travelled six hours by bus to see Modi in Varanasi told our reporter, *'Modiji toh desh ko bachane aaye hain!'* (Modi is here to save the country.) He could well have been echoing a dialogue from a Bachchan film.

~

I arrived in Varanasi in the first week of May to shoot a ground report. The campaign was at its peak. BJP leaders and workers were everywhere. In the hotel where I was staying, I bumped into Gordhan Zadaphia, the Gujarat politician who had once rebelled against Modi but had now quietly returned to the fold. I asked him what he was doing in Varanasi. 'I have been assigned the task of reaching out to Gujarati voters in the city,' he told me. The reality was that every BJP leader, big or small, needed to put in an obligatory face show before the all-powerful Modi–Shah duo. 'We had so many leaders assembled in one place, we didn't know what work to give them!' one of the BJP's campaign coordinators admitted to me later.

On the streets, the BJP's war cry, *'Har Har Modi, Ghar Ghar Modi'*, was proving contentious. The Dwarka Shankaracharya had objected, claiming that the chanting amounted to deification of Modi and was against Hindu religion. Modi had even tweeted asking his supporters not to use the slogan. And yet, when we were filming with BJP–RSS workers out canvassing on a door-to-door campaign, we heard the chant repeatedly. The moment I raised the issue with the party workers, they quickly changed the slogan. 'Har Har Modi' was dropped, 'Ghar Ghar Modi' remained in place! I am sure when our camera team left the site, the original chant would have returned. As an overenthusiastic worker told me: 'You can say what you want, Modi *hamare liye Bhagwaan barabar hai*!' (Modi is like God for us.)

An entire floor in the Surya Hotel in the heart of Varanasi had been booked by the BJP and converted into a media centre. No party is as proficient at courting the media as the BJP. The organization was near faultless. Dozens of computers, endless cups of chai and samosas, a room for interviews to be conducted—keeping the large media contingent in good humour came easy to the BJP. I must confess I was a little surprised, though, to see how even veteran journalists were fawning over Shah. 'Should I get you some extra ketchup, sir?' one of them asked, while the famished campaign manager cleaned up a plate of cheese sandwiches.

Shah was taking no chances even after the spectacular success of the nomination roadshow. He had made Varanasi his base for managing the entire eastern UP campaign in the last stretch. One day, he received reports that the party workers had become complacent about victory and weren't working hard enough. At 10 p.m. all local leaders were called and warned, 'From tomorrow, I want to see all of you out on the road, no excuses.' Shah is a great believer in the power of a door-to-door campaign in true RSS volunteer-style. Each leader was told to ensure that no house in their area was missed.

Kejriwal, by contrast, did not have the money power—certainly nothing to match the BJP election machine. Nor, this time, the media support. He had arrived in Varanasi by train in mid-April and set about trying to climb the steepest mountain of his political career. Just before arriving in Varanasi, Kejriwal had also travelled to Gujarat, where in a show of political bravado, he had marched almost up to Modi's residence in Gandhinagar, apparently to seek an appointment. Clashes with BJP workers, detentions and acts of stoning had met him in Gujarat, where armed with a notepad he was seen jotting down the number of dysfunctional schools and badly staffed clinics to arrive at his conclusion of a non-existent Gujarat model of development. Kejriwal's Gujarat trip may not have yielded political gain on the ground but was a symbolic show of strength—he was unafraid to enter the lion's den.

In Varanasi, Kejriwal did manage to create a stir initially—with his campaign gaining some visibility after his supporters took on the BJP on the streets—but it was soon obvious that Varanasi was not Delhi. Many of his volunteers had come from other states. They were simply not familiar with the narrow by-lanes of this city where every alley has a different character. 'I think we underestimated the scale of what we were up against,' confessed an AAP leader.

The one group which seemed taken up by the AAP white topi were the Muslim weavers. Travelling through the weaver bastis, I was confronted by the sense of hopelessness that stared at the Indian Muslim in this election. The local artisans could spin magical saris, but their lives were caught in a cycle of neglect and relative poverty. A superior quality Banarasi sari could range from Rs 30,000 to Rs 50,000 but the artisan would be lucky to earn Rs 5000 for his month-long effort while working out of a cramped little room. It was a terribly unequal world.

That sense of inequality had seeped down to political choices as well. The Congress, the weavers felt, had let them down. A number of promises and packages had been announced, but little had trickled down to them. The SP and the BSP exploited them as a vote bank with no obvious reward. A Modi-led BJP frightened them. 'Woh toh danga karvatein hain' (He stages riots). The AAP was a more enticing prospect. Wearing an AAP badge and cap, one weaver told me, 'Kejriwalji hamari bhasha bol rahe hain, BJP ko wahi ek takkar de sakte hain' (Kejriwal is speaking our language, only he can give a fight to the BJP). Yet Kejriwal's dilemma was that if he became a Muslim-focused party, the AAP would alienate the Hindus. The message of the public transport-using, sleeping-on-the-footpath common man up against a business-class Modi with his powerful corporate backers was far more politically expedient.

I accompanied Kejriwal on his campaign into the villages around Varanasi. In searingly hot temperatures, he seemed to be up for the challenge. 'Modi is a *hawai* neta, he comes in and out on choppers. I am a *zameeni* neta, on the ground,' he told me. His election rhetoric had a familiar ring: '*Modi Adani–Ambani ke saath juda hua hain, woh paisa banayenge, aapko koi phayda nahi hoga*' (Modi is in partnership with Adani and Ambani. They will make money, you will get no benefit). But in rural Varanasi, this line of attack was misplaced and just did not resonate. No one I spoke to in the village had heard of Ambani or Adani.

I asked Kejriwal later whether he felt he had erred in contesting from Varanasi. After all, his presence meant that the entire AAP volunteer machine had been diverted to this single constituency. 'No, I don't agree. We had to fight Varanasi to send out a message—we wanted to show we were not scared of Modi,' he countered.

The BJP, too, wanted to prove a point. Worried by the AAP factor at the start of the year, they now wanted to teach him a lesson. 'The real battle in Varanasi was always as to who would come second and who would lose their deposit. We wanted Kejriwal to lose his deposit, that was our goal,' the BJP's Kohli told me later.

Modi was never going to lose Varanasi. The big question was what would be the margin of the win. I remember meeting a few Delhi-based social activists who were campaigning against Modi. 'He can be defeated—you media people have all been bought over by him,' one vociferous lady told me angrily. I protested the accusation but realized I was never going to win this debate. Wearing ideological blinkers, I fear, can lead even rational people to think irrationally at election time.

A more logical explanation for the Modi wave in Varanasi was provided to me by the owner of Keshav Paan Bhandar, the city's most famous paan shop. As he lovingly prepared a *meetha* paan for me, I asked him why he was voting for Modi. '*Bhaisaab, agar woh pradhan mantri bante hain, toh Varanasi ka kuch to bhala hoga*'

(If Modi becomes PM, Varanasi will at least benefit in some way).

Like many other parts of India, Varanasi, too, was living on hope. In the land of Bismillah Khan and its 'Ganga–Jamuni *tehzeeb*', as they would say in Urdu, '*Ummeed par duniya kaayam hai!*' (The world lives on hope.)

~

The election in Amethi took place on 7 May. Varanasi was scheduled for the 12th. Only forty-one of the 543 seats were now left in what had been an agonizingly long nine-phase election. It was into this last stretch that the BJP now poured its entire might. 'This was now carpet-bombing in a multiple of ten,' is how one BJP leader summed up the last week of the campaign.

Modi was now addressing as many as six rallies a day, focused on the three remaining states of UP, Bihar and Bengal. The advertising campaign was intensified, with the frequency of the ads being increased. Every few minutes, a TV screen in one of the poll-bound states would have Modi staring at the camera, touching his heart emblazoned with a BJP badge, and saying, '*Aapka diya gaya vote seedhe mujhe ayega*' (Your vote will come directly to me). 'We wanted to make the candidates irrelevant—this was now only about Modi for PM,' is how a BJP strategist described the presidential-style campaign thrust.

To try and ensure that their leader touched almost every battleground constituency, Team Modi played their final *Brahmastra*—Modi in 3D. The idea had originated in the 2012 Gujarat assembly election campaign. That election, like so much else in Team Modi's 2014 strategy, served as a laboratory for innovative ideas. The 3D technology had been patented by a UK-based company, Musion. The India rights were acquired and a team of 200 foreign and Indian technicians worked for almost six months to perfect the broadcast. It was first attempted in December 2012 when Modi's fifty-five-minute speech made from his political base in Gandhinagar was broadcast in fifty-three locations across twenty-six cities. 'We were able to cover lakhs of people across thousands of kilometres in one go. It had a terrific impact,' says Prashant Kishore of CAG who headed the team which planned the concept.

I watched one of the 3D shows during the 2012 Gujarat elections from just outside Vadodara. Gujaratis, like most Indians, love their cinema. This was like a political movie being played out in front of them, with Modi as the star. Just the technology which showed Modi appearing with a glow around him was enough to make the crowd feel this was 'paisa *vasool*'. Some members in the audience would move towards the screen, trying to touch Modi, and then scream excitedly when they realized this was only a cinematic image of their leader.

Now, in the general elections, the Gujarat experiment was taken nationwide. While in April, Modi would do a 3D rally once every three to four days, in the last stretch, he was doing nearly one a day. As a result, he was able to touch over 1300 locations, 325 of which were in UP alone. 3D was also used to reach out to remote places. 'We even managed to get to the upper reaches of Uttarakhand. It was a logistical challenge, but we did it,' says a Team Modi member.

This was quintessential 'shock and awe' campaigning, Modi-style. Two studios were set up in Delhi and Gandhinagar for Modi's 'outreach'. A crew of 2500 members handling 125 3D projector units were involved and more than 7 million people reportedly witnessed the 3D shows over twelve days. In the 2012 assembly elections, Modi would appear in 3D in an almost static position on a flat screen; this time, the technology team innovated and attempted to capture every movement, including someone serving him a cup of tea, or a towel being asked for to wipe the sweat. 'We wanted Modi to appear as lifelike as possible to heighten audience excitement,' is how the 3D adventure was described to me. I later asked Kishore how much they spent on each 3D show. He wouldn't tell me but BJP sources said it was amongst the most expensive elements of the campaign. 'Upwards of Rs 200 crore' is one figure I was given. Whatever the final amount, the purpose had been served. Modi was, literally, everywhere.

∼

On 8 May, Modi was to conclude his Varanasi campaign with two rallies and then participate in an aarti by the banks of the Ganga. But twenty-four hours before his arrival, the local administration denied him permission—citing security concerns—for a rally in Beniabagh in the heart of the city and for the aarti.

Free from his campaign in Amritsar, senior leader Arun Jaitley was now supervising the final push in Varanasi. Incensed by the administration's decision, he decided to go on the offensive. A legal defence was prepared, and a letter sent to the Election Commission and the district magistrate's office. The local BJP was told to stage a dharna in protest. 'We genuinely felt that the administration was under pressure from the SP government not to allow Modi into the city,' Jaitley told me later. The fact that the DM, Pranjal Yadav, was a Yadav only gave added ammunition to the BJP propaganda machine, with a rumour being quietly spread that he was related to UP's ruling family.

By the time the DM relented, it was too late. The BJP was keen to turn adversity into advantage. Playing victim, Modi accused the Election Commission of bias and acting under political pressure. The Chief Election Commissioner V.S. Sampath is a quiet, low-profile man with a non-confrontational persona, very unlike some of his predecessors, such as T.N. Seshan. The charge of bias left Sampath nonplussed. 'We have tried our best to ensure a free and fair elections—why is Modi talking like this?' he asked me when I called him up for a reaction. Sampath, too, was slowly learning that Modi was not your average politician. His instinctively combative nature meant that even the Election Commission would not be spared his ire (as another CEC, J.M. Lyngdoh, had discovered in 2002).

Modi was determined to have the last word. Landing in Varanasi, he chose to go on an impromptu roadshow through the city right up to the party headquarters. If the nomination journey had been a march of triumph, this was a final act of defiance. On 24 April, the masses had come out in large numbers. This time, the streets were dominated by BJP supporters in saffron caps. I asked Jaitley if the roadshow was also another 'well-planned' event. 'Well, you can't expect a political party to stay silent if we are denied our right to hold a rally,' was his prompt answer.

From day one of this election campaign, the BJP, unlike the Congress, had never missed an opportunity to seize an opportunity. Varanasi's DM, intentionally or otherwise, had provided them with one last moment to exploit. On the final day of the campaign, Rahul Gandhi went on a similar roadshow through the city's streets. It looked imitative and, frankly, a little late as always. Rahul once again lived up to the rather harsh description of him as a 'tubelight'.

~

Modi concluded his 2014 campaign by addressing his last rally in Ballia in eastern UP. His publicists were quick to provide the details. Their leader had done 437 rallies and covered more than 3 lakh kilometres since being anointed the BJP's prime ministerial candidate in mid-September. But if he was tired, he wasn't showing any signs of it.

On the way back from Ballia, he stopped at Varanasi airport where his trusted aides, Jaitley and Shah, were waiting for him. The troika who had shaped the BJP's 2014 campaign then flew back together to Delhi. 'There was a feeling of deep satisfaction amongst all of us. Narendra was convinced that victory was ours and Mission 272-plus would be reality—there was no self-doubt at all,' Jaitley told me later.

On arrival in Delhi, Modi made a quick stopover at the RSS headquarters at Jhandewalan where he met the RSS chief Mohan Bhagwat. It was a reminder that even as a prime ministerial nominee, he was first and always a swayamsevak. It was also perhaps a thanksgiving to Bhagwat. After all, the Sangh with its well-drilled cadres had come out in almost full strength to provide the organizational support and feet on the ground for Modi and the BJP in this election. Indeed, the RSS had pulled out all the stops— grass-roots organizers, campaigners and mobilizers—perhaps as enthusiastically as it had done in the JP movement against Indira's

Emergency. With a targeted door-to-door campaign, they had been Modi's last-mile warriors.

The same night Modi flew back to Gandhinagar. The most gruelling campaign in the history of Indian elections was over. Modi had run a marathon with unbelievable stamina. 7, Race Course Road, the most cherished address in Indian politics, was now well within his grasp.

10

It's a Tsunami!

Narendra Modi was due a late lie-in on 11 May. It was possibly the
first Sunday in eight months when he didn't have to hit the road and
deliver another *bhashan* (speech). But for a swayamsevak, old habits
die hard. Even though his first appointment was only after 8 a.m.,
Modi was up by 6, leafing through the morning newspapers and
government files. I had been trying to speak to Modi for a fortnight
now but to no avail. Normally, Modi would reply to a missed phone
call. But in the rush of the last phase of campaigning, it seemed he
had no time for even a short conversation. Vijay Nehra, additional
secretary in the chief minister's office, had promised that he would
try and connect him on Sunday.

Finally, at around 10.30 a.m., the chief minister called back.
'Should I be congratulating India's next prime minister in advance!'
was my first response. I could hear a slight laugh on the other end.
Our big post-poll survey results were to be out the next evening and
Modi was anxious to know the findings. *'Kya number de rahe ho,
Rajdeep?'* (What number are you giving?), he asked. 'My sense is
our final number will be anything between 270 and 280, sir,' I told
him reassuringly.

Modi didn't seem too pleased. 'We will reach 300 seats—wave

hai, wave,' he said. I agreed with him. 'Yes, I also feel 300 is the likely figure, you are sweeping north and west India, sir.' *'Yeh jo Dilli main baithe political pundit hain, inko kaho studio ke bahar jaaye!'* (Ask your Delhi-based experts to move out of the studio), he suggested. And then he suddenly broke into English. 'First time since 1984, you will have a majority government in Delhi.'

There was an authoritative tone to his voice, almost as though he was already the prime minister. I tried to needle him a bit. 'What about Jayalalithaa, Mayawati or Mamata, will you take anyone's support?' I asked. *'Kissi ki zaroorat nahi padegi* [We won't need anyone], it will be a clear verdict!' Before I hung up, I had one final journalistic shot. 'Narendrabhai, you did not give your old friend an interview during the campaign. I hope you will at least give me one once you become prime minister!' Modi parried the request with *'Ab Dilli mein milenge!'* (We will now meet in Delhi.)

Delhi was already preparing for a change in guard. The only real question was whether Modi would cross 272 comfortably and have an absolute majority or need outside support. Airtel chief Sunil Mittal was hosting a dinner that evening for a few close friends at his Amrita Shergill Road bungalow. To make the evening a little exciting, he announced a competition, asking his guests to come up with the final BJP tally of seats. Whoever came closest to the actual number would get a Franck Muller watch as a reward, the one furthest away would have to host the next dinner.

At the dinner were politicians, media barons and corporate tycoons. Only one of the guests, Meenakshi Dass, from a prominent business family, gave the BJP by itself a figure close to the magical 272 number—her guess was 266. Even Arun Jaitley's figure was a more modest 245 seats. The media leader at the dinner table gave the least—less than 200 seats. So much for us journalists having our ear to the ground!

Even the RSS was playing it safe. An internal poll done by a Sangh supporter had placed the BJP around the 230-seat mark. 'We may need to do some post-poll alignment,' an RSS leader told me. Perhaps it was wishful thinking, since not everyone in the saffron brotherhood was joyous at the prospect of a colossal victory by a dominating personality. In Gujarat, pumped up by repeated electoral victories, Modi tended to ride roughshod over not only his own party but even the Sangh.

Yet there was also genuine concern in a section of the Modi camp over voter turnout numbers. Across India, the turnout had risen, in some states rather dramatically. 'This was the one X factor that worried us. We were just not sure who had got this additional vote,' a BJP strategist admitted to me later.

A senior journalist who met Sharad Pawar the day before the results said that the NCP leader was still hopeful of a hung Parliament. 'I could sense he was still hoping that if the BJP ended up with around 200 to 220 seats, then smaller parties like his could play a major role in government formation,' the journalist told me after his meeting with Pawar.

Some Congressmen were still living in denial. When I spoke to a Union minister and suggested that 300 seats for the NDA couldn't be ruled out, he laughed: 'You guys will never learn. You got it wrong in 2004 and 2009, you will be proven wrong yet again.' A New York-based banker friend had a similar concern. 'Waiting anxiously for your exit poll tomorrow night, Rajdeep. I just hope you guys won't do a 2004 on us!'

Ah, 2004! The election that had virtually buried the science of psephology, or poll forecasting. No one had predicted that Vajpayee and Shining India would lose power and the Congress would form a coalition government. Frankly, by the last phase even then, there were signs that the NDA was on the decline, but no one wanted to stick their neck out and actually predict a Vajpayee defeat. Two states in particular—Andhra and Tamil Nadu—had swayed that verdict. This time, the locus of the conflict had shifted to the north. The final numbers in UP and Bihar would hold the key to whether India would really get its first single-party government since Rajiv Gandhi's landslide in 1984.

~

Exit polls are now an integral part of the great Indian election carnival. Many viewers are sceptical about the findings, but there are very few who don't track the numbers. From Dalal Street to North Block, TV sets get switched on when the numbers are being announced.

My former boss at NDTV, Dr Prannoy Roy, is the guru of poll forecasting in India, building his reputation by getting the 1984 elections spot on. Prannoy, an economist by training, had a childlike enthusiasm for numbers. I'd watch him and his 'partner in crime' Dorab Sopariwala, a delightful old-style Mumbai Parsi, scribble away on a sheet of paper, making all kinds of calculations.

Prannoy and Dorab took polling seriously and had developed the concept of Index of Opposition Unity (IOU) as a statistical measure. It had been evolved by looking at the Congress as the principal pole of Indian politics and then determining the potential of victory or defeat based on how united the anti-Congress Opposition was. The IOU method had worked in the 1980s. In the more competitive elections of 2014 where the Congress was no longer unassailable, new formulas were needed. Prannoy and Dorab, in fact, had almost lost faith in poll predictions after the 2004 miscalculation. Even on their programmes, they'd often issue a statutory warning—'Look, you can always get this wrong, it isn't as if any of us have a magic formula.'

It's a warning that my other psephologist friend Yogendra Yadav would also often give. 'This isn't a maths sum, Rajdeep—can we please tell our viewers that.' Yogendra was more academic in his approach—he liked to see himself as a political scientist first, a number cruncher only later. His team at Lokniti in CSDS had evolved a more refined system for a post-poll survey, one with a smaller sample size but which involved going to people's homes with a questionnaire. 'Whether out of fear or bravado, people sometimes can tell a lie outside a polling booth as to who they have voted for— they are less likely to do so in their homes,' was Yogendra's logic. The bigger challenge in any random sampling system remained—how do you convert vote percentages in any poll into seats? That was the statistical jugglery which could trip up a pollster.

Indeed, despite the attempts at a more rigorous exercise of measuring voter behaviour, exit polls faced a severe credibility crisis in the 2014 elections. For some self-styled pollsters, providing numbers to a television channel had become a business opportunity. A sting operation just ahead of the 2014 election campaign had revealed that some pollsters were ready to fudge the numbers if required. A senior politician once told me in all seriousness, 'Rajdeep, television channels can fix ratings and I can fix a poll!'

Personally, I was troubled by the tamasha that exit polls had become. It felt as though the months of effort in reporting and analysing an election were being reduced to a single number. If you got your exit poll number right, then it was as if your entire election coverage was validated. If you got it wrong, then you were scoffed at, and all the good work done previously was consigned to oblivion. It was almost as if the soul of journalism was being mortgaged to the marketplace—every channel had to do a poll because that was what the viewer supposedly wanted.

I will never forget the trauma I went through during the 2012 UP elections. Our exit poll had predicted a comprehensive win for the SP and a rout for the Congress and the BJP. But in the first hour on results day, the BJP was actually leading, with most of the leads coming from postal ballots and early counting. That was enough for a senior BJP leader to come on air and demand an apology from Yogendra and me. 'You should apologize to the people of India for having misled them. Your poll has been proven to be totally wrong,' the BJP leader insisted. For the BJP, for whom a so-called 'bias' in the English-language media is a favourite theme, asking for an apology from the media comes very naturally. Yogendra looked shell-shocked, fearing his integrity was being questioned.

By afternoon, the final results were out—the Samajwadi Party had indeed swept the polls, the BJP had been routed, our numbers had been proven absolutely correct. I wish the same BJP leader had appeared on our prime-time evening bulletin that day. I might have been tempted to demand a similar apology from her for her all-too-ready suspicion of the media and its motives.

Traumatic or not, we were all rushing to kick off the exit poll race. Election Commission rules prohibited announcing any findings till the last vote had been cast. So at 5.30 p.m. on 12 May, once the final round of voting was done, every channel began blasting their poll results. Some screamed louder than others, but for once most of the polls were pointing in one direction—a victory for the Modi-led NDA. Only the scale of the win differed.

ABP News predicted 281 seats for the NDA, NDTV 280, TV Today 261 to 283, India TV 289, CNN-IBN 274 to 286. Times Now was the only channel to suggest a hung Parliament with a figure of 249 to the NDA, while News 24 was the outlier—their poll predicted a massive 340 seats to the NDA. All polls predicted the Congress-led UPA struggling to cross the 100-seat mark.

The News 24 poll (which would eventually come closest to reality) was done by someone called Today's Chanakya. This esoteric sounding gent who had named himself after the canny ancient scholar was, a little more prosaically, a certain V.K. Bajaj. I had first him met more than a decade ago, during the 2003 Rajasthan elections. He was from Bikaner and had come to see me with a packet of the town's famous *bhujia*.

'Sir, Vasundhara is winning the elections. I have an interest in predicting elections, please give me one chance!' he told me. I took the bhujia but was a little dismissive of his claims to be a pollster. He thrust a piece of paper in my hand with his findings. They turned out to be pretty accurate. Every time there was an election, he'd SMS or email me his numbers. More often than not, they were right (yes, he got some wrong too!). I asked him what his trade secret was, especially since he didn't have a sample size for his poll. He'd just smile and say, 'I have my nose to the ground, sir!' VK, as I called him, was proof that no one had a monopoly on being a successful pollster. No wonder people in India take the *satta* market seriously too!

One of the other problems with exit polls is quite simply this— the winning politician comes on air and praises your poll, the loser calls you biased. The 12th of May was no different. The Congress, in fact, had gone so far as to say that the exit polls were rigged and unscientific, and none of their leaders would participate in a TV debate on the findings.

The BJP leaders were predictably ecstatic, while the so-called third or fourth front leaders were a little nonplussed. 'You may have no role now to play,' I told Derek O'Brien of the Trinamool. 'Let's wait till the 16th, then Mamatadi will show her cards,' was his measured response. The exit polls showed the Trinamool, AIADMK and Biju Janata Dal doing strongly, but not in a position to be kingmakers.

The real kingmaker, it seemed, was Amit Shah. Most polls were giving the BJP fifty or more seats from the decisive battleground state of Uttar Pradesh. Shah came on our programme that night once the findings were out. 'Your poll has underestimated us slightly. My final number is 295 to 305 for the NDA,' he claimed in his trademark no-nonsense style. I asked him if he was willing to put a wager on it. '*Rajdeepji, yeh sab chodiye, hum 16 May ko baarah baje baat karenge!*' (Forget about bet and all that, we will speak on 16 May at 12 noon).

Frankly, I agreed with Shah's assessment. I had argued with our statistician, Dr Rajeeva Karandikar of the Chennai Mathematical Institute, that maybe we should be edging the NDA closer to the 300-seat mark. 'Rajeeva, if the BJP is getting 40 per cent votes in UP, they will sweep the state,' was my argument. Rajeeva, a brilliant statistical mind, wanted to be a little careful. 'I agree, but maybe sometimes it is better to be cautious,' was his advice. Perhaps we erred on the side of caution because the ghosts of 2004 were haunting all of us.

They certainly weren't haunting Shah. The politician who had first predicted that the Modi wave was becoming a tsunami was ready to have the last laugh.

~

Within hours of the exit poll results being announced, all roads led to Gandhinagar. Fellow politicians, bureaucrats, industrialists and well-wishers were all keen to have a word with the man who was set to become the country's next prime minister. But, as was typical of him, Modi met very few visitors. He had always kept a sparse house—it's a home with minimal furniture—and he didn't want to be flooded with bouquets and garlands. At least, not yet.

Among the first to call on him had been Gadkari who had flown down from Delhi for what was being described as a 'courtesy call'. Within the BJP, the joke was that the former BJP president wanted to just mark his presence ahead of the Cabinet formation. 'Everyone was already eyeing meaty portfolios,' a BJP leader claimed later. Modi, as always, wasn't revealing too much. He instead suggested that a wider consultation could begin on the road ahead. 'I can come down to Delhi if you want,' he had indicated to Gadkari. Gadkari had got the message. Forty-eight hours later, he along with party president Rajnath Singh and senior leader Arun Jaitley were winging their way to Gandhinagar. Significantly, Sushma Swaraj wasn't present, while Advani had been ignored altogether. The balance of power within the party was now firmly ensconced in and around Modi. He didn't need to come to Delhi—Delhi would come to his doorstep.

The four leaders held a preliminary discussion on government formation and what would be a possible calendar of events in the next fortnight. 'We didn't discuss who would be getting what portfolio, but we did look at the larger political picture that would emerge after the verdict. And yes, the assumption was that we were winning the elections,' Jaitley later told me. If the BJP was eyeing power after ten years, the Congress was slowly reconciling itself to defeat. The party was now clutching at straws. 'Do you really think we will get less than 100 seats?' one minister asked me anxiously.

On 14 May, two days before the verdict, Sonia Gandhi threw a farewell dinner for Dr Singh and his wife. The prime minister had announced his retirement in January and this was an opportunity for the party to simply say thank you. It was a thoughtful gesture by Sonia and almost all the Union ministers and CWC members were there. A lavish spread had been prepared (one minister told me the kebabs were excellent). Dr Singh was presented with a silver plaque and a citation signed by all his Cabinet colleagues and there was a shawl for Gursharan Kaur. The Congress released a two-minute video thanking Dr Singh for ten years of leadership. If there had been any recrimination over things that had gone wrong, it appeared that at least for this one evening, they had been forgotten.

And yet, what should have been a special moment for the Congress party and Dr Singh was hijacked by the news that Rahul Gandhi was absent from the function. 'Where is Rahul?' was the media chorus outside 10, Janpath. Trying to avoid the forest of cameras, the Congress, it seemed, had no answer. An hour later, the AICC issued a press statement saying that Rahul, after a hectic three-month campaign, had taken a short break and was 'out of town'. He had reportedly already met the prime minister over the previous weekend and expressed his gratitude in person.

The damage had been done. The Twitter-friendly Omar Abdullah was among the first to react. 'If you knew he was not attending the dinner and he had explained his absence to the PM earlier, please put out a statement before the news breaks.' So, where, indeed, was Rahul? As usual, the Congress wouldn't divulge his whereabouts. Dubai was one guess. 'Far East' was another surmise (apparently, in a yoga camp in Myanmar, we were told by one CWC member). It all seemed rather strange. It was bad enough that Rahul was never in town on his birthday while Congress workers lined up to greet him; now, he had chosen to skip a dinner which the Congress party, of which he was vice president, was hosting for their prime minister. It was not just poor form; to the outside world, it smacked of plain and simple bad manners. Sonia, I was later told, was angry at Rahul's no-show but could do little about it. 'The fact is, the one person in the Congress she had no control over was her son—he could overrule her,' a senior Congress MP told me later.

In an election season where so much had gone wrong for the Congress party, this was one final embarrassment they could have done without.

∼

The 16th of May was like any other excruciatingly hot summer day. Life, though, was easier for me since I was to be in an air-conditioned studio for the 6 a.m. live coverage. Driving to the studio in the early hours of the morning, my mind was transported to the first election I had done on television. The 1996 general elections marked my television debut—then we were doing the elections for Doordarshan. If counting day now was a bit like a T20 match, then it was like a five-day Test match.

We had Dr Roy and Vinod Dua—a unique and stellar English–Hindi combination—holding forth in the studio. Private news television networks had still not taken off, so we had a virtual monopoly over viewership. The nation was, literally, watching us. It was also a pre-electronic voting machine era—the results would come through very slowly and the entire exercise went on for three days, like a slowly unfolding Hindi film drama. In fact, to keep the audiences engaged, Doordarshan would break the election coverage with old movies.

I was reporting out of the Congress headquarters for those seventy-two hours; among my colleagues in the field were Arnab and Barkha. One episode sticks in my mind of that time. On day three of the coverage I got a call from Kamal Nath, the senior Congress leader. Nath had been denied a Congress ticket after his name surfaced in the Jain hawala scam. He was convinced that the hawala charges had been a conspiracy by then prime minister Narasimha Rao to edge out all his political rivals. As the results were coming in, it was apparent that Rao was on his way out. Nath wanted his revenge.

Around 8 in the evening, he called me and said he wanted to do a live interview with me from the Congress headquarters. I warned him that the party viewed him as a persona non grata, and might not allow him to enter the premises. 'Don't worry, Narasimha Rao is history, my friend. Today I will expose him before the nation,' he told me. Sounds like a scoop, I thought, and invited him to join the telecast.

An hour later, a slightly inebriated Nath arrived at the venue. We did a live interview where he, as promised, lambasted the Rao government. There was only one hitch—this was Doordarshan and Rao was still technically prime minister of India. A few minutes into the interview, I was getting frantic signals to cut the live telecast. Nath, though, was on a roll. 'History has taught Rao a well-deserved lesson. Thank God the country is rid of him!' It is perhaps the one and only occasion when the prime minister has been spoken about in this manner on Doordarshan!

That was, of course, eighteen years ago. Now, we were into another general election in the age of private television where dozens of news channels were in frenetic competition. At CNN-IBN, we genuinely believed we had assembled what we liked to call 'the best team in politics'.

There was Swapan Dasgupta as the premier right-wing voice and someone who had an inside track to Modi; the liberal historian and public intellectual Ramachandra Guha was among the rare breed who spoke as well as he wrote; Manini Chatterjee of the *Telegraph* offered a punchy counterpoint to Swapan's Modinama; P. Sainath, a Magsaysay award-winning journalist, had documented rural India better than anyone else; Kumar Ketkar offered a robust old-style Nehruvian perspective; and just in case the right wing felt outgunned, we had the straight-talking political economist, Surjit Bhalla, who I would often term as being 'on the right of Atilla the Hun!' Our number crunching was done by Prof. Karandikar while the political inputs were handled by Dr Sandeep Shastri of the Lokniti team, whose enthusiasm would usually lift my spirits. The only member of our original election panel we were missing that morning was Prof. Dipankar Gupta, the leading political sociologist who had the great skill of making his point forcefully without raising his voice.

The panel had come prepared to stay in the studio for several hours. 'Don't worry, we have lots of food and drink organized to keep you going,' I assured them. In the end, it was all over in the first three hours. The first round of leads that come on a television programme are usually from postal ballots, so one can be easily misled by the initial numbers. But within half an hour of the counting having started, a clear trend had begun to emerge.

The BJP was well ahead in most seats in north and west India from where leads were now coming thick and fast. At around 9 a.m., we had a flash saying Rahul was trailing. My first instinctive response was—could Smriti Irani be the Raj Narain of 2014 (the socialist leader had defeated Indira Gandhi in Rae Bareli in 1977)? Then, we had another news flash—Supriya Sule, Sharad Pawar's daughter, was trailing in Baramati. Surely not, I muttered to myself, the Pawars had been winning the seat for four decades now. From Thiruvananthapuram came the news that Shashi Tharoor was also lagging behind. Would the BJP actually break its duck in Kerala? Every Congress minister, except Kamal Nath and Jyotiraditya Scindia, seemed to be losing in the first round of counting.

But the big story was undoubtedly coming from UP. By 9.30 a.m., we had trends for almost fifty seats from the state. Except two (Sonia Gandhi in Rae Bareli and Mulayam Singh in Mainpuri), the BJP was ahead in all the rest. Shah was right, I said on air, this could really be a political tsunami.

At 9.32 a.m., I asked my producers to flash the big breaking news on the video wall—NDA set to win the 2014 elections; Narendra Modi poised to be India's next prime minister. News television works like a herd on major news days. Within minutes of us putting out the flash, every news channel in the country had followed.

A few hours later, the noise had settled a bit. Rahul Gandhi had recovered and was now leading in Amethi. He would eventually win by just over a lakh of votes, unlike 2009 when he had won by an impressive 3.70 lakh votes. Supriya Sule had edged ahead as well, as had Shashi Tharoor, but both their victory margins had been drastically reduced. There were no comebacks, though, for a majority of the Congress ministers. The only important BJP leader to bite the dust was Arun Jaitley in Amritsar, defeated because he had miscalculated the depth of anger against the Akalis.

There was little of interest left elsewhere. In Andhra Pradesh, the other key battleground, it was Chandrababu Naidu in Andhra and Chandrasekhar Rao in Telangana. 'You must come for the swearing-in,' Naidu's assistant SMS-ed me within minutes of the results being announced. KTR, son of Telangana's first chief minister, would send me a similar invite a few days later. I, as always, preferred to stay at home.

Meanwhile, there was another battle within a battle—Mamata Banerjee and Jayalalithaa were engaged in their own private duel about who would finish third. Eventually, Jaya would nose ahead, but neither Amma nor Didi were in any position to change the course of events in Delhi. The other potential prime ministerial pretenders had been almost wiped out. Mayawati, quite astonishingly, had drawn a blank. Mulayam Singh had won just five seats, all won by family members. Sharad Pawar's NCP was down to just five seats, Nitish won just two, Kejriwal's AAP bagged only four seats, all of which came from Punjab.

The biggest defeat was of the Congress. The mighty party of the freedom movement was down to just forty-four seats, its worst ever performance. Not even the 1977 post-Emergency debacle had been this terrible. In all the states where there was a direct fight with the BJP, the Congress was demolished. An SMS joke doing the rounds suggested that if you travelled along the highway up north from Mumbai, the first Congress constituency you would touch was Amritsar!

The BJP, on the other hand, had quite remarkably won 282 seats on its own, the first instance of single-party majority since 1984. UP had been swept—a quite astonishing seventy-three of the eighty seats were in the BJP–Apna Dal kitty. The party won all the seats in Rajasthan and Gujarat, its alliance won forty-two of the forty-eight seats in Maharashtra and thirty-one of the forty in Bihar. Of the seventy seats where the polling percentage had gone up by more than 15 per cent, the BJP and its allies won as many as sixty-seven. On our map in the studio, north, west and central India had only one colour—and it was saffron.

This was a rout. If it was a T20 match, they might have called it off after just the first power play.

~

Modi, as always, had got up very early that morning. If he was excited, he wasn't showing it. He was a bit like a CBSE topper who probably knew he was going to get cent per cent but was just waiting for a final confirmation. He did his usual morning meditation and had a very light breakfast before placing himself before the television screens. His team was providing him constant inputs by the minute. He, too, knew in the first two hours that it was all over.

'India has won!' his aide tweeted from his account. Even in victory, he hadn't forgotten the power of constant communication. Or of symbolism. A little after noon, he emerged from his residence and drove to meet his mother, Hiraben. The first television image post-victory was well-thought-out—Modi sitting on a chair being blessed by his mother and surrounded by a few other smiling relatives. Narendra, who had left home as a teenager to become an RSS pracharak, had now returned, if only for a photo op, as the prime minister designate. It had been a truly remarkable journey.

His first public comments after the victory were made at a thanksgiving speech in Vadodara, one of the two seats he had contested from. The margin was a near-record 5.7 lakh votes. In victory, he appeared statesman-like. Immaculately dressed, as always, in a trademark beige and white half kurta, he said, 'I want to tell all my fellow Indians that in letter and spirit I will take all Indians with me.' These were not the words of chief minister Modi—this was prime minister Modi talking.

Modi promised he was here to stay. 'I want to make the twenty-first century India's century; it will take ten years, not very long.' As the ever-faithful crowd in their Modi caps cheered him on and screamed, 'Modi, Modi', the showman was in full form. 'Achhe Din,' he said loudly. The near-hysterical crowd bellowed back, 'Aa Gaye!'

A little after 8.30 p.m., he had his last public function of the day, and as it turned out, as chief minister too—a speech to another crowd of admirers in Ahmedabad. In 1971, Modi had come to the city to work in the anonymity of his uncle's small canteen before moving up the political ladder. Now, he was back. This was another homecoming to remember. His tired voice was beginning to crack but he was determined to have a final word. *'Desh chal pada hai, hamein kadam milana hai'* (The country has begun to march ahead, we have to match its steps).

The mood at the Congress headquarters was in sharp contrast. The party had put up small tents with coolers for journalists to protect them from the heat, with special arrangements for food and refreshments. They need not have bothered. By early afternoon, the locale wore a deserted look. Winners love to come on television, losers are good at the disappearing act.

A little after 4 p.m., Sonia and Rahul Gandhi made an appearance before the television cameras outside the party office. Both of them congratulated the new government and accepted responsibility for the defeat. 'The people's mandate is against us and I humbly accept the verdict. As Congress president, I take responsibility for it,' said Sonia. Rahul echoed the sentiment, but the weak, almost goofy, grin on his face looked inappropriate for the occasion. Neither of them referred to Modi by name. That would happen a few days later. Clearly, some of the bitterness of a long campaign hadn't dissipated.

And yet, watching the images of a victorious Modi saluting the people and a humbled Congress leadership accepting defeat with grace, my mind went back to a meeting I had with the Pakistani prime minister Nawaz Sharif in Jeddah in 2004. Sharif at the time was in exile, living in a rather opulent palace-like structure, having been forced out of the country by General Pervez Musharraf. As we sipped Kashmiri kahwa, Sharif sounded wistful. 'Rajdeepji, your democracy is truly special. One government comes in, another goes but there is no vendetta or bloodletting. Look at us in Pakistan. I am here in Jeddah, Benazir is shuttling between London and Dubai. Neither of us can return home. You are a lucky country!' Indeed, we were. It is a terrible cliché, but the truth is that every Indian election is a constant reminder of the genius of our democracy. 2014 was no different.

~

Evening prime time on counting day is usually reserved for the big
newsmakers. A little after 9.30 p.m., we had the biggest newsmaker
of the day after Modi—Amit Shah. If Modi was the Man of the
Series for having successfully driven an unrelenting presidential-style
campaign with his charismatic persona, then the effective election
micromanaging by Shah made him a deserved Man of the Match.
Without the stunning triumph in UP, the BJP would have probably
been forced to look for post-poll coalition partners.

Shah had not watched much TV since the morning. When a
journalist visited his rented house in Jangpura in south Delhi at 8.30
a.m., he was just waking up. It was only after 9 a.m., when he was
certain of which way the wind was blowing, that he actually switched
on the news. Even then, his first preference was for a channel that
was showing the UP results.

With every result from UP, Shah felt an increasing sense of relief.
He had been predicting as many as sixty seats for the BJP from the
state, but the trends showed that the party was set to even cross
that mark. His only disappointment was that his friend Jaitley had
lost. His first port of call after the numbers were out was to Jaitley's
house. It was the one dampener to what had been a spectacular
performance.

I asked Shah how he felt to be projected as the Man of the
Match. 'Rajdeepji, yeh meri jeet nahi hai, yeh har karyakarta ki
jeet hai!' (This is not my win, it is the victory of each worker). Had
he anticipated such a big win, I asked. 'Sach kahen toh hamein
bhi anuman nahi tha ki itni badi jeet hogi. Yeh toh vakai mein ek
tsunami hi hai! (Even we did not anticipate the scale of this win,
this is truly a tsunami)', he said, with a smile that was getting bigger
by the minute.

We finished our news coverage at around 11 p.m. After a long,
gruelling day in the studio, I was ready for an Old Monk with
coke. But one more call remained to be made. I telephoned Modi's
residence in Gandhinagar to congratulate him. The operator who
picked up the phone said Modiji was in a meeting and would call
back. At midnight, I tried my luck one last time. The operator was

apologetic. *'Sorry, Saheb sowa chali gaya'* (Saheb has gone to sleep).

The boy from Vadnagar with the blazing eyes and burning ambition was going to be the prime minister of India. An RSS swayamsevak was to take over as the country's chief executive. Long years in politics, the determined building of a massive personality cult in the face of the hard rock of controversy, had resulted in this extraordinary achievement. Narendra Modi deserved a good night's rest.

Epilogue

Narendra Modi was sworn in as India's fifteenth prime minister—and the first to be born after Independence—on 26 May 2014, dressed in a cream kurta and brown sleeveless jacket. The swearing-in ceremony had a typical Modi touch. Rather than holding it in the stuffy Durbar Hall which can barely accommodate 500 guests, Modi chose the grand forecourt of the Rashtrapati Bhavan for the occasion. Rajpath was lit up—it was a public spectacle played out on live television. The professional event managers in Team Modi were told to work closely with the Rashtrapati Bhavan to ensure that the ceremony went off flawlessly. Clearly, the new prime minister wasn't convinced that the government officials alone would get it right!

In his moment of ultimate triumph, the guest list suggested a genuine attempt at appearing inclusive. More than 3000 invites were sent out—I received one as well, though, sadly, being in the studio, I couldn't attend. But many of Modi's election rivals were present—Sonia and Rahul Gandhi were in attendance, as was Mulayam Singh Yadav. His former mentor L.K. Advani, too, was there. Only days earlier, an emotional Modi had wept in Parliament's central hall while formally accepting his party's leadership; Advani had cried as well. It seemed for a fleeting moment like a tearful reunion of the old and new orders within the BJP parivar.

The election campaign had seen the Ambani–Adani duo being targeted as beneficiaries of Modi's largesse—unmindful of the criticism, both families were there in full strength. Modi hadn't forgotten his Hindutva roots—sants and sadhus and even the controversial Sadhvi Rithambhara made a rare public appearance. The Hindi film industry was represented by Salman Khan who had flown kites with Modi in Gujarat as part of a PR blitz. And cricket legend Sunil Gavaskar was there in his capacity as BCCI's interim president. Modi's family, though, was not invited—once again underlining his complex private life that he had kept wrapped away from the public glare.

Modi, as he had done through the election campaign, had choreographed the swearing-in into a major news event. Just a few days earlier, in a powerful symbolic gesture, he had invited all the SAARC heads of state, including Pakistan's Prime Minister Nawaz Sharif, for the occasion. It was an unprecedented invite and a diplomatic coup—India's new prime minister was making a case on day one itself to position himself as a statesman and leader of the South Asian region. He had also sent out a subtle message to the West, especially the United States, which had targeted him in the aftermath of the 2002 riots, that their stamp of approval was not a priority. The new prime minister would make the neighbourhood his principal foreign policy thrust. Even when he did later accept an invite to visit Washington, he saw it as being entirely on his own terms. The US had denied him a visa for years, now they had bent before him—he felt vindicated.

The SAARC invite caught the ministry of external affairs (MEA) off guard—they now knew they were dealing with a prime minister who would not be chained by protocol. The SAARC initiative was a brilliant move, raising Modi's stature. Even the anti-Pakistan Shiv Sena was silenced, aware it couldn't be seen to play spoilsport. The only hitch was the extreme outdoor heat—Sharif, used to five-star comfort, could be heard complaining that he would have preferred an air-conditioned environment.

Modi was sworn in along with forty-five ministers, twenty-four with Cabinet rank. The original list, I was told, had been prepared by Modi's key point persons, Arun Jaitley and Amit Shah, then vetted by the RSS. The final touches, including portfolio distribution, were done by the prime minister himself. The choices reflected the limited pool of talent available to him but also Modi's domineering style of functioning. Jaitley, whom he implicitly trusted, was given the heavyweight finance and defence portfolios. Sushma Swaraj, whom he did not trust, was given MEA only at the last moment as a compromise. Smriti Irani, who was now seen as a Modi protégé, got the prestigious human resource development (HRD) portfolio, enough to spark off private criticism from others who felt left out. There was even a suggestion that Modi had elevated Smriti because he wanted to send out a message to Sushma that she wasn't the only woman face of the BJP. Piyush Goyal, who had starred in the campaign, was given an integrated energy portfolio (coal and power) while Gadkari had to be content with surface transport. 'All road contractors from Maharashtra will now be heading to Delhi!' was the joke in Delhi's power corridors on Gadkari's appointment.

Advani and the old guard were, yet again, not obliged. The BJP patriarch had been pushing for a constitutional post—'Make me the Lok Sabha Speaker' was his plea. Modi put his foot down— the tears in Parliament's central hall were replaced by the chilling pragmatism of power. A decision was taken that no one above the age of seventy-five years would be given a ministership. 'We can always make them governors if they wish,' Modi told an aide (eventually, Advani and Dr Murli Manohar Joshi were even removed from the BJP parliamentary board).

The allies were put in their place as well. Ram Vilas Paswan had been hoping for a 'wet' ATM ministry—he was given the relatively lower profile consumer affairs ministry. 'Paswan's past meant that the prime minister was suspicious of him—he doesn't want anyone in the government who will affect his clean image,' a Cabinet colleague later told me. The Shiv Sena, too, asked for more—but it had to be content with the heavy industries ministry. Modi wanted to send out a clear message that he was the Big Boss—this wasn't a UPA-II-like government where allies could decide ministries. And he certainly wasn't going to be bullied like a timid Manmohan Singh. The only demand he acceded to was from Rajasthan Chief Minister Vasundhara Raje who was peeved that no minister from her state was in the original list despite the BJP sweeping the state; thus, Nihalchand Meghwal was made a minister of state.

Left out of the government was Arun Shourie, one of the finest minds from the political right, who had openly backed Modi's prime ministership. A few days before the Cabinet formation, I had interviewed Shourie and got the distinct sense that he was preparing for a comeback. He spoke with great passion of how he believed the new government should function. He had parked himself in the national capital hoping for a call-up. It never came. Apparently, Shourie's old enmity with Jaitley had done him in—even in victory, there were still ghosts of a Hindu Divided Family that haunted the BJP.

Also haunting Modi was his own past as an autocratic leader who ran a government in a highly secretive manner. He had governed Gujarat as a virtual one-man show, with an excessively centralized chief minister's office where bureaucrats were often more powerful than ministers. New Delhi is not Gandhinagar—just the scale and dimension of the challenge makes it imperative that the leader empowers the Cabinet and delegates work. But apart from Jaitley and a few others, Modi wasn't convinced about the abilities of many of his Cabinet colleagues. Instead, he wanted to send out a message to the bureaucracy that they would be his prime assets.

A senior bureaucrat who attended a secretaries' meeting with Modi came out most impressed. 'He said he would fully back us for any decision we took, and if there was any problem, we should not hesitate to directly contact him,' the bureaucrat told me. The choice of bureaucrats in Modi's PMO reflected his approach— low-profile and experienced individuals who would never try and overshadow their boss. Many of them were bureaucrats whom Modi had successfully worked with in Gujarat. There was no space in the Modi PMO for a Brajesh Mishra-like figure who was seen by some as the virtual de facto head of government during Vajpayee's tenure.

While the bureaucrats seem satisfied, the ministers clearly are not. First, Modi expects them to work long hours. A minister who was relaxing at home at noon got a sudden wake-up call when a PMO official rang her up and said she was expected to reach office by 9 a.m. every day. Each ministry was asked to put up a detailed presentation before the PMO, listing out their tasks in the first year. 'The days of long lunches for our *mantris* are over,' was the buzz in Shastri Bhavan. A certain discipline and accountability in ministerial functioning can only be welcomed.

Second, Modi is determined to exercise tight control over the Cabinet system. When Rajnath Singh, the official number two in the government, wanted a particular IPS officer as his private secretary, the Modi PMO struck down the appointment. The officer concerned had served in a similar capacity with the Congress's Salman Khurshid. 'Rajnath was fuming but couldn't do anything about it—no one can challenge Modi,' a BJP leader later told me.

Third, there is a certain fear factor that Modi has instilled in his Cabinet colleagues, the fear of the Supreme Leader watching their every move. I had first-hand experience of it when I had to interview a minister for this book. As I was approaching the minister's residence, I got a call from one of his aides. 'Please, can you come from the back entrance?' When I met the minister, he insisted that we not speak in his main hall but in the garden behind the residence. 'You never know which room is bugged nowadays!' the minister warned.

Another story, possibly apocryphal, is that when Prakash Javadekar, information and broadcasting and environment minister in the Modi government, was on his way to the airport, he got a call from the PMO. 'Sir, you are wearing jeans for an official trip— you need to be dressed formally,' he was warned. Javadekar, who reportedly rushed back to change, denied the story when I asked him about it.

Like the ministers, the media, too, finds itself constrained. In Gujarat, Modi had preferred routine information department handouts to any extended interaction with journalists. Now, he has brought the philosophy of keeping the media at arm's-length to Delhi. No high-profile media adviser has been appointed, but Modi's long-serving assistant Jagdish Thakkar is in charge of sending out official press releases in a clerical fashion. As they did throughout the general elections, Modi's Twitter team puts out news updates and photographs with clockwork precision. Ministers have been explicitly told not to speak out of turn or appear on television debates, and instead focus on one-way social media engagement on a strict 'need to know' basis. 'In UPA-II, we could call up any minister at any time and they would respond. Now, everyone wants to be very discreet,' a senior reporter tracking the government told me. The more liberal and transparent UPA-II media set-up had led to a near-anarchic situation where ministers would often speak out in conflicting voices. By tightly controlling the information and restricting media access, Modi, it seems, wants to recapture the executive space that the Manmohan Singh government might have ceded to agenda-setting prime-time television, but the fear remains that a limited news can also promote a more opaque governance. The belief is: less news = less chaos. But let's also not forget: more opacity = less freedom.

He's even stopped the tradition of having a large contingent of journalists accompanying the prime minister on foreign visits. I had enjoyed travelling with Vajpayee on quite a few occasions. Yes, the air travel was a bit of a luxury—you were plied with plenty of free booze and chocolates, all, of course, at the tax payer's expense. Air India would put its best foot forward on the prime minister's plane— the hospitality was matchless. I must confess to having seen a few of my fellow journalists do almost everything but report on these trips. One of them had to be literally pulled away once from a night club in Paris in a drunken stupor before the police was called in.

But for serious, professional journalists the long flights also gave us a chance to interact with key government officials and build relationships in an informal setting. It gave us an insight into a prime minister's functioning beyond the forbidding corridors of South Block. Vajpayee once even advised us on which were the best places to eat in New York! Modi, though, is not a bon vivant—the pracharak in him has little time for discovering the many charms of New York. 'Why do we need to oblige the media?' was the cryptic question he posed to an official who tried to make a pitch for the journalists. Perhaps Modi has a point—it is time to end the junket culture that bedevils a section of the Indian media.

It's not just the media—the judiciary has also been put on notice. By fast-tracking the National Judicial Commission Bill that seeks to restore the primacy of the executive over judicial appointments, Modi is attempting to redraw the balance of power between the judiciary and the executive. The danger is in throwing the baby out with the bathwater—in recasting the relationship is the political class attempting to subvert judicial independence? The memories of the dictatorial Indira years in the 1970s haven't entirely dimmed.

In a sense, Modi is perhaps closest to Indira Gandhi in his personality-driven leadership style, an imperious attitude that ensures that institutions remain subservient to the individual (even Teachers' Day has been sought to be harnessed to the cult of Modi). His run-in with Congress-appointed governors is a good example. Precedent does suggest that political appointees are expected to resign when a new government emerges. But the manner in which Modi has gone about it suggests a certain contempt for the governor's office. At least two governors—including former Gujarat governor Kamla Beniwal with whom Modi was engaged in a running battle in Gandhinagar— were packed off to Mizoram, leaving the chief minister of that state to complain that Aizawl had become a 'dumping ground' for inconvenient constitutional authorities.

Much like Indira, Modi in power is in no mood to reach out to the Opposition. The Congress has been determinedly pushing for the Leader of the Opposition post; the government has steadfastly refused. The BJP claims it's going strictly by rules framed by the Speaker's office and parliamentary convention which say a party must have at least 10 per cent of the total strength of the Lok Sabha to qualify for the status of Leader of Opposition. The Congress needs fifty-five MPs, it has just forty-four. 'When we had very few numbers in Parliament, did the Congress ever give us the Leader of the Opposition post?' a BJP minister asked me.

But this battle goes well beyond just the numbers. Right through his election campaign, Modi had spoken of a 'Congress Mukt Bharat'. It wasn't just about defeating the Congress but decimating them to the point where the party would cease to exist. By denying them the primary Opposition space, Modi has sent out a firm message that the Congress's claims to be a truly 'national' party are now under serious scrutiny.

Indeed, while a triumphant Modi seeks to stamp his authority on government with a streak of ruthlessness, the Congress leadership needs to lift the morale of a party that is in deep depression. A question that was first posed after its 1977 debacle is being heard with even greater frequency now—is the Congress finished?

$\sim$

Within a few weeks of leading his party to defeat, Rahul Gandhi was flying off abroad. June can be awfully hot in Delhi, and Rahul clearly wanted to beat the heat. But it wasn't just the rising temperatures he wanted to avoid—it appeared that he didn't want to confront the growing disquiet being felt within the Congress.

When the sixteenth Lok Sabha was convened, the expectation was that Rahul would be the Congress's leader in Parliament. Instead, he shied away from taking up responsibility once again—the seventy-two-year-old veteran Congress leader from Karnataka, Mallikarjun Kharge, was chosen instead. Kharge, a Gandhi family loyalist, has won a record ten consecutive elections, but the truth is, he isn't going to set the Yamuna on fire. By choosing to opt out, Rahul had once again demonstrated an inability to lead from the front. Even his self-styled political guru Digvijaya Singh was disheartened. 'When the going gets tough, the tough must get going. Rahul is making a mistake by not taking up the challenge,' he told me. Privately, Congress leaders whispered that maybe Rahul didn't want to sit in the front row of the Lok Sabha where he would be caught out if he dozed off!

A contrast could be drawn with Indira Gandhi who had found herself in a similar difficult position after the 1977 election disaster. She was jailed, her party split, she was written off, and yet, quite remarkably, she made a comeback in three years, her fighting spirit best exemplified by the enduring image of her on an elephant striding across the floodwaters of Belchi in Bihar to meet marooned Dalit villagers who had been brutally attacked. Even Sonia had shown some of that political courage when she refused to buckle under the foreign origin propaganda against her. It is the kind of resolve which Rahul, it seems, is incapable of demonstrating. The *Economist*, in a scathing piece, wrote: 'Rahul, who had been long groomed for leadership, is a dud: earnest, but lacking in energy, ideas, strategy, and, crucially, the ability to connect with party workers and voters.'

Is Rahul really a 'dud'? I hardly know him at all to answer that with any certitude, but what I will say is that he has singularly failed to show any quality that marks him out as a leader who can lift a struggling party. He is probably the first member of the Nehru–Gandhi family who doesn't even command the respect of his own party men. At a lunch, an agitated senior Congress leader told me, 'We need a change in leadership, Rahul must go!' I asked him if he had any replacement in mind. He admitted there was no one he could single out right away. The only option being occasionally mentioned is Priyanka, who remains insistent that she is not entering formal politics.

To that extent, the Gandhi family remains both an asset and a liability—it holds the party together in the absence of any alternative leadership, but it also terribly retards the party's growth by creating a political culture that thrives on a nauseating sycophancy and an unwillingness to empower its regional leaders. Dynasty alone will not sustain the Congress—it needs to throw up a merit-driven, mass-based leadership that can usher in new ideas and energies.

Over the years, the 'umbrella' party that could co-opt and accommodate conflicting interest groups has badly atrophied, to the point where decay has now set in. UP and Bihar are a good example—in the two big states of the Hindi heartland, the Congress has fossilized. 'You can identify a Congressman by his age. The older they are, the more likely they are to have been Congress supporters at some stage,' is how a UP leader explained the predicament.

So, how will this ageing party, devoid of a robust organization, really combat a cadre-based party like the BJP? 'Nothing is permanent in politics, things will change in five years. Who would have thought in 2009 that we would lose the 2014 elections so badly?' is what one Congress MP told me. If this attitude lulls the Congress into complacency, then Modi could provide them with another wake-up call. Modi is not Morarji Desai, the Janata Party prime minister who was unable to hold a disparate flock together. This time the Congress is having to deal with a tough, dynamic politician who has understood what it takes not just to win power but to retain it, as he has shown in Gujarat. Challenging him will require the Congress to move beyond its time-worn slogans and identify more directly with the aspirations of a younger, more impatient India.

For example, the Congress's vision of a secular republic now faces a mounting challenge even from its traditional supporters. At a seminar in Patna, a young Muslim student leader told senior academic Pratap Bhanu Mehta that he had three questions he wished to pose to Rahul. 'I want to know, are Muslim youth less likely to suffer ordinary discrimination in Congress-ruled states? Does a Congress-ruled state like Assam or Delhi have a better record of bringing perpetrators of riots to justice? Why, after sixty years of Congress rule, do Muslims feel they have to vote on their "security"?'

The three sharply worded questions reflect the dilemma of the Indian Muslim—is 'secular blackmail' stemming from the fear of a Modi-led government enough reason to vote for a party which itself has failed to offer protection or development to minorities? The Congress cannot rely on handouts and platitudes any longer; it needs to be ready to start a mass mobilization programme by taking up issues of urgent public concern. The era of drawing-room political machinations is coming to an end. It would be premature to write the obituary of any party, but the Congress does have a long, arduous road ahead.

Other parties, too, are having to slowly pick up the pieces after the stunning 2014 results. In Bihar, we have seen the emergence of a potential grand 'secular alliance'—Nitish, Lalu and the Congress may actually come together in the 2015 assembly elections. It's an alliance which smacks of political opportunism—once sworn enemies are coming together in a desperate bid to keep the BJP out. As Lalu told me, 'Our biggest enemy is Narendra Modi. *Bade dushman ko harane ke liye kabhi kabhi samjhauta karna padta hai*' (To defeat a bigger enemy, you sometimes have to compromise). If the Bihar by-election results are any evidence, then Lalu's instinctive street-smart politics is a potential survival ticket.

Other regional forces, too, have to worry about what the rise of Modi means for their future. Mamata Banerjee in Bengal, for example, has now realized that the BJP is an emerging force in the state's politics and has even hinted, quite tellingly, at a reach-out to the left. Mulayam Singh may have to shift gears as well—the 2014 elections have shown that his brazen attempts at minority appeasement are bound to invite a political backlash. Mayawati may never ally with Mulayam, but she, too, has to move beyond the politics of fake empowerment—statues are not a substitute for development. In Maharashtra, Sharad Pawar is making a big mistake if he thinks reservations for the politically influential Marathas will be a game changer—every time you give reservations to one group, you end up alienating many others. Perhaps the only regional leaders who will feel secure are Naveen Patnaik and Jayalalithaa. The Modi tsunami has stayed away from the Odisha and Tamil Nadu coastline.

Arvind Kejriwal, too, has been humbled by the 2014 election verdict. The politician who insisted that the AAP would fight in more than 400 seats across the country is now terrified of even contesting the Haryana elections. His sole aim, he says, is rebuilding his base in Delhi. It seems a rather strange U-turn for a politician who at the start of 2014 thought he could walk on water. At least Kejriwal has shown some spunk, though—when the Modi government completed forty-nine days, he put up posters across Delhi comparing his achievements with that of the prime minister. If only the Congress and Rahul could show similar fight, politics in the country may become a little less one-sided.

That nothing is permanent in politics is best exemplified by the left's pitiable condition. In the 2004 elections, they held the balance of power at the Centre and helped shape the first UPA government. Ten years later, they have been reduced to marginal players— intellectual hubris and an unwillingness to adapt to a changing India have made the left parties almost irrelevant to the national discourse.

~

Every prime minister is entitled to an extended honeymoon period, especially one who has scored such an emphatic victory. 'Achhe Din Aane Wale Hain' was Modi's caller tune in the 2014 general elections. The Modi juggernaut was driven by an overarching sentiment of 'hope', the belief that the moment he was elected happy days of high growth, low inflation and strong, corruption-free governance would return. Hope brings with it a rising tide of expectations. When price rise remained stubborn in the first few weeks of the new government and tomato prices shot up, my driver asked me, *'Sir, woh achhe din ka kya hua?'* (What happened to the promise of good days?) When there was no 'big bang' announcement in the Modi government's first budget, his critics were quick to question his intent to reform. 'Chidambaram's budget with saffron lipstick," was noted columnist Swaminathan Aiyar's rather caustic verdict. When the Indian government blocked a WTO agreement by sticking to its stand on food subsidies, Modi admirer and right-wing economist Surjit Bhalla remarked angrily, 'A leader, operating from a position of one of the most voted governments in Indian history, should be making policy with conviction, not emulating tactics of a defunct government.'

Truth is, Modi as prime minister has so far been more cautious than he was as a campaigner, the courage to usher in drastic reform less in evidence. Perhaps he doesn't see himself as a Margaret Thatcher-like figure, as some of his supporters would like him to be—someone who will dismantle the Indian state in a manic urge for privatization. Perhaps he is more of an efficient, project-driven CEO—bullet trains and smart cities are his ideas for a new India, not labour reform or disinvesting PSUs.

As a resilient politician who has built a career with single-minded determination over several years of highs and lows, Modi likes to see himself, as they say in cricket, as a '*lamba race ka ghoda*' (ready for the long haul). 'My government is here for five, if not ten years—why are you judging me on the first 100 days?' he asked an industrialist who met him. A close aide told me that it was no different when he first took over as chief minister in Gujarat. 'He would like to fully familiarize himself with the Central government in Delhi before he starts taking big decisions,' was the explanation I was given.

But Modi must know as a shrewd politician that he was elected as an agent of change, not continuity. That is what the idea of 'hope' was premised upon. That Modi is capable of being a change agent is doubtless. A Modi acolyte tells a delicious story of his leader taking on the Planning Commission when he was Gujarat chief minister. Modi was convinced that the Planning Commission was an impediment to faster growth. So at a meeting in Yojana Bhavan, he insisted on showing all the commission members a ten-minute video before meeting them for additional grants. The video showed in stark terms why Modi believed the Planning Commission should not exist!

A similar desire to rewrite the rules was witnessed when the Modi government decided to call off Indo-Pakistan foreign secretary-level talks after the Pakistan high commissioner met separatist Kashmiri Hurriyat leaders. The Hurriyat meetings at the Pakistan High Commission had been a familiar kebab and *kahwa* ritual; the ministry of external affairs, too, didn't seem to get agitated over it. Modi, though, has drawn a Lakshman-rekha for Indo-Pak diplomacy. As a seasoned diplomat remarked, 'You just can't have cross-border firing and sari–shawl diplomacy at the same time. Modi is not Manmohan, he is not even Vajpayee.'

It is that ability to break with convention, to challenge the Lutyens' Delhi establishment, to be adventurous in his thought and execution that will define Modi's prime ministership. He is leading India's first genuine right-of-centre majority government—Vajpayee's NDA was a loose coalition arrangement—and therefore has the mandate to effect a dramatic transformation.

Will this change alter inter-community relations as well? The 2014 election verdict has revived and emboldened the RSS and its affiliates—RSS chief Mohan Bhagwat has described India as a Hindu nation and Hindutva as its core identity. A Goa BJP minister echoed the sentiment. Minority affairs minister Najma Heptullah even went so far as to suggest there is nothing wrong in calling all Indians 'Hindu'—it is a badge of national citizenship. Modi hasn't criticized or distanced himself from the remarks. In Gujarat, once he had settled down, Modi did marginalize the VHP hotheads. As prime minister, he is faced with a similar challenge of reining in his own saffron brotherhood. Will there be a genuine outreach to the minorities or will that run counter to his original persona as the face of unapologetic Hindutva politics?

During the Ramzan month in 2014, Modi did not host the traditional prime minister's iftar. 'You know he doesn't believe in these token gestures,' was how the decision was explained by a PMO official. Instead, I was reminded by the official how the prime minister's Jan Dhan financial inclusion scheme did not discriminate between Hindus and Muslims. 'Our slogan is "Sabka Saath, Sabka Vikas",' I was assured. Will that assurance satisfy minority groups who coexist uneasily between fear and radicalization?

Catchy slogans have been Modi's trademark—when he visited Kargil, he assured the soldiers on the border, '*Na khaunga na khane doonga*' (I won't take bribes, nor allow others to take bribes). A few days later, I met a senior bureaucrat and asked him whether he felt red-tapism and corruption had significantly declined in government. He just smiled: 'This is India, Rajdeep. Nothing changes overnight.'

~

On 15 August 2014, Narendra Modi addressed the nation for the first time from the ramparts of the Red Fort. Only a year earlier, on Independence Day again, he had begun his audacious bid for prime ministership by virtually challenging Manmohan Singh to a public debate. Now the challenger was prime minister. Wearing a short-sleeved kurta and a red Rajasthani safa, Modi reverted to his success mantra in the 2014 elections—a masterful orator directly communicating with the voter. In an extempore speech peppered with ideas and an infectious energy, Modi spoke of himself as a 'sevak' and an 'outsider' in Delhi. He focused on sanitation and 'toilet building' as a national mission, and rhetorically asked, 'What kind of prime minister stands at the Red Fort and talks about toilet building?' This was quintessential Modi—breaking with tradition, almost challenging the ruling class to reorder its priorities.

He even threw up a 'Make in India' catchline, an invitation to the world to make India a manufacturing hub. He called for a ten-year moratorium on divisive politics and asked for parents to check rising crimes against women by educating their sons. And yes, he did promise to disband the Planning Commission. The tedium of using the 15 August speech to pay ritualistic obeisance to past achievements was forsaken. Instead, Modi was offering a glimpse at a future aimed at growth and harmony. The rousing speech received a thumbs up—Television Audience Meter (TAM) ratings show that it was watched by a viewership three times higher than the 2013 Independence Day speech. Modi had pressed all the right buttons—now, importantly, he needs to walk the talk.

Only a few days before Modi's virtuoso performance, his general election Man of the Match, Amit Shah, was also given his reward—he was made the BJP president. For someone who, just eighteen months ago, was facing an extended prison sentence in a fake encounter case, it was an astonishing turnaround. Indeed, never before have two leaders from the same state outside of the Hindi heartland come to dominate national politics in such a sudden and dramatic manner. As a bureaucrat laughingly told me, 'I hope that we now at least get a half-decent Gujarati restaurant in Delhi!'

Shah has his task cut out—he has to be a bridge between party and government but, importantly, also ensure that his winning formula of the general elections is sustained in the state elections as well. In his first speech as party president, he set out the BJP's goal. 'We must capture power from Jammu and Kashmir to Kerala, from Nagaland to Gujarat.' It is an ambitious project, but after his stunning success in UP, Shah seems to believe he has the organizational machine to deliver the results. Certainly, his eye for detail and micromanagement mark him out as an ideal election strategist.

And yet, the Shah model of fighting elections has also thrown up real concerns of a worrying revival of communally divisive politics. His decision, for example, to make the party's rabble-rousing Gorakhpur MP Yogi Adityanath one of his star campaigners in UP has sent out a signal that saffron politics is an intrinsic part of the BJP's UP strategy. Western UP continues to simmer in the cauldron of religious polarization. The UP BJP wants to make an election issue of 'love jihad'—a dangerous term being used to suggest that Hindu–Muslim marriages are based on forced conversion. In Jammu and Kashmir, the call for a 'nationalist' government which will seek to abolish Article 370 is also disconcerting—politically sensitive issues cannot be settled in a cavalier manner. 'We are playing with fire,' warns a security official who has worked in the valley for years.

The apparent shift in strategy from the 'development driven' pattern to a sharper 'Hindutva' identity politics has already backfired in a series of by-elections since the general elections. The triumph in the 2014 general elections was driven by a recognition that the BJP needed to reinvent itself, adapt to a changing India by making governance and rapid growth its core issues, with Modi as the face of change. While the prime minister seems to have been astute enough to the embrace the new paradigm, some of the Sangh's foot soldiers seem a step behind. Unless, as some political observers suggest, the dualism of a prime minister who is striving to appear statesmanlike and a party leadership which is more ideologically rigid is part of a well-crafted double act by the Modi–Shah duo. Moreover, the BJP's decision to break ties with its twenty-five-year-old ally, the Shiv Sena in Maharashtra, only suggests that the duo are convinced that the mandate of 2014 was for a Modi-led BJP government, and not for an NDA-like coalition. Unilateralism, it seems, is the new mantra for the BJP leadership

Modi and Shah, controversial but successful—easily the two stand-out politicians of 2014. Their rise will continue to attract sharply divided opinion. Modi, for example, will always be seen by his critics with a measure of scepticism. Eminent social scientist Ashis Nandy had written an article in the *Seminar* magazine in 2002, recalling an interview he had done with Modi as a pracharak in the early 1990s: 'It was a long, rambling interview but it left me in no doubt that here was a classical, clinical case of a fascist . . . all set within the matrix of clear paranoid and obsessive personality traits.' Modi's supporters reject the Nandy thesis. As one of them, a remarkably hard-working politician, told me, 'Modi is a remarkable politician with a human touch and communication skills who has consistently fought and won over adversity. He represents the triumph of Indian democracy.'

This is not an appropriate time to either demonize or deify Narendra Modi. His prime ministership is, after all, work in progress. What is certain, though, is that Verdict 2014 has placed India at the cusp of change, with the future direction pregnant with a range of possibilities, good and bad. If a Congress under Nehru ushered in India's republican Constitution, a BJP led by Modi could well redefine the idea of India, or at least the way it is governed.

Appendix 1

2014 Election Result: Some interesting aspects based on Election Commission of India (ECI) figures

- Out of the 282 seats that the BJP won, in 137 it secured more than half of the total votes polled; moreover, in 169 seats the party's vote share was greater than the vote shares of parties that finished second, third and fourth put together.
- 73 per cent or nearly three out of four BJP victories were by margins of over one lakh votes.
- BJP's success was mainly against the Congress as nearly three out of five BJP victories were against it.
- For the first time the BJP's national vote share was greater than that of the Congress. Even in the national elections held during the Vajpayee years, the Congress had been ahead of the BJP in terms of overall vote share.
- Punjab is the only state in the country where the BJP's vote share declined since the 2009 election. Among all the states, the BJP's highest vote share increase in percentage point terms was in Uttar Pradesh at +24.8.
- BJP and allies won 67 out of 70 seats where voter turnout went

up by over 15 per cent since 2009. In six states, the BJP secured more than half of the total votes polled. These are Gujarat, Uttarakhand, Rajasthan, Madhya Pradesh, Goa and Himachal Pradesh.

- In six states, the BJP won each and every seat on offer. These are Gujarat, Rajasthan, Delhi, Uttarakhand, Himachal Pradesh and Goa.
- One in three seats won by the BJP is from Uttar Pradesh and Bihar.
- The BJP won two-thirds of the highly urban seats (37/57) and more than half of the rural seats (178/342); Congress could win only two seats that had an urban population of over 75 per cent, Ernakulam and Ludhiana.
- Out of the 44 seats that the Congress won, only 13 were won by margins of over one lakh votes; seven were narrow wins by margins below 10,000 votes. In as many as 178 of the 464 seats that the Congress contested, the party's candidates secured less than 16.66 per cent of the total votes polled, hence losing their security deposit.

2014 Election: Some interesting points based on Centre for Study of Developing Societies (CSDS) Surveys

- Narendra Modi's popularity (people's preference as prime minister) at the time of the Lok Sabha election was nearly twice that of Rahul Gandhi, Sonia Gandhi and Manmohan Singh put together. Modi was preferred by 36 per cent of the voters, whereas Rahul, Sonia and Manmohan together totalled 19 per cent.
- Modi's popularity jumped by nearly two times (from 19 per cent to 36 per cent) between July 2013 and April–May 2014; Rahul Gandhi's increased only marginally from 12 per cent to 14.
- For the first time in a national election, more Hindu Dalits and Hindu Tribals voted for the BJP than the Congress; Congress was ahead of the BJP only among Muslims and Christians.
- While about two out of every five Muslims voted for the Congress,

Hindu Upper Caste support for the BJP was one out of two.

• **The** BJP secured about 36 per cent votes among the youngest/ first-time voters (18–22 years); the Congress got less than half as much (17 per cent).

• BJP's relative unpopularity among women voters continued in 2014: 29 per cent women voted for the BJP as opposed to 33 per cent men, a difference of four percentage points. In 2009, the difference between the two was of two percentage points.

Note

ECI figures and CSDS Survey data analysed and compiled by Researchers at Lokniti, Centre for the Study of Developing Societies. ECI figures for the 2014 Lok Sabha election accessed and downloaded from http://eciresults.nic.in/. Survey data is from the following election studies conducted by Lokniti, CSDS:

1. National Election Study 2014, Post Poll, conducted in 26 states; sample size: 22,301.
2. National Election Study 2014, Pre Poll, conducted in 21 states; sample size: 20,957.
3. Election Tracker January 2014 conducted in 18 states; sample size: 18,596.
4. Election Tracker July 2013 conducted in 18 states; sample size: 19,062.
5. National Election Study 2009, Post Poll, conducted in 29 states and one union territory; sample size: 36,641.
6. National Election Study 2004, Post Poll, conducted in 29 states and two union territories; sample size: 27,189.
7. National Election Study 1999, Post Poll, conducted in 20 states and one union territory; sample size: 9436.
8. National Election Study 1998, Post Poll, conducted in 18 states and one union territory; sample size: 8133.
9. National Election Study 1996, Pre Poll, conducted in 20 states and one union territory; sample size: 9602.

During all the above-mentioned surveys, face-to-face interviews with randomly selected voters from the most updated electoral rolls were conducted by specially trained field investigators. All National Election Study Post Poll data sets have been weighted by the actual vote shares garnered by the main parties/alliances in the respective election.

Appendix 2

Tables based on actual results (Election Commission of India—ECI) or survey data (Centre for Study of Developing Societies—CSDS)

It was a comfortable victory; 73 per cent or nearly three out of four BJP victories were by margins of over one lakh votes.

Victory margins (votes)	Seats won by BJP
3 lakh and above	42
2–2.99 lakh	74
1–1.99 lakh	90
50,000–99,999	44
25,000–49,999	17
10,000–24,999	6
Less than 10,000	9
Total	282

Source: CSDS Data Unit

For the first time the BJP's national vote share was greater than that of the Congress; even during the Vajpayee years the Congress had been ahead of the BJP in terms of overall vote share.

Year	Congress's lead over BJP in terms of vote share (percentage points)
1984	+40.61
1989	+28.17
1991	+16.60
1996	+8.51
1998	+0.23
1999	+4.55
2004	+4.37
2009	+9.75
2014	-11.74

Source: CSDS Data Unit

In six states, the BJP's vote share on its own crossed the 50 per cent mark.

State	Percentage of votes secured by BJP on its own
Gujarat	58.7
Uttarakhand	55.3
Rajasthan	54.9
Madhya Pradesh	54.0
Goa	53.5
Himachal Pradesh	53.4

Source: CSDS Data Unit

NDA's strike rate was above 90 per cent in nine states; cent per cent in six states.

State	Seats won by NDA / total seats on offer
Gujarat	26/26
Rajasthan	25/25
Delhi	7/7
Uttarakhand	5/5
Himachal Pradesh	4/4
Goa	2/2
Madhya Pradesh	27/29
Uttar Pradesh	73/80
Chhattisgarh	9/10

Source: CSDS Data Unit

In the southern part of India too, the BJP gave its best-ever performance.

Year	Seats won by BJP in South India	Vote share (%)	States & UTs from where it came
1984	1	1.9%	AP
1989	0	2.0%	–
1991	5	9.9%	Karnataka (4), AP (1)
1996	6	8.8%	Karnataka
1998	20	15.4%	K'taka (13), AP (4), TN (3)
1999	19	12.5%	AP (7), K'taka (7), TN (4), A&N Islands (1)
2004	18	14.2%	Karnataka
2009	20	12.0%	Karnataka (19), A&N Islands (1)
2014	22	15.6%	K'taka (17), AP (3), TN (1), A&N Islands (1)

Source: CSDS Data Unit
Note: South India includes Andhra Pradesh (AP—undivided), Karnataka, Tamil Nadu (TN), Kerala, Puducherry, Andaman and Nicobar Islands (A&N Islands) and Lakshadweep.

BJP retained 103 of the total 116 seats it had won in 2009 and snatched 109 from the Congress.

Seats that . . .	
BJP retained since 2009	103
BJP snatched from Congress	109
BJP snatched from Congress allies	12
BJP snatched from Others	58
Total	282

Source: CSDS Data Unit

BJP won two-thirds of the urban seats and more than half of the rural ones; Congress could win only two seats with an urban population of over 75 per cent (Ernakulam and Ludhiana).

Category	Total Seats	Congress		BJP	
		2009	2014	2009	2014
Rural (less than 25% urban)	342	116	27	66	178
Semi Urban (25–74.9% urban)	144	67	15	32	67
Urban (75%+ urban)	57	23	2	18	37

Source: CSDS Data Unit

Congress's disastrous performance.

Congress . . .	Seats	
Contested	464	Lost deposits on 178 seats
Won	44	Only 13 won by margins of over 1 lakh
Came second in	223	157 of these were lost by margins of over 1 lakh
Came third in	65	Got less than 15% vote in 35 of these
Came fourth in	117	Got less than 5% vote in 70 of these

Source: CSDS Data Unit

Congress fared disastrously even in Reserved seats.

Category	Seats	Congress		BJP	
		2009	2014	2009	2014
Reserved (SC)	84	30	7	12	40
Reserved (ST)	47	20	5	14	27
General	412	156	32	90	215

Source: CSDS Data Unit

For the first time in a national election, more Dalits and Tribals voted for the BJP than the Congress.

Year	Dalit vote for BJP (%)	Dalit vote for Congress (%)
1996	14	34
1998	14	28
1999	14	30
2004	13	27
2009	12	27
2014	24	19
	Tribal vote for BJP (%)	Tribal vote for Congress (%)
1996	21	42
1998	21	32
1999	22	46
2004	28	37
2009	24	38
2014	38	28

Source: National Election Studies conducted by CSDS

Note: Figures weighted by actual vote share of parties in the respective years.

While the Congress performed poorly among Dalits and Tribals, the Muslim support for the party was 38 per cent, the same as it was in 2009.

Year	Muslim vote for Congress (%)	Muslim vote for BJP (%)	Muslim vote for Others (%)
1971	59	0	41
1996	36	2	62
1998	32	6	62
1999	40	7	53
2004	36	7	57
2009	38	4	58
2014	38	8	54

Source: CSDS Data Unit, National Election Studies conducted by CSDS

Note: Figures weighted by actual vote share of parties in the respective years.

Muslim support for Congress was much greater in states where it was locked in a straight contest with BJP.

States with ...	Muslim vote for Congress (%)	Muslim vote for BJP (%)	Muslim vote for Others (%)
Cong vs BJP direct fight (Bipolar)	73	19	8
Cong vs BJP vs Others (Multipolar)	37	7	56

Source: National Election Studies, 2014, conducted by Lokniti, CSDS

Note: Bipolar states are Himachal Pradesh, Uttarakhand, Chhattisgarh, Madhya Pradesh, Gujarat, Rajasthan and Maharashtra (BJP–SS vs Cong–NCP).

On the back of massive and unprecedented support from Hindu Upper Castes and OBCs, the overall Hindu support for the BJP touched an all-time high of 36 per cent, rendering any minority consolidation behind non-BJP parties almost ineffective. Never in the past had Hindu support for the BJP crossed the 30 per cent mark.

Year	Vote for BJP among Hindus (%)
1996	23
1998	28
1999	27
2004	25
2009	22
2014	36

Source: National Election Studies conducted by CSDS

Note: Figures weighted by actual vote share of parties in the respective years.

Modi's popularity (36 per cent) at the time of the Lok Sabha election was nearly twice that of Rahul Gandhi, Sonia Gandhi and Manmohan Singh put together (19 per cent).

Choice for PM	2014 NES Post Poll (%)
Narendra Modi	36
Rahul Gandhi	14
Sonia Gandhi	3
Mayawati	3
Mulayam Singh Yadav	2
Arvind Kejriwal	2
Manmohan Singh	2
Others	9
No opinion	29

Source: National Election Studies, 2014, conducted by Lokniti, CSDS

Question asked: After this election, who would you prefer as the next Prime Minister of India? (This was an open-ended question and no names were offered to the respondents.)

Modi's popularity jumped by nearly two times between July 2013 and April–May 2014; Rahul's more or less stayed where it was.

Choice for PM	Jul 2013 (%)	Jan 2014 (%)	Mar 2014 (%)	2014 NES Post Poll (%)
Narendra Modi	19	34	34	36
Rahul Gandhi	12	15	15	14
Sonia Gandhi	5	5	3	3
Mayawati	3	2	2	3
Mulayam Singh Yadav	2	2	2	2
Arvind Kejriwal	-	3	2	2
Manmohan Singh	6	3	2	2
Others	14	10	10	9
No opinion	39	26	30	29

Source: National Election Tracker surveys and National Election Studies, 2014, conducted by Lokniti, CSDS
Question asked: After this election/the 2014 Lok Sabha election, who would you prefer as the next Prime Minister of India? (Do not offer any name and record the exact answer and consult PM codes for coding.)

The BJP trailed the Congress in terms of vote share before Modi was declared as PM candidate, and overtook it in the months following the announcement.

	BJP's vote lead over Congress (percentage points)
July 2013 (Survey)	-1
January 2014 (Survey)	+7
March 2014 (Survey)	+10
May 2014 (Actual)	+11.8

Source: CSDS Data Unit

Gender divide over Modi: Women supporters of Modi were much less than men supporters.

Gender	Want Narendra Modi as PM (%)	Want Rahul Gandhi as PM (%)
Men	41	16
Women	30	13

Source: National Election Studies, 2014, conducted by CSDS

The BJP's relative unpopularity among women voters continues: 29 per cent women voted for BJP as opposed to 33 per cent men. In 2009, the difference between the two was two percentage points; had only women voted, the BJP may have fallen short of majority.

Year	Women–Men voting gap for BJP (percentage points)	Women–Men voting gap for Congress (percentage points)
1996	-3	+1
1998	-5	+3
1999	-3	+5
2004	-1	+1
2009	-2	+1
2014	-4	0

Source: National Election Studies conducted by CSDS

Modi was preferred as PM among the young voters much more than among the elderly.

Age Group (years)	Want Narendra Modi as PM (%)	Want Rahul Gandhi as PM (%)
18–25	42	16
26–35	38	15
36+	32	14

Source: National Election Studies, 2014, conducted by CSDS

The BJP's lead over the Congress in terms of votes secured was least among the elderly voters aged above 55 years (eight percentage points) and greatest among the youngest voters aged between 18 and 22 years (nineteen percentage points).

Age group	Vote for BJP	Vote for Cong
18–22	36	17
23–25	33	20
26–35	33	20
36–45	30	18
46–55	30	20
56+	27	20

Source: National Election Studies, 2014, conducted by CSDS

Dissatisfaction with the UPA government kept rising over the last three years.

Satisfaction with performance of the UPA-II government	Satisfied	Dissatisfied	Net satisfaction
July 2011	49	31	+18
July 2013	38	40	-2
Jan 2014	35	50	-15
Mar 2014	42	48	-6

Source: State of the Nation survey, 2011, and National Election Tracker surveys, 2013–14, conducted by Lokniti, CSDS

Anti-incumbency also kept increasing.

Should the UPA govt get another chance?	Yes	No	Pro/Anti-incumbency (% points)
July 2011	37	35	+2
July 2013	31	39	-8
January 2014	26	52	-26
March 2014	23	54	-31

Source: State of the Nation survey, 2011, and National Election Tracker surveys, 2013–14, conducted by Lokniti, CSDS

UPA-II was extremely unpopular compared to the two previous governments.

Year/Government	Should the Central govt get another chance?	
	YES	NO
2004/NDA	48	30
2009/UPA-I	54	45
2014/UPA-II	23	54

Source: National Election Studies conducted by CSDS

Price rise, corruption and a desire for development seem to have been the reasons for strong anti-incumbency against the UPA-II government.

	Single most important election issue (answers to an open-ended question)			
	Inflation (%)	Development (%)	Corruption (%)	Employment (%)
July 2013	11	9	6	5
Jan 2014	18	9	7	6
March 2014	19	15	12	7
April 2014	19	17	12	8

Source: National Election Tracker surveys, 2013–14, and National Election Studies, 2014, conducted by Lokniti, CSDS

Price rise perhaps made the BJP overtake the Congress for the first time among the poor.

Year	Poor for BJP (%)	Poor for Cong (5)	BJP lead over Congress among the Poor (% points)
1999	20	29	-9
2004	19	26	-7
2009	15	26	-11
2014	24	20	+4

Source: National Election Studies conducted by CSDS

UPA-II was seen as a very corrupt government by 45 per cent of the respondents, up from 34 per cent in 2013.

How corrupt is the UPA-II government?	2011	2013	Jan 2014	Mar 2014
Very corrupt	28	34	45	41
Somewhat corrupt	42	42	30	32
Not at all corrupt	5	4	6	8
Can't say/No opinion	25	20	19	19

Source: State of the Nation survey, 2011, and National Election Tracker surveys, 2013–14 , conducted by Lokniti, CSDS

Some more points based on Election Commission of India (ECI) figures:

Out of the 432 seats which AAP contested, in 414 the party's candidates secured less than one-sixth of the total votes polled, hence losing their security deposit.

AAP candidates secured less than one per cent of the total votes polled in as many as 265 seats. In other words, in a little over three out of five seats that the AAP contested, the party could not even secure one per cent of the votes.

Number of seats where AAP vote share was . . .	
Less than 16.66% (lost security deposits)	414
Less than 10 per%	411
Less than 5%	397
Less than 2%	355
Less than 1%	265
Less than NOTA vote share	260

ECI data recomputed by CSDS Data Unit

Some more points based on survey figures:

Narendra Modi's popularity (people's preference as PM) was greatest among the youngest voters (43 per cent) and relatively much less among the elderly voters (30 per cent). Modi's lead over Rahul Gandhi was also the widest among the youngest voters (29 percentage points) and narrowed down among elderly voters (17 percentage points).

Age group (years)	Want Modi as PM (%)	Want Rahul as PM (%)	Modi's lead over Rahul (percentage points)
18–22	43	14	+29
23–25	40	17	+23
26–35	38	15	+23
36–45	36	14	+22
46–55	33	14	+19
56+	30	13	+17

Source: National Election Studies, 2014, conducted by CSDS

Appendix 3

All India Lok Sabha Result 2014

Slno	States	Total Seats	Turnout %	Congress		Congress Allies		BJP		BJP Allies		Left		BSP		Others	
				Won	Vote %	Won	Vote %	Won	Vote %	Won	Vote %	Won	Vote %	Won	Vote %	Won	Vote %
1	ANDHRA PRADESH*	42	74.5	2	11.5	0	0.0	3	8.5	16	29.1	0	0.7	0	0.8	21	49.4
2	ARUNACHAL PRADESH	2	78.6	1	41.2	0	0.0	1	46.1	0	0.0	0	0.0	0	0.0	0	12.7
3	ASSAM	14	80.1	3	29.6	0	2.2	7	36.5	0	0.0	0	0.8	0	0.0	4	30.9
4	BIHAR	40	56.3	2	8.4	5	21.3	22	29.4	9	9.4	0	1.5	0	2.1	5	27.9
5	GOA	2	77.0	0	36.6	0	0.0	2	53.4	0	0.0	0	1.2	0	0.0	0	8.8
6	GUJARAT	26	63.6	0	32.9	0	0.0	26	59.1	0	0.0	0	0.2	0	0.9	0	6.9
7	HARYANA	10	71.4	1	22.9	0	0.0	7	34.7	0	6.1	0	0.4	0	4.6	2	31.3
8	HIMACHAL PRADESH	4	64.4	0	40.7	0	0.0	4	53.3	0	0.0	0	0.8	0	0.7	0	4.5
9	JAMMU & KASHMIR	6	49.7	0	22.9	0	11.1	3	32.4	0	0.0	0	0.0	0	1.5	3	32.1
10	KARNATAKA	28	67.2	9	40.8	0	0.0	17	43.0	0	0.0	0	0.2	0	0.9	2	15.1
11	KERALA	20	73.9	8	31.1	4	10.9	0	10.3	0	0.5	8	40.1	0	0.4	0	6.7
12	MADHYA PRADESH	29	61.6	2	34.9	0	0.0	27	54.0	0	0.0	0	0.4	0	3.8	0	6.9
13	MAHARASHTRA	48	60.5	2	18.1	4	16.6	23	27.3	19	24.0	0	0.5	0	2.6	0	10.9
14	MANIPUR	2	79.6	2	41.7	0	0.0	0	11.9	0	0.0	0	14.0	0	0.0	0	32.4
15	MEGHALAYA	2	68.8	1	37.9	0	0.0	0	8.9	1	22.2	0	0.7	0	0.0	0	30.3

No.	State	Seats	Turnout %	Congress Seats	Congress Vote %	Cong. allies Seats	Cong. allies Vote %	BJP Seats	BJP Vote %	BJP allies Seats	BJP allies Vote %	Left Seats	Left Vote %	Others Seats	Others Vote %
16	MIZORAM	1	61.7	1	48.6	0	0.0	0	0.0	0	47.2	0	0.0	0	4.2
17	NAGALAND	1	87.8	0	30.1	0	0.0	0	0.0	1	68.7	0	0.0	0	1.2
18	ODISHA	21	73.8	0	26.0	0	0.0	1	21.5	0	0.0	0	0.5	20	51.0
19	PUNJAB	13	70.6	3	33.1	0	0.0	2	8.7	4	26.3	0	0.5	4	29.5
20	RAJASTHAN	25	63.4	0	30.4	0	0.0	25	54.9	0	0.0	0	0.6	0	11.8
21	SIKKIM	1	83.4	0	2.3	0	0.0	0	2.4	0	0.0	0	0.0	1	95.3
22	TAMIL NADU	39	73.7	0	4.3	0	0.0	1	5.5	1	13.1	0	1.1	37	75.6
23	TRIPURA	2	84.7	0	15.2	0	0.0	0	5.7	0	0.0	2	64.0	0	15.1
24	UTTAR PRADESH	80	58.4	2	7.5	0	0.9	71	42.3	2	1.0	0	0.2	5	28.5
25	WEST BENGAL	42	82.2	4	9.6	0	0.0	2	16.8	0	0.0	2	29.6	34	43.5
26	A.&N ISLANDS	1	70.7	0	43.7	0	0.0	1	47.8	0	0.0	0	1.1	0	6.8
27	CHANDIGARH	1	73.7	0	26.8	0	0.0	1	42.2	0	0.0	0	0.0	0	27.5
28	DADRA & NAGAR HAVELI	1	84.1	0	45.1	0	0.0	1	48.9	0	0.0	0	0.0	0	5.4
29	DAMAN & DIU	1	78.0	0	43.3	0	0.0	1	53.8	0	0.0	0	0.0	0	2.3
30	DELHI	7	65.1	0	15.1	0	0.0	7	46.4	0	0.0	0	0.1	0	37.2
31	LAKSHAWDEEP	1	86.6	0	46.6	0	0.0	0	0.4	0	0.0	0	1.5	1	51.5
32	PUDUCHERRY	1	82.1	0	26.3	0	0.0	0	0.0	1	34.6	0	1.7	0	37.1
33	JHARKHAND	14	63.8	0	13.3	2	10.9	12	40.1	0	0.0	0	1.4	0	33.2
34	CHHATTISGARH	11	69.4	1	38.4	0	0.0	10	48.7	0	0.0	0	0.6	0	9.9
35	UTTARAKHAND	5	61.6	0	34.0	0	0.0	5	55.3	0	0.0	0	0.3	0	5.7
	All India	543	66.4	44	19.3	15	3.7	282	31.0	54	7.4	12	4.8	139	29.7

*Undivided Andhra Pradesh

Congress allies: BPF (in Assam), RJD (in Bihar, Jharkhand), JMM (in Jharkhand), NCP (in Maharashtra, Bihar), BVA (in Maharashtra), IUML (in Kerala), RSP (in Kerala), SJD (in Kerala), KCM (in Kerala), RLD (in Uttar Pradesh), Mahan Dal (in Uttar Pradesh), JKNC (in J&K)

BJP allies: Shiv Sena (in Maharashtra), RPI-A (in Maharashtra), SWP (in Maharashtra), RSPP (in Maharashtra), TDP (in Andhra Pradesh), SAD (in Punjab), LJP (in Bihar), RLSP (in Bihar), Apna Dal (in Uttar Pradesh), PMK (in Tamil Nadu), MDMK (in Tamil Nadu), DMDK (in Tamil Nadu), RSPB (in Kerala), Independent (in Kerala), HJC (in Haryana), NPF (in Nagaland), NPP (in Meghalaya), AINRC (in Puducherry)

Left: CPI(M), CPI, AIFB, RSP (except in Kerala)

Acknowledgements

Writing a book is a bit like a political party attempting to win an election: it cannot be a one-man show even if the author's name is emblazoned on the cover. This book wouldn't have happened without the dynamic Chiki Sarkar of Penguin asking me to write it and my remarkably poised editor Nandini Mehta ensuring that I stayed the course. Journalists are used to deadlines, but we usually write 1000 words; a 100,000-plus-word book is very different. Without Chiki and Nandini's gentle prodding, I'd have been lost.

A special thanks to all my journalist friends and colleagues who so readily shared information and insights. Whoever says we have lost the spirit of camaraderie in this ruthlessly competitive world? To the many others who agreed to part with their wisdom, my thanks: some of you are quoted in the book, others have chosen to stay off record. Thank you also to all the politicians who contributed to the book: we tend to lampoon our netas too easily, but trust me, a majority of them are rooted and knowledgeable. I didn't have a formal researcher, but Monica Sarup at CNN-IBN was always there with background material. The team at CSDS, especially Professor Sanjay Kumar and Shreyas Sardesai, were, as always, terrific with election data and analysis. A special mention for my assistant

Surinder Nagar, who is my man Friday (and Saturday and Sunday!). Surinder even gets the credit for the jacket photograph.

I have been privileged to have had great friends who have stuck by me through good times and tough times. I want to especially thank Ramachandra Guha, who was the first to encourage me to write and the closest I have had as a mentor: I know of no other public intellectual so generous with his ideas (and with his hospitality, at his wonderful home in Coonoor). Thanks to my friend Shikha Trivedy for believing I had a book in me, and to Sameer Manchanda and Piyush Goyal for always being there for me. I have been fortunate in my early years to have worked with editors and media leaders who gave me two rare gifts for a young journalist: freedom and opportunity. So thank you to Darryl d'Monte, Dileep Padgaonkar, Radhika and Prannoy Roy. And the legendary R.K. Laxman who gave me my first journalistic lesson: the art of communicating in simple language.

Most of all, thank you to my family. My daughter Tarini who taught me all I needed to know about how to use the computer, while my son Ishan kept reminding me of the need to be steadfast in my writing (I guess medical students learn to be focused at an early age). To my mother Nandini, indomitable professor, who is perhaps my biggest (at times, only) fan and who gave me my early learnings in life. To my late father, who was a champion Test cricketer and my hero. I wanted to be a cricketer; he just wanted me to be happy in whatever I chose to be. Shonali, Taimur, Aman, Mummyma, Chitra and Bhaskar Ghose—thank you all for always being there.

Last of all, thank you to Sagarika, beloved wife and friend. She is the original author in the family and I guess she had more unflinching faith in me than I had in myself that I could actually pull off a book. I can only hope that you, the reader, will be generous with this debutant who remains simply a newshound in heart and soul.